Earth Day
Vision for Peace, Justice, and Earth Care

Earth Day
Vision for Peace, Justice, and Earth Care

My Life and Thought at Age 96

JOHN MCCONNELL
The Founder of Earth Day

Edited by JOHN C. MUNDAY JR.

RESOURCE *Publications* · Eugene, Oregon

EARTH DAY: VISION FOR PEACE, JUSTICE, AND EARTH CARE
My Life and Thought at Age 96

Resource Publications
An Imprint of Wipf and Stock Publishers
199 W. 8th Ave., Suite 3
Eugene, OR 97401

www.wipfandstock.com

ISBN 13: 978-1-60899-541-7

Manufactured in the U.S.A.

Contents

Foreword

From the individual's birthday to the observance of United Nations Day, from personal human rights to universal brotherhood, from the family and the city-state to the international community, at long last the concepts of Earth Day, of world patriotism, and the family of man have come into being!

May there only be peaceful and cheerful Earth Days to come for our beautiful Spaceship Earth as it continues to spin and circle in frigid space with its warm and fragile cargo of animate life.

—U Thant

FORTY-ONE YEARS AGO, JOHN McConnell proposed the idea of Earth Day, a global holiday devoted to the care of the Earth and promotion of peace among nations. He sounded a call that has gone around the world, and generated worldwide awareness of our fragile planet. His Earth Day and his Earth Flag have come to symbolize our responsibility for Earth care.

My father, Secretary-General U Thant, recognized the importance of Earth Day. My father was the 14th signer of the Earth Day Proclamation, prepared by John McConnell on June 21, 1970. Within a year of the first Earth Day celebration on March 21, 1970, in San Francisco, my father signed a United Nations Proclamation on February 26, 1971 to set the spring equinox as Earth Day at the UN. I was greatly inspired to read the Earth Day Proclamation written by Mr. McConnell, and signed by many leaders of thought, in which it said, "International Earth Day each year can provide a special time to draw people together in appreciation of their mutual home, Planet Earth, and bring a global feeling of community through realization of our deepening desire for life, freedom and love, and our mutual dependence on each other."

There is a famous photo of the Earth taken from the Moon by the astronauts of the Apollo 8 mission. The documentary film "An Inconvenient Truth" by Al Gore opened with that photo. I have a copy of that photo in my home. The message under the photo reads, "As others see us, clearly, One World." That photo is on the Earth Flag developed by John McConnell in 1969. Today, all over the world, people fly the Earth Flag with the photo of Earth from the Moon. It symbolizes a vision of a world where global citizens have developed a spirit of One World. This message has guided the activities of the U Thant Institute since its inception.

The First Day of Spring was designated as Earth Day by Mr. McConnell. Mr. McConnell described Earth Day as "the day of nature's equipoise, when we celebrate the wonder of life on our planet." The annual ringing of the Peace Bell at the United Nations building that symbolizes peace, justice, and cooperation, at the first moment of Spring when day and night are equal around the world, reminds us of our belonging to this global community. It gives us a deep sense of collective ownership, and strengthens our commitment to take responsibility to safeguard the natural endowment of the planet Earth and its resources in the interest of future generations. Thus, the ringing of the Peace Bell has become synonymous with Earth Day.

At the first celebration of Earth Day at the United Nations, on March 21, 1971, my father sounded an alarm that "our small planet is perishable" and stated his concern that there is an inherent risk of obliterating all life on Earth with the deterioration of our natural environment. "Man's future and man's environment must be conceived and managed wisely if he is to survive and to prosper," my father warned as he noted the challenges facing the planet, including poverty, food shortages, urbanization, the squandering of natural resources, and pollution, among others. But he believed that "humanity will be united by the common dangers we all face." Celebration of Earth Day, he said, is now necessary to promote that awareness and to remind us of the fact that "our Planet Earth is in crisis."

Forty years ago, my father saw the urgency of the need to solve the environmental problems facing the planet Earth. He said on many occasions, "these are problems we have hardly begun to face, and yet the hour is already very late. As we watch the sun go down, evening after evening, through the smog across the poisoned waters of our native earth, we must ask ourselves seriously whether we really wish some future universal historian on another planet to say about us: 'With all their genius and with all their skill, they ran out of foresight and air and food and water and ideas,' or, 'They went on playing politics until their world collapsed around them.'"

With the conviction that the UN should play a vital role in preserving and enhancing the life on the planet, my father in May 1969 proposed "the creation of a global authority to deal with the problem of the environment." In a statement at the Preparatory Committee on the Conference on the Human Environment on March 9, 1970, at the United Nations, he declared, "never in the twenty five year history of the United Nations has there been a problem of more relevance to all nations than the present environmental crisis." He added, "The crisis of the environment could be the challenge which might show us the way forward to a responsible and a just world society—a path which, for all the efforts of the United Nations in the political crisis of our time, has so far eluded us."

The UN Environment Programme (UNEP), with its mission "to provide leadership and encourage partnership in caring for the environment by inspiring, informing, and enabling nations and peoples to improve their quality of life without compromising that of future generations," is in concert with that of my father's vision. It is also Mr. McConnell's conviction that "peace and justice on Earth can come about only when all peoples recognize the importance of our planet as our common home." Mr. McConnell believes that Earth Day is the vehicle for promoting peace and justice among nations.

When I rang the Peace Bell at the UN Earth Day ceremony in 2007, I said "Today is the beginning of spring here in the Northern Hemisphere. It marks the beginning of new life." Each year on Earth Day we reaffirm that the newness of life involves caring for our planetary home and simultaneously caring for each other. We are bound by a common interest in survival. My father always believed in the oneness of humanity. He believed that conflicts don't result from differences in beliefs alone but from lack of education. Mr. McConnell has likewise advocated using Earth Day to educate all groups in society about the interdependence of peace, justice, and cooperation in Earth care.

When I established the U Thant Institute in 2003, its mission was to reflect my father's ideals, to advance peace through the virtues of tolerance, cooperation, understanding, and compassion.

The Institute's mission is to foster awareness that there is only One World and one human family, and to encourage others to join hands in preserving our Earth and striving for a more harmonious existence on it. As all of us have equal rights and privileges to benefit from the Earth's life, it is the responsibility of every one of us to take care of it for our own survival and for our future generations. Every year when we celebrate Earth Day we affirm our partnership in fostering international understanding.

In 2009 we celebrated the centennial birth anniversary of my father and his life. During his work as the Secretary-General of the UN, he set forth world peace programs on the environment, population, economic wellbeing, and education. He conceived his role of the Secretary-General as a moderator and harmonizer with patience, and someone who constantly had to understand "the other person's point of view." This idea is promoted in John McConnell's profound admonition that we should agree where possible, and "leave room for our differences." I am grateful to learn that John McConnell's story here shows that his entire life has been guided by a mission to promote peace among peoples, and care of our common home.

This book is John McConnell's story of Earth Day, and relates all the other activities of his life that have advanced the Earth Day concept.

I have much respect for the lifelong work of John McConnell. He has generated a renowned collection of ideas for advancing peace and justice, including Earth Day, the Earth Flag, and the Earth Day Proclamation, the concept of an Earth Trustee, the Minute for Peace, and the Earth Magna Charta. With unrelenting drive and energy, he has promoted these ideas over a half-century, leading people devoted to peace, justice, and environmental stewardship. As seen in this autobiography, Mr. McConnell strongly articulates these relationships. He explores features of the world's governmental, political, and economic systems that have led to exploitation and violence instead of meeting people's needs. Mr. McConnell shares a vision for world peace with my father based on the ideals of tolerance and compassion.

I encourage you to read this life story of a most remarkable man, and to join in the causes which have energized his life.

Aye Aye Thant
Westport, CT
USA

Preface

Earth Day is built on peace, justice, and care of Earth—

- You can't have peace without justice, and justice requires care of Earth.

- We are excited about our work. We live on an amazing planet with a web of life.

- To continue the human adventure, our priorities are to care for Earth, to eliminate injustice, and to leave a planetary inheritance to future generations.

- The practice of what I have proposed, if implemented, would eliminate poverty all over the world.

Acknowledgments

IT WOULD BE IMPOSSIBLE to list all of the many leaders and laymen whom I met through the years who influenced my thinking and effort. Among those who are better known were President Dwight Eisenhower, Eleanor Roosevelt, Billy Graham, United Nations Secretary-General U Thant, Under-Secretary-Generals Robert Muller and C. V. Narasimhan, President Jimmy Carter, Sheikh Yamani, Shimon Peres and Mikhail Gorbachev.

To the many who through the years have helped me by phone, fax, and funds, my deep felt thanks.

In regard to the Earth Magna Charta, I wish to especially thank George Gallup Jr. for his encouragement and help. Also Coretta King, who participated in our 1979 Earth Day Ceremony and who called my attention to the book by her husband, *Strength to Love*. Thanks to David Stephen and the office of the United Nations Secretary-General for special assistance. I also express my appreciation to Mary Harrington, a volunteer in Boston, and to Angi, daughter of our former Earth Society Foundation president, Hans Janitschek, for transcribing preliminary drafts of the Earth Magna Charta. Also, to Hans Janitschek for his friendship and assistance through the years, and Carmen Colombo of WOWZone.com, for initially helping me put my material on the Web. Robert M. Weir is very much appreciated for having written a detailed biography in *Peace, Justice, Care of Earth*. My thanks also to Swarthmore College and its Peace Collection, for receiving and indexing my archives. I am most grateful to Aye Aye Thant for contributing the Foreword. Finally, I want to thank Dr. John C. Munday Jr. for making it possible for me to tell my story.

To my wife, Anna, go my deepest thanks and love. Her devotion has sustained me.

This book is a collection of my writings and memories. I hope the reader will not be disturbed by some repetition here and there.

1

Introduction

I AM BEST KNOWN for my role in starting Earth Day in 1970. Its purpose was "peace, justice, and the care of Earth." We obtained thirty-three Nobel Laureates as sponsors. We aided environmental efforts and helped end the Cold War.

As you will see in this book, early in life I went on my own search to find what life is all about. In later years I was aided by top scientists, philosophers, and leaders of the Christian, Jewish and Muslim religions.

I came to the conclusion that to save our planet and have a future we should come together where we agree and leave room for our differences. People forget their differences—or peacefully accommodate them—when they have an urgent common cause they can all support.

We are faced with inexplicable mystery when it comes to why we are here and what life is all about. Many religions around the world claim to provide answers. The Native Americans had an appreciation of the importance of animals, trees, birds, and sky, reflected in the beautiful statement of Chief Seattle. Their religion and their beliefs about the mystery of life reflected those views. The Founding Fathers of the United States got some of their ideas from them.

Many theories try to deal with the enigmas of life. The problem is that we focus on their conflicting views. While we must acknowledge our differences, we should look for common ground and ever seek to unite in matters where we agree.

But no one seems to provide a way that will appeal to every creed and culture—and enable us to avoid global catastrophe. Our problem in this era of data explosion is the different points of view—and their importance in the total picture. We seem to be at the end of humanity's brief history. We need a miracle to bring about the drastic changes needed to provide a sustainable future and continue the human adventure.

The result of my life experiences has led me to the need for the whole human family to see and appreciate the wonderful miracle of the web of life that covers our planet. While we are confronted with inexplicable mystery regarding what life is all about, we recognize that to have a global future, every major creed and culture must join in an all-out effort to avoid global catastrophe. We must now take care of our planet—and do it in a way that will bring just social benefits to the whole human family. There must be global independent efforts for a sustainable future.

While many leaders of other religions support Earth Day and its Earth Trustee agenda, I feel I can share something from my experience that comes from my personal faith. In our devotions one morning, my wife and I were reading from the Gospel of John where Jesus washed his disciples' feet and indicated that if he, as their leader, humbled himself to serve them, they should show the same love to others. This reminded me that the most powerful message Jesus gave was, "Love one another." His words and actions define the meaning of love. He demonstrated by his life what this meant.

In this time of global confusion, injustice, violence, and war, an understanding of the meaning of this real love will result in right actions to save our planet and provide the human family with a new beginning.

Our planet is in crisis. The state of the world and what should be done is important to everyone. Governments, think tanks, and leaders in science and religion are all expressing their deep concern. Bill Moyers provided a look at the whole planet and its grave problems in his "Earth on Edge."[1] The question is, "Can we face the facts, and take action quick enough to avoid catastrophe?"

At critical times in the past, as the founder of Earth Day, I have obtained attention for ideas that aided the peaceful exploration of space, the ending of the Cold War, and the understanding of the importance of the environment—the skin of life that covers our globe. I now contend that instead of global disaster, we can, with the vigorous actions I propose, a moral equivalent of World War II, diminish pollution, violence, and poverty, and provide a promising future for the whole human family.

---

1. The program "Earth on Edge" premiered on PBS on June 19th, 2001.

Much of what I have said and done is on my website, http://www
.earthsite.org. But to better understand the background and reason for
my ideas, this book will include the details about my life, and how I
came to the views that I share. I would say that I am a pragmatic idealist.
My wife would say that I am a visionary.

I have long been urged to write a book about my life and what I
believe is the state of the world—its dangers and opportunities. This
book will attempt to tell about my life adventure—the famous people
I have met, the things I have done, my efforts to see the whole global
picture and to inspire actions that would benefit people and planet—and
to avoid global disaster.

The story of my life can increase understanding of my views.

While I hope that what I have to say appeals to the philosopher and
scientist, most important to me is that all readers who agree with my
views will do something about them. My purpose is to bear witness to
the truth; not only the truth about facts, but the truth about which facts
are most important.

Among the many people who influenced my thinking was S. I.
Hayakawa, whom I knew in San Francisco. He wrote a book in 1941
titled *Language in Thought and Action*,[2] which followed *Tyranny of Words*
by Stuart Chase in 1938.[3] From Dr. Hayakawa I learned that communication required an attitude of openness to be meaningful. I have repeatedly found important ideas and values in religions and philosophies with
which I disagree. I have no hidden agenda. My purpose is not to convert
people to my particular creed, but to share what I believe is important.

When confronted with the facts, people of every creed and culture
agree that our most important task now is to act as responsible trustees
of planet Earth. I believe the Earth Magna Charta (see chapter 36) describes the best way to be Earth Trustees.

WRITING A BOOK

Lately, I have been reflecting on my ninety-six years of life. I must warn
you that when you get to be ninety-six, you undoubtedly have problems
with hearing and memory. It's a little frustrating. I was ninety-six years

---

2. Hayakawa, *Language in Thought and Action*.

3. Chase, *The Tyranny of Words*.

old on March 22, 2011, and I will be writing from my memory—but it can be confirmed by the many documents available.

People my age tend to make mistakes in the details of what they think happened in their youth. My wife has organized the records we have of my past and they are helpful. However, many of the records I once had have been lost. I encourage young people to keep a diary or journal—and hold on to them. I did for a while, but I was not consistent and unfortunately much of what I did write about myself has been lost. When I think of the difficulties I have experienced in my life, it is amazing that I am even alive.

I have never written a book before, but I have hundreds of articles, newspaper clippings and letters that my wife has been putting in order. A little sample of this is on my website, http://www.earthsite.org. I want to try in this book to provide the many friends and supporters—of my Earth Day/Earth Trustee agenda—some items that will help unite global efforts for peace, justice, and a sustainable future.

In these pages, I want to provide different perspectives on the human adventure. They call attention to important matters in which we can agree and unite in a common cause for a sustainable future. At the same time we must recognize our differences and how to accommodate them.

Since my early youth I have been deeply interested in "What Life Is All About." This was the title of a tract written by my father, evangelist J. S. McConnell Sr. Recognizing the amazing mysteries of life, as I sit at this computer, I ask myself the question, "Are the thoughts that come to me just the data that has been stored in my brain? Or are they influenced by input from another dimension of reality? How much of a factor in what I do and say is my particular belief in God?" I will address these questions in the book, but will focus on the here and now—the state of the world, its past, present, and possible future.

Other factors in my thinking are the people I have been privileged to meet. While many in humble circumstances have influenced my thinking, I have learned from many world leaders who met with me and showed interest in my views. Years ago these included Eleanor Roosevelt, President Eisenhower, Werner Von Braun, and Edward Teller. Later, my interests took me to other leaders in science, economics, religion, and government, and to major books on these subjects.

This book will state my views, and how and where their adoption has benefited people and planet. It will seek to give an in-depth reason for them.

The following brief statement expresses what I believe is most important for the world right now. The details in the rest of the book will help you understand the importance of the statement below as it describes my life, my thought, and my actions.

THE MOST IMPORTANT IDEAS

I have had a sense of mission since my early youth. From early childhood I have had a burning desire to know what life is all about. The way I thought and the experiences I had all led, step by step, to my vision of Earth Day as a global holiday for the whole planet.

My father, who was an evangelist, made me think about why we are here and where we are going. It seems to me my whole life has been a search to learn what life is all about.

The themes that have emerged as the most important for the human adventure are "peace, justice, and the care of Planet Earth."

Love (creative altruism) will bring the greatest personal and global benefit.

Life is a mystery. The more you know the greater the mystery. The world is filled with good and evil. The evil far outweighs the good.

But there have been times and places where the good was dominant. The world is headed for doom. But I believe in miracles. With today's technology, a good idea for Earth's rejuvenation—if effectively demonstrated in any part of the world—could cover the globe and provide a new beginning for planet Earth.

Bill Gates and others have provided the computer technology that benefits the world. Efforts for peace, justice, and a sustainable future together with modern technology can have a huge impact for a better future.

Three major things in my life made a global difference: In 1957 it was my proposal for a visible Star of Hope Satellite. In 1963 my "Minute for Peace" got global attention. And in 1970, Earth Day helped unite efforts for "peace, justice, and the care of Earth."

Many years ago I presented a plan for a World Peace Blitz that would remove the causes of war and create a climate for peaceful progress and justice for all. This was designed to spark the positive aspects of war (common purpose, loyalty, crisis, challenge of great risks, heroism) and channel them into a dynamic campaign for peace, justice, and stewardship of Earth throughout the world.

THE OLD WORLD IS DYING

But in the dying new life is stirring.

Even in dogmas of prejudice and pride, wherever people are involved there are always a few who will re-kindle the fires of love and truth. Too often they have been alone; too often the fires of new love have died. But now in our new world of global communications, they are feeding on each other and spreading.

Now is the time for each person of goodwill to choose peace; courageously, confidently, vigorously: to speak, to pray, to work for peace.

Not the false and temporary peace that is forced by the power of the sword, but the real and lasting peace that is won by the power of the spirit; by compassion, understanding, cooperation, and good will.

The old world is dying. But a new world is aborning, a world that transcends the old with promise of new beauty, power, freedom—and perhaps a cosmic destiny of unimagined grandeur.

A GLOBAL CALL TO ACTION

In this new millennium it is imperative that the whole human family mobilize for a moral equivalent of World War II. All people who receive this message are urged to quickly choose what they will do. Think about it, talk about it, and then act.

Be aware that today global institutions induce individuals to accept as truth what is forced upon them by institutional propaganda, which keeps people from thinking for themselves. Don't let powerful people in political and social institutions make your choices for you or take away your self-confidence.

The Earth Trustee idea, part of the original Earth Day on March 21, 1970, provides the key that appeals to thinking people and can do the most good. Now, every individual and institution must seek to eliminate pollution, poverty, and injustice by Earth Trustee choices in ecology, economics, and ethics.

Thousands of group projects are already helping people and planet. Their impact can increase dramatically by uniting in a global Earth Trustee Campaign with one common cause—the rejuvenation of Earth.

Human greed, injustice, and folly have almost ruined our planet. But with the aid of new technology, a vigorous global effort can repair the damage.

Until now, Earth Caretakers have been a sad minority. The most powerful institutions (global corporations and rich governments) have usually put financial profit and personal gain first. The resulting social and environmental damage is disastrous. But the Earth Trustee vision and action by individuals and institutions can change things for the better. The Earth Trustee vision provides a way for everyone to tap the best in thinking and in personal faith.

Earth Day is an opportunity for *all* world leaders to call for daily prayer, meditation, and heartfelt dedication to the care of Earth—to think and act as Trustees of Earth. World leaders should act now, urging that everyone oppose violence with non-violence—Martin Luther King's effective solution. Those who believe in the power of prayer can prove the power of their faith by their vigorous efforts for peace, justice, and a sustainable future. Leaders in other areas of public trust ideally will do the same. The March 20 Earth Day is the day to focus attention on what can be done.

When people think and act as Earth Trustees, they will show a reverence for life, and for holy places. In this way people can prove the benefit of their religious faith in a future life, by their actions in this life.

Earth Day and its Earth Trustee agenda put the Golden Rule to work: Do unto others as you would have them do unto you. Here is a chance for people of all religions to show their ethical values by being Earth Trustees and practicing reverence for life in word and deed.

DOOMSDAY—OR OPPORTUNITY

The following example shows how our money and greed-driven culture is ripping apart the last strands that still hold the planetary web of life together. But we have a choice. What will we do? What will you do?

Will this new millennium bring the doom of civilization—or a new beginning for our planet?

Evidence compiled by experts points to global disaster. The facts are succinct in *Paradise for Sale: Parable of Nature*, a book by Carl N. McDaniel and John M. Gowdy.[4]

The book documents how the quest for money and the misuse of science and technology exhausted the natural wealth of Nauru, a tiny island in the Pacific. The profit–first–mentality rendered Nauru a "Paradise Lost" for its natives and habitat. The authors compare the devastation of the small island to what is happening worldwide. But while Nauru has become a charity case, to whom will the world turn for charity?

Nauru is a microcosm of the rest of the world. The only chance for civilization's survival is a rapid change of attitudes and actions that will rejuvenate our planet.

THE WAY TO GLOBAL ACCORD

And to a Peaceful, Prosperous Future

Today, many world leaders in government, business, science, and religion are seeking the way toward global understanding and harmony on our planet.

The great enigma is their failure to focus on the annual event and its agenda which has thus far made the greatest contribution to "peace, justice, and the care of Earth"—in spite of limited attention.

In the last forty years, the Earth Day observances at the United Nations on the March Equinox got attention for efforts that were promoting a sustainable future. They were also one of the key factors in ending the Cold War.

Today, there are thousands of scientists and scholars of every kind in think tanks and universities looking at different aspects of the world and its mysteries, but ignoring what we already know. They publish thousands of books and fill the Internet with their data. But with the huge amount of data we now have a new problem. We find that every time data doubles, wisdom diminishes.

In this book I want to look at the big picture—the state of the world; the different aspects of global problems and opportunities; the differing perspectives due to race, culture, religion, wealth, poverty, education, and genes. In all of this we are affected not only by our nature, but by the nature of our institutions.

4. McDaniel and Gowdy, *Paradise for Sale.*

Another important item is to remember that while words can be important, they are often imperfect vehicles of our thoughts. The best way to convey what is meant is by giving an example. Also, many religious scholars believe that when you hear a speaker who is "anointed" or "charismatic," it will fasten saving impressions on your mind and be followed by action.

What I say and do are the results of all the factors in my life. However, I contend that what headed me in the right direction and resulted in my amazing life adventure and accomplishments was the inspired passion I obtained as a child—to know what the miracle of life is all about.

The more I learn, the greater the mystery. But along the way I believe that I found in Earth Day and its Earth Trustee agenda the key to global accord and peaceful progress.

Leaders who want to promote peaceful progress should look at the history of the March equinox Earth Day, and how I came to my conclusions. Apply what is learned. This will further understanding and global unity. Earth Day is designed to promote important matters in which we agree—with room for differences in other matters. The Earth Trustee agenda of "peace, justice, and the care of Earth" will tap the best in religion, ethics, and public policy, and help efforts for global accord.

2

Searching for Truth

SOURCES AND ATTITUDES

WHERE DO WE GET our ideas? I don't know when I wrote the following, but I just came across it a few days ago. (I believe there was more to it than the one page I found.)

This morning in meditation a number of ideas seemed to come together, and I decided to record some of them while they were still fresh in my mind.

What triggered my thought was the overwhelming explosion in the media of conflicting ideas about politics, religion, the state of the world, and the human condition. This is a time when people have far more information than any time in history, and still there is such confusion that it's difficult to sort out what the most important facts or values are. One of the basic problems here is the contentious arguments on radio, TV and in magazines about who God is, who man is, and what life is all about, plus arguments about politics and money.

It seems to me that in order to find some reason or some hope, we need to look for a few firm fundamental facts that can serve as a basis for understanding what's happening in the world and what we can do about it.

I was thinking of the Bible verse that says, "No man hath seen God." God himself is a mystery. Today, in looking for answers, because of their culture, environment, and circumstances (and many unexamined assumptions), people come up with different hypotheses about the nature of reality. Too often they state their opinions as if they are proven facts; for example, "I know I'm saved, I know there's a future life, I know there's a God." What they often mean is that they are completely convinced of this. If they mean scientific proof, then many able, informed, and good people with different answers are either stupid or irrational.

In our search for reality, for truth, it's important to identify the things that are recognized as most factual. For instance, we agree that we exist. I know that there are some that believe existence is just an illusion of the mind, but most will agree with the ancient observation, "I think, therefore I am." We agree that two plus two equals four. These are not just hypotheses, or articles of faith; they are scientific facts, important basic facts.

Now when we go beyond that and say, "Where did the universe come from?" then we become involved with amazing mysteries that are so overwhelming that the greatest minds down through history to today differ on the answer. It's well for us to seek an answer and find one that satisfies us or gives us comfort, but it's good to be a little humble or modest in our opinions, to recognize that what we are talking about is not proven fact, but we're talking about unproven hypotheses. However, many times it's important and useful to have working hypotheses.

We differ about the mysteries of life—the amazing coincidences that occur and influence our thought and actions. But we can and should agree on the need for "peace, justice, and care of Earth" so we can continue the human adventure. To do this, we must vigorously come together where we agree and leave room for differences on matters where we differ.

OUTER AND INNER SPACES—SCIENCE AND ART

The images, that words convey differ with people of different cultures and experience. At first I could not imagine "outer spaces." There was just "outer space" (singular), the infinite area outside our planet.

Then the idea was given that each planet and star was in a different space—or place—and I could accept the idea of outer spaces.

Assuming that inner space refers to the place where ideas and emotions exist, I could now imagine inner spaces, containing separate ideas, images, and associated feelings.

An additional dimension of inner spaces would be in spiritual or metaphysical phenomena, which are beyond accepted logic and proof of science. In our scientific age, logic requires a cause for every effect. Some claim there are no miracles. So, metaphysical or religious miracles, which are repeatedly documented, must involve something other than materialism. While physical evidence of miracles is available, their causes are a mystery—not provable by scientific methods. The source of religious or metaphysical phenomena could be referred to as inner spaces, another dimension of reality.

With new windows of opportunity and new icons of science and art, illustrated by cyberspace, we now have a bridge to understanding inner and outer spaces, a way to peaceful cooperation and progress in the human adventure.

The icon that will appeal to all is the Earth itself. Religion, science, and art can join hands on nature's Earth Day when we celebrate spring's renewal with deepening awareness of our relation to all of life. Then every person will think and act as a Trustee of Earth. We will then see anew the wonder of life as we heed the key words spoken 2000 years ago: "Love one another."

3

The Global View

EARTH—OUR NEST IN THE STARS

TODAY, THE ASTRONAUTS AND cosmonauts have provided a global view of our planet. Through their eyes we have stepped back and viewed our planet from afar with new eyes. "We set out to explore space—and discovered Earth!"

We are now aware that one fragile planet is our home, the home of one human family. Now we have a chance to see in our diversity a unity that will enable us to fairly adjust our differences with new solutions unseen in the past.

In all decisions we must now consider how they affect people and planet, locally and globally. We must now consider how our decisions affect the nurture and protection of Earth and the rights of individuals to the use of our planet. Seeing the whole picture will help us make the right choices. Earth is our inheritance and our responsibility.

There is common agreement that our progress in technology has been used to make money, with little regard for preserving the thin skin of life covering our globe, which makes life possible.

There are now thousands of projects around the world to aid "peace, justice, and the care of Earth." The problem is, the actions that cause pollution, injustice, and violence far outweigh the good we are doing.

CAN WE SAVE OUR PLANET?

The basic problem is that human conduct is destroying our planet. The basic question is, "Why is this happening and can it be corrected?"

Whether viewed as divine providence, or the nature of the design of life, for millions of years the life on this planet constantly developed and improved. In the spread of ecosystems we find constant enhancement in life of every kind: beautiful birds, fish, animals, insects, plants, and trees. But in this potential paradise we find the rather sudden acquisition of power by *Homo sapiens*. Whether we call it sin, egoism, or some other name, we find human societies with growing power, societies whose greed and selfishness have introduced an element of destructiveness that has grown and spread until it now threatens the life of the planet. The danger has today reached a point where our increased technology, population, systems, and science have converted the development and improvement of life to destruction.

A current example is found in the balding of Earth. Forests and, in many cases, whole species of trees and plants are being destroyed by the choices of human beings. Competition for timber, wood to burn, grazing, and misdirected community and highway planning, as well as pesticides and other chemical pollution, have destroyed over half of the Earth's green cover, a major source of oxygen on our planet.

There is a growing concern about the natural processes of life, processes that improved life for millions of years and now are being ignored and recklessly destroyed. The artificial chemical and mechanical solutions to eco-problems have often inhibited and in some cases destroyed nature's capacity for self-recovery.

These questions are important because now it is evident that the future of life on Earth is being determined not by natural processes or divine influences that improved life in the past, but by the decisions and choices of human beings, choices that are being made without regard for Earth's billion-year success story. As a result, our choices are not serving the improvement of life on our planet, but are instead causing its degradation and destruction.

Is there a factor in the human psyche that will doom our planet? Is there a chance of changing or transcending this factor so that the development and improvement of our planet can continue? Whether caused by original sin, a design deficiency, or an enigma of human nature, a change must be made if we are to have a future.

To put these matters in clear perspective, we need to correct the generally accepted view of the "survival of the fittest," that in the development of life on our planet raw competition was nature's method of improvement. As a result, many accept a "dog eat dog" philosophy in human conduct.

At every stage of development of consciousness, balancing mere competitiveness is a growing cooperation and affection. Affection between mates and between parent and offspring is a key emotional element in the character of higher forms of life. In some mysterious way the well-being of Earth's total life is constantly engendered by subtle cooperative acts that preserve and improve not only the life of the individual but the life of the species, and, in turn, the life of the whole planet. Competition and cooperation have worked together for Earth's benefit.

With man's growing ability to look at both the past and the future, and to choose, comes the necessity of tempering competition, greed, and selfishness with concern and consideration for the whole family of life on our planet.

Now we ask the question, "Is this possible?" Fortunately we find individuals in every culture who demonstrate creative altruism. Throughout history caring individuals have sought the well-being of their neighbors, the nurture of their natural surroundings, and the protection and care of our bountiful planet. The degree of commitment and action varies from person to person, but the capacity for creative altruism is certainly evident in the human family.

So, to answer the question, "What can we do about the destruction of life on Earth?" we suggest the following:

As individuals and groups turn to the problems at hand, to problems of pollution, inequity, inequality, or waste, let us find reinforcement and a connection with other groups who independently are striving to achieve the same goal—to be responsible custodians and caretakers in every part of our planet; to do this with a deep commitment to life, to one another, to the good, or to God if we have a faith that works.

STATE OF THE WORLD—AND WHAT TO DO

> Oh wretched mortals, open your eyes.
> —Leonardo da Vinci

The Internet has made the world more aware of the wide range of differences about most everything. This is a time when information technology provides a thousand perspectives of global dangers and opportunities. Constantly there are new data that provide another view.

Scholars from science, religion, and philosophy have different perspectives on what is important and what life is all about. However, there is common agreement about some things.

Many scholars agree human history will soon come to an end unless there is a major change in human conduct. New technology makes it possible for massive destruction by a few seeking revenge for a real or imagined wrong.

Most can agree that to continue the human adventure we must get behind a common cause all can support. To move in the right direction we need a sense of global community, built on the recognition that we have an amazing planet, covered with a skin of life. There are abundant raw materials, natural resources, and technology. With wise use of our technology we can eliminate pollution, ignorance, and poverty, and provide a sustainable future and a good life for almost everyone.

To succeed, we must not repeat the mistakes of the past. Human history has a long record of more evil than good. While the world has long had examples of good, there are far more examples of evil. We need a moral equivalent of war to tip the balance in the right direction, a grand global effort for the rejuvenation of Earth and a future of peaceful progress.

This must be done in a way that is fair and that will enable all to participate, with greater benefit for those who render greater service.

No individual, corporation, or government is capable of organizing the whole world for this task. But a general description of the policies and actions needed is available. The "Earth Magna Charta" (in chapter 36) points the way. The keystone of the Earth Magna Charta is the Earth Trustee idea: Everyone has a right to benefit from Earth's natural bounty, and an equal responsibility to help take care of it. The Earth Magna Charta provides enough information for any group, institution, or government body to initiate an Earth Trustee effort. Often there are projects that are already pursuing the Earth Magna Charta goals.

Along the way we have to look at the state of the world and understand the problems we face. Our view will depend on what we are looking for. An economist will look at the economy. A politician will look at governments. A theologian will look at religion. People around the world will reflect different views.

People working in these different areas have not had an agenda that would link their independent efforts in a common goal.

When people concentrate on where they agree, they have peace. When they concentrate on where they differ, they have war.

New York City can serve as an example of our problem. It has attracted people of every creed and culture. In a sense it is the capital of the World: home of the United Nations, TV networks, newspapers, magazines, and books with global circulation. Wall Street and major corporations are located there.

Margaret Mead said that the problem is not only the nature of people, but the nature of their institutions. In all of the above, the goal of most individuals and institutions is to make money. A man said to his son, growing up, "Make money, honestly if you can, but son, make money."

There is little awareness of the history of our institutions, and how human greed and lust for power produced structures and policies that are evil and reward deception. The stock market and the banking system are prime examples. The people who control the banks and major corporations are a key factor in the control of the world. Today the most powerful individual or institution is the one that has the most money. What could and should be most powerful are the voices that speak for peace, justice, and the care of Earth's amazing web of life.

What this book lays out is a world view and action that can appeal to the most people and do the most good to bring about the desired future. Earth Day and its Earth Trustee agenda provide the way to a better future. The formula for the Earth Trustee agenda will encourage links and mutual efforts where there is agreement and leave room for differences.

THE WAY TO A PEACEFUL, PROSPEROUS GLOBAL FUTURE

Survival of life on our planet is in serious jeopardy. By its actions humanity has condemned Earth life to extinction. There is urgent need to understand the cause of this mindless decision and the means to reverse it.

The basic problems are:

Addiction to War: Throughout history, nations have fought one another over their differences. Had the money devoted to war been spent for education about the proven ways to peace through understanding and non-violent resolution of conflict, today we would have a world without war.

Ignorance: We lack good information about ourselves, about individuals, groups, and nations that appear to threaten us, and about choices in spending and lifestyle that will sustain instead of destroy vital natural resources and processes.

Selfishness: We are beset by our own shortsighted self-interest, lust, greed, and ambition.

Rationalization: There is no limit to the good arguments that people make for a bad cause.

The overall reason for poverty, pollution, and war is the lack of a well defined agenda for peaceful progress that will appeal to all. As a result, adversaries lack a basis for peaceful resolution of differences, and fall into conflict that endangers the human adventure.

Discussions too often neglect areas of honest accord. Peace efforts then stall in spite of international laws and United Nations agreements and resolutions. We need to stress where we agree and what we have in common.

Various groups produce long statements about steps to take toward a peaceful prosperous future. The statements often have a good overview of values needed. Through the years we have had dozens of conferences with similar statements.

But they lacked what is essential—a short statement that would embody the attitudes and actions needed for a global effort. This could be followed by different approaches to details of implementation.

The solution was provided by the original Earth Day and its Earth Trustee agenda for peace, justice, and a sustainable future. We ask individuals and institutions to all choose and support some project that will benefit people and planet. Call it an Earth Trustee project and share reports of your efforts and their success.

The remedy, briefly stated, is to *obtain from adversaries support for the basic goals on which all can agree.* Acknowledge the possibility of good intentions on all sides and that we all have varying degrees of selfishness and hypocrisy. Recognize that most conflict is the result of bad information about everyone's best interest, or about what is fair for all parties concerned.

The greatest danger is the power struggle among nations with different ideologies and military strengths. How can the problem be resolved?

All the adversaries claim good will for all people on Earth. Each claims a better life for people who follow their persuasion.

Regardless of where the truth lies concerning the advantages and disadvantages in each case, there is overwhelming evidence that no one has yet demonstrated a fair, free, and healthy society. Crime and greed in one form or another are rampant in all countries.

A halt to partisan rhetoric is desperately needed. Let us now focus on a set of common purposes to which all can agree. Open channels of communication are needed to honestly report progress on all sides in achieving these goals.

A set of objectives to help meet these requirements is set forth in the following Earth Objectives:

Earth Awareness: Attention, recognition, love, and devotion to the care of our planet.

Earth Care: Stewardship of Earth in every block and neighborhood.

Sharing Earth's Natural Bounty: Providing homesteads, land, or equivalent value in house or apartment for every homeless family; seeking equitable access to land and raw materials, the gifts of God.

Toward these objectives, pertinent facts need to be recognized:

The Problem of Special Privilege: There should be agreement that every individual has an equal claim to Earth's natural resources and raw materials. These unearned assets—the gift of God—are the inheritance of all Earth's children. This claim could be recognized by providing free homesteads for all needy families and individuals. After accomplishing this, further special royalties from owners of oil, minerals, and land could provide a minimum income for everyone. These items should be recognized as the inheritance of the whole human family. No human made them, and all people have an equal right to benefit from them.

Fair Use of Money and Credit: Good information is needed about the functions and uses of money and credit. Questions need to be answered: In the complex array of financial institutions and systems, who has the control? Who makes the decisions? Who benefits and how? For example, in the United States, to whom is our multi-trillion dollar debt owed? Who are the people who benefit from interest paid on this debt? Where is the money? Where did it come from? Do we have an honest, fair medium of exchange and a just form of ownership? Great changes are needed to reward workers who render useful service, instead of schemers and deceivers whose power is corrupting the marketplace.

Right information about these questions would result in corrections that would provide a more equitable economic system. Surely we can agree that the goal in every society should be fair access to, and opportunity for, useful work, trade, and benefits. Right information is needed globally about what is being done to achieve these goals.

Making Religion and Philosophy Work for Peace: Efforts should be made to obtain from all religious and ideological groups a list of their ethical and moral teachings, separating them from the abstract, unproven, though perhaps useful, beliefs about the unknown. Life is filled with profound mysteries: Is there a God? Life after death? Faith or metaphor provides meaning and hope for many. And there are amazing manifestations in answered prayer, spiritual healing, ESP, and psychic phenomena. Our leap of faith may be the right way, accompanied by inner conviction and certainty. But our differences with others in these matters cannot be settled by the hard facts of science, at least not yet.

Though we may have differences about our beliefs, we should agree and support actions where there is common accord. Almost every religion and philosophy teaches the Golden Rule. Stewardship and care of Earth is taught by all. Making these the most important priorities for common support will bring harmony and peace.

A major cause of our problem is sin and selfishness. Religions, the grace of God, and enlightenment address these problems. Proof of their value will be the extent to which they halt degradation and destruction of Earth's life and instead bring stewardship and care of Earth. To accomplish this they will need to add to their faith good information and responsible actions. This will also lessen prejudice and diminish deceit.

Through these endeavors and a massive Earth Campaign, those who care will, by God's grace, overturn the mindless decision of humanity to extinguish life on Earth, providing an opportunity for rejuvenation and a peaceful, prosperous future for our planet.

STATE OF THE UNION

Presidents of the United States have hardly helped to stave off disaster. President Clinton, for example, failed to grasp the nature and extent of our global crisis, and on the other hand the opportunity for change—what would have been an historic change from "Earth Kill" to "Earth Care." He ignored the importance of the original Earth Day and its Earth Trustee agenda.

America enjoys its greatest prosperity, but at the expense of a major part of the world. Its system of money and power robs the suffering poor that are in the majority in many countries.

While America pioneered democracy and laws to further freedom and justice, most of its resulting wealth has been spent on vast military weapons and programs for ways to kill people. The terrible record of war and injustice during the past millennium is still with us. You cannot pick up a newspaper without some headline about violence, injustice, and conflict.

Action must be taken that will provide a future, something to live for. The idea needed is the simple truth, good and bad, about our planet. Its appalling past must be recognized as we seek to realize the positive potential of its people.

People are the problem. With a new vision they can be the solution. Wake up world. A great future is possible now!

The core concept needed by Earthkind for a better tomorrow is the need to be Trustees of planet Earth, to take charge and take care of our planet with fair benefits for all. To accomplish this, five major items need to be addressed: ecology, money, property, government, and inner life.

Let us begin with *ecology*. A first priority is protection and care of the environment—Earth's raw materials and natural resources, including creatures large and small. All individuals should be encouraged to have or support an Earth Care project, to do as much for their planet as they would do for their country. The whole world can further this purpose by joining in the observance of one great global holiday—Earth Day on the March equinox. When the Peace Bell at the United Nations rings at the moment spring begins, people of every creed and culture can strengthen a global sense of community by their silent prayers and positive thoughts, by their heartfelt commitment to think and act as trustees of planet Earth. A real understanding of Earth Day, and its purpose in peace, justice, and the care of Earth, will bring commitment and Earth Trustee actions.

Second is *money*. We must provide an honest, fair, medium of exchange and equitable access to credit. A money system is needed that will facilitate barter or exchange with the advantage to workers and producers instead of to money manipulators. Money should be a means for exchange with minimum cost to the user. Where there is adequate security for a loan there should be no interest charged, only a charge for the cost of the transaction. A simple change in the Federal Reserve would make this work. Money should be available in exchange for a legal lien on adequate tangible assets, and available in a fixed percentage of assets that will meet the need for money flow without inflation. A fair money system will bring benefits to everyone.

Third is *property*. Planet Earth is humanity's inheritance. We must recognize the rightful claim of every person to inherit an equitable portion of Earth's natural bounty. Land, or a portion of money from the sale of land, can and should provide every family on Earth with a habitable homestead—a farm, a house, or an apartment. Fair property rights will bring security to everyone. Taxes should be based on the value of land, not improvements.

Fourth is *government*. To achieve a balance of freedom and order and check the power plays of national governments, local communities must be given a larger responsibility for peace and the care of Earth. Let towns and cities link with each other—locally and across national boundaries—in major, vigorous independent programs to foster understanding and cooperation in solving social and environmental problems.

A "Council of World Towns and Cities" is needed for these purposes. This can bring the measure of unity we need in our diversity and help foster the trust needed by nations to achieve lasting peace for all peoples.

Fifth is *inner life*. One of the greatest causes of conflict in history has been the conflicting views of different religions (including ethical atheism). At the same time it is religion that has most effectively fostered humanitarian actions. Can the obvious benefits in different religions be approved and supported without approving that part of their creeds with which we differ?

Most people have an allegiance to a creed dealing with the mysteries of life. Creeds explain why we are here. Is there a future life? Is there a God? Answers to such questions often provide meaning and incentives for a virtuous life. But each person must temper his belief by recognizing any virtue he sees in people who have a different hypothesis about the mysteries of life.

Most seekers of truth share the conviction that love is the greatest wisdom. The Creator must have infinite wisdom. Therefore the Creator must be a God of love. By emphasizing our common search for love and light and basic points of agreement—including the importance of the Golden Rule, creative altruism, integrity, repentance, forgiveness, and recognizing our differences—we can, with a touch of humility, reinforce the values we share. Inner experience can then fuel mutual efforts for a better life, a better world.

Heralding a program for Trusteeship of Earth with these redemptive changes would quickly bring new attitudes of trust and hope—a change of heart worldwide. Efforts for completion of a safe disarmament will then succeed. The money saved can provide a great education for the next generation.

Is it possible to turn things around, to turn things right side up? Yes. The means of great change are at our fingertips. With the aid of the telephone, radio, TV, computers, and websites we can, here in America, inspire a new global climate for opinion that will enable us to harvest Earth's bounty instead of suffer from fear-induced scarcity and greed.

In scattered places all over the world, a few people are demonstrating solutions to major problems. Mostly unknown to each other, they are showing the way. Let America launch a global campaign for the redemption and renewal of planet Earth. Let us headline the creative actions and the ideas new and old that are healing and nurturing our planet. Let each of us spread the word: *Wake up world—a great future is possible now.*

OUR COSMIC QUEST

We are at the point in history where we may discover some answers to basic questions that have puzzled the great minds of the past. What is the purpose of the vast cosmos? Why are we here? Where are we going? Why are we addicted to war? Is there life on other planets? Are there other dimensions of reality? We are overwhelmed by the magnitude of the mysteries.

In the present explosion of information and knowledge, from the discovery in space of immense black holes to tiny finite quarks, the one thing that keeps coming back is the mystery of love. When we see a mother holding a baby, and when, in the most tragic things that happen, here and there we see individuals of compassion and love, the mystery strikes home to our heart.

While there are many unanswered questions, many scientists believe that love is a part of the cosmos. It has been shown in an intriguing way how molecular and biological elements often come together, attracted to one another for mutual benefit and creation of something new. When we work together for mutual benefit we are building on the very nature of the universe. Consciousness of this fact will enhance our efforts. Love of God and of his creation will bring personal and global benefit.

A help to many is belief in a Supreme Being. There must be a self-conscious Creator, otherwise I am in some sense superior to the source of all that is. God must have infinite wisdom. The greatest wisdom is love. And we know the wisest people are those who love. God must be a God of love.

As we probe the great mysteries of the universe, both physical and metaphysical questions, we are at a point in history where there seems to be the possibility of getting some fundamental, practical answers to the basic questions about who and what we are, and the role of our planet in the scheme of things. Humanity and the global web of life may play an important role in the destiny of our galaxy! It is of great importance that we continue the human adventure. To do this we must correct the things that we know are wrong in our attitudes and actions, so that we can continue to explore the unknown.

EARTH MIRACLE

You can be part of the greatest miracle in history: the miracle of Earth's rebirth.

Imagine a world of freedom and order with no war and a healthy environment. Imagine economic incentives for improving the quality of life, where the pleasures of inheriting a portion of our beautiful planet are shared by the children of the poor, as well as by the children of the rich!

Close your eyes and picture the world as a Garden of Eden, cared for in pride by all the people of our planet, with the best of Earth's thousands of cultures each adding its sparkle to Earth's changing patterns of beauty. Great new cities with clean power and air. New towns with numerous parks amid nearby wilderness areas. No population problem.

A constantly improving technology, in harmony with nature, serving to better the quality of life. In this new world, man would spend his major time in learning, and loving, and exploring the new meanings of mind and spirit and the great mysteries of the cosmos.

All this and much more can happen in your lifetime!

BIRTH PANGS OF EARTH

In the present birth pangs of planet Earth, there is turmoil and suffering. Everything is being shaken and the things that are false are being exposed. The moral and mental bankruptcy of all the leading nations is clearly seen. The masks are cracking and the hypocrisies in business, politics, and religion are everywhere evident.

But underlying all this is humanity, and a growing awareness that Earth is giving birth to something new, something pure and good.

A new breed of man is being born, individuals that hear the call of destiny and obtain their direction, not from the thrones of power, but from their own inner voice. There is a new consciousness expressed in terms such as "Spaceship Earth," recycling, meditation, renewal, and harmony with nature. New models and systems and plans for the future are emerging. Young Earth-Builders are at work with a new honesty and a peaceful vitality. A real Earth People movement is in the making.

The key to making the Earth Miracle happen is for the enlightened few to find each other, to deepen their commitments, communicate, and encourage one another, and to intensify their Earth-building activities. Already mankind has available the ideas, the technology, and the initial skills for building a dynamic world culture. The awareness of this is rapidly spreading. We are approaching the "critical mass" where spontaneous regeneration will begin.

EARTH PEOPLE

Who are they? What are they trying to do?

The idea of Earth People grew out of Earth Day and the conceptual revolution that followed. Earth People are individuals who have embraced the new ecology world view, and are seeking harmony with nature and with one another as the only solution to the grave environmental crisis of our polluted planet.

The new concepts that draw them together are set forth in the Earth Day Proclamation, written June 20, 1970, and signed by Secretary-General U Thant and other humanitarian leaders for International Earth Day on March 21, 1971.

No special organization is being formed to further this movement. There is nothing to join. To indicate their participation, individuals may fly the Earth Flag, wear an Earth Patch or Earth Button, and sign copies of the Earth Day Proclamation. The extent of participation is up to each individual, but all Earth People are urged to join some group that is vigorously working to heal and build our planet through programs related to ecology, wildlife conservation, and population. Earth People Centers (see chapter 17) have been set up in some places to help Earth People exchange information about local needs and actions.

Earth People recognize that only those who do their part to help take care of Spaceship Earth have a right to use and enjoy this wondrous planet; only they have the right to be called "Earth People." As world citizens, they realize that it is the highly technological societies that are responsible for the crisis in which we find our planet, and they realize that we must start at home to solve the problems that we all face.

EARTH BUILDERS

Earth People are Earth Builders. Be an Earth Builder. Join the silent Earth Brotherhood, the invisible global community of people who are experiencing a new consciousness of love, of oneness with all nature and with one another. Join the new breed of honest men and women who are seeking to peacefully build the Earth for the glory of God and the joy of all creation.

Picture our Space Ship Earth swiftly moving through the vast regions of space on a great mission that is only dimly understood thus far by the most enlightened minds. Your help is needed in the search to understand and fulfill that mission. Your consciousness counts in helping provide the total enlightenment and energy for the task.

While our situation is desperate, our purpose here is not to appeal for help from space, nor from amorphous institutions such as governments, corporations, religions, and other groups. Our purpose is to reach concerned individuals with convincing evidence that we can help ourselves; that you and I and other individuals can act together in a special way, with sufficient vigor, to change all society from the destruction of Earth to its nurture and care. All that is needed is understanding of what is required, and a strong dedication to our task. Everyone can help save our planet.

The way to begin is simple. Begin each morning with a period of silent meditation, prayer, or reflection. Think of the friends in this life and beyond who have influenced you for good—for love, beauty, honesty, courage, and faith. Realize a connection with them and others who come to your mind. In deep gratitude accept the joyous love you feel welling up within you—love of family and friends, love of God, joyful thoughts of beauty in nature, music, children—and tears. Bring into this divine ocean of grace all your anxieties, fears, selfishness, and failures. Accept the healing and help that at that moment is yours for the asking. And then rest in the great peace that will follow. In that great silent peace you will have gentle clear thoughts—a still small voice within—telling you the immediate actions you can take to help build a new Earth.

4

Efforts for Peace—and the Fate of the World

THE ESSENCE OF MY THOUGHT AND MY EFFORTS

EARLY IN LIFE I went on my own search to find what life is all about. This brought me in touch with leading scientists and stimulated my appreciation of a scientific view of everything. In later years I was aided by top scientists, philosophers, and leaders of the Christian, Jewish, and Muslim religions.

The search to know more about everything, which my father engendered, led to my friendship with an outstanding scientist, a chemist named Albert Nobell. With the help of money obtained from George Pepperdine (of the Pepperdine Foundation and the namesake of Pepperdine University), in 1939 we established the Nobell Research Laboratory in Los Angeles.

Our work there brought me in touch with scientists at Cal Tech and resulted in dialogue with them about space exploration, and the search for peaceful uses of atomic energy. In 1958 I attended the Atoms for Peace Conference in Geneva where my proposal for a visible Star of Hope Satellite attracted attention and support.

I came to the conclusion that to save our planet and have a future we should come together where we agree and leave room for our differences.

THE WAY TO PEACE AND PROSPERITY ON PLANET EARTH

We need a global goal with strong global appeal.

What can help us most is an idea that can be understood and that can change the situation. The problem is not other people or other countries. The problem is all of us. As the comic-strip character Pogo said, "We've met the enemy and he is us."

Today, we need an idea that will turn things around all over the world. We need a concept that can bring a global change of attitude—if you will, a global change of heart.

I want to present that idea to you right now: *All that is needed is for each of us, in his or her own way, to be a trustee and caretaker of planet Earth, seeking the nurture of Earth's life and fair benefits for all its people.*

This is an agenda that will appeal to all. There will be differences about details and priorities. But the way to peaceful progress is to share views of where you agree and where you differ, and to leave decisions about implementation to local communities.

For example, present differences at the United Nations about abortion will not be resolved at the global level. But leaving this matter to local governments and institutions can enable the United Nations to proceed in matters where all agree.

Stephen Hawking has answered key questions about time and space in the universe. What we most need to understand is the nature of our planet and the human family who will determine its future.

We are now in the greatest global crisis in human history. "Crisis" means danger and opportunity. Never before has it been possible for so few to kill so many. Devilish weapons are now available to angry dissidents.

In our global society we have many creeds and cultures—with differences and limited mutual understanding. The world is filled with real and imagined injustice. The 9–11 terrorist attack is only a tiny sample of what can happen.

During the brief period of my life I have seen more and more evil at work worldwide. It has reached a point where some scholars believe civilization is doomed and will come to an end in the next few decades.

On the other hand, our amazing technologies make possible communication and the rapid spread of solutions all over the world.

THE WAY TO A BETTER FUTURE

To turn the world right side up and provide a future for ourselves and our children, we need to look at the big picture.

Throughout this book I seek to describe what we know about the state of the world, the nature of people and planet, and the factors that must be addressed in order to provide a future of peace, justice, freedom, and prosperity.

To be practical, we must first look at the enigma of human ignorance. Most people want to do the right thing. But they choose the words and actions that cause conflict, waste, pollution, and injustice, and diminish freedom and order. "Father, forgive them. They know not what they do."[1]

An example: The United States and its Christian majority spend billions for bombs and pennies for peace. Were the money that is now devoted to our vast military establishment given instead to global education that would foster peace, justice, and a sustainable future, there would be no more wars and we could have a future of peaceful progress.

The biggest enigma to me is the way President George W. Bush invited Christian leaders to the White House to pray that he would make Christian choices in his administration. Then he did the opposite of what Jesus taught. He wanted their backing as he stepped up the killing of people he claimed were our enemy.

Jesus said, "Love your enemies,"[2] and was the world's greatest example of nonviolence. Martin Luther King Jr. said "He who is devoid of the power to forgive is devoid of the power to love."[3]

I credit the measure of success in my efforts for peace to my Christian faith. At the same time, I applaud those of other religions who also work for "peace, justice, and the care of Earth."

When it comes to ultimate questions regarding reality, we are confronted with profound mystery. I have no proof of what will happen when I die. I have no videotape of Heaven. But I am impressed with the local and global results of actions by devout Christians who put their faith to work.

It is interesting to note that those who have done the most to benefit people and planet have been those who believe in a future life. While

1. Luke 23:34.

2. Matthew 5:44.

3. From "Loving Your Enemies" by Martin Luther King Jr., a sermon delivered at the Dexter Avenue Baptist Church in Montgomery, Alabama, at Christmas, 1957. Martin Luther King wrote it while in jail for committing nonviolent civil disobedience during the Montgomery bus boycott.

only a small minority of those who claim to be Christians do what Jesus taught, without them the world would be far worse than it is. Jesus told us to love one another and forgive one another.

To choose a better future we need to understand not only the nature of people, but also the nature of institutions. Few people realize how much their words and actions are the result of what they see and hear—on TV, radio, and newspapers—and now on the Internet. Then there is the influence of your school, religion, and the nature of the culture in which you live.

In all of this what gets attention is the result of who has the money. One of the tragic problems is that the mass media do not accent the positive. They make more money when they accent the negative. A TV anchor man told me the easiest way to keep up their ratings was to identify with people's hate, fear, greed, and lust. Turn on the TV and you will see the result.

Add to this the nature of our banks, corporations, and stock market, and you see that money is made, not in ways that further justice and freedom, but in ways that make millions for the people who best control the system. Lord Acton said, "Power tends to corrupt, and absolute power corrupts absolutely."[4]

But again, most people want to do the right thing, and it is ignorance of the big picture that prevents peaceful progress on our planet. We must come together where we agree, leaving room for differences.

A GLOBAL EARTH TRUSTEE CAMPAIGN

Let's spell out the global solution that will appeal to the most people and do the most good.

We must get the backing of powerful leaders and big money who will reward the best examples of Earth Trustee actions. Institutions of every kind will find in my Earth Magna Charta the policies and agenda that will best serve this purpose.

Foundations are urged to provide grants for the best examples of Earth Trustee actions. Media can do their part by featuring what they see as the best examples.

A key objective is a change in the global state of mind, reflected by mass media, that will inspire the best in people and institutions.

4. Acton, letter to Bishop Mandell Creighton.

Get these ideas to religious, business, and political leaders of every kind. Offer a heartfelt prayer that we will succeed in a global effort to think and act as responsible Earth Trustees, with liberty and justice for all.

The best place for an Earth Trustee example would be the city of Jerusalem—holy to Christian, Jew, and Muslim.

We need a miracle. But I believe in miracles!

5

My Family History

THE FAMILY LINE

JOHN SAUNDERS McCONNELL (EVANGELIST J. S. McConnell) was my father. He was born in Seattle, Washington, on January 9, 1892, and died in Ahwahnee, California, in 1966. His father was Rev. T. W. McConnell. When I was small, Grandpa McConnell told about going to Oregon in a covered wagon with my grandmother, and how the Indians they met did not attack them because he prayed and trusted God.

Dad was always bragging about the fact that we are descended from pioneer stock. In my youth I heard many stories about how we were related to Daniel Boone (as descendants of a brother of Daniel Boone), and descendants of Red Conn, an Irish king. In my early youth the whole feeling about pioneering, the pioneer spirit, was in my blood.

When I was about ten years old, we were living outside of San Diego, California. I remember walking down a dirt road in San Diego, and picking up a scrap of paper that had a poem on it. It said,

> Lord, give me the strength of the pioneer
> And the faith of his hardy soul!
> Provide me with courage to persevere;
> Make me fight till I reach my goal.
>
> Let weaklings indulge in a sheltered life
> Where they curse when their luck goes bad,
> But fit me for battle, with storm and strife;
> Give me brawn like my fathers had!

> I want to be known as a man who wins,
> As a fellow with nerve and pluck
> Who finishes everything he begins,
> And as one who can whip his luck![1]

I still remember the poem and feel it contributed to my drive and persistence.

GRANDFATHER T. W. MCCONNELL

The capability of Internet search engines constantly amazes me. I knew that my grandfather, T. W. McConnell, was a preacher, a Baptist minister, and had preached in Los Angeles. I put his name in the Google search engine and found the following which I had not known. Here is one of the records from an Apostolic Faith website:

Evangelist T. W. McConnell's Testimony

About twenty-eight years ago, I went into a meeting to break it up, and the Lord broke me up. My conversion I never could doubt. I was called to preach and refused, and went on for a number of years trying to get away from the call. Finally I obeyed the Lord, and started in to work for him, but not to preach. The Lord sanctified my soul. Then I commenced to try to preach. About two years after, the Lord appeared to me in a dream. He so filled me with his Spirit that people were not able to stand up before me, for a time. A few days after, he told me to give up my business, and make my wants known to him, and not to man. I obeyed. The Lord supplied my every need, and was with me in revival meetings and in healing many that I prayed for. But I heard of people receiving the Holy Ghost and speaking with tongues. I came to Los Angeles to investigate, and found it was a fact, and earnestly commenced to seek the Lord for the baptism with the Holy Ghost. And the Lord, knowing my heart, came and took possession of me and spoke with my tongue. I want to say to every person, test God and you will never deny the baptism with the Holy Ghost.
Experience in Trusting God for Needs.
The first time I was out of wood after the Lord had shown me to trust him, I asked the Lord for wood and the wood did not come. The Lord had shown me that I could not ask for flour till

1. Hawthorne, "Make Me A Man!"

it was gone. I went down into the basement that morning and found some hard knots that had been laid aside and had enough wood for that day. The next morning I asked the Lord for wood. The wood did not come. I picked up enough chunks and chips to do that day. The next morning, I went to the Lord and said, "Father, there are no more chunks and chips, we are out of wood. Send the wood." I went down to the city and forgot all about it. Did not think of it, until I returned home, and my daughter said, "Papa, who brought the wood?" I told her that "she need not trouble, the Lord would send it." But she said, "Some man brought wood, who was he that you sent it by?" I thought she was joking, but she said, "Look in the box and in the basement." I went down and found a large load of wood all ready for the stove and just the length that we used in our stove.

I did not know for some time who brought the wood; but one day when holding meetings in South Seattle, a man invited me home with him, and while at dinner he said, "I want to tell you something that happened to me. I was crossing the bridge with a load of wood. My wife had written out a bill of some things that we had to have, and I needed feed for my horses. I was taking this load of wood in to get the groceries and feed. While out on the bridge and no one near me, an audible voice said behind me and just above me, 'Take this wood to McConnell.' I looked around me and there was no one near me. I said, 'I cannot take this wood to McConnell, I have got to have the groceries and feed,' and drove on. The voice said again, 'Take this wood to T. W. McConnell.' I said, 'How can I take this wood to McConnell; I must have these groceries and feed for my horses.' And the third time the voice spoke, and so strong that it scared me, and I answered, 'Well, I will,' for I believed it was the Lord talking. There was no one about. I went and made inquiry, finally looked in the directory and found where you lived. I drove to the house and unloaded the wood, then drove back home as quickly as I could, loaded up some wood that I had and drove back to town, sold my wood as soon as I reached town, got my feed and groceries, and from that time I have prospered as never before."

T. W. M.[2]

---

2. T. W. McConnell, "Evangelist T. W. McConnell's Testimony."

EVANGELIST J. S. MCCONNELL

My father, John Saunders McConnell Sr., was one of the founders of the Assemblies of God. My father was called "the fiery Irishman." I have many memories of my father—many memories of things he said and did that were inspiring. He preached a great sermon on 1 Corinthians 13, the love chapter. The sermon is reprinted in the appendix. At times he did many things that demonstrated love for his family.

My father used to teach that God is love, and love by its nature wants to give love and receive it. Therefore he created man with free will (a necessity for love), knowing that by the very nature of free will, man would make selfish instead of loving choices.

But then, when man's selfish choices led to evil results and separation from God, to save man God gave his Son to suffer in man's stead. His Son taught man the way to peace—to love the Lord our God with all our soul, mind, and strength, and our neighbor as ourselves.

BIRTH AND CHILDHOOD

I was born on March 22, 1915, in Davis City, Iowa. Apparently it was a very small town. My parents were Pentecostal evangelists who were touring the country. They stayed there for awhile. Someone gave them the use of a house and that's where I was born. I was their first child. I am grateful for their love and teaching in my early years.

While I have always preferred to call myself John McConnell, the full name my parents gave me was John Saunders McConnell Jr. My mother, Hattie (McLaughlin) McConnell, traveled with Dad and they never stayed in one place very long. She told me she was grateful for the house that was provided by Christian supporters of Dad's ministry when she announced she was going to have a child. But when I was a few months old they moved on.

One story my mother told about me concerned my interest at an early age in songs they sang. Dad had written many songs, most all with a message. When he built a tabernacle in Walla Walla, Washington, in 1920, he wrote the Airplane Song.[3] Airplanes were new then. (We used to spell it "aireoplane.") The song said,

---

3. Published in 1930 in a hymnal as "The Heavenly Aeroplane." See the poem in the Appendix.

> One of these nights about twelve o'clock,
> This old world's gonna reel and rock.
> Sinners will tremble and cry for pain.
> And the Lord will come in His aireoplane.

One day I was playing in the yard, when for the first time I saw an airplane. I ran into the house and cried, "Mommy come quick! Jesus is here."

I am also reminded of the song we used to sing, "Rose of Sharon, now blooming I see. Rose of Sharon so precious to me . . . ." Uldine Utley, a teen-age evangelist, had a magazine called "Rose of Sharon." I knew her family and for a time traveled with them. In her New York meeting, she packed out Madison Square Garden.

We are all affected by our childhood experiences and memories. I was fortunate in having loving parents. They were strict, as most parents were back then. On one occasion I was seated on the platform behind where my father was preaching. He was puzzled by the smiles on the faces in the audience. Then he looked behind him and discovered I was standing there imitating all his gestures. I've forgotten whether I got a spanking that time. I did on many occasions.

However, Dad showed wonderful affection for me and all his children. There were eventually six—three boys and three girls. I was the oldest and often had to take care of my younger brothers and sisters. When we were holding meetings in Indianapolis, Indiana, I was taking care of Paul, my baby brother. I put him in my wagon and was able to take the wagon right into the library. He was asleep and it gave me a chance to read some books, which I loved to do.

A newspaper reporter from the *Indianapolis Star* was in the library and took a picture of me in my Boy Scout uniform, reading a book, and Paul asleep in the wagon beside me. My parents were dumbfounded to see the photo in the newspaper the next day. (We have a copy of the newspaper article and photo.)

THE EARLY YEARS

I was fortunate in the experiences of my early life. In my earliest memories, I remember that we traveled a great deal. My interest in nature was partly the result of the fact that we traveled so much. While my father's meetings kept us on the move, visiting churches in every part of the country, I benefited from the people I met and the wonderful experiences of seeing the wonders of nature, from the Redwoods in California, and the snowfall in Maine, to the beaches and Everglades in Florida.

At the time of my sister Grace's birth (I was about three years old), my father explained to me that I was going to have a baby sister and I was going to get to see her. He drove me in his Ford car to see my baby sister. Just before that, for the first time in my life, I had seen a black child. I was very excited, so I asked my Dad, "By the way, is she going to be black or white?"

Another memory that I have is that a member of our church in San Diego worked at the Balboa Zoo and used to take me there. His son and I would play with the baby lions, which was a great thrill.

A Bible scripture that especially influenced me was "Seek first the kingdom of God." Since God is love, we should seek the rule of his love and wisdom on our planet.

Beginning at age six or seven, and since then through the years, I have learned more and more about what this could mean. My ever-inquiring mind continued its search through the ups and downs of my life adventure. I made mistakes and committed sins, for which I had to ask God's forgiveness. But I kept coming back to my desire to understand and further a kingdom of love and peace on our planet.

I have an amusing story in regard to what you remember when you're young. I was about ten or eleven years old. This was in Seattle, Washington. My parents had friends over who had a bunch of girls. We were put in my room to talk or play. They got to talking about who could remember furthest back. It was really interesting. I wish I had a recording of it.

Finally, they asked me how far I could remember back. I said, "I remember back to the day before I was born."

They said, "What!?!" I said, "I cried all night for fear I'd be a girl."

To put my memories into context, I have to talk about my father. As one of the founders of the Assemblies of God, my father felt called to new fields, to minister as an independent Pentecostal minister. So we were always traveling. We never stayed in one place more than a few months.

I recall that when we were in Seattle, there was a church where my father was preaching. I got in trouble because one day I wandered off to another room of the church and fell asleep in the corner. When it came time to go, they couldn't find me. They finally found me.

Back in those days, we didn't understand how we're conditioned by our creeds and our cultures. Black people were like a different race. My father was very liberal for those days. He'd have colored singers come and sing and he'd preach for colored churches, but they were always separate from white people.

FAMILY INFLUENCES

Our lives are influenced by the factors in our experience, in our upbringing and in our environment. These influences are integral to our attitudes, our drive, and our will. One of the influences in my life was that my father, when I was very young, talked to me and said that we should think about Jesus.

When I was converted, I even had the baptism and spoke in tongues. I never spoke in tongues after that.

Other people were converted, and for them it was an emotional experience. But my father said, "John, I want you to understand what I preach and what I say and what I do, but I want you to think for yourself. We are confronted with mystery. You must find out what to believe in your own way." He kept preaching in his sermons, "What's life all about?" But he wanted me to seek the answer to that question in my own way.

Because my father was a Pentecostal leader and later an independent evangelist, and in my early youth we were constantly on the move, I lack formal education. What little I had consisted of grade school in many parts of the country. I did have one year of high school and one year of college. My schooling was rather irregular. I remember that in Texas I had a real easy time, because before that I attended school in Vancouver, Canada, and the standards in Vancouver in the second or third grade were higher. In Texas, they advanced me a full grade.

During those early years, I witnessed many miraculous cases of healing and answers to prayer. Later in my life I tried to look at all of these events, along with psychic phenomena, from an objective scientific standpoint. But the more you know, the greater the mystery.

I recall in San Diego a Sister Nuzum, who worked in the Mexican district in order to evangelize and help Mexican people. She was an elderly woman. One day I was complaining to her about a big wart I had on my toe. She said, "Well John, you know if we will pray, Jesus will take it away." She used to talk in a very personal way about her relationship with Jesus.

She prayed for my wart. The very next day, I was going to school barefoot (because of the wart, my shoe wouldn't fit), and somebody ran across my foot with his shoe. The foot was bleeding and I was taken into the principal's office, where I discovered the wart was gone. The spot quickly healed.

Along the way, I was imbued with a strong interest in reading. When I was about fifteen years of age, during the Depression in Oakland, California, I got a job working part-time in the public library. I'll never forget Miss Morgan, the librarian, who took an interest in me and got me interested in outstanding books on classics, science, and nature. I remember reading all of the books by Earnest Thompson Seaton. He was a great naturalist. Many other books helped my thinking. I was really taken by the pioneers that lived on the frontier.

Then I got a job when I was about seventeen with the American Correspondence School. They offered an educational program that we sold for a very small amount of money. They would send lessons for you to give your children. It was like home schooling. I made pretty good money doing that. The sales were good in out-of-the-way places. I covered territory all over northern California and southern Oregon. And I was so taken with the natural beauty.

Later we lived on Oregon's West Coast. My father bought a piece of land from a real estate operator who had bought it. There was room for about 50–100 lots, by dividing the piece of land into small areas. We sold it at a good profit. But then we found out that the man who bought it from us made a lot more money.

That convinced me that the best way to make money was to look for a place where the population is moving, and buy land there and hold it, and you would double and triple your money. Through history that is how the big money was made. I was really persuaded of this, and I wish I had followed it, for I'd be wealthy today.

My search for the meaning of life led me, during teen-age years and afterward, to explore science, religion, and philosophy. My father's ideas influenced me even after I left home. At one point, around 1939, he wrote a tract, "What's Life All About? Why are we here? Where are we going?" About that time, I was a partner with Albert Nobell, a chemist, in the Nobell Research Laboratory in Los Angeles, California. While my formal education was limited to one year in high school and one semester in college, our work brought me into personal contact with leading scientists and their books.

I attended Pepperdine University. While attending I sometimes played tennis with the president, Hugh Tiner. The founder of the University, George Pepperdine, was then the silent partner in our Nobell Research Foundation, providing most of the funding. My meeting him is an interesting story. We needed funds for our laboratory. Mr. Pepperdine was founder of Western Auto Supply Co. He formed the Pepperdine Foundation which had an office on Wilshire Boulevard. One Sunday, I passed the Foundation and decided to stop. When I looked through the door, I saw that someone was in the office. I knocked and the person who opened the door was George Pepperdine. He invited me into the office. This began a wonderful friendship.

During the Depression, I helped build a highway. I dug ditches and did hard labor at various times. Later, I was ordained by my father, and I preached in churches across the country. During the war I was a conscientious objector.

6

Traveling with the Evangelist

IN MY EARLY YOUTH, my dad, J. S. McConnell, always took his family along in his evangelistic endeavors across the country. Dad was advertised as "the fiery Irishman" and was a dynamic speaker. He could quote great portions of the Bible. We would all help with singing and in other ways.

I still remember the words of dozens of songs we sang. They come back to me when I need their help. One that pops into my mind right now is the following:

> So, I'll travel on, before my feet grow weary.
> I must hurry on, to the celebration in the sky.
> Where sweet music sounds, I'll find my loved ones waiting,
> Waiting, to welcome me, to the Jubilee in the sky.
> I'll never have a worry, never a care,
> Friends all around me, joy everywhere.
> There'll be a grand reunion when I get there,
> And, Oh How happy I will be.
> So, I'll toddle on, I hear sweet voices calling,
> Calling, for me to come, to the Jubilee in the sky.

I don't have a really good voice, but I can sing dozens of gospel songs from memory. Many of them were written by my father. Some were by my mother. One song of hers that has been a great help to me has these words:

> Oh, the faith that works by love
> Will move the mountains when we pray.
> Oh, the faith that works by love
> Will turn the darkness into day.

I wish I had more of the records of Dad's life. All I have is a scrap book, a few tracts, his book, *The New Covenant*, and his Bible, which is filled with his notations and cross-references. I also have the following article, "Power from on High—What Is It?,"[1] an article by C. G. Finney in a tract I found in my father's things after he died. Handwritten on its cover is a brief note: "God has not changed since Finney's day and is willing to give you all He gave Finney and keep His power on you as He did on him. Let's meet conditions."

I recognized the handwriting. It was that of Sister Nuzum. She was a member of the church where my father was the pastor. She was a very successful soul-winner. She was also a close friend of the family, and we often had her to dinner at our home. This was when I was in first grade.

In the tract, Charles Finney said he came to the Lord ". . . on the morning of the 10th of October, 1821." He was powerfully converted in the morning, and the same day received overwhelming baptisms of the Holy Spirit. The major immediate result was the power to witness to others and fasten saving impressions on the minds of men. When he lacked this power he would humble himself, and with prayer and fasting cry for help: "The power would return with all its freshness."

One of my many memories of Sister Nuzum is this: When I had to feed the chickens she went with me. A chicken was drinking water and would repeatedly raise its head as it drank. Sister Nuzum said, "Other creatures appreciate what God provides. Look John, every time that chicken takes a drink she raises her head in thanks to God."

Through the years I have held on to Finney's tract. I repeatedly forget about it, but then when I come across it I read it again. It always leads me to rekindle my prayer life and faith. "Thank you, Sister Nuzum."

GOSPEL CAR

As mentioned, my father was one of the founders of the Assemblies of God. In their archives is a copy of a photo that shows Dad and Mother standing in front of their Gospel Car. This vehicle was their home as they went across the country preaching the gospel. The words "GOSPEL CAR" were on the side in large letters. The car had hard rubber tires and chain drive, and a two-cycle engine. Dad used to say it was air cooled; it would go about twenty miles and then he'd stop and let it cool. The Waco

---

1. Finney, "Power from on High."

Bridge in Waco, Texas is in the background of the photo. The year is 1912, three years before I was born. The photo is the first photo included in this book. The second photo shows the group including my parents that convened to organize the Assemblies of God in 1914.

When I was growing up, we initially traveled by car, then by car and trailer, and then in Los Angeles a rich man gave Dad a kind of bus that was built on a Pierce Arrow chassis that had been lengthened. It had enough built-in accommodations that our whole family could eat and sleep inside. A little railing circled the top, which had a rowboat you could take down when you were at a lake. We used this vehicle for traveling; we went across the country in it and stopped at different cities and had meetings in different churches. We had contacts with all kinds of full gospel and Pentecostal churches. Dad packed out big auditoriums.

We went to New York, and on Coney Island we parked by the boardwalk. We'd get up on top of the bus with its rowboat. Usually it was upside down and we'd turn it right side up. It made a compelling attraction. We would sing and then Dad would preach to people on the boardwalk.

Among the people who were converted was a wealthy woman who put us up at her home. I'll never forget that. She gave us everything. Dad received money from people who liked what he was doing.

My father started something for Jews called "God's Powerhouse," right on the boardwalk, on the street that ran alongside. The aim was getting the Jews in there. He wouldn't mention Jesus; he spoke in very general terms about love and power in your life.

While in New York City, Dad preached at the famous Cornell Memorial Methodist Church. We had a place where we lived right near the church. Dad held a revival there and packed out the church.

The pastor was Lincoln Caswell, who would give special programs where he would impersonate Abraham Lincoln. With Dad was the Tindley Sextet—six sons of Charles Tindley, a famous black singer and minister. He had them all trained in singing. Tindley wrote "We'll Understand It By and By." The Tindley Sextet was featured in my father's meetings. This was around 1930.

We have clippings of the photo that appeared in New York papers that shows the Tindley Sextet in the row boat singing, and I am in coveralls with a fishing pole. I put a string on the pole with a clothespin at the end, and would put the leaflet telling about our meetings in the clothespin, and pass it on to people on the street.

I remember that in the meetings the youngest son, E. Thurwalden Tindley, would tell the story of how his father wrote the song "Nothing Between." He said it was written at the time of his father's death; his father had his six sons round his bedside, where he shared the song's message with them. This was the message he wanted his sons to remember.

Then the son would sing "Nothing Between," and when he came to "Keep the way clear, let nothing between," at the word "way" his tenor voice would go an extra octave higher. It was sensational and there wouldn't be a dry eye in the audience.

The son was offered a role in Green Pastures on Broadway (a musical comedy that earned a Pulitzer). He turned it down, because he was interested only in living the gospel of Christ, as he was a Christian.

We'd go downtown in Times Square with the Tindley Sextet singing on the top of the car. It stopped traffic, and we were on the front pages of the newspapers. The police had to come in and get us to move. We weren't breaking any laws, but it was causing traffic jams. That got publicity.

Dad knew how to get publicity. He had catchy titles to advertise his sermons, such as, "Hell discovered 60 miles from New York."

Another memory of mine is about Willis Shank and the wonderful times we had together. My father was holding a meeting in Seattle. It was during the Depression and I was shopping in a Good Will store. The clerk was Willis Shank. We immediately became friends. I had contacts with a radio station, and we started a gospel radio program called, "The Radio Gospel Train." It was very successful and we were invited to many churches.

I remember our theme song:

> I'm traveling, with Jesus, on the Radio Gospel Train.
> I'm happy, and rejoicing, on the Radio Gospel Train.
> Soon we'll reach the Union Station.
> Heaven is my destination,
> For I'm traveling, with Jesus, on the Radio Gospel Train.

I know that later on many "evangelists" got money in the wrong way and misused it. But I have only good memories of what my father said and did in his meetings concerning money. One thing my father preached, and I failed to practice, was we don't go into debt. We don't assume that God will pay off a debt. Assumption is different from faith. That's where, at times, I made a big mistake. It's easy to borrow money.

VIGNETTES OF LIFE

Security these days is much different than when I was young. When I was about sixteen we were in Seattle, and President Franklin Roosevelt visited the city. There was a parade, and he came along in the motorcade. I was kind of adventurous, and as the car came along, I ran out on the street and jumped on the running board! No problem, and we went down the street. My friends were dumbfounded when they saw President Roosevelt coming down the street, with me waving to them.

The President didn't pay me any attention. He was busy waving to everyone.

FAMILY LATER ON

My mother was a good wife and went along with my father. Much later on, they were divorced, but still later they remarried. My dad lived to be seventy-four. My mother lived to be one hundred.

7

Setting the Bearings

BEFORE WORLD WAR II

A ROUND 1939 I MET Albert Nobell, a chemist, who ran the Nobell Research Laboratory in Los Angeles, California, which later became the Nobell Research Foundation. I served as vice-president and business manager of the Foundation. I was about twenty-four.

Albert Nobell was brilliant. He had worked for Monsanto, one of the big chemical firms.

We developed a thermosetting plastic, and designed the first plastic plant on the West Coast for its manufacture. To help in conservation of nature we developed a plastic using walnut shells. Through other research in the laboratory seeking uses for waste products, my concern for ecology grew. We sought inventions that would save energy. Our work brought me in personal contact with leading scientists and their books.

DURING WORLD WAR II

Through work with the Nobell Research Laboratory, I had conversations with Edward Teller, the inventor of the atomic bomb. He agreed with my idea of focusing on the fact that all people are part of one human family. Our venture into space aided this new world view.

However, Teller was Jewish and motivated by his fear of Hitler's followers. He saw Hitler as a threat who must be destroyed before any action for global understanding and peaceful progress could succeed. He did suggest that a student exchange program with Germany and Russia could lead to understanding and peaceful resolution of conflict. I tried to get attention for that idea, but did not succeed.

But when I argued after the war that the atom bomb was not the way to peace, he said that we should fund a program that would enable every college student to have one year of college studies in a foreign college, especially behind the Iron Curtain.

I shared this with members of Congress, but nothing happened. In 1944 I also met with senators to create a prayer room in the Capitol.

AVOIDING MILITARY SERVICE

I joined the Merchant Marine after the United States entered World War II. It was one of the things I did when I was struggling with my conscience about what was the right thing to do. I felt it was not right for me to be free of danger while people were risking their lives, even though they were, in my mind, ignoring the commands of God and the ways of God. At that time, the greatest danger was in the Merchant Marine. And so I went into the Merchant Marine. I was careful to choose ships that were not carrying military cargo, but carrying good things to people. I worked in the boiler room. It was hot work, shoveling coal into the boiler. And I preached all services on this vessel.

I'll never forget two occasions. From our ship we once saw the sinking of a couple of other Merchant Marine ships by submarines. On the other occasion, another ship went out of control, and veered around and came into us. It didn't do enough damage to cause us to sink. But the other ship was next to us. I'll never forget; I had the impulse to jump onto the other ship for no good reason at all. I've often wondered what would have happened. My life would have been different if I had made that leap.

I was in the Merchant Marine a little over a year. I shipped out from New York on July 10, 1942, and was honorably discharged from the US Coast Guard on August 4, 1943, for service in the American Merchant Marine in Oceangoing Service. During that time my home of record was Oakland, California. This discharge was not officially given until 1989.

I came back from the Merchant Marine for one trip home. I was expecting to go on another trip, and so I came home for a visit. It just happened to be when authorities were checking up trying to find me, and I was picked up and inducted into the Army.

My present wife, Anna, says she has never understood how I got inducted into the Army while working in the Merchant Marine.

I blame myself; you have to communicate the right way with people. When I went before the draft board, it was my chance to sound off to them. I expressed my convictions very firmly. I was preaching to them, and of course that turned them off completely. They decided that they would "take care of" this "character" (me). They disallowed my conscientious objection and insisted that I go into the service.

I had George Pepperdine, founder of Western Auto Supply, multimillionaire, founder of Pepperdine College, come and testify on my behalf. They still said I had to go into the Army. I really admired George Pepperdine for supporting me.

So, I was inducted. But I refused to take the oath during induction. I went through the procedure against my will. All the way along I kept saying that I did not agree to this. I was put into basic training. The draft forced me into conflict with the Army.

The thing I'll never forget that was so real to me was the following: I was on the Army rifle range. They gave me a rifle. They made us lie on the ground and point the gun at a target I was supposed to hit, and I was an excellent marksman. The target was a figure of a man. I was supposed to get as many bullets as possible into the figure. Suddenly that figure turned into the face of Jesus, who said, "Inasmuch as you do it to them, you do it to me." I decided that soldiers, whenever they kill, they're killing Jesus.

I flatly refused to fire the rifle. So, I was put in the stockade.

GOING AWOL

I stirred up trouble in the stockade by trying to preach to the guards, and for that I was placed in solitary confinement. I was limited to bread and water. I refused the bread for eleven days, losing forty pounds. I was without light or heat in what they called "the black box." Afterwards I was released and charges against me were dropped.

What sustained me in this soul-wrenching experience were the words in a song by the daughter of Catherine Booth of the Salvation Army. Over a hundred years ago the daughter was imprisoned in a French cell where she had to fight off the rats. While there she wrote, "Blest beloved of my soul. I am here alone with thee. And my prison is a haven, since thou sharest it with me."

Given my opposition to military service, I sought a discharge. To me my induction was plainly unfair because I had been serving in the Merchant Marine, and also was a preacher, legally, when I was drafted.

And I was only on short leave from further service in the Merchant Marine. The thing that made me go AWOL, finally, was that while getting authorized for discharge I was given an office job, doing office work, and I overheard the man over me say, "Oh, that John McConnell, we're just going to put this paper (the paper authorizing a discharge) aside, and do it after the war."

Concerning my classification and my discharge, it should not have been done the way it was. I did not get a dishonorable discharge. And I did not get an honorable discharge either. I got the middle one.

Because my discharge from the Army was delayed, here is what I did to avoid further service. My first wife, Mary Lou, and I bought a sailboat down in Sarasota, Florida, and took it out of the country in war time. We lived on the boat for two years.

SAILING TO HONDURAS

In 1945, Mary Lou and I sailed our 38 ft yawl ("The Christian") into the region of the Bay Islands near Honduras. We eventually reached the harbor at Oak Ridge, Roatan, Spanish Honduras. This was a very dramatic adventure, as I had left the United States because I did not approve of our support of World War II.

All things work together for good to them that love the Lord. A few days into April 1945, we landed on this beautiful little island, Roatan, not knowing where we were, but deeply grateful for the sight of any kind of land. Sixteen days before, we had been sailing a few miles out of Tampa, Florida, when we experienced in succession a calm, engine trouble, and then a storm that broke our boom, ripped some of our sail, and blew us several days we knew not where.

We did not have any proper navigation instruments. I couldn't get a sextant. But I happened to have a copy of Gatty's Raft Book.[1] Just a little booklet, it told you how to determine your position at sea with just a yardstick and a piece of string. You may have needed a clock of some kind.

I used it to get my position within a few miles. With it we were able get a very rough idea of where we were. We found the storm had brought us somewhere down to the Caribbean Sea. When we came near the Bay Islands, I aimed at them using Gatty's Raft Book.

---

1. Gatty, *The Raft Book*.

After repairing the torn sails and lashing a splice on the boom, we rigged enough sail to take us slowly south under a gentle east wind. We hoped to strike land somewhere along the coast of Honduras. And then we saw land. I knew it was off the coast of Honduras, and there were three little islands. The islands were called Oak Ridge, of all places, because I had been involved with some scientists working on the atom bomb at Oak Ridge, Tennessee.

As we approached one of the islands, we supposed the people would be Spanish speaking, so seeing a fisherman in a little sailboat, we headed our boat for him. Mary Lou was all ready with three sentences in Spanish to find out where we were and where the nearest village was. To our utter amazement he answered in English, and we found, among other things, that these islands, though Spanish territory, were once British territory and to this day are old English speaking. So by Divine Providence we were able to get busy for the Lord as soon as we arrived.

I remember Port Royal with its ruins of an ancient fort. That was our first landfall, when we arrived at the island. Its small bay provided a perfect escape from the storm that accompanied our arrival. I discovered there was only one man living there. But he told me about Oak Ridge and we left in a few days to go there.

On arrival we found ourselves in the lovely little harbor of the town of Oak Ridge. Our engine was fixed, we made arrangements to obtain a new boom, and the people of the village (numbering about 1500) received us with open arms. A steady stream of children paddled out to our boat with gifts from the neighboring homes. Over several days we received more than ten kinds of cake, besides eggs, bread, sweet potatoes, plantains, three kinds of bananas, green and ripe coconuts—of which we were both very fond—as well as grapefruit, limes, and candy.

We lived on our boat while there. The people were friendly and prided themselves in the food they served when we visited their homes. It was good and quite different than anything we had tasted.

It would be great if I could find anyone who remembers me. There must be some record of the six months or more that we were in Oak Ridge.

We were very good friends of the mayor. I don't remember his name, but the mayor repeatedly had us to his home. I also remember the old English they spoke was different than I had heard. He "awksd" me what my name was.

During our visit the people told me their fascinating history. Among other things they had dual citizenship. When the islands were ceded to Honduras, it was with the understanding that the people could keep their British Citizenship.

A boat builder there was constructing a small vessel using a special wood that resisted worms. The planks were fastened with wooden dowels. The people had great imagination and initiative.

One of the residents gave me the keys to a doctor's office that had been closed since he died. He was their only doctor. I learned much from the books about medicine he had left behind.

On one occasion we were sailing around the island and were becalmed. I had an engine, but I rarely used it and it was not working. A large boat whose owner was Captain Morgan happened to pass by our sail boat, and he offered to tow us back to the harbor—which he did.

PREACHING IN HONDURAS

God must have sent us to this isolated community, as we found that they had a nice church and a fair Sunday school, but no minister. I was invited to preach at this little Baptist church. We preached at the church and I believe a revival was on the way. One night some of the folk had to paddle a mile and a half against the wind to be in the service.

When I spoke at the church in Oak Ridge, I mentioned that I had known some of the key scientists working on the idea of an atomic bomb. I told them of the incredible damage such a bomb would cause. A week later, news of the Hiroshima atomic bomb was reported on radio, and people were amazed that I had spoken of such a possibility.

The people said they had been praying for a pastor and invited me to be that person. I spoke each Sunday at their church while I was there. We also started a school. Oak Ridge, Roatan, brings back many wonderful memories.

I was introduced to the people as "Reverend Miracle" and it surely was a miracle the way God brought us there.

I thought that with the boat I could make money taking people for a cruise. A man who was an outstanding sailor offered me a chance to go on a cruise somewhere, I forget where. I got concerned because his favorite pastime was to show how close he could sail to a rock—with my boat!

Some Christian church up in the states carried a story about what we were doing, and sent us an offering of several hundred dollars.

I was fascinated with the sea life down there. I will never forget using underwater goggles and seeing all kinds of amazing fish. It was very exciting. I could see so far underwater.

At one point I had a wonderful experience going up the Rio Dulce river in Guatemala. I can remember the howling monkeys on the canyon walls. I had to anchor my boat up the river because the hurricane season was coming on, and I was going back to Guatemala City. So I took my little dinghy, and I rowed back down the Rio Dulce to Puerto Barrios. I rowed through the night. It was a beautiful moonlit night. A porpoise kept me company. He discovered that when he came swishing by, he turned my dinghy around a little bit. He kept doing it more and more, until he had my dinghy going around and around. After he tired of his play, he went on. Every possible effort should be made to protect the dolphins.

Here is how I got back to the States from Honduras: Mary Lou got pregnant. At that time the war was over. I had proof of my citizenship, and so we were able to fly back into the States.

Concerning the boat, at first I left it down there. Then when we went back, I arranged for its sale. I've often wondered whatever happened to it. At the time, I was being pursued by the authorities, because I was one of those that had deserted from the Army.

PRISON TIME

For going AWOL, I went to prison in California, but only for a matter of months. Wilson Van Dusen was the psychologist responsible for giving me the Rorschach and other tests at Fort Ord (Monterey Bay, California) when I was in prison. A few years ago he wrote me and challenged me to keep my focus on God.

I believe many of the greatest victories over difficulties have been the result of religious belief. In my own case, in reflecting on my life and what influenced me, I have thought of the time I was in prison after the war, because of my opposition to World War II, and my religious views on war and what should be done about it. In prison I had good and bad experiences.

Most of the prisoners were black. To keep us busy, or perhaps to give us exercise, we were ordered to march around the prison yard. Some had been loyal soldiers on the front lines, but were late in returning from time off to see their families, or were being punished for minor infractions.

On this particular evening, they had kept us marching for hours and many of us were angry. Spontaneously, someone in the ranks started singing a Negro Spiritual. Soon we all joined in. The song helped me then, and had a lasting effect on my life. I remember well the words and the tune, and the memory often comes back to me and helps in my life journey.

Negro Spiritual

Up above my head, I hear music in the air.
Up above my head, I hear music in the air.
Up above my head, I hear music in the air.
Now I know, Yes I know,
There's a God somewhere.

The greatest music comes from faith in God. From Gregorian chants to Negro spirituals, the Christian finds support for his faith. Let atheists study and sing the great hymns, and they will experience a change of heart!

The messages in songs inspired in Heaven are the best means of changing War Makers to Peace Makers and of turning hate into love.

FOLLOWING PRISON

In 1954, some time after my release, I was briefly a registrar for Lincoln Law School in Oakland, California. Later the same year, I became a representative for the American Correspondence School.

In 1956, I became interested in newspaper publications. I moved to North Carolina and co-published *The Toe Valley View* with Erling Toness. Right after Sputnik in 1957, I wrote the editorial on Star of Hope, which began my direct involvement with ideas that would go round the world.

In 1959, Erling Toness and I moved to California and we founded *The Mountain View*. During that time, I wrote an editorial urging a joint venture with the USSR in space. Also, I was traveling and working on the Star of Hope project.

In August, 1960, Toness and I formed a limited partnership in charge of *The Mountain View* because of my involvement in the Star of Hope project. This was severed in December 1961. After that, I became the Northern California director for Meals for Millions, providing food for Hong Kong refugees fleeing Communist China. We organized a parade in San Francisco that raised $60,000 for multi-nutrient meals.

8

Family Life

MY FIRST FAMILY

I MARRIED MY FIRST wife, Mary Lou Clarke, in Los Angeles in 1943. Mary Lou was beautiful, talented, and a wonderful wife. However, after the birth of our second child, it was discovered that she was schizophrenic. This may have been triggered by my difficulty with the Army. She filed for divorce in 1953, which became finalized in 1954.

Our first child was born in 1946. She uses the name Coronella Prudence Heather Keiper, but her real name is Constance Blythe McConnell. Unfortunately, she inherited the schizophrenia.

Our second child, Cary, was born in 1949. He lives near San Diego and is doing well.

A SECOND FAMILY LIFE

Anna and I were married in 1967. We first had a son, John Paul, born in 1968, who died when Anna was pregnant with our daughter, Christa, born in 1970. John Paul was a beautiful mongoloid who died of a viral infection in 1969.

Christa is now married and living in Colorado. From my journal entry in January, 1978, I recall her childhood and how I sang to her at bedtime. Here is the story in present tense:

> For years I have been singing "Magic Songs" to Christa as she goes to sleep. For several years this was every night, but during the last couple of years I just allow occasional songs, perhaps one or two a week.

The stories are each different and spontaneous with occasional rhyming when it works out. While related in a singing voice, with changes of mood or key, there is no real musical structure. The only requirement for them is that they contain something "magic."

Christa continues to want these songs. Last night's "Magic Song" is an example:

Andy, a small boy, liked to stroll through the woods near his house. But his brother had warned him not to eat any of the mushrooms he found, because, while some were good, others were deadly poison—and some had strange magical effects.

Andy found some mushrooms he knew from previous descriptions were "Magic." So he ate some and they tasted so good he ate them all up.

Then suddenly he felt his body starting to grow. And to his amazement he kept getting larger and larger until the tree he had been standing under only came up to the top of his toe. And still he kept growing until his body extended out in space past the Moon.

The Moon looked just the right size to play basketball and he saw in the distance a cosmic playground with a basketball court. So he had a great time playing basketball with the Moon.

Then he started picking stars out of the sky, for he saw they were bright shiny marbles. And he played a great game of marbles in the cosmic playground all by himself.

As he got up to go he saw the Earth floating by and stuck it in his pocket.

And then he woke up!

NOTES FROM 1970

April 27, 1970

My wife Anna is expecting a child the end of May (29th). Until last week, the pregnancy has been quite normal, but last Thursday night Anna had pains, which were repeated and finally resulted in bleeding Saturday morning. We took her to Roosevelt Hospital in Manhattan, making the trip from her mother's home in Bridgeport, Connecticut. Dr. Luchinsky examined her and ordered her to bed. Apparently there had been a slight breaking away of the placenta.

The general feeling among Anna's friends (and Anna) is that the baby will be a girl. Last night, I was closing my eyes, opening my Bible at random, and letting my finger decide the Scripture I would read. Turning to different Scriptures (five or six), the question in my mind was, "What is the mission of this child; will our new baby be a boy or a girl?" The final verse I turned to was Luke 1:57. My finger was on the verse, "Now Elizabeth's full time came that she should be delivered: and she brought forth a son." (One of the previous verses was Ps 22:9–10, where David speaks of his birth.) This same day we received a letter from my mother saying she had dreamed of Anna having a baby boy. However, our child was a girl—not a boy.

When the mind is at rest and honestly seeking God's will, it is amazing how often opening the Bible at random will result in a Scripture bearing on the subject in mind. This has happened to me dozens of times. A few months ago I was concerned about finding some Scripture that would bear on the concept of planetary inheritance which I had developed. With this specific question in mind, I prayerfully opened the Bible, and my finger rested on Ps 115:16: ". . . the earth hath He given to the children of men." (This is one example of many.)

While superstitious use of this practice will lead (and has often led) to fanaticism, nevertheless, our searching for the "Way" is often aided in this manner. The way it operates seems in some degree similar to the I-Ching.

April 30, 1970 (Wonderful anointing in prayer this morning.)

As we love God, we want to be one with him. In becoming one with him, the problem of keeping our freedom and at the same time surrendering our will is solved. For we discover our greatest freedom is found, not in *freedom from him*, nor to be free from God's will, but in *freedom with him*. As we become one with him we begin to participate in his freedom, the freedom of the Creator—in whose image we were created. There is far more freedom within the constraint of God's will than there is without it.

September 28, 1970

Coordinating one's thoughts, feelings, and experiences in the planning of the future is difficult in a busy life. Improvement would undoubtedly be aided by some brief written record, so that a more accurate perspective of the past can provide a better guide to the future.

A person's journey through life, especially the *inner* journey, can be aided by occasional reference to past insights and experiences. Since the passage of time so easily clouds the conscious memory, and sometimes distorts or erases its images, this written record should serve a useful purpose.

MOVE TO DENVER

Diary Entry, 2002

We have just completed a major move, from New York to Denver. This morning in my time of meditation I felt I should take action on something I have long neglected—a daily or weekly diary. In this I will try to report the items in my personal life and in the world that have my attention. And it will provide material for the story of my life [in this book].

My wife and I arrived in Denver on June 21. Joy Mason, sister of our son-in-law, picked us up at the airport and brought us to our new home. Our new address is 4924 E. Kentucky Circle, Denver, CO 80246. (Phone Number: 303-758-7687).

It is a small cottage, part of a cottage complex run by three church organizations. We pay only $500 a month for rent, and this includes many services: a central office building with library, exercise facilities, and meals available at noon each day. We are entitled to one free meal a week and other times pay $6.

This is a kind of a new beginning for us. I hope and pray I will find one or more individuals in this new environment who will see the importance of the thought and actions in my long life— and use them to head the whole world in a better direction.

STRANGER THAN FICTION

October 27, 2002, Idledale, Colorado

Today is a beautiful day. My wife, Anna, and I dropped what we were doing yesterday and rushed to St. Joseph's Hospital. Our daughter, Christa, had called the night before to tell us she had given birth to her expected child. The child was a girl—7 lb, 10 oz. They have named her Hannah Rose, and of course we wanted to see them.

It was a wonderful visit. Afterward, her husband, Paul Mason, drove us to their home here in the foothills above Denver. We are putting things in order for Christa's arrival with the baby, probably tomorrow.

I'm taking a break to put down some of my thoughts about the amazing story connected with this child's birth.

We all have coincidences in our lives. Some, more than others. What I am about to tell you is a number of seeming coincidences that are indeed "Stranger than Fiction."

Back in the 1960s I was promoting a global "Minute for Peace." This began December 22, 1963, when we ended the thirty day period of mourning for President Kennedy, who had been killed on November 22. I was responsible for the idea of Minute for Peace and had persuaded CBS to produce and broadcast the "Minute"—which carried the voice of Kennedy with the words he had spoken the year before at the United Nations: "Never have the nations of the world had so much to lose or so much to gain. Together we can save our planet . . . ."

This brought global headlines and the support of UN Secretary-General U Thant. I then produced a series of Minutes for Peace that carried the words of world leaders about the ways to peace.

To help me in this, a beautiful office at the top of the Chrysler building in New York was donated by Fred Tomlin, a man whose company was devoted to public relations. He invited me to a reception in his Connecticut home, where a young woman came up to me and said, "Now I know why I came to this event. I was told that I would meet the man who is the reincarnation of George Mason—and I sense that you are him."

Now I did not believe in reincarnation, and still do not. But my background in scientific research made me curious.

She offered to take me to Williamsburg, Virginia, which had the original church that George Mason attended. I agreed and we made the trip.

I was shown a pew with a seat marked as the one where George Mason sat, and at the suggestion of my friend, sat for awhile in that seat. On the way there I was shown a statue of George Mason, and it bore a resemblance to me.

Out of curiosity I studied the life of George Mason, and found that his ideas appealed to me.

But at the time, I had been reading how a person's handwriting reveals a great deal about the person. When I looked at samples of George Mason's handwriting, there was no similarity to mine.

I do not believe in reincarnation. But George Mason's ideas about justice, freedom, and order played a part in my coming up with the idea of Earth Day—which I founded in 1970.

And, when our daughter Christa married Paul *Mason*, I asked him if he were related to George Mason, and found that he is a direct descendant! So my granddaughter Hannah Rose is a descendant of George Mason.

I don't know what it all means, but it is truly "Stranger than Fiction."

CHRISTMAS 2002

Anna Writes a Christmas Letter—

Many wonderful changes for John and Anna have occurred during 2002.

As I'm writing this note at our kitchen table, I'm glancing out of our seven foot window expanse (three windows together) at snow (2–3 inches) covering lawns and trees. Our walks were plowed and shoveled starting at 7 am. It's in the teens and twenties today.

Most of you know that our daughter Christa and son-in-law Garin Paul helped us move to Denver, Colorado at the end of June. Garin drove the Ryder truck—Christa and our 9 year old cat Erasmus accompanied him.

Once Erasmus settled into our little two bedroom cottage, he decided this was a wonderful retirement place! After two months of saying "No" to a leash in order to go out, he's finally said "Yes" and enjoys taking Anna out for a walk!

John enjoys the second bedroom as his office. He is very busy promoting "peace, justice, and the care of Earth" mainly through his computer website.

Another wonderful blessing is the birth of our third grandchild, Hannah Rose, on October 25th. Our two grandchildren, Kaitlin and Robbie, are John's son's (Cary's) children. Hannah Rose is Christa and Garin's daughter (Anna's first biological grandchild).

John will have cataract surgery on December 9th (left eye) and December 23rd (right eye). We pray that the operations will be successful.

Our prayers are that each one of you and your loved ones will have a wonderful Christmas and New Year 2003.

Love from both of us.

CHRISTMAS STAR

Wise Men Still Seek Him

My Life—A Christmas Story

As I write this, Christmas 2002 is just a few days away.

Never was there a darker night. The mighty war-makers of our planet dominate the sky with their devilish weapons, designed to make skeletons of people. Human history is a long record of war, hate, violence, and fear. Now it is at its worst.

But at this moment of impending doom for the whole human family, I hear on the radio, "Hark, the Herald Angels sing . . . Peace on Earth, good will to men." I see on my desk the Christmas card with the Star of Bethlehem. There is also a painting of a three-mast schooner under full sail and with it the words "Wise Men Still Seek Him."

When I was a boy in Oakland, California, I loved to visit the small observatory near our home. They would let me look at the Moon and the amazing vista of space.

Later in my life I made friends of leading astronomers. At one point, we had the astronomer who discovered Comet Kohoutek with us on a Queen Elizabeth II cruise. I came to realize that life is an inexplicable mystery. The more scientists know about the cosmos, the greater the mystery.

But the greatest mystery is the mystery of love—best illustrated by the Christmas story of the birth of Jesus.

This was heralded by a new star and shepherds hearing the Angels singing about his birth. "Hark, the Herald Angels sing, Glory to the newborn King. Peace on Earth and Mercy mild. Heaven and Earth now reconciled."

As a child I loved the Christmas Story and ever since have sought to learn and follow the teachings of the "Man of Galilee."

My wife, Anna, and I were married on Christmas Day. And the magic of Christmas has enriched our life together.

In 1957 right after the first Sputnik, my weekly newspaper in North Carolina, *The Toe Valley View*, urged the launching of a visible "Star of Hope" satellite to foster global peace. The article was picked up by the Associated Press and carried by newspapers worldwide.

The Star (of Bethlehem) with the Story of Christmas was a factor in my 1963 "Minute for Peace." This daily Minute on radio and TV aided peace efforts in succeeding years, and later led to

Earth Day efforts around the world that fostered peaceful resolution of conflict, and cooperation for "peace, justice, and the care of Earth."

At Christmas time we hear wonderful carols. When we listen with our heart they enrich our lives and help make us peacemakers. Jesus said, "Blessed are the peacemakers."

While the wealth and the power of the mighty is devoted to war-making, the power of the faith that comes from love is far greater. Let the peacemakers of the world unite with faith and real love of friend and foe. Prayer, faith, and love can bring the miracle of new life and a new beginning for our planet.

This Christmas is also special to me because our daughter Christa just had a new baby girl. And here at Christmas time I was able to hold in my arms a beautiful miracle of life—my granddaughter.

I was reminded of the wonderful song Ervin Drake wrote and sang at one of our Earth Day ceremonies at the United Nations:

> . . . Every time I hear a newborn baby cry, or touch a leaf, or see the sky.
>
> Then I know why . . . I believe.

Have a blessed Christmas. Let's give top priority to support of peacemaking efforts and elimination of the root causes of violence. Live your faith—and expect a miracle!

CHRISTMAS 2003

Christmas Message, 2003

It's probably the fact that one's working habits slow down as one gets older, but Anna has never been so late in Christmas baking or Christmas cards. We don't know if our greetings will get to you before Christmas, but we want you to know we're thinking of you.

We've had a lot of joys this year. Hannah Rose has been a delight. It's been fun watching her grow. Another joy is watching Christa and Paul's nurturing of her. Hannah Rose will be fourteen months on December 25th. She's been saying "Grandpa" for months now. Anna's been wondering when "Grandma" would come! It was loud and distinct a lot of times last week! Also last week, when Christa went out of the kitchen-dining room, Hanna Rose said, "Bye bye Mama." She does say "Papa" and a number of other words, plus loves to read her books.

Another joy that was not slow in coming is Bethany Anne, born Nov. 26th at 9:30 pm—6 lbs, 15 oz. (Christa got into the hospital a little before 9:00 pm.) Christa and Bethany Anne spent Thanksgiving in the hospital, while Paul, Hannah Rose, Paul's parents, Denny and Chris Mason, his sister, Joy Mason, his grandma Kathy, and John, and Anna had a lovely dinner in Idledale (Paul and Christa's home).

Hannah Rose and Bethany Anne are thirteen months apart, which will keep Christa and Paul busy for a while! We now have four grandchildren with John's son Cary's children in California—Katie thirteen years and Robbie six years.

John is very busy promoting the fortieth anniversary of Minute for Peace Day—December 22, 2003. He's gotten a lot of response through the Web. His site is www.earthsite.org.

Anna ripped the disk on her right side on March 25th. She opted for physical therapy instead of an operation, and has done so well, that about six weeks ago the therapist said Anna didn't need to continue coming for the therapy. Since Anna had been doing about a half hour of exercises per day at home since the mid 1980s, a few more added on didn't faze her.

Both of us are healthy and love living here.

We wish you and your loved ones blessings for 2004.

John and Anna

9

People I Have Met

THE PENTECOSTAL MOVEMENT

A CURIOUS COINCIDENCE YESTERDAY was my coming across an old address book and seeing the name, "Betty Arthur." It had been many years since I had spoken with her. Over fifty years ago she and her mother, Mrs. Hal Smith, had been good friends of our family. They were active leaders at Angeles Temple, the church in Los Angeles headed by Amie Semple McPherson, founder of the International Church of the Foursquare Gospel.

I doubted the old number would still work, but tried it, and Betty answered. We had a wonderful visit on the phone.

One of the people I met through my father's evangelism was Uldine Utley, the child evangelist. She was only fifteen years old at the time. She became a dynamic preacher in Fresno, California. Dad encouraged her and her parents to go into evangelism, and they went across the country holding meetings. She ended up in New York, and packed out Madison Square Garden.

Later, Uldine had a nervous breakdown, and ended up in a New York mental hospital. I found out about it, and was very upset. Her parents got permission to take her to their nearby home for a visit. Instead, they got me to drive them to California, thereby keeping Uldine from going back into this mental hospital. They didn't like the conditions there.

MEMORIES OF BISHOP PIKE

I have been asked to share my memories of Bishop Pike. I was active in San Francisco back in 1963. We ended the period of mourning for President Kennedy with a "Minute for Peace" on radio networks on December 22, 1963. Bishop Pike encouraged my efforts, and I had many meetings with him.

The Bishop was a brilliant man. He could give a talk without any preparation that would be better organized and presented than sermons by others that had hours of preparation. He sought truth with a passion, and reminds me of my father.

In 1966, I was in New York staying at the Biblical Seminary. I learned that Bishop Pike was visiting the city and went to see him at his hotel. He asked me to his room, and happened to mention that his son was going to London and was in the next room asleep.

A few days later I was wakened in the middle of the night with a terrible feeling that someone I knew was dying. In the morning, I happened to meet a woman friend in the elevator. She said, "John, I had a terrible nightmare last night. In this vivid dream I went to open my door and there was a ghost-like skeleton."

The next day there was the story on the front page of the papers telling about the suicide in London of Bishop Pike's son. The woman I had talked with in the elevator had in the meantime called a girl friend in another city and told her of her nightmare. This friend just happened to be the girl friend of Bishop Pike's son.

A short time after this I was back in San Francisco, and I tried to see Bishop Pike. I called his office at the Cathedral, but was told it was his last day at the Cathedral and he could not take a call. I said it was urgent and would they let him know I was on the line. He took the call and we talked. He told me he had no time for so-called psychics, but a Madam Twigg in London had called him and insisted she had been in touch with his son and mentioned items that no one but his son knew about. He was curious.

I don't know what happened with Madam Twigg, but a short time later I was visiting Santa Barbara and learned there was a prayer meeting at a local church. I felt I should attend it, and in a discussion period I mentioned the death of Bishop Pike's son. Present was a George Daisley who spoke to me at the close of the meeting. He said he now knew why he had come to the meeting—he was a psychic and had been in touch with Bishop Pike's son.

I was struck by the coincidence and thought this was a chance to learn more about psychics. Mr. Daisley told me he would give me a sitting at no cost. So, the next day I visited him where he was staying in a guest house at the Bob Hope Ranch.

I took along pencil and paper, and when he supposedly established contact with "the other side," I took down what transpired.

He said he was communicating with my sister. It seemed unlikely that he knew I had a sister who had died in a fire when she was nineteen. Her name was Hope. He said she was so happy to contact me and asked me what I would like to say to her. What followed was interesting. But the answers I supposedly got from Hope were to me unsatisfactory. I asked who else was there, and the answers were evasive. I no longer have the record of what I wrote, but nothing of real importance came from this séance.

However, George Daisley managed to have Bishop Pike see him, and the Bishop later talked to me about it. He said that there were some mediums who seemed to obtain information in a séance that could only come from a departed soul. The problem is, what was the source? He mentioned to me that in India they claim there are "akashic records" in some other dimension of reality where everything that happens on Earth is recorded. Some believe it is demons seeking to lead people astray.

You could go on endlessly with possibilities, but to me it is one of those things that are unknowable. Hundreds of books and research by hundreds of scientists bring us no closer to an answer.

I was saddened by the tragic death of Bishop Pike, which occurred later in the Holy Land. So much in this world is perplexing. But life is bitter sweet. Let's be aware of the evil in life but choose the good. I like the lines of the song my friend Ervin Drake wrote: "Every time I hear a newborn baby cry, or touch a leaf, or see the sky, then I know why . . . I believe."

STORIES OF PEOPLE

I remember one woman who was concerned about the space program. She worked as a nurse in a hospital. In her culture they used to have a belief that women giving birth at a certain phase of the Moon had an easier birth.

Then she heard about our landing on the Moon. Later, when they had some problem in the hospital, she asked, "What in the world did they do to that moon?"

10

Religion and Philosophy

THE ULTIMATE QUESTION

WHAT IS THE MOST important question facing humanity?
When I was a boy, my father, who was an evangelist, often preached a sermon on "What's Life All About?" This is the ultimate question that confronts us. Why are we here? Where are we going? Why is there a universe?

The question is a big one. When it comes to ultimate questions about spiritual or metaphysical matters, we are confronted with profound mystery. Intelligent people from different creeds and cultures come up with conflicting beliefs. There is a massive amount of data about the human adventure—hundreds of good books have been written about our planet and its people. In many cases they complement one another, but often they present conflicting views, partly because no one mind can assimilate all the facts.

> Wisdom, imagination and virtue is lost when messages double, information halves, knowledge quarters . . . .[1]

There is just too much information for even the greatest genius to pull it all together. At the same time, there is broad recognition around the world that civilization is at the greatest crossroad in history. We have grave problems that could result in the demise of humanity. At the same time, we have amazing progress in technology and scientific discoveries that wisely employed could bring a new utopia.

1. Benking, personal communication.

Now is a good time to look at the whole picture: human history, its failures and achievements, and its present dangers and opportunities, and see whether, or how, we can continue the human adventure.

Why do I feel qualified to address this issue? I am not a scholar, scientist, or theologian. Perhaps my effort will encourage others more qualified to address the issue. On the other hand, I have a long history of interest in the subject and have been called sensitive and creative by some leaders in public life. As founder of Earth Day, I have tried to see the whole picture.

To address this issue we need to recognize two levels of reality, the physical and metaphysical. Through the years scholars have come up with different, conflicting ideas about what is real and what is important. There are many differences over the existence or nature of God, the soul, life after death, and the possible purpose or cause of creation. While there are phenomena that suggest another dimension of reality, conflicting explanations lack scientific confirmation.

We generally agree the cosmos exists. There is considerable agreement that creation requires a creator. Extensive mathematical experiments with giant computers have demonstrated that order cannot come from chaos. There is chaos in the cosmos, but within the chaos we find beauty and order at work. There must be a God somewhere!

The wisdom needed for creation is greater than anything we can imagine. It would be easier for an ant to understand the mind of Einstein than for a person to understand the mind of God. On the other hand, many scholars consider the greatest wisdom we know is the wisdom of love. God must be a God of love.

Dorothy Sayers' classic, *Mind of the Maker*,[2] makes a great case for the idea that in his creation God is like a playwright. Shakespeare said, "All the world's a stage." Examining the drama of history we find many amazing stories of tragedy and triumph. The greatest story ever told was about the "Babe of Bethlehem." Belief in what Jesus said and did has repeatedly played a vital role in social progress, better relations, and great music!

When it comes to the question, "What caused the cosmos and why are we here?" there are many hypotheses, but no answers that intelligent minds can agree on. In matters of religion, opinion depends mainly on place of birth. I was born in the state of Iowa and became an

---

2. Sayers, *Mind of the Maker*.

evangelical Christian. The Dalai Lama was born in Tibet, where people believe in reincarnation.

In 1996 it was my privilege to meet the Dalai Lama in Budapest. I expressed my warm appreciation of his efforts in behalf of peace and the stewardship of Earth. But in our conversation I also said, "I want you to know I do not agree with your belief in reincarnation. However, I do not have a videotape of what it's like in heaven and I do not believe you have an X-ray of a soul waiting for reincarnation." The Dalai Lama laughed and warmly agreed with me.

Truth cannot contradict itself. In trying to get around this fact, many today are contending that all truth is relative—that the Hindu, the Christian, and the atheist just see the truth in different ways. Many claim that "there is no absolute truth." The fallacy of this is quickly seen if one adds that, for example, the Nazis just had another way of looking at the truth.

Another view given little attention, but widespread, is that there is no answer to religious metaphysical questions. A friend of mine, who supports my environmental efforts, will not discuss religious questions of life and death, because he "will not waste his time on things that are unknowable." His case is a strong one. But I have found that in my own case and the witness of many others, a belief or faith that provides greater meaning for life is of great benefit, even though in all honesty we must recognize that it is only a working hypothesis.

In all of this we are dealing with phenomena that have many different possible explanations. Some believe miracles of healing and answers to prayer are simply the result of psychic ability. We are confronted with amazing phenomena from different countries that cannot be explained by medical science.

There are strong arguments for another dimension of reality beyond what we see. But thus far, it does not lend itself to scientific methods of proof or broad agreement.

Let's act on what we do know and can agree on. We agree on the need to take care of our planet and take action to eliminate poverty, pollution, and war in this new millennium. Any help in life that your religion provides can be commended, without necessarily agreeing with your creed.

Let's put first the important matters in which we agree. Then we can avoid catastrophe and rejuvenate our planet in this new millennium.

To be successful, we now need a moral equivalent of World War II. The way to achieve this is the Earth Trustee way, set forth in "The Earth Magna Charta." Then peaceful progress will enable us to continue the search to know, "What's Life All About?"

FINDING THE ANSWER

There are many factors that affect a person's life adventure. I am best known for my role in starting Earth Day in 1970. We aided environmental efforts and helped end the Cold War.

But these activities began, as you will discover on my website (http://www.earthsite.org) and throughout this book, when I went on my own search to find what life is all about. The details of that search deal with every major branch of human knowledge. While much was gained from articles, books, and mass media, real understanding came from my conversations with major leaders in science, religion, and philosophy, and with heads of government. Sometimes an exceptional unknown individual would share valuable insight. I was aided by top scientists, philosophers, and leaders of the Christian, Jewish, and Muslim religions.

In the middle of the last century I had meetings with Norman Cousins, who was then Editor of the *Saturday Review of Literature*. He had just returned from a visit with Albert Schweitzer in Africa. Just this year, I was looking at the copy I have of Schweitzer's *Out of My Life and Thought*.[3] At the close of the book, he said that after all his research he had come to the conclusion that life was inexplicably mysterious and filled with suffering.

But he went on to say that there is a will to progress in human society, and the problem is to bring to it a reverence for life.

Over the years, my ever-inquiring mind continued its search through the ups and downs of my life adventure. I made mistakes and committed sins, for which I had to ask God's forgiveness. But I kept coming back to my desire to understand and further a kingdom of love and peace on our planet.

My search led me to explore science, religion, and philosophy. But my life-long search has resulted in total mystery regarding the big picture. Scientists have no explanation of eternity or infinity on which they can agree.

3. Schweitzer, *Out of My Life and Thought*.

But they do agree that the future of the amazing skin of life that covers our globe requires responsible stewardship of Earth by its human inhabitants, with words and actions that promote harmony with people and planet.

I came to the conclusion that to save our planet and have a future we should come together where we agree and leave room for our differences.

THINK FOR YOURSELF

No one seems to realize that in today's world almost no one thinks for himself. Everyone's mind is being manipulated through mass media by someone with money power, fame power, government power or corporate power. It is tragic that hardly anyone seems to know about this.

The organized political, social, and religious institutions of our time persuade individuals not to arrive at their opinions by their own thinking. Their convictions merely reflect the ready-made opinions of the power elite.

Teach your children the importance of morality and faith. But as they get older they should be taught the importance of thinking for themselves. This gains importance when you realize that everyone will sometime in life have an original thought or idea that no one else in the world has ever thought of.

THE CHOICE IS YOURS

The manifestation of God's love and grace seems to be accompanied by such a variety of explanations—many apparently contradicting each other—that it seems obvious there is no plan or effort on the part of an omnipotent Mind to reveal the truth, scientifically and logically, about other realms of reality. This includes life after death, transcendental consciousness, life on other planets, other planes of reality, and so on.

At the same time there is overwhelming evidence of realities independent of and seemingly contradictory to present material scientific knowledge, such as spiritual healing, ESP, and out-of-body experiences.

The one teaching of all higher religions is that God is love (and all love is of God). Until there is a real scientific breakthrough, or demonstration of the nature of higher realities, it would seem prudent to let every seeker choose the path or way he or she believes will best channel the life and love of God into our material world.

In view of some "field force" and "astral body" phenomena, it may be that the faith and love of individuals is in some way fashioning the realms of the Spirit, which in turn determine the course of material progress and evolution. In some powerful and mysterious way, our *not knowing* the scientific explanation of spiritual reality *facilitates* our free choice in fashioning the future, with love and faith. Perhaps at a higher level of evolution we shall see clearly some of these higher realities as we continue our cosmic quest.

In the meantime I would take all the so-called mystics and prophets with a grain of salt. They may each contribute knowledge of some facet of love and life, but none I have heard excel the practical insights and demonstrations that Jesus brought.

TO BELIEVE OR NOT TO BELIEVE

About Unbelief

We all believe that we exist (as Descartes said, "I think, therefore I am"). There is common recognition of the physical world, that is, of people and planet.

The difficulty is the metaphysical mystery: What caused the cosmos? What's life all about? We desire meaning and purpose in life.

The scenario that offers the most hope is the story of the love revealed through the life and words of Jesus. Some do not accept the gospel accounts of his miraculous birth and resurrection. But whether fact or metaphor, or part of both, we find in this historic drama the greatest wisdom and love, revealed through the example of an ideal family.

Joseph, the father, was a man who led and loved. Mary was a woman who loved and led. Jesus was a child who listened and showed unlimited love which he accredited to his heavenly father.

Ever since, the greatest benefactors of human welfare have been those who believed what Jesus said and did, or were influenced by the record. Recent examples include Mahatma Ghandi, and Martin Luther King Jr.

I cannot imagine the source of the cosmos, and the love at work in its chaos, being inferior to me, given that I am conscious of and concerned about what I create. The source of all must be the ultimate leader, conscious of *His* (father=leader symbol) creation.

While the mystery remains, I can no longer reject belief. To do so would be illogical.

This belief does not "limit the spectrum." It broadens the spectrum. Jesus says, "Walk in the light and more light will be given."

RELIGIOUS DIFFERENCES

Once my father was preaching, and a woman came up to him afterward. She said, "I enjoyed your sermon, but you don't go far enough."

He replied, "What do you mean?"

She said, "The Bible says to love your enemy, and the Bible says, the devil is your enemy. You should love the devil."

She had gone on to devil worship. You can turn things upside down.

Despite religious differences, there are similarities among the religions. For example, the Bible and other religious books say similar things. The Koran articulates duties that are similar to what Jesus said.

We have only one Earth. On the other hand, at our present level of awareness, we're headed for doom. I don't know what the future will bring. But I know that unless we have a miracle, we're headed for doom. If there's a God, now is the time for intervention.

And I think what would help is what is written about love, that is, altruism. A book was written on love in terms of altruism, *Love Can Open Prison Doors*.[4] I knew the author, Starr Daily, personally. He was a marvelous man. He had committed murder and was in prison. Because of his Christian experience of salvation, he was working miracles in the prison. As a result, they turned around and released him.

It's amazing how many people I've contacted that have read that book.

COLLECTIVE SPIRITUAL POWER

Can love conquer hate? Can faith conquer fear?

Psychological and psychic factors are perhaps the most decisive in determining human events. Certainly Hitler rode the crest of a raging wave of hate rising from the depths of the human psyche.

---

4. Daily, *Love Can Open Prison Doors*.

Is it possible that in man's unconscious, feelings of love or hate in a large number of people can coagulate and focus their power on a single object, resulting in either fatal or redemptive effects?

Are the tragic assassinations of great leaders who were doing good the result (at least in part) of these little understood but very real factors?

Are the actions of mentally disturbed people sometimes the result of collective hate that has found a waiting trigger to release its evil energy?

Can the healing power of love and faith prevent these kinds of tragedies?

Did the waning spiritual support of Dr. King by his followers result in a failure of spiritual or psychic protection at the time of his death? Could the deaths of John and Robert Kennedy and Martin Luther King been prevented by those who knew how to pray with love and faith for their protection, but didn't?

Can thoughts of strong feeling affect other minds tuned in on the same subject?

Does not the existence of ESP, spiritual healing, and other phenomena suggest a non-material energy at work in human affairs?

Can it be possible that a high intensity faith and love in one individual can add to a collective energy in the unconscious of other people concerned with a particular person, or problem? Can this energy neutralize, heal, or overcome opposing attitudes of fear and hate?

We know our actions affect other people. Do thoughts and prayers about altruistic goals also affect other people?

If they do—and I believe they do—then Earth Day this and every year provides a great opportunity, to halt humanity's rush toward disaster and create a global state of mind that will foster Earth's rejuvenation. I hope you will think about this or pray about it and do what you decide is best.

Reflection on these and other related thoughts may lead us to consider the tremendous power that is available through each person's inner mind or self. A high intensity love, free from all hate or bitter feelings about any person, may add to the collective energy that is working at the deepest levels of psychic reality, to thwart chaotic energies and achieve a higher level of spiritual life on our planet. Every concern that is transformed through prayer and meditation to love and faith is working directly for renewal of Earth and Earthkind.

The test of whether faith is real is the action that follows to back it up. Faith for peace in Palestine will be accompanied by a search for facts, and a generous giving of time and money to relieve suffering and to aid peaceful actions for ending conflict. At the same time, the problem in our technical age of great distances between our acts and their results can be countered by inner awareness of psychic feedback from the results of our thoughts and actions. A sensitive pilot then might have a problem dropping a bomb, because he would feel the pain of the injured. And the taxpayer who pays for the bomb would feel the prick of his conscience. The awakened individual will heed the inner feedback and seek to make his actions consistent with his best thoughts.

In this consideration of the direct power of thought and mind, we are not suggesting a super-duper-computer at work in the unconscious. Perhaps in part this is the way it works. But a better and more human analogy, which brings us closer to the awesome mysteries of the unknown, was provided by the amazing carpenter-teacher Jesus, who told us two thousand years ago to think about God and talk to him as a loving father.

In these days of scientific research, we have probed tiny particles of the atom, explored the moon and neighboring planets, and searched distant solar systems without finding any physical signal from the Creator, who if he exists must be as much and more than we are. Nevertheless, we find that the acceptance of the idea of a divine loving father aids the growth of profound non-material realities, such as courage, faith, love, compassion, kindness, wonder, awareness of beauty, and joy. The record of history attests this over and over again. Perhaps some day our probing and our search will solve some of the mystery and bring a better way. But for now, most people find that talking to their heavenly father obtains the best results in experiencing the inner power of universal love. It is more effective than talking to nobody, or to some nebulous supreme unknown.

The amazing thing is that it works. Faith in a heavenly father can increase our inner capacity for love and for sending healing thought to other troubled minds.

But regardless of the different formulas and brand names, or no names, employed by people of different beliefs, the importance of love is recognized by all. We desperately need a united effort by all groups, churches, temples, mosques, schools, and clubs—young and old—to apply the power of intensive loving thoughts and deeds to the fierce indecencies of war and violence. To this end we should appropriate at least a few billion dollars for research on how the proven powers of meditation and prayer can be used more effectively to promote understanding, cooperation, and peace. Breakthroughs in psychic research should be vigorously pursued and applied to freeing men and nations from their obsessions, freeing them to create in love the peaceable kingdom.

FAITH AND WORKS

One time in New York I briefly attended a Sufi meeting at the St. John Cathedral House. The speaker, their leader from India, radiated love and light, and led in meditation that was hypnotic and peaceful. It seemed to me that he was a channel for loving energies from another realm. But to me the proof of the pudding—the important question—is "How is this contributing to the material and physical goal of Earth's renewal?"

It may be that every yoga feeling and thinking love is somehow healing the minds of men and improving their actions. But I am more impressed by seekers who pray or meditate in the morning and then go out to bake or sew or build or clean, in harmony with nature and with God's requirements for Earth's resurrection. I would be far more impressed with a mystic who found a new practical energy source, or invented a new efficient way of producing protein, than all who work miracles of ecstasy, out of body experiences and levitation.

I believe peace and love found inwardly should be creatively put to work outwardly.

Jesus said, walk in the light and more will be given.

Perhaps we can best reach the peak where we will see the new dawn, by carefully walking now in the faint light of the stars and moon!

11

Personal Faith

THE FOUNDATION

I CONSIDER MYSELF AN evangelical Christian. I believe what the Bible teaches about the birth of Jesus Christ, that he was born of a virgin, and that he rose from the dead. And I believe what he had to say about a future life. I believe the Sermon on the Mount points the way to the best future in this life and whatever lies beyond.

But I must be honest and note that my belief is a hypothesis about profound mysteries in which there are varying kinds of arguments for and against. This is a far cry from setting them out as established facts. It occurs to me that if we had scientific proof that there is a future life, and that all who accept Jesus as their Savior are going to live in this future life and have all the benefits that are described about heaven, why, that would be the same as God saying to a person, "Now, if you'll love me, I'll give you a million dollars." That seems to be the wrong way to obtain love.

The promises that are made in the Bible have been believed by people who have been deeply affected or moved by discovering in someone's life, or in the Scripture, an appealing answer to difficult questions. Some have seen miraculous results in their life and the lives of others they know through belief in the Christian gospel. This is great, but the doctrine they credit for results is their hypothesis—for people with different doctrines have also seen miraculous results and demonstrated love and wisdom in their actions.

I accept as true the teachings of Jesus and believe my faith plays a vital role in my life. At the same time, the altruism Christ inspired in me is found in many people of different religions and political beliefs. I have prayed that Jesus, or some angels, would make a public appearance and settle the question of their reality and the nature of other possible dimensions of reality. Disappointed, I focus on what we must do to continue the human adventure with all its mystery. And my faith still works—I continue my faith in Christ because it has brought the greatest benefit in my life.

SEEKING AND LISTENING TO GOD

Let me share with you some of my own struggle to understand what life is all about. When I was a child, the teaching of my father (an evangelical minister), which greatly influenced me, was based on the words of Jesus, "Seek first the kingdom of God." That meant you were to seek for the rule and reign of God's love in your life and in the world. While my life has had its ups and downs, I keep coming back to this. I testify to the great benefit that comes from constantly listening to the "still small voice within."

The influence of my father, and E. Stanley Jones who advised me, Billy Graham whom I visited at his home, Frank Laubach who was a Christian missionary who developed the literacy program titled "Each One Teach One," and many wonderful less well-known friends, all led me to believe that we could have the presence of Christ with us. The more our faith in his presence, the more the awareness and guidance of his Spirit in our life.

At a recent meeting of leaders from India, I was a featured speaker. I shared with them the fact that I try to spend time in prayer every night before I go to sleep. I pray that I will be aware of God's presence through the night and my first thoughts when waking will be about him and what I can do to please him. Then through the day I try to maintain awareness of his presence and listen for the still small voice that sometimes speaks to me with an idea—quite apart from my natural reasoning. One of the leaders spoke to me afterwards and said that was the best thing he had heard in a long time.

At times, the presence of Christ has been very real to me. Back near the end of World War II, at a time when I was facing the most difficult decisions of my life, I was sailing my 38 ft yawl from Florida to Honduras. It was a beautiful star-lit night and I was thanking God for his help in what I was doing. I seemed to feel an arm around my shoulder and experienced an inner glow.

On November 24, 1965, I wrote,

> The State of Grace I feel today has come to me many times. I wonder what I should do about this. Of course I'm deeply grateful for the joy this brings. And it seems to me it would be desirable to live in a constant State of Grace, conscious of the presence of the Holy Spirit—aware of the pain in yourself and others, but in ecstasy through awareness of the exquisite beauty to be found in unexpected places—sometimes to see the lotus in the mud. To have a conviction there is a destiny—a purpose in life, a mission for each man and woman. To feel the Love of God—a profound mystery that enables all of life.
>
> It seems to me I should seek to maintain this State of Grace and view all people, all problems, all opportunities in the light of its illumination.
>
> Thank you, Father.

Sometimes, however, there are doubts. In 1972 I wrote, "I cry for God. He eludes me. But sometimes in my worst disappointment, a miracle occurs that makes me feel he is near. I am even doubtful that he even exists. I don't even know what or how or where he is. But I cry for God. And as I search I grow—and I know."

Through the ups and downs of the years I have found benefit from practicing or believing that the presence of Christ is with me. And on rare occasions I experience amazing answers to prayer. I struggle over and over again with the question of what it all means. Is it real, *or*, as some would say, the power of positive thinking? The mystery remains. But in my case, in spite of repeated disappointments, faith is repeatedly confirmed.

Through the years I have come to realize that the more I am aware of the presence of Christ, and the more I feel his presence with me, and the more I keep my mind open to the little mental suggestions that seem to be from the Holy Spirit, the more I will make the decisions that are best for his glory and his kingdom.

What is important is constant awareness of the presence of God, and appealing to God for wisdom in the choices we make. When it comes to the ultimate mysteries of life, the meaning is captured not by the scientist, the philosopher, the psychologist, or the theologian, but by the poet, the artist, the musician, and the child. Not by the wisdom of the intellect, but by the wisdom from above, which comes to those who listen to the whispers of conscience, to the tap of love in the beating of the heart.

In my morning devotions there are varying degrees of success in sensing the presence of God. Sometimes I feel empty and go ahead, in praise and worship and reaching out for answers. On the other hand, occasionally there are experiences where I feel flooded with the love and praise and glory of God.

One morning I was thinking of all the difficulties that I have in the mission I am pursuing. It seemed to me that I cannot find, anywhere, individuals who have a grasp of the total picture of the state of the world, of civilization, and of science and our awareness of the cosmos, in what is happening both in religious circles and economic circles, in business and in education (I think of the university presidents on television), and in political efforts—I hear no voice that is speaking of the whole, that is tapping the awareness that is available today, that could with vision and with effort bring a great change in the history of the human family.

As I struggled with these difficulties, I asked myself the question, why is it that I don't have one or two people who completely share the vision I have? Going back to the question of what is wrong in my own efforts, I have misgivings about the failure to see the money provided that is needed for just the bare essentials, and where I can best use my efforts and my thinking. I tend to scatter in too many directions.

Also, as I continue my adventure with Christ, I often wonder if I am following my own idea, or is it really the voice of Jesus speaking to me when a thought comes. However, to know his purpose, we must do his will.

MEDITATION AND THE PRESENCE OF GOD

Earth People should consist of individuals who communicate easily with each other. Their times together should be times of accord, good feeling, "in phase" with each other.

In tuning in during meditation, each person can draw strength by thinking of other participants—friends—who are in accord.

Then, as awareness of the Spirit grows, the self, with all its faults, its sin, its pride, should be lifted into the consciousness of The Presence. The surging love that follows should be directed in mind to the personal relationships where there is conflict, misunderstanding, and jealousy, and as the Spirit leads, to distant individuals, especially those in high places whose choices can help lead the world toward peace.

About noon one day in 1967, I was in my office reading an article in *Faith at Work* on "How to Get Along With People" by C. S. Lewis. I suddenly was especially aware of the presence of God—a warm feeling of illumination, love, and grace. Tears flowed. I wondered if some one of our inner fellowship was praying for me at that moment. And at the same time I felt that this flow of the Spirit should be directed to others. Seeking guidance, I especially thought of Senator Kennedy. He had been on my mind because of his speech on Vietnam. I prayed that this Presence flowing through me would be directed to him and strengthen his will and illuminate his mind. I also gathered in my mind those individuals with whom, through Minute for Peace, I felt a conscious daily link in spirit— Brother Mandus, Pastor Prange, and others. I seemed by these thoughts to increase the power of this Presence and its flow to Senator Kennedy. I added in my thoughts the desire that it might also go to any other person—even some one unknown—who needed and could receive it.

About fifteen minutes later, in an effort to better understand this phenomenon of the Spirit, I went to the phone and called a friend, Sara B. I had spoken with her the day before and felt that she may have partly caused this or participated in it. She answered the phone, and said she had at that very time been praying for me and Minute for Peace, and had also thought about Senator Kennedy. Over the phone we joined in prayer about the war in Vietnam and Senator Kennedy. I again was deeply moved by the sense of God's presence.

However, in this telephone prayer, I unintentionally mentioned someone with whom I felt my friend might have a strained relationship. Immediately, there was a diminishing of the "Presence." I later wondered whether this was just in my mind or something picked up from my friend.

It seems to me that joining only with those who are in one accord with you, and focusing on areas of accord, helps to open our spirit to receive this power. (In Acts they were of one accord, one heart, and one mind when the Holy Spirit came.)

In seeking this love-power of the Holy Spirit, it seems helpful to exclude those with whom you are not in rapport. This should not be a rejection of them, but a recognition of our imperfections, or perhaps of the limitations and differences in our ways of communications. After the Holy Spirit comes in his fullness, we overcome this limitation and understand each other, even when we speak in different languages!

Of course, even in a circle of deep fellowship, there will be differences and difficulties. We must seek to deal with these in love "without dis-emulation." Explore, recognize, and discuss them. But keep detached. There should be no desire to condemn or convert. A spirit of condemnation corrupts the soul. We should not condemn our adversary, our neighbor, or ourselves. Hate condemns—love forgives.

This attitude of detachment, extended to the self, will heal the split that is in each of us. It is in this way that sin and pride in our lives are overcome. We don't change an evil by either fighting or ignoring it.

To get rid of it in our self, we must first be a detached observer. In doing this we discover that which is of God in ourselves, along with longings to know him more, and at the same time we probe the shadows where our sin and pride exist. Right action results from right thinking. Courage to change for the better—to choose the right way—is given to us when we walk in the light of God's forgiveness and grace, letting that light shine on our misdeeds. Then we must consciously lift our whole being—all that we are—into the healing presence of God, not anxious, not guilty, but recognizing that as we bring our whole being into God's love, and keep it there, he will work the changes needed to make of us the creation he desires.

Then, free from condemnation, we can choose to change without self-righteousness, with humility, gratitude, and growing in love, realizing that in common with all humans we ever miss the mark. (We must not judge how far the other person is missing it.) But we can ever draw nearer to it as we recognize our sin, our shadow—our missing the mark—without condemnation. Then, filled with the grace and joy of the Spirit, more and more we will overcome sin and manifest the righteousness of God.

LIFE SUPPORT FROM FAITH

The one thing that I'm grateful for is faith. I don't know whether it's in my genes or a gift from the Holy Spirit. My father's tract called "What Is Life All About?" was permeated with the idea that everyone should think for himself and that we should learn for ourselves what life's all about. Of course, for him, his Christian faith was "What Life Is All About." And I'm grateful for the effect this had on my life.

Belief in God's love and wisdom makes us feel important. Awareness of the magnitude of God's creation brings awe and humility. In life, the pulses of challenge and response may be healthy or sickly, peaceful or violent. By the same token, tension can be creative and purposeful, or mindless and destructive. The factor which makes the difference, which frees the mind of anxiety in moments of great tension and concern, is the inner core of faith that is ever aware of God's loving presence.

At my age now, after all my research and studies through the years, I'm glad that I had thirty-three Nobel Laureates sponsoring Earth Day. I've had discussions with top scientists. Sometimes I'm sorry that I know so much because it takes away from the simplicity of one's faith. I've come to feel that my religion back then was the reason for the miracles that happened and the benefits that I saw.

Some scientists would say, however, that it was the power of positive thinking, or that it was the influence of all kinds of things. I don't agree with that. I stick to my Christian faith.

I have a deep-felt belief in the Christian gospel. I believe in the resurrection of Christ. I believe in the Virgin birth.

But to me that is a hypothesis. In our laboratory, we used to say that we go ahead and do things with a working hypothesis, although we didn't have proof that we were right.

One thing that is unique about the Christian faith, which is missed by the New Age movement and by pantheism and by other creeds or beliefs that suggest that we are all God or that we are all part of God, is the explanation of the phenomenon of what I call sin, whether it's greed or hate or fear or violence. This phenomenon is certainly real. I never had any patience with the extreme Christian Scientists who said that sin is all an illusion of the mind. I find that sin is very real.

At the same time, in the record of history where I have looked, I find that the people whose lives have contributed most to peaceful progress, or to love or to virtues we seek, have been people who recognized sin in themselves and felt deeply about it. They repented of it and were aided in their repentance through their whole portrayal of Christ's death, suffering, and resurrection. For them, this was all part of what this global play is all about.

Where people come to a different conclusion, or explain things in a different way, if we are open and creative, we can find points of accord, points of agreement. These should be so precious that we accommodate our differences.

In the case of Jesus Christ, there was never anyone more loving, kind, thoughtful, and aware. His words all through the Gospels are filled with compassion and love. Nevertheless, hypocrisy was one thing he could not stand. He spoke of "You serpents, you generation of vipers, how shall you escape the judgment of hell" (Matt 23:33).

GUIDANCE AND PRAYER

In addition to using our intellect the best we know how, in making decisions and in acting, another very vital element is our spiritual life, and the intuitive part of life that goes with it. People who are not religious or Christian often tap what is intuitive, but this is an area of special importance to the Christian. We read in the Bible how people were influenced by their dreams. I know in my own life there are times when I have an inner feeling that I believe is related to guidance from the Holy Spirit.

In my Christian background, which included the influence of my father, I have had many experiences. An important influence on my thinking is the feeling that comes from many great songs. My mind is filled with their memory. I think of all the wonderful songs that came to the evangelical movement; my father wrote some of them.

Read the history of "Amazing Grace" and how it was written. The writer was a man who was a slave trader, and was converted to Christ, and became a great witness for freeing the slaves.

Another song comes to mind from the 18th century:

> Forgiveness, forgiveness, forgiveness is free
> No matter how sinful, how vile you may be
> Oh come to the savior, oh come to the savior
> Oh come to the savior right now.

In the Welsh Revival this song caused thousands of conversions and actions that resulted in a spiritual awakening in England and America. Social justice spread. Converts included scholars who established our major universities. I must add that other religions can find in their history similar records.

I have moments of discouragement. I pray to the Lord to keep me going. I spend an hour in prayer every day.

When the busy world about me is so filled with toil and care
And the Spirit's gentle voice is quite unknown
And I slip into my closet and the Savior meets me there
And I spend an hour before the Father's throne
Oh, that happy secret hour I spend with Jesus
What communion have I with Christ alone
How my heart is caused to burn by the lessons that I learn
In that happy secret hour before the throne.

Some times at the end of the day, I say:

Now I lay me down to sleep
I pray the Lord my soul to keep
Tell me in my dreams I pray
What I should do at break of day.

When I pray to God for help in deciding how to do what needs to be done, I remember verses from different songs that bring encouragement:

There's an answer on the way right now
There's an answer on the way right now
Daniel heard the angel say, there's an answer on the way
There's an answer on the way right now

All my days and all my hours
All my will and all my powers
All the passion of my soul
Not a fragment but the whole
Shall be Thine, dear Lord
Shall be Thine, dear Lord

I know the Lord will make a way for me
I know the Lord will make a way for me
If I live a holy life, shun the wrong and do the right
I know the Lord will make a way for me

Faith is the hand that touches God
Until His heart of love is moved
To meet the world's dark need
His grace and power to prove

God hearkens to our faintest cry
When looking from above
He sees behind the prayer we pray
The faith that works by love

Oh the faith that works by love
Will move the mountains when we pray
Oh the faith that works by love
Will turn the darkness into day.

Here is a specific prayer that I pray:

Oh, Lord may your love and light shine on my life today
And guide me to the words I should speak and the things I should do
That will further your Kingdom and bring a great spiritual awakening
All over the world.

ANSWERS TO PRAYER

When I was a child, I saw many people that had terrible diseases or were crippled. I remember one miracle involving a nephew of my father. We were out stomping in the woods and he somehow broke his arm. You know that you have to take a boy who has broken his arm to the doctor. But my Dad took the arm that was broken and bleeding. He put it back and strapped a couple of boards on it. We prayed for the Lord to heal it. And it healed perfectly! These things just don't happen today. And there are many other cases where people had all sorts of problems and the answer was prayer.

Another case that impressed me developed one night before a meeting, when my father gathered the family together to join him in special prayer. This is one memory for think tanks to ponder. My father said that we have a bill we need to pay the next day. It must have been a little over $100. He said, "The way the offerings have been going, I don't think we'll get enough money to take care of it." The offerings had only been running about $50. Back in those days, you could buy for five cents what you pay $2 for today. He mentioned the exact amount of the bill. He asked us to pray that the Lord would provide the money for us, that the offering would take care of it. So we prayed.

That night, they took up the offering. Afterward, it was my job to count the offering. I counted the money. I couldn't believe my eyes. Then I recounted it three times because I couldn't believe it. It was to the penny of what we had prayed for.

DEALING WITH THE UNKNOWABLE

At some time we all think about what will happen when we die. While no one has a video tape of what it's like in heaven, or in other dimensions of reality, most people have some belief about it.

I happen to consider myself an evangelical Christian. I cling to my faith because of its benefit. In trying to reconcile what I have learned from responsible scientists about the Earth and the universe with my Christian faith, I use an idea that came from my days in the Nobell Research Laboratory in Los Angeles. When you get a good result, but cannot explain how it works, call your formula "A Working Hypothesis" and keep using it.

I accept the words and life of Jesus as my working hypothesis. Belief may be contrary to present scientific evidence, but my belief works. The more I study the words and works of Jesus, the more I feel and show the love and understanding that helps the projects I have created and supported.

At the same time, I support the efforts for a better future by people who follow other faiths. I have cooperated with people of other beliefs for common purposes. I make room for our differences in belief.

Earth Day and its Earth Trustee agenda helps us get our priorities straight.

DEATH AND IMMORTALITY

Eventually we face the matter of what happens when we die. There is a tendency for Christians to accent the importance of being baptized and going to church and doing some good things so that when you die, you'll go to heaven. The difficulty is that in this day of science, we know that the Earth isn't 6,000 years old as some Christians believe. Science says the Earth is billions of years old, and when you get into the question of eternity and infinity, we're confronted with ideas beyond our comprehension. When you get to my age, you know that you may only be around a few more years, so you start to think of what happens when you die.

Is there life after death? I believe there is. There are all kinds of phenomena that suggest its possibility. But we lack valid experiments that prove its existence, or why, when, and where it happens. The evidence is interesting, but without far more evidence, there are many possible conflicting explanations. For instance, with the help of a famous psychic,

Madam Twigg in London, Bishop James Pike appeared to have conversations with his son, who had committed suicide. The son appeared to talk of things that only the father knew, and, in some cases, items the father had not thought of for years. But in my conversations with Bishop Pike at that time, he told me he was not completely convinced, for one of the possibilities he had thought of was that all the memories of his son could be in some kind of Akashic Record in another dimension of reality—and it was that data that he was contacting.

In psychic phenomena—especially about the spirit world—the data are amazing, but they somehow always elude firm scientific explanation. Of course, most psychics are just plain frauds.

Consciousness is a vital reality and we need some beliefs or hypotheses to relate to it, and where possible to use our belief or experience for good. Intuition, or "word of knowledge," ESP, spiritual healing, and answers to prayer, all demonstrate that there is more to life than the scientific, physical world.

But in most cases our explanations are vague hypotheses. I was told that one of the astronauts in space conducted ESP experiments with people on Earth. The results indicated that his thought traveled faster than the speed of light. These things stimulate further research. In the meantime, let's accept proven phenomena and use them when we can, but avoid dogmatic statements about unproven explanations.

We all have questions pertaining to God and life after death. While these questions are important to most people, we do not have an accepted scientific basis for certifying which answers are true. I don't have a documentary video of what they are doing in heaven. However, faith in life after death has a powerful value. I once heard a group of prisoners in a jail all join when one of them started singing, "What are they doing in heaven today, where sin and sorrow are all done away." It brought me to tears. And of course no one can prove heaven doesn't exist.

We must recognize our differences and work together where we agree.

During a ride in a car with Robert Kennedy Jr., we talked about life, and life after death, and eternity. We have different creeds and different hypotheses about what the future may bring.

But we do have convincing evidence that the planet exists, and that we have life here. During our lifespan here, we have the potential for pain and for happiness and joy. To give meaning for our passing this way, we should explore more deeply the meaning of life, love, and truth, and prove the creative possibilities that exist in the human mind and in human society.

People that demonstrate the love of God in a marvelous way, and have wonderful answers to prayer, seem to need to focus on a future life, not worrying about what is wrong with this present life, because they feel what is important is eternity and heaven. To me, the Christian hypotheses about life after death, and about what the future will bring, have been a part of much of Christian history that has brought great benefits right here on Earth. History includes the Welsh Revival, the Wesleyan Revival, and early American revivals, where attitudes changed and people started relating to one another, creating a spirit of community and cooperation. They made great changes and did wonderful things right here on Earth. Jesus said, "Thy kingdom come, thy will be done on earth, as it is in heaven."

I believe we should separate our creed about the future from the agreement that we can all share about the present physical planet. We can all agree that we should be responsible to take care of things in the here and now, and change the social systems that are doing so much damage. We can provide real fair opportunity for people.

EASTER FAITH

Easter provides a great opportunity for a new beginning. Get attention for Earth's resurrection, and America will lead the world into a better future. We know America and the world are facing terrible problems. Easter provides the solution!

Our country was founded by devout Christians. They headed our country in the right direction and it became the envy of the world.

Of course, if you look at the complete record, one could say that we stole the land from the Indians. We keep talking about peace, about the Declaration of Independence, and our Constitution, which is to foster freedom and peace. We have a measure of peace, and we have a measure of freedom. But underneath all of this is something terribly corrupt.

Now as I say that, again the enigma is the great good that has been done. The people who first came over here established our universities. Most people don't know that our leading universities, Princeton, and Yale, and so on, were founded by devout Christians. And their purpose was to spread the Gospel. They're hardly doing that now.

In all of these things I come back to the fact that we are at a point in history where unless we reject our habit of war, why, we're headed for doom. We talk about a new millennium, a new world order, and a new age from a different perspective, a different viewpoint. Unless we can see a global change in the state of mind of the human family, in ten to twenty years, civilization will come to an end.

On the other hand, we have new technology and the beautiful truths that come from the lights along the way, and particularly the brightest light of all—the Star of Bethlehem—and the truths that came through Jesus. In my mind, what Jesus said and did brings attention to the Golden Rule.

Jesus said, "I am the way, the truth and the life," and embodied the meaning of truth. The understanding of the importance of truth and its connection with God led to the wise policies and actions that followed the founding of America, and it became the envy of the world.

But in recent years secularism has corrupted our country, teaching that there is no absolute truth. Everything is relative and there is no need for a belief in God. Cynicism and corruption are the result.

We need a miracle. Every Good Friday, let us ask America to join in heartfelt repentance and prayer—with a new commitment to peace, justice, and the care of Earth. On Easter we will confirm our commitment as we celebrate the resurrection of Jesus Christ. With heartfelt faith we can then join in each doing what we can to aid Earth's resurrection.

God will hear our prayer and aid our efforts. We will see a miraculous change for the better in America and all over the world.

To one and all: Spread the word. Help get global attention for our opportunity to make every Easter a Resurrection Day for the whole world.

THE LORD'S PRAYER

In my quiet time one morning in July, 2002, I thought of the Lord's Prayer. At one time my father preached seven sermons on the Lord's Prayer.

It seemed to me that the seven items in the prayer (Matt 6:9–13) provide a basis for global redemption. We need to recognize and affirm:

1. Omnipotence of God: "Our Father which art in heaven."
2. Holiness: "Hallowed be thy name."

3. Our goal: "Thy kingdom come. Thy will be done in earth as it is in heaven."

4. Faith for provision: "Give us this day our daily bread."

5. Forgiveness: "Forgive us our debts as we forgive our debtors."

6. Guidance: "Lead us not into temptation."

7. Deliverance: "But deliver us from evil."

8. "For thine is the kingdom, the power and the glory."

My trouble for many years has been that I wanted to see and get global attention for the big picture: the cosmos, the state of the world, what life is all about, and the agenda that would appeal to people of every creed and culture and provide a future for people and planet.

Now I think I have the way. The Lord's Prayer: *the key to everything.*

The Lord's Prayer provides a way to deal with all the ideas about philosophy, science, religion, history, government, education, etc. They can each be better understood with the help of the Lord's Prayer. There could be hyperlinks to website notes that deal with particulars. Also, hyperlinks to music and glyphs that increase understanding.

GOD AND PAIN

In 1967 I was alone in the apartment, with a very deep sense of the presence of God. I was thinking of how I could see two people at one time—be aware of them, or link in mind with two or more people in other parts of the world, who would feel the connection and think of me.

And I was thinking that God could do the same on an infinite scale, and is aware of all his children. That Jesus through this illumination realized the full potential of his mind and Spirit and thereby provided an intermediate consciousness—the Christ consciousness—of mankind. Through him and his extended awareness we move toward an understanding of God.

Suddenly, in the midst of this meditation, a burst of insight came to me which in a great measure answered the outstanding enigma of life—the problem of pain. It moved me deeply, to the point of a great weeping for joy. It seemed to me that in permitting mankind to exercise his freedom in exploring what is to man "the unknown," and allowing him to bear the consequences of material and spiritual mistakes and the resulting pain (Buchenwald, martyrs, etc.), God is preparing man for a unique role in creation.

If it is true that God is constantly creating ever new forms out of the stuff of his universe, and if it is true—as we see in this life—that this can result in evil as well as good, then it is essential that the beings that would best aid in furthering this exploration of the unknown and his continuing creation, should be prepared by the experience of experiment—choice— and the resulting good or evil which are found in this life.

In this, for the first time, I see a possible value that would justify God's permission of pain as we know it and see it in the lives of his children. Perhaps only in this way can they be prepared for their great role in eternity, in eventual probing of that which is in some measure unknown, even to God, and in participating with him in the great cosmic drama of his ever-continuing creation.

HEAVEN AND HELL

It would be an interesting question to put to an audience, how many believe that they are going to exist after death, and that they will be conscious in some way? Then, how long will this continue? Will it be a thousand years? Okay, how many believe it will continue a million years? How many think that there will be sometime when this ends? By that time, they are beginning to think. Do they think it will continue a trillion years, or a trillion trillion years?

Suppose each grain of sand on the beach represents a trillion years. Now we're talking about a rather stupendous period of time. Will your existence continue that long? If so, do you think that there will be any meaningful recollection of what happened during your life here on Earth? If so, you'll have to have something equivalent to a brain much bigger than the Earth, even with microelectronics. I'm being ridiculous, but when it comes to dealing with eternity, we have no answers.

By the same token, we ask questions about heaven, about the beyond. If there is life after death, what kind of mansions do our loved ones have in heaven? Do they have radio or TV? What kind of clothes do they have? How do they do their laundry? Do they live without food, and if so do they miss the pleasure of eating? What about sex? These things are left without explanation. We don't have a videotape of heaven showing our loved ones and the kind of life they are enjoying.

On the other hand, people talk about folks who are not fortunate enough to hear a convincing message about the Gospel, and therefore die without accepting Jesus Christ as their personal savior, and are condemned to hell. Now they don't go into the matter of what they mean by hell. When it comes to eternity and infinity we are dealing with such staggering mysteries that we really can't cope with them. The more you know, the greater the mystery.

I remember the story of a woman who took some matches and burned her little child's hand to teach her not to steal. When she was denounced for her action, she said it was better for her child to burn for a few seconds from a match, than to have to end up going to hell where she would burn for millions of years.

When we talk about hell, the burning fire of hell, do we mean that the person in hell will feel the pain of burning—not for a few minutes, not for a few hours or days, not for only a thousand years, but for millions and billions and trillions of years? We're talking about eternity, and the idea of eternity is that there is no end to it. When we think about the future we are dealing with great mysteries. As far as the Bible is concerned, it often speaks in metaphor and in parables. In fact we are told that Jesus never spoke without a parable. He was constantly using symbols to get at profound truths that could not be directly described. No man hath seen God nor can we see him.

I remember the story of a little boy who was drawing a picture, and his mother asked him what the picture was about and he said, "Oh, this is a picture of God." And she said, "But nobody knows what God looks like." To which he replied, "Now they will." Well, I think our conceptions of God are in some ways just as limited. We can have only a tiny inkling of what he is all about. But that tiny inkling can be the most wonderful thing in the world.

EVIL

Here is one possible explanation for why evil exists. Since God is love, he desired creatures like him that would love him. To do this, he created man in his own image—an independent creature made to love and be loved.

He knew the nature of independence was such that it would be used to do that which was forbidden. He knew that when he told Eve not to eat the fruit from a particular tree, she would disobey his command.

This would sever their relationship, but provide a way to win her love, and the love of all human beings. You cannot force love, you must win it.

He was then able to win their love by having his Son suffer the death (separation from God) that Eve's sin had caused.

So sin—selfishness, greed, hate—entered the world. But the death and resurrection of Jesus provided a way for love to triumph over evil.

THE WORDS OF JESUS

I was thinking one late January morning in 1981 about the influence of the words and teachings of Jesus on my own life. I thought, I would like to see a book or booklet that contains nothing but the words of Jesus. Or, it would be great if a book were written about what he said and did, based on the historical information that is available today, and that explained the culture and various meanings of terms and phrases. The book could feature the words of Jesus with notes that annotated the items to which I have referred.

There would be a special section that would list the commandments of Jesus (see in the appendix the reprint of the booklet by my father) and the promises of Jesus. Then the book would develop highlights in his life and words. It would conclude with comments about the words, teachings, and life of Jesus made by leaders down through history, reflecting their different opinions.

Jesus gave 147 commandments, and the Gospels are filled with his wisdom and commandments. We need to meditate on what they really mean. You get different meanings from time to time. But more and more, we're moving in the right direction.

In my mind the words of Jesus lead to the best benefit in conduct, and the best benefit for people and planet (speaking in very broad terms). I think that one person who was attuned to this essential thing was Mother Teresa of Calcutta.

The greatest benefit can come from going back to the story of Jesus. Regardless of the intellectual difficulties in acknowledging his divine birth, or resurrection, or the many miracles that are described, we do have evidence that there are miracles. We do not understand them. They seem to contradict everything that we know intellectually about science, about biology, nevertheless, they exist. They are documented.

The question is how can we tap the power of love, of compassion. What we need today is ultimate altruism, the kind that was demonstrated on the cross by Jesus, and by saints and martyrs through the years. We need this ultimate altruism, this deep sense of meaning beyond the immediate circumstances we face. We need to feel that there is meaning in life, and meaning in the cosmos. While it is a mystery, we can come closer to understanding it through the icons, the symbols, the metaphors, the poetry, through graphic illustrations that touch our emotions and our hearts. As we do this, we begin to see that here and there and everywhere there are people who are coming together, who are bridging gaps in understanding, and the power of love is at work.

> Footsteps of Jesus, that make the pathway glow
> We will follow the steps of Jesus, where 'ere they go.

PRAYER FOR GUIDANCE

Dear Heavenly Father, with all these things and many, many more things on my mind, I find it difficult to make the clear choices that are needed to get things done. But You have said that "if you abide in Me and My words abide in you, you can ask what you will and it will be done." Oh Lord, I ask for Your wisdom, for Your guidance, from moment to moment: who I should speak to, what I should write, what I should say, where I should go. Oh God, my circumstances have too much chaos. Only by Your guidance can I find the way. Jesus said, "I am the way, the truth and the life." Help me, Oh Lord, to see the way I should go. And increase my faith. You said that "if you have faith as a grain of mustard seed you can say to this mountain be removed," and there are mountains of obstacles all about us. But, through the wisdom and power of Christ's word we ask that these mountains be removed. One mountain that I face is the lack of funds, the lack of someone to get money and manage it, and to pay bills. These mundane things must be responsibly managed. I need someone. I can't do everything myself. Bring the help. Provide the way. And, Oh Lord, help me to abide in You. May I live the life of the song we used to sing:

> All my days, and all my hours
> All my will, and all my powers
> All the passion of my soul
> Not a fragment, but the whole
> Shall be Thine, Dear Lord.
> Shall be Thine, Dear Lord.

12

A Personal Diary

THE ROLE OF PRAYER IN MY LIFE WORK

THROUGH MOST OF MY life I have devoted time every day to silent prayer, expressing my intense desire to know and do God's will. We used to sing a song, "Accent the Positive, Reject the Negative." To do this you must be aware of the negative. While I have had many answers to prayer, most of my prayers are unanswered (especially in the case of my need for more funds to aid my work).

While prayer has been a part of my life since childhood, its role was best defined in something my wife came across in our records of the past. The year 1964 was a time when the Minute for Peace that I had started in 1963 was gaining global attention. At that time it was my good fortune to meet Tessie Durlach, an elderly woman who invited me to visit her. This resulted in our having regular meetings, where at her suggestion we would join for a period of silent prayer and meditation. During this time we would each write down what came to us and later talk about it.

In January 2000, my wife began going through voluminous records from the past and came across the copy of what I had written about prayer at that time. There are eighteen typewritten pages and on the first is a title, "The Meanings of Peace." The following includes some of these meditations, from the diary.

DIARY

I have often recorded in a diary the thoughts I have received during prayer and reflection. Here is a sample of my meditations, from April 6, 1964 to November 12, 1966. During this time I was actively promoting the Minute for Peace program:

April 6, 1964

The new utopia: The institutions of society should seek to aid, not hinder the purposes of evolution (see *The Phenomenon of Man*[1]). Man can choose the destiny of his society, and should do so. With this in mind, our great universities should seek to define the structure for a new Utopia, bringing into this effort the findings of the behavioral scientists.

August 3, 1964

Money—Promissory Notes:

When checking accounts are permitted, repetition of deposits in other banks creates unearned assets (increments) for the banks. Any unearned asset should go to the equal benefit of all people, not just to the bank.

Loans—a negotiable instrument (note) of an individual is equal in value to the negotiable instrument of the bank (money). The bank has no more right to charge interest for a loan of money than its customer has a right to charge interest for the loan of his note. The only proper charge is for evaluation of the note and the risk it involves—the insurance needed for reasonable risk. Otherwise, note and money should be an equal exchange.

January 25, 1965

Self-righteousness is one of the great blocks to world peace. Our efforts to find accord fail because we condemn the Soviet leaders for their deceit and ill-formed plans. Because we see the evil in their system and actions, we feel we are better than they. This is our great mistake. God judges each man according to the light that he has. Where more light is given, more right action is required. Using this scale of judgment, America, with its rich heritage of freedom and grace, is far more guilty of sin than the USSR.

Our terrible crime rate, neurotic militarism, and gross materialism are a few reminders of our awful hypocrisy. When I listen to the unjust ranting of Soviet Ambassador Nikolai Federenko in

1. de Chardin, *The Phenomenon of Man.*

the Security Council, I am reminded of how much I could have done to further peace in the world that I have not done. I am sure that in the eyes of God I am more guilty than Federenko. Realizing this, I cannot condemn him. I must humbly say, "Let us both give all our strength to the actions we agree will bring lasting accord."

August 21, 1965

Sometimes our thoughts lead to action; sometimes they are an escape from, or a substitute for, action. Nevertheless, most action is the result of some kind of thinking.

September 19, 1965

"Peace is not the absence of war; it is a virtue, a state of mind, a disposition for benevolence, confidence, justice" (Spinoza).

"Peace is not made at the council table, or by treaties, but in the hearts of men" (Herbert Hoover).

Minute for Peace messages will not use empty clichés and sentimental phrases that bring a pseudo-agreement, void of thought or understanding.

Minute for Peace will speak for accord. In controversy, it will seek and praise the words and actions that express sincere accord. Minute for Peace recognizes the need to express conflicting opinions in a free society, but it sees its role as a constant reminder of the goal of accord and cooperation, which is essential for peace.

Minute for Peace endorses the idea of a continuing search to provide the widest possible freedom of action by individuals, groups, and nations, but maintains that this should be more than equaled by a counter force seeking and affirming unity and cooperation. In order to achieve peaceful progress, the major energy of society—in money, talk and time—should be directed to areas of agreement and cooperation.

Let unity be the mainspring and controversy the balance wheel. The work of Minute for Peace is to wind the mainspring of agreement and accord with words of peace, with headlines for happenings that inspire good will and cooperation.

October 20, 1965

Can prayer bring world peace? Millions of prayers have not prevented wars. Prayer is more effective when it is specific. To pray for peace, one must be informed and focus on a specific situation and the key individuals involved.

Without organized hate, war is impossible. Within five years Minute for Peace can make organized hate impossible.

November 8, 1965

Minute for Peace will become a High Court of Conscience—the conscience of the world. Instead of waiting for a "Golden Age" in some nebulous future, why not make it a reality now? The means are at hand. If we act vigorously now, by the turn of the century we will see a world of prosperity, peace and beauty, far exceeding the wildest dreams of even a generation ago.

These are some of the practical possibilities. The springs of freedom and creativity will be released in the majority of individuals throughout the world, because the world's communications media will first of all inspire men everywhere with a new vision of the sovereignty of each person. The ways and techniques of peace will take control and conduct man's conscience.

Checked by his intellect, strengthened by faith, his intuition will give him new confidence, wisdom, and a sense of his responsibility to the Kingdom of God, the Kingdom of Love. This will be aided by a daily "Minute for Peace" shared in unison around the world.

Let us not wait. Let us begin now to build the new world of tomorrow. Let us not think in the old terms of ideologies (religion, communism, socialism, capitalism). If we open the minds of men to good will and mutual trust, all social, economic, and political ideas will be encouraged as experiments for progress. Openly pursued, checked by the new honest sources of evaluation (aided by modern electronics) which mutual trust will provide, each system will gather value from the other.

Competition in the pursuit of excellence will replace the competition which arises in the pursuit of greed or power. The rule of gold will be replaced by the Golden Rule as each man checks his conscience as well as his intellect, for evaluation.

November 24, 1965

The state of grace I feel today has come to me many times. I wonder what I should do about this. Of course I'm deeply grateful for the joy this brings. And it seems to me it would be desirable to live in a constant state of grace, conscious of the presence of the Holy Spirit, aware of the pain in yourself and others, but in ecstasy through awareness of the exquisite beauty to be found in unexpected places—sometimes to see the lotus in the mud. To have a conviction there is a destiny, a purpose in life, a mission for each man and woman. To feel the love of God, a profound mystery that enables all of life. It seemed to me I should seek to maintain this state of grace and view all people, all problems, all opportunities in the light of its illumination. Thank you, Father.

November 25, 1965

I'll avoid words that incite passions, and use words that encourage peaceful understanding. The meaning of words I use is intended: to resolve differences by negotiation, conciliation, arbitration; to look for beauty and joy in human relations; to patiently endure the railings of hate by those whose injuries and hostilities have not yet been healed by friendship and love; to praise and give power and honor to the men who turn aside from the ways of greed and instead seek the greatest service to their fellow men; to stand firm against injustice, without hate or violence—sustained by the highest will and purpose the individual knows; and to have confidence that support can always be found for a just cause.

December 3, 1965

In Minute for Peace, we must turn to our conscience not as an escape from action but as a guide to action for peace. Our economy, political practices, and communications policies should all be scrutinized and vigorously changed to provide practical and effective incentives for excellence.

Who takes the initiative for a cease fire? The one who loves the most.

December 18, 1965

Psychologically, the greatest thing for peace would be a rescue of an American astronaut by a Soviet cosmonaut.

January 10, 1966

We need to turn the life of the mind and spirit of all men from the negative to the positive, opening the door in each human mind and heart to the renewing influence of the Holy Spirit and strengthening each mind by a connecting link—a fellowship—with all minds.

January 24, 1966

Live in that relaxed tension where you are sensitive to any urgency of the moment, but at the same time are aware of your place in the broad sweep of eternity, of your responsibility to prepare for the tasks of the future.

January 26, 1966

Consent with that mysterious power that holds up everything. Call it God, call it law, call it mind—the important thing is to see its powers of love, joy, and peace.

January 30, 1966

The following are some of the ways in which you can work for peace through Minute for Peace. Please check one or more. Peace is important.

1. I will telephone ten or more of my friends today and tell them about Minute for Peace.

2. Each day after lunch at about 2:00 p.m. I will invite whomever I am with (my companion) to join for a moment the increasing multitudes who are sending thoughts of good will and peace to heal the hatred in the trouble spots of the world.

3. Each morning I will take time to listen to my own "inner voice" for ideas and actions that will help build a peaceful world. This is a true Minute for Peace. Some see in it a psychological tool for brotherhood; others, a vehicle for the flow of the Spirit of God through the mind of man.

February 12, 1966

While there is a basic appeal in the idea of "One World," there is also an element of threat, to the freedom of the individual: the fear that in some way the human spirit will be suffocated unless its loyalty is expressed as an alternative to some other loyalty.

Man is not so much affected by what he has been as by what he thinks he can be.

February 18, 1966

Jesus taught by answering questions.

February 20, 1966

Scientists give answers to what scientists ask. No particular world view is used in selecting data. Perception is radically relative.

March 27, 1966

In the future the importance of each individual will be encouraged through public emphasis on the roots and value of culture in the history of every race and nation. China's turn to communism was partly a reaction from Western pressures which brought progress but tried to dictate and failed to respect the greatness of the Chinese psyche with its need for self-fulfillment.

April 10, 1966

The one thing that is common to creative minds in all religions, ideologies, and sciences is a search for meaning. In the new age approaching, there will be increased appreciation of old values and their roots in history, but the atmosphere will be such that no one will venture the final word on any subject. Automation will be used for the benefit of the doers, instead of the drones. A simple system to provide economic justice would eliminate much of the present effort to automate the present inefficiency in banking, credit, and trade.

Instead of the present global negative accent on getting, from a sense of need, the new accent will be on giving, from a sense of abundance. While there is abundance to provide a good life for all the people on this planet, this is only possible by wise and careful use of natural resources and by long range planning for their use in ways that will protect and improve our global environment. A plan for the next one thousand years is needed that will enable mankind to reuse natural resources wherever possible, and to anticipate future needs and develop new sources of energy and materials to meet these needs.

Let us first involve the thinking people of all nations in the quest for peace, through Minute for Peace. This will be followed by actions for peace, publicity for peace, spiritual and moral inspiration and renewal, and new answers to global problems.

At present the people who financially benefit the most are not those who serve most or create most, but the drones who use their mental acumen to figure the best way to take advantage of the "system."

A complete change of our taxing, banking and credit system is needed that will provide simple and effective economic justice for all. To facilitate this, the treasury of each nation should form a corporation in which every citizen would have one share of National Treasury Stock. This corporation would create the amount of money needed for trade and exchange. People who owned property could borrow 50% of the property's value. (This percentage could be less or more, to control inflation.) The integrity of every nation's National Treasury Stock would be certified by a United Nations agency established for this purpose. This money could also be converted into United Nations International Currency for use in international trade. The United Nations agency handling this would debit or credit the nation's account.

Dividends would be declared on the basis of any actual increased gross national product. This would go to National Treasury Stockholders and would be equally shared by each citizen through their one share of stock. In such a program there would be an effort to recognize the principle laid down by Henry George, that each individual has a right to an equal share in the natural (unimproved) resources of this planet. Appropriate implementation of this principle can result in every family owning their home or apartment.

They should be provided the equivalent of their basic inheritance and given an opportunity to improve it. Their success should depend, not on the ability to deprive others of their basic property rights, but on their ability to multiply what is rightfully theirs through their wise use of the benefaction of nature and through the earnings resulting from their service to their fellow man.

Dramatize this responsibility by providing personal membership in the United Nations for all individuals. This would be managed by the United Nations Association (UNA) working through voluntary Non-Governmental Organizations (NGOs). Membership would require that each person pursue his goals in life in a peaceful way, and that he encourage all organizations, including the government, to do the same. It would also require that he recognize the power of his mind in the affairs of men, that each day he spend a period in meditation, seeking honest accord with his neighbors and with all the nations, and that he send thoughts of approval and good will to all adversaries.

The best hopes and values of religions and their organizations can be realized through the United Nations. UN membership would be no threat to communists or capitalists if it called for heart-felt links of mind and spirit.

April 30, 1966

Kirk (*New York Times*) misses the point that wise men can further the causes they believe in without assuming political power. If, instead of urging ideas they approve, men would submit ideas to be examined by each man's conscience, the evils of power would be avoided. The greater the reputation, the more important it is that a leader's voice be followed by the voice of opposition and by thoughtful reflection of each man's conscience.

May 8, 1966

There is no limit to what God can do through a man who doesn't care who gets the credit. God is so charitable, he will work through open channels even though he doesn't get the credit.

May 14, 1966

Yesterday Mrs. Tessie Durlach reminded me of the value of writing down thoughts that come during meditation, obtaining more divine guidance in this way. I will try to practice this each day in the coming weeks and see how it works out for me. I tend to feel awkward or slowed down when I try to record my thoughts on paper, and usually do so only when it is important that I remember something, or necessary to find the exact words that will express an idea or feeling. There is danger in past ideas being taken too seriously and hindering the free flow of thought with ideas that are ever changing, hopefully, ever moving in the direction of the truth.

May 17, 1966

Minute for Peace: Listen to it. Think about it.

May 20, 1966

Means for neutral policy: form a board from small nations.

Wake up! Planet Earth. Don't be a mirror! Be a focus. Be a lens. Project: Peace Headline Series—stories of peaceful progress in conflict situations. Sponsored by Minute for Peace. It would obtain moral support for right action through the prayer, good wishes, and approval of participants in Minute for Peace.

May 22, 1966

Everyone wants peace. There is something everyone will do if they can be convinced it will work, and that is: think about peace.

If we can convince the public in every nation that Minute for Peace will work, it will work.

Sidney Hock on Karl Marx—

> The positive upshot of the great debate . . . is the question whether it is possible to develop on rational grounds, not from party ethics or an ethics of class, but from an ethics of humanity, a Bill of Rights for all of mankind in the light of which we can appraise the ethical behavior of parties and classes, construct a world community and reconstruct national communities that would enable them to live, and let each other live, in peace.[2]

May 25, 1966

Sensing this grace, the glory, the love, the glory of the infinite power of all good.

May 26, 1966

3-5 minute promotion spot to cite evidence for the power of individual thought. ESP. Let us not be afraid of the truth our enemies speak.

UNIP (United In Peace) Uniplan Uniperson Uniteam Uniglow Unilight right thought = right action, sensing the grace, the glow, the love, the glory of the infinite power of all good. Get telephone girls and other friends to meet each day in the Metropolitan room.

May 28, 1966

From Mrs. Durlach: quote from Paul Goodman (*Growing Up Absurd*): "That you love me makes me of value to myself."[3]

---

2. Hock, *New York Times Book Review*, 45.
3. Goodman, *Growing Up Absurd*.

May 30, 1966

The first days of the thirty-three-day Minute for Peace campaign should reach the leaders who are most developed and effective in using the methods and ways of peace. If you feel insecure, choose close friends for peace matters. If you feel secure, choose an adversary and be a bridge of understanding.

June 5, 1966

The inner glow in each individual can be increased by connecting it with the glow in all the other people of the world. This can be aided by Minute for Peace, which provides a conscious link with the glow of good will in every man.

In this way the dark barriers of fear and greed will be pierced by the rays of faith and love. This will bring a new climate where the peace builders can lead in creating a new world of freedom, order, beauty, meaning, and joy. This "inner glow" refers to the feeling of wonder, awe, gratitude, and worship that is experienced by almost everyone at some time. The most numerous examples of it are found in poets, artists, musicians, scientists (sometimes at the moment of discovery), religious mystics, gifted teachers, some political zealots, and most everyone truly in love. It is found most in new mothers and little children. It goes by many names: love, joy, turned on, salvation, Holy Spirit, serenity, etc.

June 10, 1966

Peace is not the cessation of war, which is a period of waiting for other wars. Peace is not negation. Peace is obedience to the law of life. By obedience to the law of mathematics, we acquire logical thinking. By obedience to the law of harmony, we acquire music. By obedience to the law of form, we acquire beauty. What's new, in the awareness of the human mind and its overwhelming possibly infinite potential, is this: There is power for peace in thoughts of goodwill.

Now this power can be intensified by the knowledge that each person is connected with others—through Minute for Peace, a daily minute that is strengthening good will and peace throughout the world.

You are not alone. Each time you think about peace with good will and hope, you are joining an ever increasing multitude in every land who believe world peace is possible. When enough people are aware of each other's good will and faith, war will be impossible.

Today, in countries we do not trust and that do not trust us, the word is spreading that all men of good will are one and that they are in a majority. They can each in their own way be a power for peace by joining in mind and spirit with all the others in a daily Minute for Peace, and by spreading the word of what they are doing. Today, turn on your power for peace with a Minute for Peace.

When the majority of us are "turned on," the world will see the way to peace. "Turn on for Peace'" with Minute for Peace!

July 1, 1966

> Pangere—to agree
> Pango—I agree
> Paxi—I have agreed
> Pactul—agreed
> Pacum—object of another verb, to have agreed
> Pax—Peace

July 7, 1966

There is a need for a social-economic system that will encourage self-renunciation and lead to the highest expression of love of God and fellow-man. Explore ways of adding a factor that would move present systems in this direction.

> During the next 60 seconds your own thoughts can help bring world peace. [Multiple bells] In this Minute for Peace, [UN Peace Bell] you are now listening to the Peace bell at the UN. At this moment minds around the world join in good will to strengthen peace. [End of Peace Bell] ... Now, help raise the minds of the whole world with your [Peace Bell] thoughts and feelings of peace [continue Peace Bell, fade multiple bells].

October 29, 1966

Condemn Not

A spirit of condemnation corrupts the soul. We should not condemn our adversary, our neighbor or ourselves. Hate condemns—love forgives. Right action results from right thinking. Courage to change for the better—to choose the right way—is given to us when we walk in the light of God's forgiveness and grace, letting that light shine on our misdeeds. Then, free from condemnation we can choose to change without self-righteousness—with humility—with gratitude—growing in love, realizing that in common with all humans we ever miss the mark. We must not judge how far the other person is missing it, and we can ever draw nearer to it as we recognize our sin, our shadow, our missing the mark—without condemnation. Then, filled with the grace and joy of the Spirit, more and more we will overcome sin and manifest the righteousness of God.

November 12, 1966

Calendar reform: A single solution to the calendar problem, which would maintain the seven-day week (as against proposals for a World Day outside the week) is to initiate a 13 month calendar of 28 days each, with the provision that every ten years there would be an extra two weeks on the first month.

At the beginning of each century, four weeks would be inserted to meet the needed correction of time.

<End of Meditations, April 1964 to November 1966.>

13

Living the Beatitudes

I BELIEVE THAT THE great Magna Charta of our Christian faith is found in the Sermon on the Mount (found in Matt 5–7). The basic foundation for that statement is found in the Beatitudes. There is something extremely hopeful as we look at them.

We know today people are disillusioned. Everywhere I go I see cynicism and hopelessness. "Yes, of course it's all wrong, but there's nothing you can do."

The Beatitudes begin with "Blessed are the poor in spirit for theirs is the kingdom of heaven." Another meaning of poor in spirit is brokenhearted. "Blessed are the broken-hearted for theirs is the kingdom of heaven." It is important to recognize that people in that state of mind are willing to change, to see something new and different. These are the people to whom Jesus says, "Theirs is the kingdom of heaven." By the "kingdom of heaven" is meant the rule and reign of divine love and wisdom. On Earth the kingdom of heaven means a healthy peaceful planet.

As we look at this little gem that is set in the vast blackness of space, we contemplate it and think of the marvelous planet we have inherited. People living here right now are deciding whether life on Earth shall survive, grow, and blossom, or whether it will die. We are the first generation that without any question must take charge and take care of Earth.

Once we realize, in our state of disillusionment or sorrow, of being broken-hearted, then there is a chance, then there is hope. Out of this can come the manifestation of a glorious and wonderful kingdom for our whole planet.

Then, of course, we must go on. We must take the next step. Jesus said, "Blessed are they that mourn for they shall be comforted."

When you really go deep enough inside, you're going to feel a godly sorrow. It's going to bring about a desire for a change.

That should be followed by the next step, "Blessed are the meek" (not the weak, but the meek), "for they shall inherit the earth." The beautiful thing about the Sermon on the Mount and the Beatitudes is this—it's the only way I know to be truly humble. The proudest people are those who are proud of their humility. There has to be a process that brings about true humility. The process is to recognize the grace of God, to give up your life and let God remake it, renew it, regenerate it. Out of this can come real, true humility, because you realize that all the great things that are done through you are not your doing, but God working through you.

The other thing about this is, "they shall inherit the earth." One of the great truths that has been neglected by the church and the world at large is that this Earth is the inheritance of the human family. The Psalms say, "The Earth hath He given to the children of men" (Ps 115:16 KJV).

Of course, there is a sense in which "The earth is the Lord's and the fullness thereof" (Ps 24:1 KJV). But nevertheless, there is a sense in which the human family—those who assume their responsibilities—are caretakers and custodians of this planet. One of the most important facts for us to get hold of is that we must be responsible caretakers of Earth. This is our God-given task.

Earth is our inheritance. When we say "our inheritance" we mean the inheritance of every man, woman, and child on this planet. It isn't the exclusive right of the few. It is the inheritance of every person.

Every person should have an opportunity for a stake in this Earth—for a piece of land, the benefits of the soil, the trees, and the bounty of Earth. At the same time he should recognize his responsibility to be a custodian, a caretaker—to be a steward of this inheritance. So Jesus said, "Blessed are the meek for they shall inherit the Earth."

The more we learn about biology and the biosphere, the more we realize how fragile is the thin skin of life that circles our globe. We cannot go slap bang into our job, such as building atomic plants, and spreading atomic waste. There are so many things that we have done where we failed to approach our task with a sense of wonder, care, and caution. If the benefits we are seeking for ourselves and the human family are going to be obtained without forever damaging the eco-systems—the life giving network that covers our globe—we are going to have to approach each new phase of our responsibility with a great deal of care and caution. I believe that for this purpose we need the illumination of the mind of God in all that we do.

This brings me to the next step. I would like to mention that each one must be taken before the next one can follow. Jesus said, "Blessed are they which do hunger and thirst after righteousness."

Once you experience this poverty of spirit, this being broken-hearted and pressed to the ground, and have experienced a real sense of meekness, then, it's possible for you in a healthy manner to have your appetite come back: You're going to hunger, you're going to thirst. You're going to be a real seeker.

There are here and there, around the world, God-intoxicated people—people who are intoxicated with the love of God and with the joy of life. The first thing in the morning when they get up, they enter into the presence of God with thanksgiving. They are so amazed at the grace of God, the wonder of life, and the love that is found all about us in other people, that it brings great ecstasy and joy. And, in their search to know more, to understand more, there is a deep heartfelt hunger. The hunger and the thirst is after righteousness. "Blessed are they that hunger and thirst after righteousness"—seeking the right use of things, things that reflect the goodness, the glory, and the love of God.

As people experience this hunger, it's a true hunger. There is a superficial substitute that we think is desire. People think they want this, they want that, they want other things. And then they discover it isn't what they want at all. I guess one of the most deceitful lies of Satan is the appetite for superficial things—momentary pleasures, desire to make more money, to have more power, the desire of lust. All of these superficial attractions are keeping individuals away from discovering their true heart desire.

One of the great scriptures in the Bible is, "Whatsoever things you desire, when you pray believe that you receive them, and you shall have them" (Mark 11:24). The difficulty is, people don't understand what they desire. You may think you desire something, but when you go deep enough inside your innermost being and discover your really true desire, your most sincere desire, then you can know that your desire will be granted.

So Jesus said, "Blessed are they that hunger and thirst after righteousness for they shall be filled." Every morning it's possible in your reflection, your feelings, and your thought to feast upon the truth of God—upon the promises of God, the commandments of God; to chew them, masticate them, think about them, meditate upon them, and relate them to your life experiences. As you do, the innermost craving in your heart and spirit will be satisfied.

Now it's from this experience that man is led into the next stage of development where Jesus says, "Blessed are the merciful." Before this stage, if you tried to be merciful, you would be self-righteous and condescending. We see a lot of pretense of mercy. But when you appreciate the mercy of God and have the awareness of the grace of God, then you can be truly merciful. And, of course, this is followed by the statement, " . . . for they shall obtain mercy."

If we really appreciate the significance of God's grace, of his forgiveness, and of how much damage we have done in our lives—of all of the things that we have done out of selfishness, with their unpredictable evil toll—and that God has canceled the debt, we are so grateful that it becomes impossible to condemn anyone else, regardless of what they do.

Then we shall find that, "Blessed are the pure in heart for they shall see God." Pure in heart means a whole heart. Jesus in that same Sermon on the Mount asks us to have an eye with single vision. We must not be guilty of double vision.

A whole heart is a heart where your purpose and your thinking is devoted to one thing, without anything pulling you aside. The guiding star in your life is to seek the kingdom of God, and you strive to love God with all your heart.

There is a verse in the Old Testament that says, "The eyes of the Lord run to and fro throughout the whole earth, to show himself strong in the behalf of them whose heart is perfect toward Him" (2 Chr 16:9). A perfect heart, a heart of love, an undivided heart, a whole heart, an honest heart—this is what God is seeking. Jesus said to seek the point where you can be pure of heart; this is a continuing process—it isn't something you achieve and then let it go. The impurities of the world are constantly cluttering up and staining our heart and our feelings, and there must be a continual process of cleansing, that is available through the grace of God. The marvelous thing is, the pure in heart will see God.

There are things that are unreal in the world today to the majority of people. We have a civilization where the majority of people are blind. Jesus talked about the blindness of people. They don't see the most important things there are in life.

Think about Pearl Harbor. When the attack occurred, the world had something visual that enabled people in a moment to have a great surge of feeling. Because of "Pearl Harbor," everyone, or at least the majority of Americans, got behind the flag and made all kinds of sacrifices. They were willing to leave their jobs, leave their homes, give up their salaries and go to work for a pittance, risk their lives in order to save their country.

Today, we are in a situation far worse than Pearl Harbor. And it's not just our nation—it's the whole planet. But it is not real to the people. Pearl Harbor was real.

People are blind to the fact that we face today something far worse than Pearl Harbor. Our great difficulty here is to see the reality that is not obvious to the natural eye. The natural eye does not understand the really important things.

The greatest benefit comes to an individual when, with the mind's eye, he sees the realities of the spirit. "Blessed are the pure in heart for they shall see God"—God becomes very real to them. It's such a source of faith when you get up in the morning and you feel in your mind's eye that you've caught a glimpse of God!

In my own life I was trained in a strange way to be scientific. I realize there are profound mysteries that go beyond what we see in the physical world. There are mysteries of the mind and spirit and feeling. Right now we are inter-connected globally, both by electronic communications and in our consciousness. We are one global organism in the world of mind and thought. We're all connected with one another.

This means that we're all connected with the guilt of the world. And we're beginning to realize it more and more. We have no right to be self-righteous and say we are the most moral nation in the world. Let's look at the balance sheet for a moment.

If you look at the positive things, if you listened to former CBS correspondent Charles Kuralt ("On the Road") talking about the warm, wonderful things in America, it's great! We are more independent in our thinking, more open, and we have more political freedom. In scientific and voluntary activities in the United States, we exceed in many ways what is done in all the rest of the world.

But let's look at the other side of the balance sheet. We have caused more pollution than any nation in history. The air and the water are poisoned by the acts of the people of the United States of America. We speak with great self-righteousness in condemning Ruhollah Khomeini for holding fifty hostages and we are appalled at a nation that assassinates fifty or sixty people—which is terrible. I do not mean to condone them for one moment. But in the day that one nation executes sixty people, we kill a hundred by our drunken drivers. On television we don't show the mangled bodies, the crying children, and the weeping widows; we just treat auto deaths as a passing statistic.

Look at the billions of dollars that are made illegitimately by our money brokers. One of the great tragedies in basing our whole operation on greed and selfishness is that it becomes acceptable to deprive other people of money without rendering any useful service. When a man corners the silver market and makes a billion dollars, a billion dollars has been removed from the pockets of hard working people. He's rendered no useful service. In any court of the moral law, it must be recognized that this is a kind of stealing.

So, we reward those who steal, and through inflation we rob those who work, and who render useful service. From Hiroshima to Love Canal this country is guilty of some of the most awesome crimes in the history of the world.

At the same time I want to come back and say that, on the other side of the ledger, this nation has done tremendous things to cultivate a love of freedom, democracy, and many other things that have benefited the whole human race.

But, I believe that if you put it on balance, like the writing on the wall in the Old Testament, we are weighed in the balance and found wanting.

The reason for this is that we have forsaken the moral law. We do not any longer think in terms of good and evil. In the Old Testament a prophecy about Jesus stated, "Butter and honey shall he eat that he may know to refuse the evil and choose the good" (Isa 7:15). Throughout the Old Testament, butter and honey signified the promises and commandments of God. So to that individual who determines in his life to steer this difficult course, God promises his presence, grace, and power.

"Enter by the narrow gate; for wide *is* the gate and broad *is* the way that leads to destruction, and there are many who go in by it."[1] (Matt

---

1. *The Holy Bible, New King James Version.*

7:13). We've been following the broad way where there is no right or wrong. There is no hero. There is no heroic epic. There are no great roots in our souls. We've lost the guiding star.

Therefore, our society is permeated with corruption from top to bottom. The redemption of society is now impossible—except for the grace of God. But the wonder of it is that Jesus said, "Blessed are the broken hearted for theirs is the kingdom of heaven."

The mysteries of the birth of Jesus, of who he was, are beyond the province of science. Our knowledge of natural science and biology would make the Virgin birth seem impossible. But in dealing with the great mysteries of mind that transcend matter, faith helps our search for meaning. In scientific research the most beautiful hypothesis always proves to be the right one.

In the drama of human history, nothing is more beautiful than the Christmas story. I am convinced that there was a man that lived whose name was Jesus. The man Christ Jesus put a face on the mystery of love. Historically, there is overwhelming evidence of that. I know that what he said and did and taught that was recorded by his followers is so great, this man I would follow to the ends of the Earth.

14

Implications of Faith

FAITH OR COINCIDENCE?

People sometimes say about a miracle that it's just a coincidence. That leads me to the matter of what is a coincidence. What influenced my thinking a great deal was Bible numerics. I knew Ivan Panin. He had come to Canada from Russia and had converted to the Christian faith. He was studying the Scriptures and was interested particularly in the book of Numbers.

He noted that in ancient times, the letters of the alphabet were used for numbers. People of that day didn't have separate numerals to represent numbers as we have today in English. For example, "A" was 1 and "B" was 2, and it went up to 10, 20 and so on. With just a few letters, you could have a big number.

Panin examined the Bible. He found that there was an amazing combination of 7s in the first verse of Genesis. After reading Panin's work on Bible numerics, I went to my concordance to look up different words. First, I found that the name Jesus added up in the Greek to 888. The number 7 is perfection and the number 8 is new life and new beginnings. Hebrew babies were circumcised on the eighth day.

What dumbfounded me was that records show that the name Jesus was used exactly 888 times in the Greek New Testament. Now some say that years later a scholar refuted that claim, and thought that the value was a few numbers off. But at least in my experience, the claim was correct, and I actually counted twice, using an analytical concordance, to make sure how often the word Jesus occurred in the New Testament.

Panin used to say that coincidence is interesting. He said something like this: "You might walk down a beach and find three little rocks that have rolled up onto the beach and they form a perfect triangle. That's an amazing coincidence. But if you walk down the beach and see the little stones that had rolled up and spelled out the Twenty-third Psalm, in a million years, that would not be a coincidence."

Remarkable coincidences are part of the mystery of life. I have experienced many "coincidences" that some would consider a divine miracle. Whatever the explanation, I know that back in 1969 I prayed about an idea I had. I then felt led to pick up my father's Bible, open it at random and put my finger on any part of the page. I don't make a practice of such things, but on this occasion the scripture I got was Ps 115:16, "The earth hath he given to the children of men."

This was right after I had written a brief article, "Planetary Inheritance," contending that the natural earth is the property of the whole human family. While no one has any rights to the results of other peoples' labor, everyone has equal claim to Earth's natural bounty—oil, gold, and land. The scripture I got in the Psalms was the one scripture in the Bible that best confirmed this.

Thus, every day, in my morning time of silent prayer, I fervently ask God to guide my thoughts and actions that day. I pray for guidance in what I say and do. While I almost always feel I have somehow failed (my actions rarely succeed in achieving what I pray for) I am encouraged by little coincidences that seem more than a "coincidence."

Some days ago, I was thinking about my early experiences in my Christian faith and the many scientists who seem to provide logical proof that these can only be "an illusion of the mind." For some strange reason I thought of my grandfather, T. W. McConnell. He was initially a Methodist minister. I felt led to check and see what would happen if I made a search in Google.com to see if anything came up about his name. Several came up from 1906 records of the Los Angeles Azusa Street Mission. My father had told me about the Mission. But I never knew my grandfather was ever there.

Answers to prayer continue to show me that there is more to life than what science can see.

FAITH AND SCIENCE

As we enter a new millennium, more than ever before people of every creed and culture want an answer to the ultimate questions that have troubled civilization through its history.

What is life all about? Why are we here? Where are we going?

Science and religion have sought answers and end up with only more questions. Beliefs of every kind abound. There are many theories that try to deal with the enigmas of life. Religions have at times caused wars and violence, but while at their best, they have brought harmony and peaceful progress in the human adventure.

But no one provides evidence that all fair-minded parties can agree on. No one has presented a video tape documenting the existence and nature of heaven, or other dimensions of reality. If you showed me a video tape of what it's like in heaven, then I would know that you had scientific proof that there's a heaven.

I don't know that there's a heaven. Semantics is the problem. When you say that you "know," you actually mean you have a strong belief. We have no scientific evidence that can be agreed on that there is life after death, let alone another place called heaven.

We don't even know what the soul is. There have been scientific studies indicating that you are more than flesh and blood. But scientists all disagree on what the evidence shows.

Now the trouble is that with the help of genius scientists, such as Stephen Hawking, we are told that what happens in the cosmos is just a logical result of scientific laws—and there is no room for miracles or answers to prayer.

For scientific examination concerning great philosophic and religious questions, materialistic science does not provide the right tools and we do not have sufficient data to work with. Science is unable to explain the simple phenomena of coincidence; numerous coincidences defy the laws of probability. Miracles of healing are repeatedly documented. Life seems to consist of more than mechanical laws. The universe is more than a machine. In examining metaphysics—the area of mind and spirit—we accomplish more by viewing life as drama, rather than a structure of physical materials. The vital thing is not the bodies and the costumes, but instead the story.

FAITH AND MYSTERY

I was thinking of the Bible verse that says, "No man hath seen God." God himself is a mystery. Today, in looking for answers, because of culture, environment, and circumstances (and many unexamined assumptions), people come up with different hypotheses about the nature of reality. Too often they state their opinions as if they were proven facts. For example, "I know I'm saved, I know there's a future life, I know there's a God." What they mean is that they are completely convinced of their opinions. If they mean scientific proof, then many able, informed, and good people with different answers are either stupid or irrational.

For example, if you try to "scientifically" examine the Gospel record about Jesus, then you ask the question about the Virgin birth, "Where did the sperm come from? Was the Holy Spirit a Being of some kind that produced human sperm and impregnated Mary, resulting in her pregnancy?" The moment we start thinking this way we get into all kinds of difficulty. We are confronted with no data and complete mystery.

This does not mean we should reject the story. There are many possible explanations, but the story without explanation has stirred the hearts and minds of young and old for centuries, inspiring altruism with its personal and social benefits.

But in seeking to understand the cosmos, we are confronted with the mystery of space, and of time. Nobody can understand how long time is, or when the universe started. Scientists have all these theories, but they are just theories, and they are always replaced by other theories.

Our planet is like a nest in the stars. It has an amazing skin of life. The more we study life, the more dumbfounded we are, from butterflies to germs and quarks.

If we try to see the whole picture, I don't think there is any mind capable of comprehending it all. If we probe deep enough into any question, about the world, or about people or about life, we reach a point where we're confronted with inexplicable mystery. That's the great enigma.

We can keep on going, spinning theories about reality and the nature of the world, about time and space, and about everything mental.

We quickly get involved in the big questions. As a result of all this unknowing, all kinds of pseudo-religions spring up that teach other dimensions of reality.

At one point I was intensely interested in Christian Science. Did you know that a former president of IBM was a Christian Scientist?[1] Walter S. Lemmon—I came to know him. At one point, his top aide was one of my top supporters, and donated $5000 to help promote my ideas. All his top executives were Christian Scientists.

I got real interested. He persuaded me to look at Mary Baker Eddy's books. Related to her approach is the religious view of people who employ positive thinking.

In the world of the mind, there are so many phenomena. I don't know how we have the power of thought, and the power of positive thinking. Some people think that thought travels faster than the speed of light. I think this is a statement which is unprovable, but it is interesting to think about.

A COMMON FAITH

Our age has seen an overwhelming explosion in the media of conflicting ideas about politics, religion, the state of the world, and the human condition. This is a time when people have far more information (and misinformation) than any time in history, and there is such confusion that it's difficult to sort out what are the most important facts or values. One of the basic problems here is the contentious arguments on radio, TV, and in magazines, about politics, money, who God is, who man is, and what life is all about.

It seems to me that in order to find some reason or hope for the future, we need to look for a few firm fundamental facts that can serve as a basis for understanding what's happening in the world and what we can do about it.

In our search for reality, for truth, it's important to identify the things that are recognized as most factual. For instance, we agree that we exist. I know that there are some that believe existence is just an illusion of the mind, but most will agree with Descartes' observation, "I think, therefore I am." We agree that 2 plus 2 equals 4. These are not just hypotheses, or articles of faith, they are scientific facts, important basic facts.

Now when we go beyond that and say, "Where did the universe come from?" then we become involved with amazing mysteries which are so overwhelming that the greatest minds down through history, and

---

1. Bardfield, "Short Wave Station WRUL."

today, differ on the answer. It's well for us to seek an answer and find one that satisfies us, but it's good to be a little humble or modest in our opinions; to recognize that what we are talking about is not proven fact, but hypotheses, unproven hypotheses.

Yet we need to recognize, for the destiny of our planet, that all over the world we have an incredible amount of data concerning things we can all agree on. Scientists agree on all sorts of things—quasars and black holes and quarks, for example. To identify the key points of agreement for the whole human race, and then to identify what is urgent, is terribly important for the human family. As we do that, we will continue our quest, our journey, to deal with the mystical, the metaphysical, and the spiritual.

BEING PRACTICAL

If our perspective of the world is simple, we can keep straight what is important. We do know the one thing that is practical—we do know that certain knowledge, certain actions, and certain practices, bring the best benefits. If you are a farmer, and you till the soil and get rid of pests, you get the benefit of all kinds of miracles in nature. On the other hand, if you ignore the problems, you suffer the consequences.

There are so many diverse facts that have to do with this present world, that if we just try to be practical and make the best of the knowledge we have, we will succeed. We should just use a little common sense to base our actions and our views on what we know, rather than on what we believe, and there's a difference.

I've never been a scientist; I know that there are scientists that don't believe in God. But I've never met a scientist who is neutral when it comes to right and wrong, with things that are obviously right and wrong.

We come back to the fact that many philosophers recognize that much of what we say and do has to be the result of our belief, of our faith. And faith is not knowledge. Faith is affected by what we know, but there is a big difference between what we know and what we believe.

I think it helps if we have religious faith. The faith that inspires the greatest actions is the faith in what Jesus said and did. I can wholeheartedly assert all of the teachings of Jesus, and still in all of this I'm exercising faith. Faith is the substance of things hoped for, but not the substance of proof—scientific evidence.

There is a possibility that God is trying to speak to me through the many coincidences of my life. That's where faith comes in, and I feel it at times.

On the other hand, I have to trust, because things about God are not simply proven.

A RATIONAL FAITH

When I was a boy it occurred to me that man is unique: He is a self-conscious creature. He knows that he exists and he knows what he is thinking. He reflects on the past and thinks about the future.

However, it would be presumptuous, to say the least, to imagine that we are the only creatures in the universe that have these amazing abilities. It seems probable that other creatures have this ability and that there may be, in some part of the universe, far greater creative ability and consciousness.

Above this ascending order would be God, the First Cause, the first and highest creative self-conscious Being.

Logic demands a cause for every effect. The more we learn about the cosmos, the more our amazement at both the chaos and order we find. Science now acknowledges there can be no creation without a Creator. Chaos cannot cause beauty, order, music, and meaning. To create art or music, human beings need intellect and emotion. The Creator of Earth and stars must be far superior to us in mind and consciousness. There must be a self-conscious Creator. In other words, the Creator of all must certainly be conscious that he exists and be conscious of his creation.

Otherwise, I would be in some sense superior to the source of all that is, that is, superior to the God Who Is!

Further, if his love and wisdom are infinite, he must know that I exist.

The Creator must have great wisdom—and our wisest men have seen love as the greatest wisdom. The Creator must be a God of love.

So there are many arguments that can be made that there is a Creator and that he does know and love his creation. All the world's major religions teach love and the Golden Rule, or creative altruism. Even atheists, who believe in morality or ethics, teach creative altruism. The one thing we can expect of the Creator is that he is a God of love.

There is, to my way of thinking, no religion that provides a more beautiful definition of love—with a Creator who is the very essence of love, a heavenly father—than that described by Jesus. So important is this that he said, "By this shall all men know that you are my disciples, that you have love one for another." Jesus was the living expression of God's love.

Some people think of God as the all-encompassing, incomprehensible, indescribable Essence, The Infinite Potential. This reflects the beliefs of Helen Shucman and Bill Thetford, who "scribed" *A Course In Miracles*,[2] which was first published by Robert and Judy Skutch. At the time of publication, Judy Skutch invited me to a meeting with a small group at her home in New York. She introduced me as "the person who most influenced my thinking." Later, when I saw where she was going with her ideas, I tried to show her how wrong she was, without success.

While I accept that what Jesus said is true, the difficulty is that I am confronted with contrary philosophical arguments that exist in the world. I believe the best proof of our faith is not what we say or what we claim, but what results from our taking steps in our faith. In that area, we find general agreement.

Attitude is very important for what people take from life. There are some people who have a deep affinity for wildlife—for nature, for trees, for plants, for flowers. Some women are consumed with a passion for growing beautiful flowers.

When everything boils down, I think what is important to me as an individual is to contribute to the betterment of people and planet—to the skin of life that covers our globe, and to the welfare of the people that live here, and that's the Golden Rule. Every major religion agrees with the Golden Rule or something similar. Most people agree that love, honesty, and virtue are important.

We read in the Bible that we were created in God's image. And the meaning of that is, obviously, that we were intended to be creators. And so we should create, to connect our creation with the love of God. Then we will create things that will benefit people and planet.

I'm grateful for my Christian faith and the reverence for life it has engendered. I pray to God and I think he hears my prayers. I have seen miracles and miraculous answers to prayer; on the other hand, I've had disappointments in not getting an answer to prayer. Sometimes miracles happen and I give him thanks. But I cannot understand the unanswered prayers and the pain and suffering that millions of people experience.

2. Shucman and Thetford, *A Course in Miracles*.

The one thing that I see as important now is that we make sure that the human adventure continues. But no one seems to provide a way that will appeal to every creed and culture, and enable us to avoid global catastrophe. We seem to be at the end of humanity's brief history. We need a miracle to bring about the drastic changes needed to provide a sustainable future and continue the human adventure.

To do that we must come together on what we are most certain of, and what we can do about it. That is what I have summed up in the history and the meaning of Earth Day, and its Earth Trustee agenda of pursuing peace, justice, and the care of Earth. The power of love, and the power of the Golden Rule, and the power of mind and Spirit, when they are used for what Jesus intended—as shown in my experience and in what I've accomplished—that's what has inspired me.

God must exist. But Dear God, why don't you show yourself in an unmistakable way, and tell the whole human family why we are here and what we should do?

Strangely, my heart is filled with deep anguish—and exhilarating hope.

FAITH AND PERSONAL DEVELOPMENT

Now abstractions can have a validity of their own. As I pursue my own particular belief or understanding, there is no need to be timid, uncertain, or insecure. For part of my belief is that results come from confidence and wholehearted commitment to what I believe. But I can still be open and capable of change if a better hypothesis is presented to me.

In fact, I believe the greatest belief comes from the greatest honesty. Recognizing that, yes, life is a great mystery, I'm confronted every day with puzzling enigmas. But in seeking the truth, in seeking the way, in seeking to have a fuller understanding of love, I have found the greatest help in the words and actions of Jesus as recorded in the Gospels. And as I go searching through other scriptures in the Bible, and other great writings in history, I find the elements that provide a tremendous possibility of a beautiful meaning and integrity in all of life.

Discovery of more and more reality seems to be part of our destiny or purpose. I don't fully understand why we are left with so many questions unanswered, why it is that we can't have an angel come down and explain things to us, or a radio message from a distant star or planet. But we do find that the honest seeker of truth, who practices what he learns, and who examines the story of Jesus, as found in the Gospels, will find a basic answer in his search for truth and love. Then he can turn to the other scriptures, and the experience of Christians, and have his faith reinforced and understanding deepened. Saints down through the ages have demonstrated the meaning of what Jesus taught.

Now, of course, in the above I am reflecting on my own hypothesis or faith. But every major religion is a search for truth, by advocates of their particular hypothesis. Most important is the impact of their belief on their conduct—their honesty, confidence, fairness, compassion, and creativity. We will have a peaceful, prosperous future when we all come together where we have common ground, and leave room for our differences.

FAITH AND FREE WILL

Faith is a valid necessity because of the uncertainty principle.

In the most important questions about reality we are confronted with mystery and conflicting evidence. This is one reason intelligent people differ. If there were no uncertainty, intelligent people would base their creeds and actions on scientific, documented proof with which all reasonable people would agree. There would then be no need for faith. Certainty would make doubt impossible and faith meaningless.

The Bible says, "Faith is the evidence of things not seen." When faith is followed by miraculous answers to prayer, with no perceptible physical cause for results, the only possible explanation is an unseen power at work. The fact that faith gets results makes faith the evidence of unseen power. The best faith is the faith that works by love—love of God and people.

Faith is not proof that the operative creed is true, for people of different creeds get answers to their prayers. But working faith is proof that the confident action of the mind has brought results occasionally (not consistently), resulting in healing or other answered prayer that cannot be rationally or scientifically explained.

If there were no uncertainty, all intelligent people would belong to the same religion and vote the same way. The uncertainty principle makes free will possible.[3]

---

3. This section originally published in *The Christian News*, February 22, 1993, p. 19.

IS MAN A MACHINE?

As we become more and more acquainted with the mechanics of the computer, the similarities with our brain lead to a mechanistic view of life—that we are all just tiny components in a vast computer reacting to stimuli—often meaningless. But there are other considerations—man is also the programmer. Provided with information, he contributes consciously and unconsciously to the total system, adding questions and information that reflect his mental and spiritual maturity. It may be that, in his present stage of soul development, most or all of the knowledge he transmits is already known to the system. But it may well be that each individual is in preparation for a future role, where, with God and for God, he can probe the unknown, taking the stuff of the universe and drawing on his knowledge of love and physics to create and form new structures of life and beauty, all to the glory of God.

One of the most disturbing developments in recent years is the successful prediction of election results through opinion polls conducted with the help of computers.

Poll results are obtained, apparently, from very small samplings of different groups with similar environments and influences. This seems to suggest that people are nothing more than machines. Their choices in the voting booth will be the result of the propaganda, prejudice, and emotional influences of their particular environment. Control these, and you can control the way they will vote. Insight, intuition, and independent judgment seem to be a rare exception in today's society.

Research should be conducted to find the creative few who don't necessarily follow the poll pattern. Find out what is different about them, and find out if it is possible to encourage their qualities of independent thought and human sensitivity in the rest of society. For instance, it would be interesting to find out if they spent more time in meditation and reflection, in the enjoyment of nature, studying basic concepts in their education, participating in sincere works of charity in their community, and so on.

As long as a computer can measure the mind of a man, he has lost his meaning as a person. The great inner struggle to make the right choices will cease to be meaningful when a computer can predict what they will be. The fault is not with the computers. The answer is to rediscover the divine in man.

FAITH AND THE BIBLE

We are far more aware than people were 2000 years ago. On our planet, we know of one human family. Now there are studies that indicate the whole human family came from the black man in Africa; I don't know who will refute that in the future. The idea that the plan of God was revealed to the Jews—that has certainly been refuted very effectively from a scientific perspective.

There is, however, much in the Scripture to consider. I've come to the conclusion that, when it comes to prophecies in the Scripture, we are dealing with symbols. God may know that we are individuals intended to be creators, to create things that will benefit ourselves and the world and the people on it. We are led to accomplish this best from the teachings in the Bible. In my mind I am coming to this from a Christian standpoint. Everything under the sun is taught in the Bible.

However, to me there are all kinds of inconsistencies in the Bible. Consider the case of Saul— God punished him for not killing all the women and children when he went into a certain city and conquered the Amalekites.

I don't know how the kingdom of God will be brought on this planet, whether through God's working through man, or God coming back to set up his kingdom. I don't think we should be arguing about it. What's important is what we say and do now.

The things that we are faced with are so much more important. We have a corrupt money system, a corrupt lust for power on the part of people who claim to be Christian, and we have the corrupt stock market and all the evil things that it is doing. What gets me the most is that the nation which is recognized as the great Christian nation has spent more billions and billions of dollars for diabolical weapons and new ideas of germ warfare and all kinds of things to destroy life. If America spent one-tenth of that for what Martin Luther King and other people who believe in peaceful resolution of conflict have advanced, why, we wouldn't have any more wars. I think that the stupidest thing in the world is for us to further the idea of making skeletons of our enemies, instead of making them friends, which the power of love and the power of prayer have demonstrated is possible over and over again.

FAITH AT WORK

I first saw faith at work sixty years ago as men and women met together each week at Calvary Episcopal Church, in New York City, to reinforce each other's faith. Miraculous solutions came to human problems, and over the years I have nursed a growing conviction that the power of faith can be applied in practical ways to our global as well as our personal problems.

Those were wonderful days when we had our "Faith at Work" meetings. When Sam Shoemaker spoke at those meetings, there was always love in his voice.

The Rev. Sam Shoemaker was an Episcopal rector at Calvary Church in New York City and later at Calvary Church in Pittsburgh. He was credited with being a co-founder of Alcoholics Anonymous by the A.A.'s Bill Wilson. The degree, details, and importance of Sam Shoemaker's impact on early A.A. were virtual unknowns until author Dick B., an active, recovered AA, devoted eleven years of research and writing to these subjects. His books will show you the enormity of spiritual words, ideas, and language Shoemaker contributed to A.A.'s spiritual program of recovery. Shoemaker helped the Bible, Christianity, and the power of God come alive in the Twelve Step program of the 1930's.[4]

In the Faith At Work meetings, we were taught to not only speak to any stranger we saw in the regular Church Service, but also to invite them to lunch and then witness to them about how our personal lives had been aided by putting our faith to work.

Among the many names I remember was that of Irving Harris. He was a wonderful friend. E. Stanley Jones gave me helpful advice on where I should live and what I should do. Dr. Trueblood gave me contacts in the White House, and I was able to meet with Senator Hatfield and others in Congress regarding prayer and peace.

I remember especially Frank Laubach. I not only knew him, but later shared the platform with him in another church where we both spoke. I feel my life greatly benefited by his telling me a very simple idea. Here is the simple idea Frank Laubach shared with me. We should make sure that every night when we climb in bed that our last thought, the last thing we think about, is Jesus, and our love for Christ. This should always be a time of prayer, with faith that he is with us, he will be with

---

4. See Dick B., *New Light on Alcoholism: God, Sam Shoemaker, and A.A.* Consistent with A.A.'s traditions of anonymity, the author uses the pseudonym "Dick B."

us through the night, and that our first waking thoughts in the morning will be about him and what he wants us to do that day. Throughout the day we will sense his presence. Our best thoughts and actions will reflect his love and wisdom.

I was re-reading Frank Laubach's little book, *Prayer, the Mightiest Force in the World,*[5] when President Carter was announced as the winner of the Nobel Prize! I had been thinking of the "Camp Farthest Out"[6] where we had wonderful sessions of prayer. President Carter's sister was there.

Following are a few quotes from *Prayer*. I treasure this little book. It reminds me of the times I spent with Frank Laubach and his providing the simple idea which has repeatedly brought miraculous results in my efforts for peace, justice, and a sustainable future.

Quotes from *Prayer* –

"We need cool heads to do the right thing—to put out the fires of hate and prejudice, if our ship earth is to survive—and prayer will quench hate, fear and panic when nothing else will do it" (p 17).

"Other weapons converted men into skeletons. This weapon must convert enemies into friends. . . . Only prayer, which releases the infinite might of God, can win this final battle for men's minds and hearts" (p 18).

"While we have pursued scientific enquiry into other directions with enormous results, we have failed to investigate and use the mighty energies which prayer can release" (p 19).

"Let strong men sacrifice their personal advantage so that all may have equal opportunities" (p 19).

"They are still trying to make selfish greed work" (p 20).

"Senator Vandenberg wrote before the San Francisco Conference that nations were striving for 'America first,' 'England first,' Russia first'—the very attitude which has caused all wars. Peace cannot be permanent until we put 'the whole world first'" (p 20).

"The world at this moment is *the resultant of the total thought forces* which have struggled for supremacy. We had these world wars because wills all over the world have been at cross purposes with the will of God and with other wills" (p 21).

There is much more in this little book about the power of prayer and the way to peace on our planet.

---

5. Laubach, *Prayer, the Mightiest Force in the World.*

6. Interdenominational Christian lay organization that sponsors week-long and weekend programs of worship and activities.

Frank Laubach said that other weapons converted enemies into skeletons, but prayer can convert them into friends. The faith that works by love can move mountains when we pray. I know it helped make the annual UN Peace Bell ceremony on Earth Day a powerful force for peace.

My faith works out in this way. One of the statements Jesus made was that you can tell a tree by its fruits. You can tell things are the results of what you think. The difficulty is that most Christians don't walk the talk.

It is a real enigma, how people of faith act. I struggle and I get angry when I think that Condoleezza Rice and President Bush thanked God that they are Christians and that they are both born-again Christians. They accept Christ as their Savior and they follow him.

But the Christ they followed is the Antichrist of my thinking. You can tell again where your heart is by where you spend your money. They spent hundreds of billions of dollars for devilish weapons of war. They didn't get Big Money to educate and persuade and convince people of the value of real love and non-violent resolution of conflict.

President Bush should have focused his attention on the fact that we are one human family all over the planet. That's a more Christian solution. It is government's lust for power, and building up armies, that leads to war. The most guilty party of all is the United States. We spend billions for the military and pennies for peace.

We wouldn't have any more wars if the United States and the powers that be would advocate what Jesus taught. I could elucidate on that at great length, because my father used to teach us what Jesus taught. As children we used to have to memorize Scripture. I wish that I had better memory. At one time, I could quote the Sermon on the Mount. Jesus said, "Love your enemies." I could go on and on. He was the living Word. We are supposed to eat and digest and live the words that Jesus spoke.

You won't find any words of Jesus telling us to kill. They twist the Scriptures to make it mean just the opposite of what it says. You won't find any of the words of Jesus condoning war or murder or killing. People have thrown forward the question about what you would do if a maniac comes to your door and threatens to kill your child. Would you shoot him? The point is, if you're living the life of faith and love, why, this would never happen.

In 1994, I was seeking to have the ambassadors of Israel and Palestine join in ringing the Peace Bell. Two weeks before Earth Day, I was praying, and the Scripture came to my mind, "The weapons of our warfare are not carnal but are mighty through God to the pulling down of strongholds" (2 Cor 10:4). In a note to myself, I wrote "Guns and missiles will not decide the future." Television will; ideas will. If we could ever focus all the energy, money, and effort spent in solving problems on reaching minds, what a great future we could have, without the violence of warfare.

RESOLVING DIFFERENCES IN FAITH

Two Levels of Reality

To obtain the measure of agreement and cooperation needed for the rejuvenation of our planet, we need to recognize two levels of reality—the physical, and the metaphysical (the area of mental and religious phenomena).

Great benefits have come from religious belief when it resulted in greater compassion, humility, and cooperation for common goals. On the other hand, religious bigotry and intolerance have been a major cause of violence and war. Now we are beginning to learn how to cooperate for common goals and mutual benefit—and at the same time leave room for differences about religious creeds.

There is no doubt in my mind that there is another dimension of reality beyond the physical. Experiences around the world with mystics and researchers provide evidence of phenomena—good and bad—that cannot be explained by science. The difficulty is that so many explanations contradict other accepted explanations. We are left with unproved hypotheses about their meaning.

It should be recognized that ultimate questions about reality are still shrouded in great mystery. This would leave room for honest differences in beliefs and interpretations about the meaning of life. This does not mean a lesser belief in one's creed, or less rejection of other creeds, but a willingness to temper one's ideology or faith with a tolerance of another person's belief, so long as their adherence does not infringe on one's freedom of choice, and so long as they foster the nurture of Earth and fair benefits for Earth caretakers, *i.e.*, Earth Trustees.

The same Earth Trustee policy applies to political parties. People-to-people cooperation is possible so long as there is acknowledgment of differences, and a careful avoidance by both sides of claiming that cooperation means support of partisan ideas or ideologies. Enlightened leaders must constantly expose any hidden conspiracies to win the minds of people, and ever seek points of honest accord.

What We Have in Common and Where We Agree

Fortunately, when it comes to the physical world, the here and now, we do have science on our side and a potential for honest agreement and action. Most people, including scientists, will agree that an Earth Trustee agenda can rejuvenate our planet and provide a peaceful, prosperous future here on Earth.

The best of our science and logic provide no answers all can agree on. Our beliefs are based on faith. While we may differ on the nature of God and life after death, we can commend actions that nurture people and planet, regardless of the person's creed.

The Earth Trustee agenda should not be a stumbling block to people of any creed who want to help "peace, justice, and the care of Earth."

When it comes to the mysteries of life, the human search continues and will not diminish. The explosion of knowledge about the cosmos is accompanied by scientific study of spiritual healing and psychic phenomena. The more we learn, the greater the mystery!

The astrophysicist, Stephen Hawking, is concentrating on how the cosmos grows. The results are astounding. However, in his last words on a TV program, "The Universe," he stated, "We are finding the answer to 'how.' When we find the answer to 'why,' we will have the mind of God."

To continue our quest to understand the great mysteries of life we must avoid the death of nature and the collapse of civilization—a real present danger. Let us now convert "Earth Kill" to "Earth Care" and make this new millennium an Earth Trustee Millennium.

FINDING COMMON CAUSE

To achieve this future requires that we determine what we have in common and look for every point where we can honestly agree. This policy will solve problems and provide new solutions.

What we can agree on, and the idea that is the key to peaceful progress, is finding a common cause. John Gardner was a great advocate of that. I knew him! He encouraged me.

And so I continue to advocate a common cause—peace, justice, and the care of earth. And when every individual is interested, then we'll make real progress toward peace. We can be interested in different ways. Our views reflect our genes and our culture and our education. There are good things and bad things in all of us. If we pursue the common goals of peace, justice, and a sustainable future, we can have the satisfaction of knowing that we will contribute to the continuation of the human adventure.

Now here's a big question mark. Will the human race have a new beginning and do what is needed for peace, justice, and care of earth? Or will our lust for power and our greed drive us to destroy the whole human race?

This is the hate that motivated bin Laden. I wrote an article that I don't think bin Laden ever got. The hate that he had would never have occurred had the Christian country, America, practiced what Jesus taught.

WHAT'S LIFE ALL ABOUT?

The world is filled with pain, greed, and injustice of every kind. At the conclusion of his great book, *My Life and Thought*, Albert Schweitzer said "The world is filled with inexplicable mystery and suffering." But he went on to say that there is a will to progress in human society, and the problem is to bring to it a reverence for life.

Religions and scientists present many conflicting explanations of the enigma. My own life-long search has resulted in total mystery regarding the big picture. Scientists have no explanation of eternity or infinity on which they can agree.

But they do agree that the future of the amazing skin of life that covers our globe requires responsible stewardship of Earth—with words and actions that will foster peace, justice, and the care of Earth.

Whatever the explanation, we do recognize we have a planet with land, water, air, and an amazing skin of life covering our globe. With our new technology and a vigorous effort—a moral equivalent of World War II—we could rejuvenate our planet and provide a great future for the human family.

To make this work we need to tap the power of prayer. Scientists as well as religious institutions have now documented evidence that prayer often gets results. Confidence, positive attitudes, and heartfelt prayer have all demonstrated their benefit. Recognizing this can change the way we think and act.

But here again, we see charismatic leaders with money and institutional backing, misusing these facts to make money, and succeeding by appealing to people's greed.

We must keep going back to the meaning of love, as defined and demonstrated by Jesus, and in varying degrees by many others throughout history.

There are many aspects to our global problems. While we in America celebrate Independence Day, its claims of freedom and opportunity are marred by our terrible misallocation of power. The billions we spend on weapons is a challenge to other countries and to terrorists to increase their weapons. Were a fraction of this spent on education and incentives for peaceful resolution of differences, we would have no more wars.

We talk about equal opportunity. But our laws favor the rich and the corporations that have the most money.

To achieve a stable global society we must recognize the nature of people and the nature of their institutions. When individuals practice creative altruism (divine love) in their daily lives, everyone benefits. When institutions (colleges, churches, businesses, banks, stock brokers, governments) apply creative altruism in their decisions, everyone benefits.

In addition, most people don't realize how many of their decisions are the result of what they have seen on television, or heard on the radio, or seen in the newspaper. Unfortunately, most mass media programs are garbage. They are funded by advertising and get attention by appealing to the worst in human nature. A TV anchor man once told me they keep up their ratings by a focus on hate, fear, greed, and lust.

In every sector of society there are those who want to do the right thing. And there are well-meaning foundations that seek to fund altruistic ventures. A great number of these are aided by their religious beliefs.

My personal religious beliefs—and much time spent in prayer—were a major factor in my successful efforts to promote joint ventures in space, and cooperation that would aid peace, justice, and the care of Earth. The proposals for the Star of Hope, Minute for Peace, Earth Day, and Earth Magna Charta were birthed in prayer.

We are at a point in history where we have the basic answers to how life on this planet can be improved. If we do what is needed to continue the human adventure, the amazing new technology may provide new answers to metaphysical mysteries. As we proceed in the new millennium, everyone should think and act as an Earth Trustee—seeking choices in all they do that will replace pollution and injustice with responsible nurture of people and planet. Our differences will diminish as we pursue this essential goal.

Let us do all we can to promote a sustainable future and observe Earth Day next year and every year in a great global celebration on Nature's special day—the March equinox.

I believe that enlightenment is a possibility on our planet. Earth Trusteeship—policies and actions for peace, justice, and the care of Earth—will enable us to avoid catastrophe, rejuvenate planet Earth, and continue the human adventure.

SUCCESSFUL PRAYER

Faith and prayer will increase by attention to answered prayer.

It is discouraging to see nothing but hundreds of cries for help on Internet prayer boards. Messages of answered prayer should be separately and effectively listed. Or a star (*) could indicate messages reporting answered prayer.

In this age of science, scholars and doctors are seeking evidence and understanding of miracles in healing and answered prayer. They can benefit when people document answered prayer on the Internet.

While most answered prayer involves people in personal contact, there is evidence of the power of united prayer for global problems. Some years ago, the Earth Day website requested global simultaneous prayer for peace in Peru. December 22 at 1900 GMT was designated for global prayer for peaceful resolution of a hostage crisis. A few churches warmly responded and 350 hostages were released the next day.

In 1994, a boy from Palestine and a girl from Israel rang the United Nations Peace Bell on Earth Day, March 20. They were then joined by viewers in silent prayer for peace in Jerusalem. Progress in the peace process immediately followed.

While there are many differences about creeds, most people of religious faith believe God hears their prayers. If you believe your creed is best, prove its value by your reports of answered prayer. The best evidence that your faith in a future life is true is to demonstrate its value in this life.

The March equinox provides a unique opportunity for all Christians to affirm their faith at the same moment in time. Jesus stated in Matt 18:19, "that if two of you agree on earth as touching anything they shall ask, it shall be done for them." Earth Day is about the stewardship role

God has given us. Genesis 1:26 says "let them rule . . . over all the earth." We must "Give an account of [our] stewardship"[7] (Luke 16:2).

It is time to document and herald the fact that many prayers are answered. When living faith engages heartfelt love, miracles often happen.

7. *The Holy Bible, New King James Version.*

15

Agreeing With Your Adversaries

EACH PART OF THE world, each culture, and each religion, has different views of what is right and what is important. My deepest concern and what my whole life has been directed to is the need for a common cause that will most benefit people and planet. We need to look for where we can agree and leave room for our differences.

AGREE WITH YOUR ENEMY

A major policy that will facilitate success in cases where differences arise is to constantly look for and acknowledge important points of agreement. In my own efforts to help resolve differences between Soviet and American leaders (which succeeded on several occasions), I persuaded both sides to cooperate in matters of importance in which they agreed— in spite of strong differences in other matters. Their joint actions in environmental matters and in space then led to better communications and aided resolution of differences.

My own view of this approach was the result of my heeding the words of Jesus, who said we should agree with our adversary, or enemy. This did not mean we should agree with something we did not believe, or to agree with what was wrong in what your adversary said or did. Instead, if you looked prayerfully with love in your heart, you could find something of importance on which you and your adversary could agree.

Focusing on where we agree can bring mutual understanding that will leave room for our differences. Good will and an honest effort can lead to something important on which adversaries can agree.

WHERE WE AGREE

Let us then agree that we all are interested in what life is all about. And that we would like to see a better future for ourselves and our children. We should be able to agree that, in today's world of cyberspace, we are all so connected that problems arising anywhere will eventually affect us. Our best chance for the future is to pursue policies and choose actions that applied worldwide will benefit everyone.

The great need in our world today is to move from conflict to cooperation. Let me define what I mean. If you carry independence too far, you get anarchy. If you carry cooperation too far, you get something like Orwell's "1984"[1] where everybody is under control. We need to return to the equinox, the amazing symbol of equilibrium, the moment when night and darkness are equal in both hemispheres. We need balance in our lives. We need a measure of independence and we need a measure of cooperation, in giving in to other people. It is in finding the right balance that we become the most productive.

So if we will open our ears and spend as much time listening as we do talking, we will discover that there is a point at which we can agree with almost anyone. The moment when we establish that feeling of accord, that we are members of one human family as discovered by the astronauts and cosmonauts, we will make progress peacefully.

WHAT HISTORY TEACHES

To understand what is best we should look at what history teaches. Since the dawn of history, every generation has seen both love and hate, fear and trust, violence and compassion. Through the centuries, one's loyalty to tribe, clan, or country was repeatedly used for fighting, and ever seeking more land, wealth, or power. Power schemes were based on the idea that success will go, not to those who are right, but to the force with the stronger weapons or the most money. Even today there are those who believe that bombs help us get "Peace through Power."

As cities joined to form states and nations formed power blocks, it was always to counter other groups having power of money and weapons. Finally, the League of Nations and then the United Nations sought peace through understanding. But the patterns of loyalty and fear of "the other" caused repeated failures.

1. Orwell, *1984*.

The failures of the past do not necessarily condemn any new effort to failure. There has been a measure of success from time to time in history, where religious faith provided altruistic love that was stronger than political or nationalistic rivalries. *This Freedom—Whence?*, by John Wesley Bready,[2] described the Wesleyan revivals of the eighteenth century that countered social injustice, political rivalries, and slavery with "Strength to Love," which later was the title of a book by Martin Luther King Jr.[3] The efforts of William Penn and the Quakers were a positive force for relations with neighbors. Also important was the success of Ghandi in India's non-violent revolution.

There are new factors in the state of the world today that, taken advantage of, could finally enlarge our loyalties to include the whole human family. The enemy would no longer be other people, but instead would be the ignorance, poverty, and injustice that are found in any part of the world. The key to defeating these enemies of humanity is the spread of solutions that are working. Now the Internet can help make this happen.

Religion at its best has taught altruism, and from time to time has fostered peaceful progress. On the other hand, in the past, differences in creeds about the mysteries of life and death have many times resulted in conflict, violence, and sometimes war. This need not be.

We all respond emotionally to icons of belief which have formed as a result of our personal experiences. One of the best men I know, a man who has saved millions of acres of wilderness forests from being destroyed, has no religious belief. He said he did not have time to study things that are unknowable. And then he added, "The worst wars in history were fought in the name of religion." He is a thoughtful man. His experience and thought had left him with this view.

On the other hand, while what he said was partly true, I believe many of the greatest victories over difficulties have been the result of religious belief. In my own case I was once in solitary confinement in the "black box," because of my religious views on war and what should be done about it.

As described in chapter 7, what sustained me in this soul-wrenching experience were the words of the daughter of Catherine Booth of the

2. Bready, *This Freedom—Whence?*
3. King, *Strength to Love.*

Salvation Army, who wrote, "Best beloved of my soul, I am here alone with thee, And my prison is a heaven, Since thou sharest it with me."[4]

Now, the meaning of these words to me is far different because of my experience than their meaning would be to others. Coming back to my environmentalist friend, the interesting thing is that while he has no interest in questions about God, and we disagree on its importance, my friend and I firmly agree and have supported each other on environmental issues. Focus on common ground will prevent going to war over differences.

The world will be a far better place when people are taught to accent the positive and work together where they agree, regardless of differences in other matters. The way to bring this about is to spread the Earth Trustee vision and agenda by word and example. Be an Earth Trustee. Have some project that will help achieve Earth Trustee goals. Persuade any group of which you are a member to adopt the Earth Magna Charta and its Earth Trustee agenda.

These efforts will help achieve a new global state of mind with hope, and lead to vigorous efforts for Earth's rejuvenation.

THE COLD WAR

Finding a common cause helped the United Nations end the Cold War. One of the reasons is that when we were in the standoff with Russia years ago, I was concerned about the danger of an atomic holocaust, because of the differences with the USSR. I was to meet Ambassador Dobrynin in Washington, who represented the USSR. Before I went to that meeting, I prayed about it. In my prayer, I thought of that scripture from the Sermon on the Mount where Jesus said, "Agree with your adversary." I told the Ambassador, "We're in danger of a misstep. If we have an atomic war, civilization will be ruined."

I feel that if you can honestly with love try to find what you can applaud in your enemy and praise it, that it opens up communication and sometimes resolves differences. You leave room for your differences.

I told the Ambassador that there would be greater understanding and a better future if we would applaud what we agree with in our adversary. We agreed that there should be more attention to the environment, and that there should be peaceful cooperation in space, and that this could help promote unity in the world.

4. Booth-Tucker, *The Life of Catherine Booth.*

He agreed with me. I gave him "The Case for Planet Earth," an article I wrote at the time. And following that, he took steps in that direction. After that I wrote an article on "Astronauts for Peace."

Efforts to find agreement with the USSR succeeded, and eventually the Cold War ended without atomic war.

IRAN AND THE HOSTAGE CRISIS

In early 1980, I composed a message focused on the Beatitudes and their relevance to human relations. The message is reprinted here in chapter 13, taken from a transcript of a tape I made at my home on February 12, 1980.

Later in 1980 I was talking with Senator Hatfield, and I told him, you know they're holding the hostages in Iran. And I believe if somebody would go there, and find ways to praise them for what they have done (in the arts and sciences, etc.), that it might help get the release of the hostages. I told him that I thought this was a great opportunity to promote global consensus among the creeds and cultures around the world in the areas where we agree and where we have things in common. And that I had been fascinated by my study of different articles with information about the March equinox, that in Iran it's their New Year; they call it Noruz. It's a day of nature, of taking care of the things of nature. Many other religions relate God to nature. Noruz in Iran was the day that you are in harmony with your neighbor and your family. You make it a day of special dedication to peace, and to cooperation and care of family and friends.

Senator Hatfield replied, "John, that's a great idea." So he helped me get a visa, and I got money. But I didn't have enough to pay for a stay—I had only enough to go there and back.

When I arrived in Iran, I had this dramatic experience. People had told me, now, you will be on your own. Some people said I wouldn't come back alive, because there was a lot of hatred between Iran and the United States.

When I arrived, I was really praying. I said, "Lord, please help me." I looked around the room when I came into the airport. I liked the look of a man behind one counter; he was an airline employee. I went up to the counter, and told him why I was there, and that I wanted to meet with their president, Bani-Sadr. He was very warm and he said, "Well, I have a cousin, Mr. Gamaroody, who is his top assistant. I can take you to him." The man gave me Gamaroody's phone number. I called up and we arranged a visit.

The very next day I saw where they were holding the hostages, and later I sent messages back to the hostages. When I got to see Mr. Gamaroody, I told him why I was there. I said, "Iran has been getting terrible publicity around the world. We need to think globally. I think it is so beautiful how you celebrate your New Year, Noruz, the way it has been for hundreds of years. You are to be alone with your family, and you are to make sure you have paid your bills and you have taken care of the plants and the garden, that nature is important, and you have to make sure that you're helping take care of the natural things in your area. And then, at the moment of the equinox, you are to be alone with your family and your god in prayer."

I said, "That's beautiful. We celebrate Earth Day on the same day, and I would like to see the whole world celebrate Earth Day the way you celebrate Noruz. And I have come here to ask you to help me." I built my case on the idea that our two countries shared one important view. We recognized the annual event that could best further a peaceful future for our planet.

And he jumped out of his seat, and he said, "Great." But then he said, "But Noruz is only four hours away, and I must go home and be alone with my family and my god." And so, here I was inspiring him to take the actions that I would like to see, but in a way that was defeating my purpose.

It's close to unbelievable, but that's what transpired. I wasn't able to get back to him, and in order not to be stuck there without money, I had to take the next plane back to the United States, and so I didn't get to follow it up properly. Later I wrote a letter to him (reprinted in the appendix).

I really believe that if I had had more money to stay there longer, I would have succeeded in persuading the Iranian government to release the hostages. I discovered that it was their custom on Noruz, which is Earth Day, to release prisoners. They always release some prisoners in honoring this special day. It was a natural opportunity.

A hostage release would have been one thing the media could not ignore. It would have gotten terrific attention. That one thing could have made Earth Day what it was intended to be.

When I got back to the United States—and this is a wild story, but so help me it is true—there were newspaper reports about my trip to

Iran. It was in the *New York Times* or the *Post*; I've forgotten which. Then I got a call from one of the reporters. I expressed a desire to go back to Iran. He said, "I've got somebody who will pay for your trip back to Iran, and go with you, and who thinks this is a great idea." I said, "Great."

The man invited me to dinner. It was a fancy restaurant. I had a nice meal. This gentleman was very interested, and we had an interesting conversation. He gave me his card too. He said he would like to meet with me again in a few days. He would have to see when it could be, and that he would get in touch with me right away.

Well, days went by, and I didn't hear from him.

There was one delay after another. Then finally I called the phone number on his card, and the number wasn't good. I went to the address, and there was no one there by that name. Afterwards, I discovered that the man who'd arranged the meeting was working for the election of President Reagan.

If you remember, 1980 was the year that Carter lost the election. Now, to add to the enigma, I had known President Carter. I used to go to prayer meetings with his sister, Ruth Stapleton Carter. We went to Camp Farthest Out. We'd go up in the hills and we'd have these meetings there.

President Carter was trying to get the hostages back. I had tried and tried to get in touch with him and failed. I didn't get through to the people that were close to him.

He had issued a Proclamation, proclaiming Earth Day as April 22. But this was after President Ford had issued a proclamation in 1975 in favor of the original Earth Day on the equinox (March 20–21). This is what makes Carter's action all the more ridiculous. If you look at the record, you'll find all this to be true. If Carter had not issued his Proclamation, and we had connected, not only would the hostages have been returned, but he would have continued as President, without any question.

The only reason Reagan was elected president and replaced Carter was because of my failure to get the hostages back. The negative hostage publicity is the reason that Carter was defeated—he failed to get the hostages back. He even tried to use military strength to get them returned.

Reagan probably didn't know anything about this. But the people who were manipulating the campaign saw to it that the hostages didn't get back. No question in my mind about that.

The Iranian mission in New York, after I had talked with Mr. Gamaroody, initiated and got the support of other UN missions for a

Dialogue of Civilizations. They had some of the great philosophers, international philosophers, talking about where we agree. And it did a lot of good.

So that is how I went to Iran—seeking peaceful settlement of the hostage crisis. Finding that the March equinox coincided with Iran's New Year celebration named Noruz deepened my appreciation of the March equinox, and how much Earth Day owed to its history.

On March 25, 1980, I gave a copy of the Beatitudes tape to Akbar Zadeh, one of the students I met during my visit to the American Embassy in Tehran where the hostages were being held. He said he loved the tape and asked if I could give it to him, which I did.

I sought the release of the hostages, but that did not happen right away. However, my visit did open up better communications between our countries, and did help in the later release of the hostages. On several occasions since then the Ambassador to the United Nations from Iran has participated in the UN Peace Bell Ceremony on Earth Day on the spring equinox—which is their New Year.

HOW CARTER'S PEACE ACTIONS DEFEATED PEACE

And How President Reagan the Warmaker Defeated President Carter the Peacemaker

President Carter still does not know why he failed in 1980 to obtain the release of the hostages in Iran. Had he succeeded, he would have won another term as President and been able to continue his great efforts for peace. Instead, Ronald Reagan—the Hollywood Communicator—became President. The War Department Dealers in Death (who make billions from weapons sales) were delighted. They were able to continue their propaganda for "Peace through Strength." Ever since then, the peacemakers, who follow the way of nonviolence, have been ignored. Now the whole world is infused with the lust for the power of weapons and is headed for destruction.

Here is the reason for President Carter's failure. In 1970 I had inaugurated the first Earth Day. The date I chose for this event was March 21, the first day of spring. This annual event, when night and day are equal all over the world, was shared by the whole world. In Iran it was their New Year, called Noruz. Throughout history the spring equinox has been a special event in many countries.

But Senator Gaylord Nelson and supporters sponsored an environmental teach-in on April 22, 1970, and named it Earth Day, which resulted in confusion about the date. The rest of the story about the founding of Earth Day is in chapter 30.

In 1975, with the help of Senator Mark Hatfield, Congress designated March 21 as Earth Day, and President Ford issued an Earth Day Proclamation designating March 21 that year as Earth Day. President Ford's Proclamation said:

> The earth will continue to regenerate its life sources only as long as we and all the peoples of the world do our part to conserve its natural resources. It is a responsibility which every human being shares. . . . Through voluntary action, each of us can join in building a productive land in harmony with nature.

(The full text of the Proclamation is reprinted in the Appendix.)

Unfortunately, on January 1, 1980, shortly before I visited Iran, President Carter issued his "April 22 Earth Day Proclamation." He ignored the fact that President Ford, supported by a unanimous resolution of Congress in 1975, had already issued an Earth Day Proclamation, designating March 21 (the first day of spring) as Earth Day. This hindered my efforts to convince Iran that our most important holiday was the same as theirs and that release of the hostages on Noruz would further our mutual commitment to the meaning of Noruz.

Had my prior repeated efforts to get the ear of Jimmy Carter been successful, with his understanding and help the hostages would have been released and he would have won the election that fall.

It is indeed an enigma, how his Earth Day Proclamation to further peace actually defeated his efforts for peace.

16

Pursuing Peace

TRAGEDY VERSUS OPPORTUNITY

Why Flight 800?

July 21, 1996

What is the purpose and destiny of human life? This question comes to my mind as I think about the TWA Flight 800 tragedy in 1996, and try to sort out the monumental problems—and amazing opportunities!—now facing humanity, that is, you, me, and every person on Earth.

The people who are pinnacles of power on our globe seem to spend all their time on the symptoms of our distress, without any awareness or concern for the basic causes.

As I write I am seated in a small back yard under a large wild cherry tree. In this Queens neighborhood the adjoining back yards have lawns and plants. I hear the caw of a crow and on looking up I see a fluffy cloud. It is a beautiful pleasant summer day.

Sounds of a siren and then a jumbo jet passing overhead remind me of the continuing search for wreckage of Flight 800 now going on. How strange that so many of the lives consumed in the plane's fiery death were such great examples of what life could and should be. In one case, twenty six outstanding students from a small Pennsylvania town, together in a great venture with inspiration and hope for the future, had their lives snuffed out.

A butterfly passing by reminds me of last night's coverage on TV of the astounding Olympics opening in Atlanta. Here, so soon after the TWA tragedy, were all the countries of the world cooperating, including Iran and Iraq and others who in the past have engaged in terrorist actions. Here in Atlanta, the home of Martin Luther King Jr., was an outstanding demonstration that the power of the spirit offers a better future than the power of the sword.

What will the future bring? Will civilization, the people on our planet, go the way of Flight 800, or the way of the Olympics? The answer will depend on our attention now to the primary question, "What is the purpose and destiny of human life?" Only if the people of good will, who are in the majority worldwide, come together with a common purpose and agenda will we avoid catastrophe on our planet.

To find this needed agreement we must limit the question to "What is the purpose and destiny of human life *on our planet*?" While life after death and the ultimate mysteries of life are of great importance, there is little likelihood of agreement on our differing creeds, except that we can agree to peacefully disagree.

THE WAY TO PEACE

RECOGNIZING THE DIFFERENCES IN creeds where they pertain to a future life or to metaphysical mysteries, Pope John Paul II in his book *Crossing the Threshold of Hope* said, "The way to heaven is to pursue peace on Earth."[1] Though it has not yet been appropriately followed up, a real breakthrough in this direction was the encyclical letter, "Pacem in Terris" (Peace on Earth) issued in 1963 by Pope John XXIII. This unique message to all people of good will was taken to heart by people of all faiths as a basic statement of the rights and responsibilities in the conduct of life and the achievement of peace on Earth.

As we focus on why we are here, we will find agreement on what our purpose and future on Earth should be, and this will help us pursue a general agenda for implementation.

To go further in seeking understanding of where we are and what we should do, it is well to look at the perspective science is giving us. While we now know there are millions of stars that may have planets, what we know about the rest of our solar system indicates life may be extremely rare. The amazing web of life that covers our globe is precious. It requires our understanding, protection, and care.

If humanity is to continue its search for meaning—meaning in the chaos of the cosmos and meaning in our hearts and minds—then we

1. Pope John Paul II, *Crossing The Threshold of Hope*.

must make a quantum leap in our thinking and recognize our future depends on our coming together in a grand peaceful effort that can appeal to all people of good will.

To avoid catastrophe and instead move toward limitless horizons we must seek common ground all can support. We must resurrect the search for meaning, the values it inspires, and the actionable knowledge it reveals in our religious faith.

A way to accomplish this is described in the Earth Magna Charta (see chapter 36). This sets forth the Earth Trustee vision and agenda, and how each person can find a niche that will contribute to its goal: elimination of poverty, pollution, and violence, with ever increasing meaning, purpose, and opportunity.

As this happens the search to understand the purpose and destiny of human life will increase and be reported through every means of communication. The new reality of cyberspace allows individuals the opportunity to contribute and interact apart from the power structures of organized religion, politics, and business. Here is a democratic opportunity to end the corruption of power that dominates the world through institutional structures. Providing information on my website spreads it to others, and then I and others all have it. With an Earth Trustee world view, sharing good ideas will rapidly spread.

The power of the spirit—love, good will, and rational thinking—can now replace the power of the sword with its hate, greed, fear, and violent deaths. The key to a great future in the information age is to spread the power of love.

GLOBAL DANGER: THE GREATEST IN HISTORY

Never has civilization been faced with such global danger. Present plans by leaders in control of military might and money can now result in global catastrophe. Only a miracle can save the human family from annihilation.

In our midst, there is love at work, and there is hate at work. If the people who know and experience the power of hate and love find a way to unite, and put as much money and effort and zeal and vigor into pursuing nonviolent methods of love and good will, globally, I believe we might change the whole global state of mind, eliminate poverty all over the world, eliminate many of the problems of the great human family, and continue the human adventure.

We'll still be confronted with mystery, but we'll have the pleasure of knowing that our children will have a chance of a good life here on Earth. And that in itself should bring satisfaction.

The great enigma is how the voices of sanity have been ignored for years. Statements by Nobel Laureates and leaders in science and religion have been ignored. Had Earth Day and its Earth Trustee agenda been acted on by nations with money and military power, the world would now be on its way to a peaceful, prosperous future. Instead of billions for bombs, wealth should be used to foster peace, justice, and a sustainable future. Had this been done, education in peaceful resolution of conflict would now cover the Earth.

Instead, it is likely that the chemical, biological, and atomic weapons now available all over the world will soon bring the human adventure to an end. Many in other creeds and cultures have suffered from our selfish exploitation of their resources. They see us as the terrorist and now think they have a way to get even.

Why do the mass media ignore the voices of peace? The "Dealers in Death," who seek more money for war, seem in control of media and the White House. There are big profits in selling arms. In the Congress there are few voices pointing to the way of peaceful progress in the human adventure.

The leaders responsible for military action against bin Laden are blind to what is important. "Hatred does not cease by hatred at any time; hatred ceases by love."[2] The way to prevent killing is not by more killing. This will only produce more terrorists seeking to get even.

Jesus said, "Love your enemies." His true followers have proven that love will point to the reason for the violence, and to peaceful actions to eliminate its cause.

You who have access to power in media and government, send this message to someone important whom you know. Add your prayer and rally support by religious leaders.

While there is profound mystery about who and where God is, a few times in history there have been amazing miracles of faith and love. We need a miracle!

---

2. Muller, *Lectures on the Science of Religion*, 194.

PEACE RATHER THAN VIOLENCE

The Way to a Peaceful, Prosperous Future.

Throughout history, boundaries of nations, with claims and counter claims, have been a major cause of conflict. But now, if civilization is to avoid catastrophe, we must find a better way.

Human history has shown that when people concentrate on where they agree, they have peace. When they concentrate on where they differ, they have war. A great common cause can diminish differences and promote cooperation.

The reason for poverty, pollution, and war is that civilization lacks a well defined agenda for peaceful progress that can appeal to all. As a result adversaries lack a basis for peaceful resolution of differences.

Discussions too often neglect areas of honest accord. Peace efforts then stall in spite of international laws and United Nations agreements and resolutions. We need to stress where we agree and what we have in common.

In most cases where war ended in peace, it was not permanent. The word "peace" should indicate common understanding and good will. Agreement to stop fighting is a "truce." Only when it is followed by understanding, good will, and cooperation, should it be called peace.

Our whole planet is at a crossroad where we are in danger of total catastrophe if we choose the wrong road. On the other hand, the right choice will provide a new beginning for the human family, with peace, justice, and a sustainable future. Now we must choose.

One road is the way of fear and violence: Kill your enemies. The other is the way of faith, the faith that works by love: Love your enemies. Find common ground. Accent the positive. Work together where you agree and leave room for differences. Love will find a way.

The only way to peace is to find common ground and work for common goals.

TURNING HATE TO LOVE

Every year in late fall, Christmas approaches. We are reminded of the Angels that announced the birth of Jesus: "Hark, the herald Angels sing," and "Peace on the earth, good will to men."

The Babe of Bethlehem became the light that turned darkness into day. This light turned hate into love. Ever since, it has inspired those who saw it to become peacemakers. A few outstanding examples are St. Francis, William Penn, and Martin Luther King Jr.

Around the world there are hundreds of groups with different creeds and cultures who have one thing in common: They are seeking to know and practice the ways of peace. They differ in many of their views, but they share one goal—to be peacemakers. Jesus said, "Blessed are the peacemakers."

The greatest success of war-makers comes when they put aside their differences and make a united effort against their enemies. It is time for the peacemakers of the world to unite all the actions that promote peace, justice, and a sustainable future. Together we can end Earth's long history of settling differences by hating and killing our enemies. Together, we can prove the power of faith and love to make our enemies our friends.

UNITED WE LIVE, DIVIDED WE DIE

Abraham Lincoln said, "United we stand, divided we fall."[3] He was thinking of the United States. Today, our problem is global and far more serious. While we proclaim we are the *United* States, and are a part of the *United* Nations, today we and the whole world are dangerously divided.

President Bush's terrorist agenda, of billions for devilish weapons to make skeletons of what he considered his enemies, was opposed by bin Laden and the terrorists who see things bin Laden's way. The problem for Bush was that the weapons we developed are now in the hands of enemy terrorists, and now the weak can destroy the strong.

In the United States there is more division and hatred than we have had in recent years. We and our divided world are headed for disaster. Only a spiritual awakening can save us. Only when we see the meaning and power of love, and praise the good in our enemy, can we unite and avoid disaster.

On November 19, 1863, President Abraham Lincoln delivered his famous Gettysburg Address. His words about the importance of freedom—"government of the people, by the people and for the people"— gave hope to America and the world.

But there was a fatal flaw in what he said and did. It is time to recognize that you cannot end violence with violence. Killing our enemies because of our differences encourages others, who oppose what we do,

---

3. Originally attributed to Aesop.

to kill us. With the awesome weapons now available, opposing violence with violence can only lead to disaster for everyone.

Most of the people on both sides of the Civil War claimed to be Christians. So did Bush and Gore during the campaign of 2000. Jesus said, "Agree with your enemy" and showed the way.

The awful carnage of the Civil War would have been avoided had people on both sides of the issues that divided them adopted the methods of dealing with differences that were demonstrated by early Quakers, and later by India's Ghandi and America's Martin Luther King Jr. They provided a common cause that brought people together for the benefit of all.

I would like presidential candidates to answer the question, "Can you two provide a common cause important and strong enough to replace history's long record of human division and violence?" This is what our country and the world needs. This is the way to end bitter partisanship and futile arguments. This is what they should be talking about.

Agreeing with your enemy surely does not mean to agree with something that is wrong. It doesn't mean that you agree with something that you don't believe. But if you reach out to others with God's love in your heart, and look for important matters in which you agree, you will find a common cause. Focus on that will bring resolution of differences and friendly cooperation.

Let's end the world's long sad history of discord and violence, and make taking care of our planet a common cause. December 31, 2000, was the end of the most evil and destructive millennium in history. But for centuries many people have tried to do what they believed was right and have kept alive the hope that the new millennium would be a millennium of peace and prosperity, and a "World Without War"!

America and many other countries devote most of their wealth to military programs. They spend billions for bombs and pennies for peace. If the money that is spent on devilish weapons of war to kill people were spent instead on peace education, ventures that foster peace, promoting global understanding, peaceful resolution of conflict, and on eliminating the causes of violence and hate, there would be no more wars. We could soon eliminate war as a way to settle differences.

When that happens, the whole human family will have a great future. We will eliminate poverty and pollution and see the best in one another. We will join one another in projects to benefit people and planet. A great common cause can make this happen.

Most governments say we must kill the killers, and they praise the soldiers who kill and sometimes die for their country thinking it is the right thing to do. It is sad to think of their misguided loyalty.

Martin Luther King Jr. said, "The ultimate weakness of violence is that it is a descending spiral, begetting the very thing it seeks to destroy." He also said,

> Darkness cannot drive out darkness; only light can do that. Hate cannot drive out hate; only love can do that. Hate multiplies hate, violence multiplies violence, and toughness multiplies toughness in a descending spiral of destruction . . . . The chain reaction of evil—hate begetting hate, wars producing more wars—must be broken, or we shall be plunged into the dark abyss of annihilation.
>
> Instead of diminishing evil, it multiplies it. Through violence you murder the hater, but you do not murder hate. In fact, violence merely increases hate.
>
> Returning violence for violence multiplies violence, adding deeper darkness to a night already devoid of stars. Darkness cannot drive out darkness; only light can do that. Hate cannot drive out hate, only love can do that.[4]

As a result, the whole world is in a state of siege with ever more fear and anxiety. We need a miracle to avoid catastrophe.

FUSION NOT FISSION

Morally and spiritually, man has been haunted by a feeling, something sensed in his dreams, that he was intended for a better world. Now he sees a glimmer of light; his dreams can now come true, and he will soon step out of the darkness into the day.

In this world of tomorrow, there will be a new respect for man's mind; a reverence for life that will express itself in a deepened awareness of the uniqueness and preciousness of each mind. As the minds of all men probe the unknown, the importance of each man's role will be more and more appreciated, for every thought is unique and adds to the total thinking of man. Even in thoughts of familiar things, the connotation is never the same, influenced as it is by temperament, environment, and experience. From infancy to old age, man's great function—the one that will lead to the greatest meaning in life—is the act of thinking. From this

4. King, *Strength To Love.*

evolves the sharing of his thoughts with his fellows, of feeling the great emotions and acting to fulfill his dreams.

We have made thousands of years of progress through fission, through conflict, discord, and violence. We have split the atom; we have split the world. But this method of progress has run its course.

Now we must turn to the method of fusion through the techniques of agreement and accord—we must heal the world.

We know that in atomic reactions fission is a source of great energy. But we discover that atomic fusion is a far greater source. Our conduct today is based mostly on controversy and competition. Man still expects to fight in order to win.

The ways of peace are different. In its Latin roots the word "peace" means "to agree." In peace, progress comes from a dialogue in which men look for similarities rather than differences. Not that they fail to acknowledge the differences (in the scientific method we note both differences and similarities), but the deepest and best communication and creativity occurs when one or more people, with a sense of wonder, are pursuing together a line of thought. With this comes insight into the essence of things. In this way both sides win.

And, of course, we know that an experience, mutually approved, lowers the barriers that separate men. Then the dialogue between individuals contributes to communication, not just of words, but of real meaning.

Seeking individual peace is not enough. We must consciously add our faith to the faith of every man. Then, and only then, can we create the global field of good will that is so desperately needed. For this task, each man's thought is needed. A daily global "Minute for Peace" on radio and TV can provide a vehicle for connecting each man's faith with the faith of all men.

It seems to me that our whole problem is a matter of energy equivalents. Our global mind (the electric-mental field which, like the Van Allen belt, surrounds the Earth) has two principal things wrong with it. On the one hand, individual minds that are the source of energy are disconnected with each other and with their source of being. On the other hand, their energy is mostly negative energy. Their thoughts are thoughts of fear and result in hate and violence. If a sufficient nucleus of human minds can connect with one another in thoughts of good will, peace, trust, and love, there can be a chain reaction—a fever of faith can quickly spread throughout the world of mind. Then the whole basis of man's conduct and progress will change. Men will seek the good in each other and see that their similarities are greater than their differences. The creative potential of each human mind will be encouraged, as each man's journey is aided by everyman's quest.

TECHNIQUES OF PEACE

Man has reached his hour of destiny when he must choose the ways of peace or die.

It is now the great task of every responsible individual to think about peace; to learn the techniques and dynamics of peaceful progress, and to put them to use at every level of human contact. In sum, each one of us today must think, pray, and work for peace. May our motto be "Let world peace begin with me."

The ways of peace require that we:

1. Open the mind to ever new possibilities of real agreement in all relations, and carefully accept each agreement when it is found, recognizing that real agreement will lead not to surrender, but to creative and peaceful adjustment of differences.

2. Surround every tension with the confidence that it will be followed not by violence, but by a new breakthrough in understanding.

3. Avoid being on the defensive or putting others on the defensive. The more defensive we are, the less we understand the real meaning of the other person's words.

4. Have an open mind in negotiations and seek conciliation without the fear of seeming fearful.

5. Recognize that words of agreement must be accompanied by a continuing dialogue of agreement and by actions of agreement.

6. Emphasize points of agreement when discussing differences.

Human relations, whether at the social or political level, can only improve where strength is given to areas of sincere accord. Finding these areas and building on them are essential to peace.

In the learning process, you can only use existing concepts to build new concepts. In a similar way, relations with other individuals or nations can improve only as we define areas of unity, strengthen them, and extend them.

For example, we had many political differences with the Soviet Union, but we were both sincerely interested in the peaceful exploration of space. By developing a major joint venture in space, with astronauts from both countries participating together, we found the Soviets listening more attentively to our ideas in related fields of education and industry. Eventually, they were more receptive to democracy. Instead of meaningless exchange of words, there was more and more communication of meanings.

We are not suggesting "peace at any price," but defining the price of peace. If, with all our strength, we seek to engage our adversary at the points of agreement, there will be no energy left on either side for conflict.

We are not proposing that disarmament precede peace, but that the techniques of peace be used to change enemies into friends. If this is effectively done throughout the world, appropriate structures to guarantee freedom and order, and to eliminate war, will quickly follow. The United Nations can then extend the blessings of liberty and peace throughout the world.

But to do this there must be bold and daring initiatives for peace. In war we react to a real or threatened attack. To prevent war, we must act before the attack with wartime vigor in a common cause. If we choose a great common cause as the area of confrontation, we will not have to fight. The "belligerents" will be kept too busy responding to the force of our cooperation in the things they believe.

If we really try, we can find at least a few points of sincere agreement with almost any one we meet. Excited recognition and cooperation at these points are the beginning of peace—with a neighbor, and with a nation.

Today's world of hate is hungry for peace. So hungry, that a relatively few individuals, demonstrating a dynamic contagious peace, could trigger a chain-reaction of attitudes conducive to peace all over the world. All that is needed is a program that will inspire understanding and confidence, and provide a global connection with other people, completely free of any coercion or dogma.

Radio and TV programs focusing on peace—free of self-serving ideologies—could feature universal thoughts on the ways of peace with brief personal experiences to illustrate them. Each listener would be invited to add his thoughts to the thoughts of others and choose the course his conscience approves.

The active listener would then join each day in a silent minute for peace—completely neutral, completely free—a global connection with other people through simultaneous awareness of every man's hope for peace and love.

FACING THE DIFFICULTIES

While it is good to accent the positive and focus on solutions, we also need to honestly face the difficulties. Whether it is the result of sinful nature, childhood neglect, or bad genes, humanity today is crippled by hate, fear, greed, sickness, crime, and misuse of money and power.

The vast majority of people believe in the Golden Rule but do not practice it. They could support the visions and actions that would bring a positive, global, state of mind, which would better enable efforts to reach the minds and hearts of those engaged in evil acts.

THE STATE OF THE WORLD AND WHAT TO DO

At this time of global crisis many people are asking what should we do.

In the last century we became more aware of the many different cultures and religions around the globe. Then our venture into space made us know that we had only one Earth, and that the future would be largely determined by the human family, which now covers the planet.

Today we have incredible knowledge and technology. If it is used for good the whole world has a better future. Misused, it will destroy civilization.

The first step is Minute for Peace. We must get rid of our mutual fear. Look at realities instead of dogmas. Then we will understand each other and work together, discovering anew the beauty, love, and trust that comes from within. If we who are capable of choosing peace will begin now, others will follow and we can make our planet a new world. The choice is ours!

What we can do. Take a minute each day for silent meditation. Look at a flower, a star, a child, and reflect on the meanings of good will and peace. Listen to what our own inner voice tells us to do. Observe a Minute for Peace when we get up in the morning, or at any time, or at one of the special minutes proposed for simultaneous observance around the world—03:00, 11:00, and 19:00 Greenwich International Time (in New York, 6 am, 2 pm, and 10 pm EST).

Miracle formula. Each day join this growing network of peace with thoughts of good will for the whole world (especially for the leaders of all nations). Accompany your thoughts with words of goodwill and with works of peace.

Learn the methods of peace. Seek what you can honestly approve in your adversary, or opponent, and praise it! Work together with him on any project where there is honest accord. Assist any international project in which you believe.

Let us get excited about overarching goals that are globally shared and strive for international cooperation in achieving them. Space, medicine, music, the arts, sports, science, literacy, food, and shelter are a few of the areas where this is possible.

Spreading the news. Request the local newspaper to remind people of Minute for Peace with a daily thought about good will and peace on their front page. Peace is important! Ask them to carry a series on the methods and techniques of peace in personal, family, and global relations. Invite our radio and TV stations to carry Minute for Peace, at one of the designated times, or any time. Suggest that each church, club, and convention open their meetings with a Minute for Peace, a minute of silent meditation with thoughts of good will for the peace of the world.

Accompany thoughts of peace with deeds of peace. We can become involved in some organization or project in our church, club, or other group, in spreading in a positive and practical way the words and works of good will and peace at home and abroad. Tip the balance for peace by sending at least 10 percent of our income where we believe it will count the most for peace.

Peace Is Coming

The word is traveling on the wings of the night.
Listen to your inner voice, the Holy Spirit, or your
Conscience and you will hear it. Peace is coming . . .
You can speed the day by the miracle of goodwill.
Begin to feel it and share it in a daily Minute for Peace –
A moment to be conscious of this Earth-home, this nest
In the stars, this family of man and its awesome destiny.

RELIGIONS AND PEACE

Many people feel their religion holds the answer to a better future. They view life from the perspective of their religion.

The religions of the world (Christianity, Judaism, Islam, Buddhism, Hinduism, etc.) are an important factor in what people think and do. Unfortunately, mass media largely ignores this fact. In the newspapers and TV programs you will find far more space for football than for religious news and events.

Love of God, love of people, love of Earth, honesty, fairness, and truth are to be found in every major religion. I may totally reject the creeds of other religions where they relate to a future life and at the same time approve their actions that heal and help people and planet. A deeply held shared goal aids communication and promotes more openness to each other's point of view, often resulting in a basic unity that helps resolve many differences, with accommodation or separation where needed. True love of God will result in love of neighbor and nature.

Ghandi said, "Pluralistic nationalism excludes the establishment of any State based solely or mainly on one religion." Jerusalem, holy to Christian, Muslim and Jew, should be ruled by peace-loving leaders from all three religions.

What a great thing it would be to see Jewish, Christian and Muslim leaders in Jerusalem thinking and acting as Earth Trustees. By focusing on our common humanity and the right of everyone to an "Earth Claim," they could provide homesteads for homeless constituents. Their actions would result in friendly communities throughout the Middle East. Soon the whole world would see the Earth Trustee solution and we would be on our way to a global peaceful future.

To succeed, leaders and laymen are asked to avoid the historic mistakes of humanity's past. Instead of emphasis on our differences, let us call attention to the important matters in which we agree. We need a vision of the future: We all want a world without war and the end of poverty. We want a stake in Earth's natural bounty, for ourselves and everyone, including the disinherited poor. Now is the time for the realization of human potential—physical, mental, spiritual—in a world of freedom and order.

To achieve this we should look below the surface at the root causes of civilization's sickness. In the past individuals identified with and were most loyal to their clan, nation, religion, or business. The narrow view of competing groups often led to conflict and sometimes war.

Most religions teach the Golden Rule and profess to favor justice and fair play (though many times their words are not followed by actions). However, we are conditioned to focus on differences. We need to find and focus on a great common cause all can support. The solution is a compelling agenda that will appeal to all and leave room for differences.

Once the primary universal goal of peace, justice, and the care of Earth is established and affirmed by leaders and world public opinion, people immersed in controversy will more constructively sort out differences and find areas of agreement.

This will increase understanding and bring better definitions of issues—how they relate, provide direction, or help achieve global goals. Then, with the aid of an enlightened, responsible mass media, the world's public opinion, a powerful force, will promote good will, peace, justice, and Earth's rejuvenation. We will all think and act as Earth Trustees.

Awareness of this led to my efforts to make Earth Day "The Great Day of Earth," a global event that could bring together the whole human family on one special day each year.

Earth Day calls attention to the Earth Trustee agenda, which calls for all to think and act as Earth Trustees, making choices to help eliminate pollution, poverty, and violence. On several occasions at the United Nations, the Earth Trustee agenda has fostered peaceful resolution of conflict, justice for all, and environmental actions for a sustainable future.

PEACE IN THE MIDDLE EAST

A major global trouble spot has been the land of the Middle East, hallowed by Christian, Jewish, and Muslim history. Historic boundaries of nations, claims, and counter claims, are now transcended by a larger more fundamental claim, the claim of every person to his or her inheritance, that is, a fair stake in the land and natural bounty of their planet. When we place loyalty to planet and respect for the planetary rights of all people above loyalty to nation, new possibilities quickly appear. What a great thing it would be to see Jewish, Christian, and Muslim Centers in Jerusalem seeking homesteads for homeless constituents in friendly communities throughout the Middle East.

As far as the Arabs are concerned, they believe that they have been deprived of their lands and feel they have suffered a great injustice which they are determined to correct. In their references to peace, they always speak of justice and peace. The record of the half-million Arabs who were kept for years in refugee camps reminds them of the outrage done to their rights in the partition of Palestine.

On the other hand, the Arab sections that are oil-rich have done little to assist their suffering brethren. Nevertheless, a people with ancient roots and culture do not easily give up their homeland. The Arabs are determined to right the injustice done them and regain their property.

The Jews of Israel maintain older prior rights as descendants of the ancient inhabitants of Israel. If their arguments were applied to the United States, Americans would be placed in Canadian refugee camps and the country given back to the Indians. Of course, most (if not all) legal claims to lands by both individuals and countries, if carried back far enough, are found to be illegally obtained through deception or conquest.

However, because of the unique role of the Jew in the drama of history, and because of world sympathies for this nation so long without a country, who in recent times suffered far more than any other people the ravages of bigotry and prejudice, the Jews' claim on their ancient land has an emotional appeal regardless of how illegal it may be in the eyes of international jurisprudence.

In considering basic human rights, other factors to be considered are the unquestioned virility of the new Jewish state, and the far greater benefits they have obtained for the dispossessed individuals and families who have found shelter in their land. They have been able to do this because of massive United States gifts and loans. The Arabs, while undergoing an economic revolution and a revolution in human rights, come far short of the progress shown by Israel, achieved with the help of the United States Government.

While property rights are the basic issue, nevertheless, the Jews have made far better use of their property. This is due to able leadership and to the immigrants with progressive education and industrial skills who were attracted to the new country. This was accompanied by great financial support from Jewish wealth in the United States and other countries.

Clearly presented, with examples of benefits, the Earth Trustee idea of global rights and responsibilities of the whole human family can appeal to Muslims as well as Jews and Christians. This is more important than their differences. Here is a chance for them to be the first to benefit and to lead the whole world into a better future.

Let both Jews and Palestinians give up their partisan claims to the Holy Land and take holy action for a better future. If the warring states in America could become a United States, surely we can obtain a United Holy Land. Those on all sides who understand the power of prayer and a common purpose must now act.

To aid the efforts for peace in the Middle East, much of what is generally accepted by people of all religions (and by humanitarians of no religion) could be put to use right now by designating a brief time (1 or 2 minutes) for simultaneous silent meditation and prayer throughout the world. This could occur three times a day (0300, 1100 and 1900 GMT) and unite the thoughts and feelings of millions in concentrated faith for peace, or purposing peace. Earth Signals (see chapter 27) could be carried by radio, TV, and Internet in countries throughout the world. The Earth Signal would consist of the ringing of the Peace Bell at the United Nations and be followed by local or global programming of peaceful music, or sounds of nature. Each listener could then add his concentrated thought and faith to that of others in a growing current of peace and love.

JERUSALEM, THE KEY

For many years the major trouble spot on our planet has been Jerusalem, hallowed by Christian, Jewish, and Muslim history.

At the moment this is written, violence in the Holy Land threatens global catastrophe. Again, there is an attempt to settle differences by the power of bombs.

The plans of President Bush and other world leaders supporting him did not work. The Peace efforts by Palestine and Israel need a new basic approach: one that will resolve the conflicting claims of personal as well as national property rights—the underlying problem.

The media must help. In October 2000, the Readers Digest published an article, "Fear on Fourth Avenue," about Palestinian terrorists. It was a gripping story. But it increased fear of terrorists and prejudice against Palestinians. In all fairness the Digest should have shown other views that promote understanding and move both Jews and Palestinians toward resolution of their differences.

Today we are more informed about the amazing wealth of our planet. Its raw materials—land, oil, gold, and other minerals, plus its great diversity of organic life—can provide a healthy, prosperous future for all its inhabitants.

Justice demands an equal claim for all Earth's people to Earth's raw materials. The Psalms tell us, "The earth hath he given to the children of men" (Ps 115:16). Our economic systems should be designed to provide each person their inheritance in their planet. Every adult should by rights have two sources of income—what they earn and their inheritance.

This could easily be accomplished by requiring all who have more than their share of Earth's land or minerals to pay two percent of its value each year to those who do not own any. Planetary inheritance would eliminate extreme poverty and with a new sense of fair opportunity encourage industry and entrepreneurial efforts. This proposal, called Earth Rights, is explained more fully in chapter 21.

The perspective involved in this proposal underlies the Earth Magna Charta and is part of the Earth Trustee agenda for eliminating the conflicts and wars that have plagued history. In the past, nations have fought over land and oil, not using justice, but military and economic might to settle their differences. Our planet is too fragile and our weapons too terrible to continue this policy.

Israel and Palestine are considered the "Holy Land" by Christian, Muslim, and Jew. Each of these religions teaches honesty, truth, and justice. Let them now come together for what they all know is right.

In this context, it is suggested that Jerusalem become a United Nations Open City where all religions and races can live together in peace. Jerusalem was to be a separately administered international entity in the original UN General Assembly resolution supporting the partitioning of Palestine.

The three principle religions that believe in a personal God are the Jewish, Christian, and Muslim. They each claim Jerusalem as a holy city and revere the historic Mosque, Church, or Temple ruins located there. In this age of science we should be objective and recognize these three religions have much in common. For their mutual benefit, let them recognize the major areas in which they agree and cooperate for equal status in Jerusalem. There, with the help and approval of the United Nations, local representatives of these three religions could manage the governing of Jerusalem.

This would help the efforts in Jerusalem to place individual planetary rights (Earth Trustee property rights) above national rights. The adoption of Earth Rights would diminish nationalism but at the same time work to the advantage of all states, for their welfare depends ultimately on the justice and opportunity afforded their citizens. It would also tend to lessen the danger and the fears of Israeli expansionism and of Arab revenge, for this new doctrine of property rights would give all a new sense of justice. A common commitment to think and act as Trustees of Earth will then transcend diverse creeds and national loyalties.

Both the Arab states and Israel would then be able to cooperate in providing an equal planetary inheritance for each Jew and Arab (and other citizens). This will inspire new moral and meaningful relationships between these ancient brothers, who, in spite of their recent outbreak of hate and violence, deeply desire conciliation and peace.

Make Jerusalem an Earth Trustee city—a world capital. Already some Muslims, Jews, and Christians are developing separate but friendly communities for their constituents. And some are beginning to learn how to accept one another. An Earth Trustee agenda for all could bring an air of excitement as they led the way to the rejuvenation of our planet. Muslim, Christian, and Jew share a belief in ethical values that can foster individual rights and responsibilities.[5]

When people think and act as Earth Trustees they will show a reverence for life, and for holy places. Moves toward conciliation were helped when Shimon Peres of Israel rang the United Nations Peace Bell, and Yasser Arafat was persuaded to add his name to the Earth Day Proclamation. Because Jerusalem is a holy place to Christian, Muslim, and Jew, here is a chance for all three religions to show their ethical values by recognizing the reverence for life taught by the others—and not claiming Jerusalem just for themselves. Their example and its benefits would quickly be followed by other cities and states around the world and provide new hope in this new millennium.

In thinking about peace in the Middle East, I feel there is special value in the words of Eduardo Cohen, who stated:

---

5. Lewis, in "The Crisis of Islam," said: "Islam is one of the world's great religions. It has given dignity to drab and impoverished lives. It has taught men of different races to live in brotherhood and people of different creeds to live side by side in reasonable tolerance. It has inspired a great civilization in which others beside Muslims live creative and useful lives and which, by their achievements, enriched the whole world. But Islam, like other religions has also shown periods when it inspired in some of its followers a mood of hatred and violence."

Clearly there are virulently racist elements within the greater Palestinian community . . . but I found a real difference between Israeli racism against Arabs, based on a feeling of racial superiority, and Palestinian hatred of Jews which is an understandable Palestinian response to the policies of the Jewish government of Israel and a continuing Jewish occupation.[6]

It is my hope that the voices of peace on both sides will now enable Jews and Arabs to make Jerusalem a City of Peace and lead the world into a new millennium of peaceful progress in the human adventure. Jerusalem is critical for global peace. It is the city symbol that reflects history's long record of conflict over religious differences. At the same time, it is the place from which peace could best spread contagiously all over the world.

PEACE ON EARTH, GOOD WILL TO MEN

To solve the problem of war and violence, the articles at "Every Church a Peace Church" (http://www.ecapc.org) urge attention for the peacemakers who have demonstrated the power of love and non-violence. There are examples through history of the way to peaceful progress. From St. Francis to Martin Luther King Jr., we find the ways that work.

The only hope for the future is a global "Peace Blitz" that will end humanity's long addiction to war. Not only every church, but every city, business, school, and institutions of all kinds must now make peace their first priority. Elect the mayor who will make your city a "Peace City." Other cities around the world will follow suit. We will end "Earth Kill." It will be replaced by "Earth Care" and a great future for our planet.

GLOBAL PEACE PROCLAMATION

WHEREAS: Diabolical weapons of mass destruction are now widely available, and the long human history of greed, injustice, violence and war must now cease, or human life on this planet will end, and

WHEREAS: Hatred does not cease by hatred, nor violence by violence, and

6. Cohen, "What Americans Need to Know."

WHEREAS: There have been many cases in history where people have demonstrated the power of good will and faith to bring understanding, forgiveness and seasons of peace, and

WHEREAS: We must reverse our policy of spending billions for bombs and pennies for peace, and

WHEREAS: We can convert conflict into cooperation by searching for points of agreement and support of common goals, and

WHEREAS: When more money and effort is spent on eliminating the causes of war than on weapons of war—the world will have a peaceful, prosperous future, and

WHEREAS: Planet Earth is an amazing planet with a skin of life that with understanding and care can provide a good life for its human inhabitants, and

WHEREAS: Businesses and institutions of all kinds must now follow policies that will reward service to human welfare—instead of greedy, deceptive policies that make money without rendering any service,

THEREFORE: We will seek to now think and act as responsible, peaceful Trustees of Earth, seeking choices that will be fair and just and provide a sustainable future for our Earth Home.

We will engage in a moral equivalent of war: We will honor those who are most effective in peaceful resolution of conflict. There will be no more war heroes, only peace heroes, those who sacrifice and risk their lives to eliminate the causes of violence.

Recognizing that Prayer is the mightiest power in the world, every day we will pray for understanding of those who differ with us and ways to cooperate in achieving the great global goal we share—Permanent Peace.

With the faith that works by love, we will expect a miracle—a new beginning for planet Earth.

BETHLEHEM STAR

"Star of wonder, star of light." Is there hope for the future? The most important thing in astronomy in history was the Star of Bethlehem. To me, it points the way to "peace on Earth, good will toward men."

The horrible events of 9-11 deepened our awareness of evil. We have a wonderful planet. But hate, fear, greed, and lust continue to make life on our planet a dismal night of despair.

However, like the Bethlehem Star, Christmas brings warm feelings of cheer. On the days just before Christmas, wherever you go, you find people more cheerful. Many radio and TV programs feature Christmas carols. The beautiful carols make Christmas a time when even people on the street smile more and are more friendly.

There is profound symbolism in Christmas, and it has inspired the world's greatest music. As we approach Christmas in this new millennium, we hear on radio, "Hark, the herald Angels sing, 'Glory to the newborn King.'" We suddenly remember the Star of Bethlehem, and "peace on Earth, goodwill to all." Our best hope for the future is found in the Angels' ancient message.

When our hearts are filled with goodwill, we see new opportunities for resolving conflicts, achieving economic justice, and finding ways to a sustainable future.

Christmas was originally celebrated on the winter solstice. This is the shortest day of the year. In ancient times people noted that in the fall, the days kept getting shorter and shorter. There was fear they would keep getting shorter until there were no days. But on the winter solstice they would start getting longer, a cause for celebration!

In folklore, and perhaps in fact, Jesus was born on the solstice. This adds to the joy of celebrating the birth of Jesus. Darkness symbolizes ignorance. Light symbolizes understanding. In John 8:12, Jesus said, "I am the light of the world."

Throughout the centuries that followed, the greatest examples of brotherhood and peaceful progress have come from individuals and groups that saw in Jesus the light of the world. As noted earlier, *This Freedom—Whence?* by John Wesley Bready documents the social progress that followed great revivals of Christian faith. Major universities, charitable organizations, and governments found in the Bethlehem story guidance and inspiration for altruistic policies and programs.

As we leave the mistakes of the past and enter a new millennium of opportunity, may the light of Christmas light our way to a better day.

The record of history clearly shows that the power of compassion, justice, and freedom in the last 2000 years was most inspired by the amazing story of Jesus, by what he said and did.

While other religions and beliefs have also fostered the ways of peace, I have found in Jesus my guiding star. In my case, the words and deeds of Jesus inspired Earth Day and my Earth Trustee efforts to provide a better future for the human family.

Pantheism, in contrast to Christianity, is the belief that has held back progress in India. Strange as it may seem, the greatest efforts to practice the Golden Rule and ability to achieve peaceful progress have come from people who heard and believed the simple message contained in the words and actions of Jesus. While people naturally view his life with different perspectives, depending on their background and culture, the people who simply read what he said and did, and independently judge its meaning, reflect the greatest benefit in their lives and their effects on others. Today the problem is that few people think for themselves.

People of different beliefs (including atheists) show varying degrees of creative altruism. I try to constantly recognize common ground and support others.in matters where we agree, but with recognition of where we disagree.

We face profound mystery when it comes to the ultimate meaning of reality—Why am I here? Where am I going? What is the meaning of infinity or eternity? I am intrigued by psychic phenomena and have explored many possible explanations. But I have no scientific proof of any explanation. One of my wisest friends says he will not spend time on what is unknowable.

The simple story of Jesus in the New Testament assists my understanding of what I should do with my life. I daily seek to know his will and way. Sometimes this is a matter of just thinking logically about what he said and did. Other times, call it moments of intuition, or his spirit speaking to me, I get ideas and instructions out of the blue, and see answers to prayer and anointing on my words.

Differences and difficulties concerning religion abound. The blacker the night, the brighter the star. It is darkest before dawn, and day will soon come.

> Star of wonder, star of light,
> Star with royal beauty bright,
> Westward leading, still proceeding,
> Guide us to thy perfect light.

A DARING STRATEGY FOR WORLD PEACE

We should be as realistic about what is necessary to achieve world peace as we are about the necessities for success in a great military campaign. In the latter, an effort is made to clearly define the goals, to assess the resources that can be used, and then to develop a strategy for success. Something of this kind can and should be done if we are going to bring about the great changes needed to achieve a world of freedom and order without the threat of war.

An understanding of a total strategy that offers a chance of success could enable the individual to see the importance of the minute yet specific contribution that he can make. An experiment showing it could work would inspire him to act.

At Pearl Harbor, the war was made real. This was followed by unity, purpose, and fervor in our efforts to defeat our enemies. Millions of men were recruited; the giant strength of our industrial complex was quickly converted to meet the needs of war. Shortly there were thousands of trucks, tanks, planes, and ships, manned by quickly trained men, moving toward battle fronts that would bring the greatest destruction the world has ever known.

An equally dramatic impact for peace is needed that will catch the attention of people throughout our country and give a sense of unity, purpose, and fervor in waging peace. If we are going to seriously meet the challenge of our time and do away with the threat of war, we must activate our industrial might, our technical know-how, and our best humanitarian concerns in a mighty effort to build schools, plants, roads, dams, and modernize agriculture—in short, to work together with our neighbors around the world, for global goals in research, education, health, and welfare. What we can do for war, we can do even better for peace.

Instead of thousands of machines to destroy, we must provide and use thousands of machines to build a better world. Of course we must use the techniques of cooperation that meet real desire and need. We should now mobilize for a massive "Peace Blitz."[7]

There is no reason why we cannot wage peace with a vigor that will demonstrate a moral equivalent to war. A forceful example is needed to overcome the negative feeling that "It can't be done." *It has never been tried!*

7. The term "Peace Blitz" was used by Norman Corwin in his radio-play "Could Be."

PEACE BLITZ CAMPAIGNS

Purpose

The purpose of a peace blitz campaign is to change the climate and activities in one or more towns in a way that will provide an appropriate example of waging peace, and which could be expanded throughout the country and perhaps throughout the world. This could be an instrument for bringing about a profound change in national policies on disarmament and peace.

The Peace Blitz Declaration defines waging peace in general terms, which subsequently need to be made specific through democratic planning and action in the local community. It calls for an attack against the causes of war, such as fear, hunger, illiteracy, poverty, and other barriers to peace. The local community would choose five or more projects for this purpose.

In order to effectively defeat the apathy and complacency which is at the heart of the problem, help should be obtained from the best possible source. A brief outline of the local plan can be sent to organizations such as CARE, American Friends Service Committee, UNESCO, or the Peace Corps, requesting suggestions for projects to implement the campaign.

Program

The objective of the campaign is to rally all the fraternal resources of the community in a twofold program. The first part of this would be a great discourse on the problems of peace.

Discourse

Discussion and study would cover the whole spectrum of ideas on peace, from the inner peace taught by religion and psychology, to such problems as disarmament and world law. Able speakers would be invited to speak in local service clubs, churches, schools, and in house meetings conducted throughout the town. Every possible aspect of peace and disarmament would be discussed and publicized, but the leaders of the campaign would not give formal support to any political solutions for peace. However, the results of the discourse would be shown in an opinion survey conducted at the close of the campaign.

Projects

The second part of the campaign would be devoted to projects for peace. The purpose of these projects would not be political action (although such action might be discussed in a "World Affairs Forum"project), but participation in activities that would further understanding, good will, and cooperation for worldwide goals that can sincerely be aided. (During the Cold War the activities of Communists would have been openly discussed along with other issues, and firmly resisted where they conflicted with the concept of democracy, but in areas of agreement—such as science, space, medicine, and student exchanges—communication and cooperation would have been encouraged.)

These projects would be designed to attract people at different levels of concern. They could include a student exchange program, Peace Corps Project, Volunteers for UN projects, Food for Peace, Books for Peace, Equipment for Peace, etc. Using the concept of the Peace Blitz in publicity and promotion would redirect feelings of hostility into positive actions for peace.

To give the feeling and the reality of strength to the program, it would be important to obtain large scale participation by the industries and businesses of the town. These are the organizations with which the average man is mostly involved. American industry was a major factor in winning our wars. Their contribution can be a tremendous advantage in winning a lasting peace. In this bold experiment they would be asked to provide help from the best of their personnel along with funds and encouragement of their employees to aid the campaign projects. Their participation should be obtained in the initial planning of the campaign. This should also apply to all the important organization leaders in the community—service clubs, churches, schools, etc.

Peace Blitz Headquarters

This headquarters would be managed by an executive director and secretary with an office and minimum budget. Its function would be to develop a suitable program structure, and public relations support for the campaign.

Coordinating Group

This group is envisioned to be comprised of responsible leaders in the community, representing the best insights of sociology, psychology, economics, political science, and religion. This body would serve as an experimental, detached group who would observe carefully the program's development, make suggestions as to the ongoing local activities, and be alert to possibilities for broad outreach related to the nation and the world.

This would be strictly an idea and consulting group, not responsible for the conduct of the program, but it would at the same time see that ideas of merit were recognized and carried out. The group would also watch for breakdowns in any part of the program and seek to remedy them.

A working committee of this group could consult with other similar groups to develop appropriate steps toward the formation of an International Council (patterned, in part, after their own function). This International Council could create a Council of World Cities (see chapter 24) and, with the help of an International Public Relations Committee, provide a structure for encouraging world friendship and cooperation. Proposals for these organizations are available.

Miscellaneous

With the backing of an ongoing program and the means of taking advantage of opportunities that arise, imaginative projects could aid the total effort. One project that would help all the others would be the collection of signatures for the "Star of Hope" satellite. Those who sign a pledge to work for peace could also indicate which project they would help.

Publicity

The success of the campaign will depend in a large measure on the effective use of the communications media. Making the local newspaper, TV, and radio an example of what can be done would serve this end directly. At the same time it would create a greater sense of purpose and responsibility in the communications media.

Conclusion

During World War II, America and the world were amazed at the spiritual and material resources brought into action when people worked together for a great goal. The strength, sacrifice, and fervor of war must be given to building a peaceful world. There already exist areas of international agreement and cooperation for world wide goals (in the United Nations, UNESCO, International Council of Scientific Unions, etc.). These must be vigorously strengthened and extended. There must be understanding and support for this from the grass roots. We can fight fear and subversion with faith, when we work together for common goals in which we all sincerely believe. Fortunately, there exists a hard core of human values: freedom, love, wonder, dignity; such values are at least dimly understood by all people everywhere. While on the one hand we must guard against the things that threaten these values, what is most important is the work of extending, around the world, the foundations that support them.

A carefully conducted pilot campaign can achieve a breakthrough in tapping untold spiritual and material resources, not by fear of war and a feverish preparation for war, but by faith and a joyous preparation for a peaceful world.

17

Pursuing Earth Care

UNDERSTANDING THE PROBLEM

H UMANKIND HAS LITTLE UNDERSTANDING for applications of the laws of nature and the principles of ecology. On our crowded planet, oil, minerals, and land are not only property, but limited natural resources. It is imperative that their use conform to environmental standards, and be distributed equitably.

The only solution to this growing problem is for local ownership to recognize and be responsive to global rights and responsibilities.

Humanity is presently mindlessly destroying the natural resources essential for survival on our planet. In addition, there is a growing threat of nuclear catastrophe. Conflicting ideas and goals, in the midst of poverty and plenty, have resulted in fear, violence, and frustrating injustice. Is our planetary play approaching "Finis?"

Survival priorities include a change from a throw-away to a thrift economy, and a basic change in values from destructive, conspicuous consumption, to constructive selectivity and simplification. The first priority for industry, to do its share, is to quickly convert to products and services that meet environmental criteria and aid the process of life. These days this is called becoming "green."

In considering the causes of "Earth Kill"—the degradation of "Earth Life"—there are misconceptions in three areas of human values and activities that should be addressed. These are property, money, and nationalism or sovereignty. Misunderstanding and the resulting misuse of these factors are responsible for much of Earth's pain and misery.

There is hope. The elements are here that could bring a sweeping change from "Earth Kill" to "Earth Care," from irresponsibility to trusteeship of planet Earth. The rapid spread of the ecological world view offers great hope for a new kind of unity in human affairs, a unity emerging from the discovery that taking care of our planet is now our first and most urgent task. Now we must seek to have all human activity affecting Earth serve this purpose.

On our planet, microbes and plants in great variety interact with birds, fish, mammals, and basic nutrients in soil, air, and water. Through millions of years of evolution they have achieved a stability based on global unity and balanced diversity. We now understand that nature's delicate balances must be understood, preserved, and aided by redirecting our technology, which is the new decisive factor in Earth's destiny.

This task can best be accomplished, not only by directly nurturing and protecting nature's environment and resources, but also by understanding nature's interdependence and the common bonds that unite all life on Earth. We can then apply these principles to our conduct—in production, trade, consumption—to all facets of human life and culture.

PURSUIT OF POWER AND CONTROL

To provide a metaphorical illustration, let us assume there is some transcendent meaning and purpose in life. (I believe there is.) After a million years of preparation, mankind has reached the point where he can, and must, take charge and manage our planet.

But the crucial problem preventing his assumption of this new role is his excessive greed, ambition, and lust—aided and abetted by institutions (business, media, governments) geared to constant excess.

The rights of passage and of graduation to become managers and custodians of Earth require a maturity that will enable us to choose the good, and refuse the evil, regardless of how seductively the evil entices us.

The pursuit of unbridled power is the broad road to ruin. The managers of Earth must have self-control, if they are to take control properly. They must be able to say, "No," to put limits on their curiosity and pursuit of evil knowledge and power, when they know it is leading the world toward disaster.

The billions spent on past weapons of war are terrible crimes against God and man. If even half the money spent on our more diabolical weapons (gas, fire, atomic) had been spent on educating people on how to take care of their planet, we would have increased instead of diminished Earth's bounty. Thus far we have failed to learn our lesson.

DADDY, SHOW ME THE BRAKES!

In late summer, 1975, a neighbor boy let my five-year-old daughter Christa ride his Big Wheel. This proved to be both exciting and dangerous.

It was a hot humid day in July. I had been listening to the radio reports about the Apollo-Soyuz link-up in space. Christa had been playing for hours in our apartment in Brooklyn, New York. Hearing the children playing on the sidewalk below, she asked if she could join them.

Concerned about possible unknown dangers for a five-year-old, I went down with her and stayed to keep an eye on her.

Our block was short. At the corner was a busy thoroughfare. Across the street was a gasoline station, repair shop for cars, and a noisy auto-wash. Periodic screeches of the elevated trains rounding a curve at our other corner added the final touch to this Brooklyn block where children play.

On the sidewalk were children from three to ten years of age, most of them five or six years old. Some of them were racing up and down the narrow sidewalk on their Big Wheels. Two mothers were on the stoops. One small boy and his sister were bouncing a large ball on a garage door. This boy smilingly agreed to let Christa ride his Big Wheel.

Christa had ridden one of these clever contraptions a few times in the past, always as fast as her excited feet could make it go. Seated low, for maximum use of the leg muscles, a small child can pump the pedals of the big front wheel and achieve a spectacular speed with this modern version of a tricycle.

It had a brake, but as Christa hurtled toward the intersection I suddenly remembered I had not reminded her about the brake. I ran toward her and shouted, "Christa, use the brake." To my relief, her hesitating hand found the brake in time.

In a way our planet Earth is like a Big Wheel. We don't know yet whether we're just going around the block or really headed somewhere. But one thing is certain, the immature Earthling, called man, has discovered the pedals and is excitedly pumping as fast as he can go, though every instinct says, "Slow down. Change course. Danger ahead."

The automobile industry, for example, doesn't know how to cut back. Unions are inflexible on reduction of wages. Useless products that waste and pollute still flood the market place. The American automobile, as now designed, produced, promoted and used, is a major cause of pollution and waste. The automobile industry has not faced up to this fact.

The solution is, of course, not a reckless halt to production of cars, but the refinement and use of alternatives that are now available. These alternatives include everything from electric cars and bicycles to bio-fuel (ethanol can be efficiently produced from various plants). With determination and a new Earth care ideology, the vital changes needed can be made, without the loss of jobs.

In the housing sector, money still pours into inefficient, ill-planned, misplaced housing on land that should be used for parks or vegetable gardens, while the poor, goaded by the "Go Go, More More" media, in their frustration sometimes set fire to abandoned buildings.

One night in Brooklyn an abandoned building in the next block was apparently set afire. We were awakened by fire engines stopping nearby. Looking out our window, we were stunned by the solid billows of flame three stories high and over one hundred feet across. The firemen were fast and efficient. Had they arrived ten minutes later the whole block would probably have been destroyed. Fortunately no life was lost.

Hundreds of fires would be avoided—human lives and millions of dollars saved—if a massive program were initiated to remove wrecked and abandoned buildings. Local efforts to accomplish this have met with failure because there are apparently insufficient funds in City Hall.

A small portion of the money now going into new energy production (offshore oil wells) would be sufficient to prevent the waste of energy, money, and manpower in the present firebug syndrome. By using the money to tear down the unusable abandoned buildings in New York City, we could save millions of dollars in government guaranteed fire insurance, save hundreds of thousands of dollars in welfare relocation payments, and greatly reduce the gasoline used by fire engines!

With another small fraction of the money now allocated for other "Go Go, More More" projects, the new empty lots could be converted into gardens and mini-parks, with here and there a neighborhood resource center for information, tools, and instructions on saving and improving what we've got. Exciting new ecology approaches to simple health-enhancing life styles would stimulate new hope in areas of despair. Encouragement and financing of neighborhood industries and city farms could provide opportunities for jobs and equity ownership by local residents.

If a little bit from the oil companies is not enough, I'm sure a twenty-percent tax on the gross income of all New York bankers and corporate executives would do the trick. They know the importance of doing more with less and should lead the way with their example!

What an inspiring sight it would be if one tiny niche of the global web of techno-organic life stopped its cancer-like growth and functioned in a healthy manner. We can hope for conservation, re-use, repair, re-cycling, urban homesteads, family planning, and optimum instead of maximum production, all contributing to protecting and maintaining a stable environment; where art, science, and real religion would prosper; where the character, independence, and inner drive of its citizens would constantly improve; and where an honest face and a bicycle were more respected and desired than a Cadillac car and a Sable fur.

If one global niche could change, soon other niches would follow.

Our problem is to see both the microcosm and the macrocosm, and their relation to one another. The increasing global demand for energy is on a scale that will soon be impossible to fill. It is already wrecking the fragile skin of life that covers our globe with pollution and destruction of nature's eco-systems. Every increase in energy brings still greater demands from new masses exposed to the disease of reckless consumption. Certainly every mother should be able to have a modern washing machine or access to a Laundromat. But in the developing countries that are suddenly oil-rich, the demand is for highways, and big cars, and all the excess wasteful gadgets that pollute and corrupt industrial society. Only a great sweeping change in human values can save the world from ruin.

Of course providing essential useful conveniences to all the people of developing countries will require a great deal of energy. Energy demand in China and India is booming. This new energy need can be met (and met with non-polluting energy) if the present waste in developed countries is stopped, and if the demands of the new consumers are rational, conditioned by a new commitment to the care of Earth. The rule must be, "Take what nature has to give; don't take what she needs to live." Not a reckless more and more, but a careful more with less.

You can get more protein out of one acre of peanuts or soybeans than from two acres of farmland used to feed and fatten beef. Proper design and insulation of a house can cut fuel bills in half. Communities designed so that employees can walk to work would save untold millions of gallons of gas.

There are promising new systems and energy alternatives. But none of these will be effectively used to improve our human condition, unless we learn how to apply the brakes to what we are doing now, to change course when our technology is destroying the Earth. Otherwise, new energy will merely hasten Earth's destruction.

I'm again reminded of the Big Wheel. Amid the new questions about the nature of the universe and the role of our tiny speck in its purpose, amid new speculations about the nature of mind and thought, and amid a new search for love and for God, one stark unmistakable fact faces us: We must apply the brakes now to our terrible over-use of technology. We must slow down and change course.

"Dear God, help us find the brakes in time."

EARTH UNDER ATTACK

Many informed and thoughtful people today find moments of dark misgivings about our endangered planet. While the world talks of new alternatives—and opportunities abound for Earth's renewal—the status quo continues.

Détente will no longer suffice, at home or abroad. Underneath the stalemates and deadlocks around the world, a fatal disease is rapidly spreading, threatening all life on Earth. This is the cancerous virus of mindless consumption, an addiction to ever greater extravagance with increasing waste, pollution, and destruction of Earth's vital life support nutrients, with impulsive purchase of many useless items, but always produced cheaply at the expense of the environment.

In spite of overwhelming evidence of critical damage to moral fiber, natural resources, and physical health, addiction to consumption is spreading globally. Arabs, Africans, South Americans, and Asians are all frantically following the tragic example of industrialized countries, seeking their profit, gain, or satisfaction by using up, recklessly exploiting, and destroying Earth's limited priceless resources. More and more people are conditioned by TV and other media advertising to "Earth-Kill" habits and practices. Industries are still mostly geared to short-sighted methods and activities that pollute and destroy the Earth.

As a result, the thin skin of life that surrounds our globe is in imminent danger. After millions of years of improvement by nature—more birds, mammals, fish, plants, trees, greater and greater diversity and stability—mankind has in a few decades destroyed over one fourth of the Earth's vegetation and caused the extinction of numerous species of birds, mammals, and plants. We have endangered many other species, such as the whale, that are essential to vital life cycles. The tropical greenhouse has been forever severed from eco-systems which for millions of years spread new species of flora and fauna throughout the world. We have put in the biosphere over two million new chemicals. A portion of these are now causing over sixty percent of the cases of cancer, which are rapidly increasing, plus untold damage to other life. We have dangerously polluted air, land, water, destroyed vital wetlands, endangered oceans, and wasted scarce non-replaceable minerals and oil.

Perhaps worst of all, and most symptomatic of our problem, we have created on our planet a devil's box of radioactive waste, an alien threat to Earth life.

Added to the environmental risk of atomic plants is the even greater danger in an unstable global society of the resulting proliferation of nuclear weapons.

In the case of atomic fission, for energy or bombs, we should have seen from the beginning that it was a forbidden apple, an unprecedented evil that could lead to death and degradation.

Now the ultimate experience of evil has been tasted. Atomic fission, with its awesome fiery violence and its insidious silent spreading death, hypnotizes us with its promise of power to destroy our enemies, and, on the other hand, power to ease our burdens with limitless energy.

We have tasted the forbidden fruit and are both tempted and terrified.

We have much to be terrified about. The radioactive wastes we dumped in the depths of the sea are already seeping from their containers. The cancerous atomic plants, like noxious boils, are spreading over the face of Earth. Transportation and storage of radioactive wastes stain our environment and compromise the integrity of our planet. Our action may cause grave problems for the next thousand generations.

We have committed a heinous crime against God, our children, and all the creatures of our once-beautiful planet.

God has let us taste the bitter-sweet fruit. But now that we know the deadly pain it brings, let us ask God's forgiveness and start to rightly use our physical and spiritual resources, with all their limitations and moral restrictions, choosing the narrow way of stewardship leading to life instead of death.

Since mankind's actions will now decide the fate of our planet, moral and ethical principles and guidelines are needed to save our Earth.

EARTH KILL

The real cause of our national and global danger is not pollution, energy shortage, inflation, proliferation of atomic plants and bombs, or poverty. These are only the symptoms.

The cause is plainly that we are seeking our profit or gain mostly by using up, exploiting, and destroying the Earth. We are conditioned to killing the Earth instead of protecting and helping the Earth.

Manufacturers are geared to killing the Earth. The use of non-replaceable minerals and other materials with little or no provision to reclaim and re-use them, and using untested or poorly tested new chemicals that spread subtle disease and death to our living environment—all these destroy forever the priceless wonders that took nature millions of years to produce.

Contractors, builders, and road makers are geared to killing the Earth—paving and covering up millions of acres of fertile soil, needlessly breaking up and destroying vast networks of eco-systems that were millions of years in the making.

Agribusinesses are geared to killing the Earth. They keep replacing nature's method of diversity and stability with intensive one-crop production, treating the resulting pests and diseases with chemical pesticides that upset nature's delicate balances and destroy bugs and birds used for natural pest control, and using chemical fertilizers that leach and deplete the soil.

Real estate developers are geared to killing the Earth, with practically no understanding or concern for nature's requirements. Forests, farmland, rivers, lakes, and wetlands are polluted or destroyed because of ill-conceived housing and development projects. These deprive children, the largest and most important part of our population, of their natural heritage. Human settlements can be designed to complement and harmonize with nature's wonders and provide a healthy environment for us, and for our children.

Advertising, credit policies, taxes, and personal habits are all geared to killing the Earth. Instead of acting as trustees of our portion of Earth, we plunder our planet and divide the spoils. We have destroyed major portions of Earth's vegetation, and pushed to extinction numerous species of birds, fish, and mammals. Reckless depletion of essential minerals and oil threatens a crisis for industry. Even the ozone, our shield from radiation, is endangered.

FROM EARTH KILL TO EARTH CARE

The choice facing mankind is now clear. Unless we start using our God-given courage, sanity, and faith to restore and protect Earth's beautiful and vital nutrients and life, we will soon all become like mindless maggots consuming the remains of our doomed Earth.

The cure for "Earth Kill" is "Earth Care." The methods and means are at hand to begin Earth's rejuvenation. But only through great personal inner commitment and a massive global campaign can we wrench free from "Earth Kill" conditioning. We must now undertake an all-out effort to protect and renew the air, land, water, plants, mammals, and other organisms; seeking our gain, not by wastefully using and destroying nature's web of life, but by carefully nurturing her living resources, and by harvesting only her abundance and cautiously using and reusing her raw materials.

If we act quickly we can avoid another dark age and begin a new golden age of hope for our children and grandchildren. Let us unite and work with all our might in a seven year "Earth Care Campaign." Help tip the global balance from "Earth Kill" to "Earth Care. "

Most people would gladly cut their car travel in half, if they were convinced it was necessary in order for their children to have a healthy peaceful life twenty years from now, and that this was part of a vital program to prevent catastrophic deaths that will occur if we continue to poison and disrupt the fragile life-giving nutrients that nurture and support us.

By a determined effort and great spirit of cooperation, we can still turn civilization around from the destruction of Earth to its nurture and care. With solar energy, wind energy, biomass, alcohol from palm oil, and other renewable energy sources, we can provide all the clean harmless energy we need. Technology changes and personal sacrifices would be far less than required in the past for a major war.

Perhaps, if we will straighten up, God will be especially good to us and help us find a simple way to harness the power of gravitation or electromagnetism. Perhaps Einstein's $E = mc^2$ was not the last word on energy and energy sources.

But it would be folly to develop more power or gain more prosperity if we are going to use it for more dope, gambling, killing, cheating, waste of resources, and degradation of Earth's fragile life.

The best way to prove to God a real change of heart is to declare a national emergency, use renewable energy, and eventually stop use of non-renewable energy including our atomic plants. With other suggestions many people have offered, we could manage beautifully.

We could then gear ourselves, and our institutions, for a total global effort to respect, manage, and nurture our planet. In a few decades we could, I believe, obtain Earth's redemption and provide a healthy peaceful prosperous life for every family on Earth.

An Earth care ethic, recognizing nature's multi-million-year success story, would seek our gain, not by using up nature's capital, but by aiding and harvesting her increase. It would require that we only produce and use products and services that nurture, conserve, and recycle the organisms and nutrients of nature, without unnatural pollution. Destructive long-lasting non-biodegradable chemicals would be avoided at all costs.

One of the greatest crimes against nature and posterity is the radioactive waste from production of nuclear weapons and nuclear energy. The best-laid plans of man have repeatedly gone wrong, but never before has man risked the future of the planet.

Here in the United States our first task in this new millennium should be to respect the rights of future generations. The resulting rationing of energy will be a small price to pay for restoration of our integrity and can stimulate efforts for stopping "Earth Kill" and retooling for "Earth Care"! Stalling halfway measures will no longer do. Time is running out. We, the human family, are the trustees of Earth, but we have thus far failed to see and accept our responsibility. Instead of continuing to plunder, we must now protect our planet.

Our religions teach the stewardship of Earth, to tend, replenish, and make it a garden. The Psalms state, "The earth hath He given to the children of men" (Ps 115:16). Man (male and female) was given "dominion over . . . every living thing that moves upon the earth" (Gen 1:28). Rev 11:18 tells us, God will "destroy them who destroy the Earth." The Psalmist said ". . . the earth is full of your riches" (Ps 104:24) and Solomon wrote that ". . . the profit of the earth is for all" (Eccl 5:19). Jesus drew attention to nature, saying "Consider the lilies of the field, how they grow" (Matt 6:28) and ". . . make the tree good and his fruit good" (Matt 12:33). He noted in particular that God is involved in His creation: ". . . Not a sparrow falls to the ground without the Father's notice" (Matt 10:29).

Most of the parables and illustrations given by Jesus were drawn from nature and revealed a profound identification with all Earth-life. He, the great manifestation of God's love, told his followers that bread from the grain of the fields, and wine, the fruit of the vine, were his body and blood, making forever holy the global miracle of vegetation that covers our amazing planet.

We must now accept our duty—or die.

This urgent appeal to reason is a challenge to all nations, especially to the United States in its third century, to begin a massive "Earth Care Campaign." We should view all of our problems—economic, political, personal—in terms of "Earth Care," and choose the practices and policies that will increase the care and understanding of Earth's web of life and stop its destruction.

The greatest power on Earth is the power of the human heart. To tap its power for our task, we must seek individual commitment to "Earth Care." We can each make a check list of personal values, practices, and habits that contribute to "Earth Kill" or "Earth Care," examining our vocation, purchases, and methods of travel. Is our work, or company where we are employed, causing pollution and waste, or instead, is it using the new designs and methods that respect and complement nature's eco-systems? When we buy, do we carefully choose the products and services that save energy, avoid pollution in production or use, and can be recycled or reused, or do we thoughtlessly buy the glamorized junk products and food advertised on TV? Do we have a job where we can walk to work? How much do we ride a bicycle, public transportation, or a car? Is our car large or small? Do we grow some of our food?

We will undoubtedly need to make trade-offs. Planting a thousand trees will compensate for pollution from a big car. The question is, when we come to the bottom line, are we on balance, a curse or a help to Mother Earth?

We cannot be moral, humanitarian, or truly religious, and ignore our responsibility to help take care of our portion of Earth. It is ridiculous to think of people, who are polluting, wasting, and destroying the Earth, being converted to the love of God and continuing to pollute, waste, and destroy the Earth. In our global emergency, a task for those who profess a love of God and man is to pursue love, protection, and care of Earth.

Of course, the massive changes that are needed also require action by groups and institutions: governments, business, media, schools, unions, religious, and fraternal organizations. Every organization can initiate an Earth care plan to implement the Earth care ethic. There are many environmental organizations and consultants available to help.

In the year 1976, the Bicentennial of the United States, several auspicious events occurred which could have contributed to the global mobilization of an effective Earth care effort. Now, more than thirty years later, they symbolize what still needs to be done.

The first event was the United Nations Law of the Sea Conference. It is imperative that we fully implement the UN common heritage resolution and establish a democratic ocean regime for the protection and management of the global sea. To this end the United States should immediately renounce its claims to the continental shelf beyond the 12 mile limit, subject to establishment of a responsible ocean regime with appropriate checks and balances. Provision in the meantime should be made to take the fees and royalties from offshore drilling and use them for UN sustainable development projects in pockets of poverty. The neediest poor should be the first to realize benefits from mankind's common ownership of the global seabed, in a program that involves them in the care of Earth.

The second event, held in Vancouver, British Columbia, in May 1976, was the United Nations Conference on Human Settlements—Habitat. Continuing UN meetings on Human Settlements should be attended by every planner and decision maker in our urban centers. Congress and the President should call attention to them and TV should cover them. Habitat programs are a global effort to provide new designs for making communities humane with homes, schools, work, and services for the four billion people that may be added to our planet in the next 25 years (in spite of progress in family planning).

Using renewable energy, caring for the oceans, and providing humane communities provides the Earth care ethic so needed by the world. If we change our course and survive our present crisis, our great-grandchildren will certainly be committed to the care and protection of Earth life.

AM I A CRIMINAL?

Whether I am Christian, Jew, Muslim, Hindu, Capitalist, Communist, black, or white, am I helping to care for Earth and its threatened web of life, or am I (perhaps without awareness), destroying life and its essential nutrients?

Am I consciously aiding "Earth Care" or unconsciously aiding "Earth kill"?

Is the work I do increasing pollution and the poisoning of Earth's vital systems of air, water, land, and life—or is it helping to heal, to build, and to restore nature's diversity and balanced growth?

Are the things I buy, my life style, and my habits increasing the demand for products that waste, pollute, and destroy life and human potentials, or are they helping create demands for production, advertising, and marketing of products and services that conserve, recycle, and restore nature's interdependent niches of living organisms?

All of us, along with all other living organisms on Earth, are both producers and consumers. Before the coming of our mindless modern technology, almost everything produced by organisms—by microbes, bugs, plants, fish, and mammals—was reused by other organisms, with nutrients exchanged and transmitted throughout Earth's global web of life.

This happened for millions of years without any conscious decision on the part of any organism and resulted in constant improvement in the variety, stability, and beauty of life on Earth. But people acquired the ability to plan and choose and do so without regard for nature's systems and requirements, that is, misdirecting technology, with disastrous results. Whales and hundreds of other mammals, plants, and birds are threatened with extinction. DDT spraying of mosquitoes in North America years ago polluted penguins at the South Pole. The vital tropical forests are endangered and oceans may die.

Now the same sense that makes it a crime to kill a person must provide a new ethic and new responsibility for the care of Earth and the protection of nature.

Don't kill nature.

Choose now how you too can avoid a life of crime against nature and instead be her helper and friend. To aid your task, join an Earth care group now.

EARTH CARE CAMPAIGN

With modern communications technology, a great new idea can quickly spread to all countries and change attitudes globally. We can expect to accomplish this dramatically with a global "Earth Care Campaign."

The idea is to take action that will provide a moral equivalent of war, to enlist the same effort and commitment to save our planet as the Allies did to win World War II.

The wonderful thing is that winning this war will not require any killing, only a change of attitude and conduct that will enable everyone—the disinherited poor as well as the affluent rich—to reap the benefit of Earth's natural bounty. Everyone will win.

The enemy is not people, but wrong assumptions that pit people against other people—unexamined assumptions that magnify and distort racial, cultural, political, religious, and ideological differences. Add to this a little greed, lust, envy, hate, and false pride, and you have the making of a boiling pot of trouble.

But in this "Earth Care Campaign," focus will be on the items in which we can honestly and enthusiastically agree. People of different cultures can agree on basic moral values and deeds though they may differ on creeds that relate to the great mysteries of life. For honest agreement and cooperation we need to separate our creeds and their claims about life and death from the ideas and actions in which we can all agree. We can agree on the need for deeds that nurture people and planet, though we differ on creeds warmly held about mind and spirit and the ultimate mysteries of the cosmos and its Creator. Of course, the best evidence of the value of our creed is the love it produces in our lives. Common to every major religion is the Golden Rule—treat others as you would like to be treated. Now we have a new common ground: awareness of our planet and our responsibility to take care of it.

Here are the items where all can agree:

1. Protection and care of sea, sky, and soil; of creatures great and small—an "Earth Care" project or job for everyone.

2. Action that will provide real opportunity for the poor and disabled to obtain food, shelter, and modern conveniences, the "Earth Care" way, with minimum pollution and waste.

3. A vital change of heart that will bring love, fellowship, and cooperation among neighbors, local and worldwide.

In this campaign every church, temple, school, service club—every group in society—will be asked to join the campaign: to set goals, plan programs, and prove their worth by their love in action, by work and success in achieving the above goals.

Every group will be urged to arrange a telephone network where possibilities can quickly spread, and needs can be shared. Radio, TV, and press will headline stories of success and the growing global unity that is bridging national boundaries and political differences. A global Earthline telephone program from the United Nations will report progress daily. This will be a three to five minute tape played twenty-four hours for pickup by radio station or individuals who dial a 900 number.

If nations as diverse as the United States, China, England, France, and the USSR could forget their differences enough to wage World War II together, is there any reason we cannot all set aside our differences enough to wage an all-out effort that will bring permanent peace and prosperity to our planet? Let us recognize our differences (diversity can be a good thing), but go all-out to do the vital things we agree should be done.

Accepting trusteeship of planet Earth and seeking, in our different ways, to provide every family a homestead with fair opportunity for work, education, and human fulfillment, can now bring a spiritual and visible renaissance to our planet.

On Earth Day, we have participation by Christians, Jews, Muslims, and people of every major religion and no religion. The point of agreement is the importance of peace, justice, and Earth stewardship in the here and now. The best evidence of the value of our faith is the good we do for people and planet.

Let us make Earth Day and every day a special day of prayer for the troubled Middle East. Peace in the Holy Land would be a catalyst for peace all over the world. Dedication and action by all is needed. The proven power of prayer can help. Let all who see this message decide what they will do.

First, let us all make Earth Day a time to forgive others and our-selves for our failures in the past. Failures have been the result of sins of omission as well as sins of commission. There is some measure of guilt in all of us.

Now is the time for the whole world to unite in the vital matters where we agree.

People of different races, religions, and politics forgot their differ-ences in World War II. Can we do less to save our planet? We ask every-one to discuss with their friends what they can do. Start an "Earth Care" project now. Together we can save our planet!

EARTH PEOPLE CENTERS

The department store is a crossroads of the community and therefore a natural focal point for launching a nationwide "Earth People" effort. What better place to make Americans aware of the planetary crisis, or to get them together in seeking solutions to the problems?

There is no more pervasive media for personal communication than the American department store. It is the most kinetic, facile, subtle, and powerful person-to-person type of media we have.

Through an "Earth People Center" and program, the department store can become the funnel for a community's environmental activity. The store will be a clearing house, a coming together point, for scattered local activities in the areas of environmental improvement. In this role the store offers a real community service, not competing with local ef-forts and organizations, but rather helping to make them more effective by channeling information and manpower, providing a central platform for these groups.

As a product-oriented society we communicate the way we feel and think through the things we buy. The growing concern for improving the environment and the quality of life requires a search for products and services that will meet the new environmental demands. A special orientation of buyers, and of leaders in public relations and advertising, is needed to help the department store fulfill its potential for serving the public interest.

To this end, the concept was developed in 1971 of placing "Earth People Centers" in department stores. The "Earth People Center" de-signed for indoor use is comprised of one major geodesic dome twenty-five feet in diameter which contains a smaller dome ten feet in diameter.

The larger dome is called the *Dome of Doing* and the smaller one, the *Dome of Being.*

The Center has three major and distinct categories of information to convey:

- Defining: what the environmental crisis is about,
- Doing: how the individual can participate in the solution of the problems,
- Being: the life that flows through us all.

People entering the Center are presented with facts, figures, and illustrations concerning the degradation of the planet and its living resources. As guests walk around the circular dome, they discover each environmental problem assigned to a particular topical area: air, water, land use, food, solid/liquid waste, power, population, and noise. Each area contains a visual explanation of the problem, organizations working in the field, who to contact, and what personal habits an individual can adopt to help alleviate the situation.

In the Dome of Doing, the Center displays educational material and shows slides and films from many nationally known environmental groups, such as the Audubon Society, Friends of the Earth, Sierra Club, Zero Population Growth, and the President's Council on Environmental Quality. Literature and information spotlighting local community actions can also be made available. The UN Conference on Man and His Environment, Earth Day, and the Earth People Proclamation are highlighted as examples of worldwide cooperative efforts to save our Earth.

In contrast, the Dome of Being creates a quiet inner space where a person can reflect upon the gifts of this world, and the gift of life that flows through all of us. This dome is kept simple, with carpets to cover the floor, and a few chairs and pillows. A small tree enclosed in a Plexiglas box rests in the center. The Earth Flag is displayed, and the Earth People Proclamation. A continuously playing CD emits the sounds of nature.

A SPECIFIC AGENDA

Our most serious problem is the accelerating destruction of our fragile biosphere. Each person, each community is a tiny link in a vast network of living organisms. Each unit, however defined, has an effect on all the other parts. It is essential for the common good that every producer and consumer meet new standards for eliminating waste, pollution, and excessive population growth.

There do exist many forces for healthy change. Individuals and groups in voluntary organizations, industry, government, and the United Nations are working feverishly to alter our present course of waste and injustice to one of stewardship and fairness.

Mankind has the knowledge and the technical means to heal and rebuild the Earth for the benefit of all people. A plan is required that will provide a coalition of effort equal to the task. Given such a plan, the production and advertising geared to the old systems of waste and pollution will change.

To this end, I would urge an "Earth Care" platform be submitted to major political parties and every candidate; that the test of every candidate's worth be the strength of his commitment to the care of Earth. It would be especially fitting in this new millennium for the United States to support this platform and take the lead in Earth's rejuvenation. Efforts will at the same time be made to obtain support of all nations for the "Earth Care" platform, and for all to seek their gain not by continued destruction of Earth's capital, but by carefully aiding and harvesting her increase, and by providing new economic incentives that will serve this purpose.

Environmental groups and agencies are presenting us with alternatives for the use of land, energy, and raw materials, and with inventive ideas for production, eating habits, travel, and dwellings. Organic farming plus backyard and patio gardening; wind power; solar cells; heat from waste products; high protein grain and vegetable substitutes for meat; homes that use Earth's warmth; bicycles, mass transit, and pollution-free cars—all are examples of increasing efforts to meet human needs in harmony with nature's requirements. All these items can be implemented by individuals.

Earth Trustees should have a plan with items for implementation by government. Consider the following program for the care and management of planet Earth, and decide where you can lend your support. An "Earth Care" platform should specify:

1. The closing of all nuclear energy plants, and stopping of shipment of nuclear energy equipment and supplies to other countries.

2.   A program to provide information and guidelines to help concerned producers and consumers pursue an "Earth Care" ethic, giving special awards for products and services that minimize pollution, avoid waste, and recycle, protect, and restore our natural environment; and supplying funds and assistance for "Earth Care" information centers in every city, where people can obtain tools and assistance for improving the quality of their lives with practices that save the air, land, water, and living things.

3.   A program for guaranteed income to be tied with "Earth Care," providing minimum funds for youth and elderly through neighborhood projects (including gardens, crafts, ecological home repairs, remodeling, etc.); and guaranteeing every person the opportunity of an "Earth Care" job with at least partial pay.

4.   Tax regulations with "Earth Care" deductions for purchases of products that pass maximum (no harm) environmental criteria.

5.   That all mass-produced products be required to meet minimum environmental criteria.

6.   That all advertising be required to state ecological effects in production and use of products offered for sale.

7.   No-interest loans for changing designs or locations of factories, stores, or homes, when the savings in energy and environmental-impact expenses can liquidate cost in twenty years.

8.   Funding for environmental organizations for production and broadcast of authenticated "Earth Care" bulletins with "Earth Care" data and progress reports.

9.   That to aid the protection and management of the global sea, nations should support a strong ocean regime and full recognition of the common heritage principle beyond the twelve mile limit.

10. That in order to inspire and obtain the vital unity and support needed for our global task, all nations be urged to reduce their military budgets by 10% in the coming year, this money to be given to help overcome poverty through national and UN sustainable development programs. If major competing nations all respond, and there is a firm indication that this will better serve world peace, a similar reduction will follow each succeeding year.

SUCCESS IN EARTH CARE

Can an "Earth Care Campaign" for the peace and health of the world succeed, when all previous efforts have failed?

There are good reasons to believe it can. Political and financial leaders know our present course is hopeless. While we still seem stuck to old methods, conflicting interests, and mutual suspicions, underneath is a growing sense of unity and global consciousness, that we're all in this together. All the nations are talking to each other. Great forces of change are at work. The new technology which, misdirected, is destroying our Earth, has also given us global media and travel, and through the space program a new view of ourselves and our Earth-home. The forces destroying our Earth are at the same time bringing us closer together.

Never have values, positions, and advantages changed so rapidly. Who even ten years ago could have imagined Arab economic power or China's new position? There is growing awareness that the only way to make the world work is through accommodation and mutual advantage. Also, much of the research and development needed to proceed with "Earth Care" is already underway. Great progress has been made by UNEP, UNDP, EPA and many others in defining our problems, and in some cases, initiating the changes that are needed. The accord by the surrounding nations to protect and improve the endangered Mediterranean Sea is just one example. Here and there young people are in effect practicing the "Earth Care" ethic.

All that is lacking is what Elton Trueblood called the three P's. We need a Purpose, a Program, and a Passion. The "Earth Care Campaign" can provide all three and bring the thousand-fold increase in effort that is needed to succeed.

The "Earth Care Campaign" is simple to understand. Its platform is strong enough to get results, but leaves room for flexibility of approach by different groups. What we have here outlined provides enough information for any individual or institution to undertake an effective "Earth Care" program. In fact, we hope that you who are reading this statement will not wait for some official "coordination" but instead will begin today your commitment and action. Coordination will naturally evolve as you spread the word of what you are doing.

If you agree that there is a severe crisis and that this "Earth Care" initiative offers the best chance you know of for success (if there is a better way, please let us know), then it is incumbent on you, if you value your life, to make "Earth Care" your first priority, and to begin each day with a dedication to your new task, to consider it in all that you do, to tell your friends, write, phone, join with others, and give of your money. In short, give as much of yourself to your task as a soldier loyally serving his country.

I believe most enlightened people will agree that unless this campaign (or something equivalent to it) succeeds in the next few years, we will be faced with a world of chaos and hell. If we succeed, we will instead begin a new age of wonder in a world of peace and promise.

18

Healing, Building, Uniting

PROTEST AND VIOLENCE VERSUS PEACEFUL PROGRESS

THE ONLY PROGRESS POSSIBLE in today's world is peaceful progress. If change is going to be in the direction of progress, then we must use the peaceful methods of change. The will to build must replace the will to destroy.

Protest is an effective way to get attention. And it is possible to protest without malice or personal condemnation, and thereby minimize violence. But every ounce of effort in the protest must be followed by ten stronger efforts to take advantage of the gains in a peaceful way; to constantly build something better wherever anything is torn down.

Protest has accomplished much good in the Civil Rights movement; it has also sown many seeds of violence—and violence must be renounced by both the power structure and the oppressed if its dire results are to be avoided. This does not mean acceptance of the status quo. Great changes in our world are imperative. It does not mean the elimination of protest. But it does mean that protest must be truly peaceful and merely a counter-point to a larger positive theme.

The new way will be not to force change, but to inspire change; not to protest the evil, but to praise the good; not to speak so much of injustice, but of new examples of justice; not the destruction of the old house (the old system), but the building of a new and beautiful home. Then it will be easy to move out of the old house, to leave the old ways.

In the new way suggested here, education about justice and peace will come, but not by cracking someone's knuckles with a ruler and saying, "That isn't the way." Instead it will come by the example of being and building justice and peace.

The theme must be that this world is a nest for you and me, and for every other person on earth, and that we will work together to make it a proper home for all of us. We, who are the forerunners of a new age, can begin in our own home, in our block, by enthusiastically joining our neighbors in some task we mutually approve that will help build a better world—providing jobs and homes and education for the people in need that we know.

Then, as we work together and talk together, we will more and more speak on the same wavelength and understand each other better. Larger social issues can then be reasoned in good faith.

Today, we are so interconnected globally that if the enlightened people of this planet would effectively communicate their best experiences and values of justice, compassion, freedom, and creative hope, a body of public opinion would spread throughout the world that would by-pass government and ideological hang-ups and bring sanity into our industry, trade, and social institutions and activities.

To further this connectedness and speed this communication, I urge that you and your friends become Earth Trustees, a simple plan without dogma or ideology, to bring about peaceful changes in the efforts for a new and better world.

Changes for justice and peace will come—not by negation, but by affirmation; not by fear, but by faith; not by hate, but by love; not by the will to destroy, but by the will to build. As we hear this truth and it is confirmed by our conscience and spread by our actions, we, the people of this planet will together obtain a new and golden age of justice, love, and peace.

ACTIONS THAT HELP

We can now halt the awful record of history with its injustice, wars, and violence. Napoleon once said, "Imagination rules the world."[1] The Internet opens new opportunities to capture the imagination of the world with a solution that can appeal to all. Projects and efforts that are achieving Earth Trustee goals can be posted as Earth Trustee actions on message boards and forums. Here is a chance for people of every creed and culture to prove the value of their faith by their works.

1. Abbott, *Napoleon Bonaparte*.

All the time, we need to *think globally*, and to get attention for what is aiding people and planet. To make sense of life locally, you need to make sense of life globally.

Our environmental problems are largely caused by small thoughtless actions. The solution is small thoughtful actions.

What people know and what they do is seldom consistent. To do what is right, we must recognize and reject what is wrong.

Let's circle the world now with a positive Earth Trustee vision that can rejuvenate our planet.

EGO AND DOING GOOD

The problem is the people who do good, but who do it to increase their own importance. In many cases, contributions are made to the need that has the most public attention, and will get the donor good publicity. The donor's actions are good, but prevent a larger good. To avoid this, some donors make their gifts anonymously (see the book, *Magnificent Obsession*[2]).

The extreme example of deception in giving is the crook who makes a donation to win the confidence of a person he wants to rob.

Clever spin doctors turn logic upside-down with their twisted thinking. People who believe in the Christmas story and try to follow what Jesus taught (including his commandment to find common cause, that is, to agree with your adversary) do far more to make life better.

BUILDING BRIDGES

I had a meeting with Prince Faisal of Saudi Arabia at the Dakota apartments, 72nd St. and Central Park West, in New York, on April 18, 1978.

This was the result of a phone call to the Saudi Arabia Consulate. When I explained to the receptionist who I was and that I wanted an appointment with Prince Faisal, she let me speak to the person handling his affairs locally, Vice-Consul Saleh O. Al-Jalajel. He said the Prince's schedule was already set, but he would see, and to please call him in the morning and he would let me know if it could be arranged.

I called at 10:45, but the Vice-Consul had gone to the Waldorf Astoria. I was referred to a number there, but could not reach him. So I went to the Waldorf Ballroom where the Prince was to speak. As I got off

2. Douglas, *Magnificent Obsession*.

the elevator, I noticed a person surrounded by several other distinguished looking gentlemen being photographed. I asked a photographer who it was, "Is one of them Prince Faisal?" He said yes and pointed him out.

I slipped up behind the Prince and got his attention. When I introduced myself he said, "Oh yes, I understand we have a meeting this afternoon." He called his Vice-Consul who gave me the time and place.

My meeting with the Prince was very friendly. At times I felt a strong mutual sympathy in views that emerged in our conversation.

I explained my long interest in finding a way to unite people in awareness of Earth and commitment to its care. I managed at one point to bring in my interest in research and that at one time I was general manager of a research laboratory. Later I published some weekly newspapers.

In the early part of our conversation, he was sympathetic to my views—Earth Care, Earth Rights, and Earth Day—but skeptical about any rapid change. He thought I was ahead of my time, that while we have had great material changes, there has been no moral improvement for hundreds of years. What appealed to him were the spiritual elements in my concepts.

He agreed that we should strive to achieve spiritual growth by application in material things. He mentioned several times the subjective nature of our religious terms and the difficulty of different cultures to get the same meaning from a set of words or symbols. We discussed the problem of the larger or ultimate questions of life and death. He questioned the wisdom of asking questions for which we knew there could be no answer, that in these, we had to rely on faith. And also the difficulty of symbols meaning one thing to one person and something entirely different to another.

He thought the idea of people joining on Earth Day in silent prayer could become very significant.

I told him of my conversations with Sheikh Yamani and Dr. Obaid. He mentioned that the Muslim faith does not recognize property rights. An individual is an agent for God and has no say in how property is to be disposed of after death. Inheritances automatically go to the children. He saw the idea of being custodians of Earth in harmony with Muslim teaching.

But in all of this, he thought major changes would take a long time, at least a hundred years. I argued that everything is speeding up and great changes are occurring in a decade or two. "Not moral changes," he said.

I mentioned the items in the *New York Times* about his organizing no-interest banks in Saudi-Arabia. He said interest was forbidden by law in Saudi Arabia, and in Muslim teaching. I felt an "Earth Bank" with no-interest loans to help the care of Earth would be a great incentive to Earth Care here in the United States. He said they had looked into the possibilities of no-interest banks here but that they would be against the law, forbidden by bank regulations. I replied that there should be some way to get around that or change it. He replied, "Yes, perhaps there could be."

When talking about a global Earth Care Program, he said that what was needed was to reduce it to something simple that could be applied by people wherever they live. I mentioned the schools, block associations, and the promotion of Earth Care in New York in each block and neighborhood. But, he said, it should be not in a small place, but in a small activity that can happen everywhere.

I presented him with an Earth Flag, summed up Earth Rights and Earth Day, and mentioned our need for $120,000 for one year, and that with it we could do an effective job, hopefully creating the "critical mass" among the more concerned, needed to bring about the contagious spread of Earth Care and the great changes vital to our future.

I then gave him a collection of papers I had hurriedly prepared for him to look at when he had time, which he said he would do.

He said he would need time to look at this whole matter, but he wanted me to know that what I was doing was "exciting" and had his strong sympathies. He added that we would be seeing more of each other. He said the contact here for him would be the Vice Consul Al-Jelajel.

The Prince did not indicate my time was up, but we had talked for over an hour and our discussion seemed at a suitable place to conclude.

I also invited him to be one of our sponsors of Earth Day and gave him a card to sign and send me if he decided to do this.

UNITING FOR THE COMMON GOOD

In an amazing statement that brought global attention, when Vice President Gore conceded the presidential election to Governor Bush in 2000, he said he would "do everything possible to help him bring America together." He added, "God bless his stewardship of this country."

Governor Bush said that this was what he was hoping for, and they did meet.

Coming together and a sense of stewardship by leaders and laymen is what we need. Action for peace, justice, and the care of Earth is now essential. Let us pray that each of us will find what we can do to aid this goal. In this new Jubilee Millennium let us do what Christmas calls for—reverence for life, and care for neighbor and nature—remembering the wonder of the child in a manger. "Peace on Earth, good will to men" is the message of Christmas.

The word "peace" (*pax* in Latin) means to agree. We now have an opportunity to find common ground that will bring us to higher ground, with new ways to cooperate for mutual goals.

We can make the new millennium a new beginning of great promise for ourselves, and the whole human family. May peace and faith for a better future reign in our hearts every New Year's Day during this Jubilee Millennium.

Individuals and groups who are working for a better future should provide examples of what their programs have done to help people and planet. We need more than words. You will find a partial record of what Earth Day and its Earth Trustee agenda have accomplished at http://www.wowzone.com/mc-lee.htm.

Examples of groups that "heal, build, and unite":

- American Friends Service Committee Fellowship of Reconciliation (FOR)
- Franciscans
- Growing Communities for Peace, Scandia, MN
- http://www.humanrightsandpeacestore.org
- Mennonites
- Maryknoll Society
- Quakers—Society of Friends

THE ROLE OF RELIGION

The great enigma of history is how different religions have contributed to peaceful progress, and at other times, the same religions have been the major cause of injustice and war. The Crusades are just one example.

On each Earth Day, we have people of every major religion join in our Peace Bell Ceremony at the United Nations. Christian, Muslim, Jew,

Hindu, Buddhist, and others join in silent prayer or meditation, a time for heartfelt commitment to think and act as trustees of Earth.

It would be especially helpful if religious leaders, as well as governments, made this a top priority. While Earth Day is focused on the here and now, religious faith gives added vigor to support of Earth Trustee efforts. When asked about Earth Day, many religious leaders have warmly endorsed the idea, but did nothing to support its observance.

When world leaders and mass media give suitable attention to Earth Day and its Earth Trustee message, the world will have a better future.

John Adams said, "Statesmen, my dear Sir, may plan and speculate for liberty, but it is Religion and Morality alone, which can establish the Principles upon which Freedom can securely stand. The only foundation of a free Constitution is pure Virtue, and if this cannot be inspired into our People in a greater Measure, than they have it now, they may change their Rulers and the forms of Government, but they will not obtain a lasting liberty."[3]

CHURCHES AND EVANGELISM

The weakness of evangelistic messages and of the professing Christian church hinders belief in Christ. Some will come to know the Jesus of evangelism and will follow him, but many will go away with a false sense of security and no real knowledge of him, because we cannot really present him in the context of so much hypocrisy.

The failure of kindred churches around the world to demonstrate the spirit and love of Christ in the present world crisis belies their profession of faith. Church leaders repeatedly state that survival is at stake, that we must have world peace, but practically nothing is being done to achieve it.

Courageous acts of compassion and faith by our churches could do more than anything else to overcome the fear, want, and mistrust that is sweeping from one continent to another.

Rather than compass sea and land to make one convert, why not call on those who profess the name of Christ to show their faith by their love. If real efforts were made to get acquainted with our global neighbors, and sacrifices were made to help the desperate families of

---

3. See Adams, "Letter to Abigail Adams," in Gaustad, *A Religious History of America*, 127.

underprivileged communities in other countries—if the spiritual, moral, and physical resources of each and every church were directed to waging peace through friendship and help to needy countries—if this were done, not to make converts or even win friends, but because in the midst of such tragic suffering the compassion of Jesus constrains us, the sincerity of such good will would carry a wave of hope around the world.

For instance, let the thousands of homes that are having prayer meetings, and surely praying for world peace, be audacious enough to invite thousands of unbelievers to come and visit them at their homes, not to discuss politics, but to experience the warmth of their goodwill and friendship, to feel the love that Christians have for strangers as well as members of their own families.

Let each church begin an all-out effort to wage world peace by doing the kind of thing that Christians agree will promote peace—visits to other countries, studies of language and culture to appreciate the unique values of other countries (on the Day of Pentecost, they spoke the language of all foreigners and were called brethren by them), missionary projects to help the sick, self-help projects, technical assistance, student exchange, and any other program of compassion and kindness where Christians can demonstrate good will to people in other countries.

Church members attending evangelistic meetings can prove by their actions that the Gospel of Christ brings major benefits. Following Christ will really make people more understanding, more loving, more friendly and capable of the faith and good will to meet the challenge of today's fears.

VISION NEEDED

The basic problem on our planet is the failure of people to look beyond the problem, see the solutions, and act on them. An ancient saying tells us, "Where there is no vision the people perish" (Prov 29:18). The Earth Trustee vision, policies, and agenda can appeal to the most people and do the most good for people and planet.

19

War

ARMISTICE DAY

Each November 11 provides an astounding opportunity for our planet's leaders to speak out about the state of the world. November 11, 1918 ended hostilities in World War I and sparked the first global efforts to eliminate war on our planet.

There is worldwide recognition of the need and possibility now to end the awful violent, destructive record of the previous millennia, with their wars, injustice, and failure to be responsible stewards of Earth's precious life. November 11 is an ideal date to ask world leaders to declare their common commitment to foster peace.

On November 3, 1999, The American Experience TV featured the life of President Eisenhower. He was a great war hero, but believed civilization was at a crossroads where it would replace war with peace, or perish. I remember well my conversations with him in which he encouraged my efforts. I treasure the photo I have of us together. He said the only solution was a moral equivalent of war: that if the money spent on armaments were spent on education for peace, there would be no more wars.

The weapons and ways of war must be abolished before they abolish us. There must be *no more wars.*

THE NATURE OF WAR

When people kill those who are killing, they are both committing murder. War is murder.

Money for the military is money for murder. Those who finance murder are guilty of murder.

Therefore, declaration of war is a declaration of intent to commit murder.

Even the death penalty is murder.

I believe no war is just. Jesus said, "It was said by them of old time, 'an eye for an eye and a tooth for a tooth.' But I say unto you, 'Love your enemies, do good to them that hate you and pray for them that despitefully use you'" (Matt 5:38, 44).

Some think that their only defense against injustice is violence. They should not use violence. Many times there is recourse to law. Others use their faith in God.

A preacher should not have to take up arms and fight. His praying and preaching will do more good than his fighting. The same is true of all Christians.

Why is it that we do not know how to appeal to the heroic in man except illegitimately in war? A person returning from a peace effort that provided homes, or medicine, or help that was building and nurturing the human family *is* a legitimate hero. We have not convinced the world that war heroes are illegitimate heroes.

If there is no peaceful way to solve problems and bring people together, if there is no way to reach the minds of people that will show them the wisdom of cooperation, of peace, of agreement, of coming together and getting excited about what we have in common, it seems that civilization is doomed.

ULTIMATE WAR

Historical forces are at work today pushing us ever nearer a world war; this time, the ultimate war—destroying the world. It is as if our planet were on a collision course with some fiery comet.

During the Cold War, Communism was the enemy. Now it is global terrorism. Instead of blaming either Communism or terrorism for the impending doom, we should think of it as a threat from outside any national or global conflicts. A military contest in which a possible winner emerges is one thing. Mutual annihilation is something different. It is not our differences that have created this second monster. The monster is something apart; it is a part of the nature of the universe. At some time man's progress was bound to reveal the A-bomb and the H-bomb. Their possible misuse would immediately threaten man.

This threat from outside is of course really a threat from inside each of us. For it is the fear in man, the suspicion and hate, that will unleash the Bomb. Our fears exciting the fears of our enemies will finally culminate in disaster—*unless drastic steps are taken to change our course!*

Perhaps a better perspective of our position could be gained if we were to visualize our doomed planet plunging through space on a collision course with a super-hydrogen bomb that will destroy it. Experience in human relations teaches us that in such a crisis people would forget their religious, racial, and ideological differences. There would rise a strong bond of common feeling with all our world neighbors.

If the growing danger can be effectively made real, a common feeling over the whole world may yet be generated in time to change the direction we are headed. Identification with the whole family of man would quickly result in steps being taken to insure man's survival on this planet.

We can meet the threat of massive destruction with massive participation in nonpolitical efforts to heal, to build, and to unite.

In every American community there are numerous activities in our service clubs, churches, youth groups, and so on, that are working through voluntary and United Nations organizations to spread goodwill and render service around the world, without any strings attached. These voluntary efforts afford a closer contact and sense of participation with what is being done, than similar efforts by national governments, and they are less likely to intensify international disputes. If these activities were stepped up tenfold in an intense campaign, not to win the "war against terror," but to demonstrate genuine world friendship, a chain reaction of good will and peaceful progress would sweep around the world. A new sense of purpose and meaning in life would rapidly grow. The growing faith and friendships of the Earth's billions of little people would soon make war impossible.

We can help one another and build bridges of understanding through scientific, cultural, economic, and social activities wherever they serve a common purpose divorced from the grave ideological differences that separate us. The success of Atoms for Peace, International Geophysical Year, Cultural Exchange, International Literacy programs, health programs, and mutual aid in farming, industry, and trade indicate some of the vast opportunities in this direction. Massive participation by the people of every community in activities such as these will encourage friendly contact with our neighbors in every country, and communicate more of our true values and less of our fear and hate. Then, the theme of loving our neighbor from the world's great religions would find its way from the depths of the human spirit and mind, and into actions that relate us to each other.

BUILDING FOR WAR, OR FOR PEACE

In an address during the administration of former President Nixon, Defense Secretary Melvin Laird referred to proposed ABM missile sites as building blocks for peace. This analogy is as distorted as referring to the suicide of Hitler as a Christ-like death. The missile sites should have been called building blocks for war.

Our Founding Fathers were more honest in terms they employed. For example, they did not call the military institution a Department of Defense, they called it a Department of War.

War involves the use of military force to obtain the objectives of a nation, be they good or bad. Peace, which means agreement, harmony, and honest accord, involves the use of reason, good will, and cooperation in seeking objectives. An unfortunate use of the word peace is to refer to the end of armed struggle as peace. Only when reason, good will, and just accord is obtained can nations have peace. Without these, any cessation of fighting is not peace, it is only a truce. In our relations with Iran and North Korea, for example, although we are not fighting, we cannot say that we are at peace. The situation is an armed truce.

In the case of our war with Japan, it was followed by honest efforts to use the methods of peace and create conditions of peace. Through General MacArthur's land reform program and the economic assistance of the United States, enemies became friends. The tragedy is that before the war, some leaders in Japan, who were sympathetic to the democratic and spiritual ideals of America, sought our understanding and assistance in vain. If before the war with Japan we had changed our negative exclusion policies and spent even one billion dollars in good will efforts to further cooperation, trade, and cultural exchange, we could have obtained a lasting peace without the awful destruction and suffering of our terrible war.

War may bring nations to a point where they are willing to discuss and pursue peace, but it is a tragic, archaic method, and it always sows new seeds for future wars.

The greater the spiritual and moral force of a people and their leaders, the less the need for dependence on arms. Given our present abundance of atomic weapons—a small fraction of these could destroy any conceivable enemy—it is a sign of extreme moral decadence to ever seek greater military strength, at a cost of billions. (If you already have ten foolproof ways to kill a man that you fear, it would seem neurotically irresponsible to then take the bread from your children in order to develop still another way to kill him.) It is time that America resorted to the best in its heritage and obtained a position of great moral and spiritual power. We would then no longer be deluded by this vain compulsion for military superiority.

VIETNAM

The terrible mistakes in Vietnam were the product of short-sightedness and ignorance. It is now plain to most Americans that we were responsible for a grave injustice to the people of Vietnam, bordering on deliberate genocide and ecocide. One small step we could take would be to make available to the United Nations money, equipment, and services that would help rejuvenate the pock-marked land and provide to each surviving person in North and South Vietnam his stake in the Earth—basic means for non-polluting food, for work, and for shelter. Let the poor in Vietnam, and then in America, be the first to obtain their Earth-right. The resulting new confidence and cooperation would more than compensate for the great cost that would be required. If as a result we could really feel together and work together, instead of killing each other and destroying our Earth-home, we could soon justify the possible 100 billion dollars such a program would cost. Perhaps concerned stockholders of American oil companies would start the ball rolling by giving 50% of their dividends to an Earth Rights Fund for this purpose.

In these challenging times, most affluent Americans would be satisfied with half their present income if the result were harmony and hope, and freedom from guilt and fear. What better way to honor the third century of our democracy than with a new birth of global freedom—through worldwide social justice and freedom from war.

MILITARY SERVICE, CHRISTMAS, AND JESUS

I wonder how soldiers in Iraq sing Christmas carols? That seems ironic. If you read the Sermon on the Mount, it says to love your enemy; agree with your adversary; blessed are the poor in spirit. I would like to see some attention for Minute for Peace and for Earth Day at Christmastime. Minute for Peace ties into Christmas. There's no contradiction here.

At Christmastime, I've been very concerned how people turn things upside down, especially the great ideas that we've inherited. If you listen to carols at Christmastime, they are such an inspiration. They're such wonderful songs and messages. The angels have announced the birth of Jesus, and if people paid attention to what he said and did, we'd have peace on Earth!

But the crazy thing is that the people who destroyed peace on Earth more than anyone have been Christians! This is such a contradiction. I don't mind speaking out about this. President Bush and Condoleezza Rice said their entire lives are devoted to practicing what Jesus taught and obeying him. They claimed that they were converted, and are Christians. They attended church. And then they went out and declared war.

The people who are going out there and killing their enemies are in effect killing Jesus. And they claim to be his servants, his followers.

One of the greatest problems in the world today is the money and expertise and manpower and time that is devoted to new devilish weapons to kill people. What is it? $400 billion a year? If we had that money to spend on education and non-violent resolution of conflict, which was demonstrated by Jesus and St. Francis and, in modern times, by people such as Martin Luther King, we would eliminate the habit of war and have a great future.

It reminds me that my mother wrote a song titled, "Oh, the Faith that Works by Love."

If people have a combination of faith and love, then great things, good things, happen. On the other hand there can be an imitation, a con, a promotion in the name of Christ that can be despicable. I don't understand how people can have such twisted thinking.

We're at a point where if the peacemakers of the world can get attention, then we can turn the whole human adventure in a different direction. We could turn our attention as individuals to peace, justice, fairness, and the care of our amazing planet.

From Christmas through to the Easter season, the time when we recall the Prince of Peace—his life, his example, and his triumph—perhaps a new look at his life can at last inspire mankind to pursue the ways of peace, love our enemies, do good to them that hate us, and with humility and compassion seek a beginning of honest accord with our adversaries.

Unfortunately, the deaths of soldiers are sometimes compared to the death of Christ. It would be well in thinking of the death of Jesus to consider how different his sacrifice was than that of a soldier. While the courage and sacrifice of a soldier is to be admired, it should be remembered that soldiers killed are trying to kill other men. (How tragic that man's opportunity for heroism through the centuries has mostly been found, illegitimately, in war.) The sacrifice and death of a soldier is far different than that of Jesus, who carried no knife or spear, who sought to kill no one and in his dying moments said of his enemies, "Father, forgive them, for they know not what they do."

In the story of Jesus taken by Satan to a high mountain where he saw the kingdoms of the world, we are reminded that through the aid of satellites and TV, we can now view our whole planet. Perhaps now we should try to see Earth as Jesus would see it—a home for the whole human family. If we will now choose the ways of peace he taught, the world can indeed become a beautiful home for all the children of men. In this new world, man will seek his brother's good. New justice and freedom will reign, and the meek will inherit the Earth.

SEPTEMBER 11, 2001, A TURNING POINT

On this day, 9–11–01, a major symbol of civilization—the New York World Trade Center—was demolished. The more than 3,000 people who lost their lives included men, women, and children from every part of the world.

In this new millennium, terrorists threaten the world. The destruction of the World Trade Center by terrorists has affected the global state of mind, and may become a turning point in history. There was a feeling everywhere that the crime was against all of us. The shock brought a sense of our shared humanity. Paradoxically, the violence of 9–11 united us in altruistic concern about the future and a desire to take action.

Many in the whole world were horrified by the heinous destruction of the World Trade Center. This terrible act was revenge by a few who thought they saw and felt the pain and suffering of multitudes, and who thought such pain and suffering was ignored by the powerful in rich America.

People with other ideologies, who have suffered from misuse of wealth in exploitation of their resources, have diabolical ideas and seek weapons to destroy us. As everyone knows, there are many small devilish weapons now available. The World Trade Center destruction is just a small sample of what could happen. Had the terrorists directed their effort to destruction of the President and Congress during the State of the Union Message, we would really have a problem.

THE MEANING OF TERRORISM

To understand what 9–11 means and what we should do at this turning point in human history, we should ponder deeply, "Can this tragedy make us all look at what is wrong in society and what we can do to correct it?" The problem is not just the terrorists but what caused them to become terrorists.

Put in historical context, we see a planet that is covered by a wonderful web of life with plants, trees, vegetation, and animals. We have inherited a great planet. Pursuing peace and justice, and taking care of our planet, can provide a great future for every people and culture.

But in the past, individuals, corporations, and governments have sometimes used hate and violence to get ahead. We profess allegiance to the Golden Rule, and must refuse the *rule of greed and military might*.

WE ALL ARE TO BLAME

The 9–11 tragedy reminds us that, in the long record of history, attitudes and policies of those in control of governments, wealth, and public media have prevented peaceful resolution of differences. Had a few powerful leaders backed the Earth Trustee efforts described in the Earth Magna Charta, the global state of mind would have favored peaceful resolution of conflict in all countries, including Afghanistan. The World Trade Center atrocity would never have happened.

Our non-action in responding to the poverty and suffering in countries around the world (including Afghanistan) has been a far worse crime than toppling the World Trade Center. Sins of omission are *the same* as sins of commission. Our sins of omission in the past were a factor in the destruction of the World Trade Center.

This is true of all who fail to do what they can to foster peace and understanding. We all are to blame. Prince Alwaleed bin Talal of Saudi Arabia was absolutely right when he said that United States foreign policy was partly to blame for the terror attacks.

The horrible destruction and human suffering caused by Osama bin Laden's heinous crime would never have occurred had governments in previous years given full support to Earth Day and its Earth Trustee agenda of "peace, justice, and the care of Earth"—which had gained support in Iran and many Muslim countries.

More than any preceding generation, we human beings all know that people of different religions and cultures are one human family. New York City is the home of the United Nations and is the media capital of the world. The city is made up of people from all parts of the planet.

Peaceful progress is the result of understanding positive human potentials and joining in a common effort to eliminate ignorance and poverty. This will foster peace, justice, and the care of our wonderful planet.

New York City can lead the world in a *moral equivalent* of World War II that will provide a future for our planet. A beginning would be for the Mayor to call for a Day of Prayer for forgiveness—recognizing that we all had a role in causing the September 11 tragedy.

WHAT TO DO ABOUT TERRORISTS

The question is "What shall we do?" Can we in our diversity of creeds and cultures find an agenda all can warmly support?

We urgently need a simple solution that friend and foe can accept. We must act quickly. We not only have great opportunities, we also have great dangers.

Terrorism will not be diminished by our threats or resort to terrorism. Violence is not stopped by violence. That only increases its spread. You do not stop hatred by hatred. You only stop hatred by love. Martin Luther King believed that and proved its power. We can, and must, destroy the causes of violence without destroying the people.

We don't want to waste our time and energy trying to destroy the terrorists. That will only motivate other terrorists to take similar action. Find the cause of the symptom and you can prevent its repetition. We can stop terrorism by removing the reasons for its existence. In all of our contacts let us foster peace by our words and actions.

Act now, acknowledge fault, and pursue Earth Trustee priorities. They appeal to people of all creeds and cultures. Spread the word with faith and love, and as this tragedy has brought the world together, let us begin a new era of cooperation in the vital matters we agree are important—peace, justice, and taking care of our planet. Now is a time to forgive others and ourselves and to join in making a new beginning for the whole human family.

Years ago two men were standing at the rail of a Mississippi River boat. One was a scholar, the other a farmer. The scholar brought up ideas about science and history, which the farmer knew nothing about. Repeatedly, the scholar told the farmer that without knowledge of such things he was losing half his life. Suddenly, the boat hit a rock and began to sink. The farmer said, "Do you know how to swim? The scholar replied, "No." The farmer said, "You're losing your *whole* life."

We need to rethink what is important.

The vital question is what to do about global terrorism before it leads to World War III and the end of the human adventure. Differences can no longer be settled by killing your enemy. Anthrax is only one of many diabolic weapons that can be used by the least powerful to kill the most powerful. Neither the United States nor the United Nations can stop terrorism. The killing of terrorists in Afghanistan and Iraq will anger terrorists in other countries and spur them to new acts of terrorism.

What *is* the solution and the best way to obtain global support for it? The only way to eliminate the awesome dangers of terrorism is to eliminate their cause. The Earth Trustee agenda can do that.

Now is the time for leaders and laymen around the world to vigorously join in a moral equivalent of World War II. In this war we won't kill people, but instead we will kill the causes of war—ignorance, hate, and injustice.

We all can make a difference. Every individual now has a responsibility to think and act as an Earth Trustee. Talk to your neighbors and friends. Join some project or group that is aiding Earth Trustee goals. Whatever power you have—money, contacts, faith—use it to foster peaceful progress and the rejuvenation of planet Earth.

Initiate a global campaign for peace, justice, and the care of Earth. Get the backing of all altruistic individuals and institutions. There are hundreds of wonderful projects around the world that are seeking a better human future.

Then call people of faith in every religion to earnestly pray, and prove the power of their faith by their works.

We will cover the world with a new Earth Trustee state of mind, and turn the greatest danger in history into a new future of peace and love.

I believe that most of the people who profess to be Christians (and people of every major religion) are blind to what is important. Jesus said, "You can tell a tree by its fruit." We have a wonderful planet, and an all-out campaign to win global support for "peace, justice, and the care of Earth" could provide a new and better future. In our media-driven society, most people have upside-down thinking.

Mahatma Ghandi said:

> When I despair, I remember that all through history the ways of truth and love have always won. There have been tyrants and murderers and for a time they seem invincible, but in the end, they always fall—think of it, always.

THE WAR ON TERRORISM

What is wrong with the "War on Terrorism"? It is a total contradiction of the moral values claimed by President Bush and the world leaders who were deceived by him.

The greatest irony was his claim to be a follower of Jesus Christ. President Bush attended church and claimed to be a Christian and to get his guidance from his faith. Jesus said we should love our enemies. Love will seek a common cause and cooperation where we agree, leaving room for differences. This has repeatedly brought peaceful progress in relationships.

In this day and age we should think globally. We have an amazing wonderful planet. It's time to wake up and for individuals and institutions to reject short-sighted greed that ignores right actions for the benefit of all.

Bin Laden saw America's awful exploitation. He took action—the wrong action—and Bush responded with *wrong action*!

This scenario was repeated in the war in Iraq.

Former President Bush said, "The terrorists are not martyrs, but murderers." He was right. But if all terrorists are murderers, then we should ask the question, "Are not all who commit willful murder guilty of terrorism?"

All wars are terrorism. On both sides in a war, those who kill their enemy are causing terror. When President Bush declared war, he was a terrorist.

It is time to get back to basics: Tell the truth, the whole truth.

Our responsibility as Christians is that when we expose what is evil, we must be sure to point to its remedy. We must never give up. Even President Bush could be converted from the false *god of war*, to the real God of peace. Remember that Saul of Tarsus, who persecuted the Christians, became Paul the Apostle.

In this age of global communications and easy access to diabolical weapons, you don't stop killing by killing.

There must be an all-out campaign to expose the hypocrisy and futility of the War on Terrorism. The only way to prevent repetition of terrorism is to eliminate its cause.

Look for any good the terrorist is doing and go the extra mile to help him. You can always find a common cause—then come together where you agree and leave room for your differences.

Such a "Campaign against the War on Terrorism" can tap the best in our religious faith and result in actions that will heal, build, and unite the whole world in the ways of peace. Talk, write, think, and act as a Trustee of Earth, and you will help bring the global miracle of a peaceful, prosperous future.

WORLD WITHOUT WAR

Is there a program now available that will eliminate future wars?

Is it now possible to achieve humanity's age-long dream of a world without war? In the evolution of history, are there new factors that can facilitate peaceful resolution of conflict and encourage freedom and order, justice, and mutual responsibility?

World peace is simpler than you think! In fact, you can speed the approaching day when fear of wars will cease.

War is always the fault of the "other fellow." All that is needed to prevent war is for you and me and everyone else to realize that we all are the "other fellow."

How can this realization come? Through Minute for Peace, a daily minute of goodwill observed in unison throughout the world. You can help spread the miracle of goodwill through Minute for Peace! Also, we can all now act as responsible Trustees of Earth. Finally, we can ask all governments to reduce armaments 10 percent each year. This money will be spent on peace education—the proven methods of peaceful resolution of conflict and elimination of its causes.

The original Memorial Day began during the Civil War by women in Georgia who planted flowers on the graves of soldiers who had died, honoring friend and foe alike. Patriotic soldiers followed their leaders and died on both sides of the battle. In the Kidron Valley of Israel, the cemeteries of Christian, Muslim, and Jew are together.

Memorial Day reminds us that enemies can become friends. It is better to choose the ways of peace before people kill each other. Each year since 1948 the President of the United States has proclaimed Memorial Day a "Day of Prayer for Permanent Peace."

While we will always remember the war heroes on the planet who gave their lives for their countries, our new world view, of humanity as one human family on one fragile planet that needs our care, requires that we encourage the heroic in men and women, not through military campaigns, but through peaceful campaigns for environmental action and social justice.

To proceed, all that is needed is global attention for this dynamic world view, which is one that all can accept and support. Science, technology, and the best in our religions—love of neighbor and love of our planet—have prepared us for this moment of opportunity. We've ended the cold war, we are less threatened by bandit states, and through efforts in the United Nations we are improving communications, understanding, and cooperation.

A quick and just settlement of ongoing conflicts will come when, in good faith, men seek deeply in their conscience for the highest good of the community and of the world, for the Creator has imprinted his order on the conscience of man.[1]

---

1. Pope John XXIII, "But the Creator of the world has imprinted in humankind's heart an order which their conscience reveals to them and enjoins them to obey," in "Pacem in Terris."

20

Crime and Punishment

CAPITAL PUNISHMENT

O N JUNE 11, 2001, Timothy McVeigh was killed by the United States, whose leaders believe revenge is a deterrent to murder. They believe the way to discourage murder is to murder the perpetrator.

The evidence does not support this view. Appropriate punishment would be life imprisonment without parole. This would leave open the possibility of society (and behavioral scientists) benefiting from what they might learn from the criminal. Behavioral scientists trying to understand the causes of criminal behavior cannot interview a man who is dead.

Life imprisonment (without parole) for murder would be far better. It would also deter murder, but more important, while preventing the guilty from repeating their crime, it could bring benefit. The convict, Starr Daily, became a devout Christian while in prison. This totally changed his thinking, and his bright mind resulted in articles and books that have been of great benefit to society.

The cure to crime is not another crime. Just as violence is not the way to end international violence, neither is violence the way to end crime.

There are unproven hypotheses about the ultimate mysteries of life, such as heaven, hell, and the afterlife. I recognize this is also the case with my Christian faith. Good people differ about the meaning of life and what the world is all about. Among those who claim the Bible is the word of God, there are conflicting interpretations, reflected in thousands of sermons and books. The worst are "spin doctors" who twist the words to mean the opposite of their obvious meanings.

I base my confidence in my Christian faith, not on scientific proof of my belief, but on the proven benefit it has brought to multitudes down through the centuries and today. And on its benefit in my life, the many answered prayers and help in my desire to be a blessing to people and planet.

Our laws have changed through the years. Many of our present laws are unjust and counter-productive.

In my view there is no "just cause" for taking a life.

Some think that capital punishment by government fulfills the justice of God. I think it's ridiculous to consider the actions of civil government, which follows different policies all over the world, to be showing the justice of God. I do not think we should follow the example of evil totalitarian governments, that regularly put people to death, and call it God's vengeance.

The tragic crucifixion of Christ provided an opportunity for God to show his great love. My father, an evangelical preacher, contended that the greatest wisdom is love. So God is a God of love. The nature of love is the desire to love and be loved. So God created independent creatures (Adam and Eve) and gave them the desire to love and be loved. The natural tendency of independence is to use it for selfish reasons, which led to the fall of man. But this provided God an opportunity to prove his love by letting his Son suffer the pangs of death on the Cross and thereby provide our redemption. In this way God won our love.

The God revealed in the life of Jesus (in his commandments, promises, and actions) showed the value he placed on human life by the drama of the Cross, and the Resurrection!

We need to get our priorities right. Jesus said, "You can tell a tree by its fruit." The best evidence in the here and now of the value of a belief about God and a future life, is how much the individual or group is doing to promote "peace, justice, and the care of Earth."

We are told in the Gospel of John that Jesus is the Living Word. His flesh typified his commandments and his blood the promises he gave. Jesus said, "Except ye eat my flesh and drink my blood, ye have no life in you." The more you meditate on his commandments, promises, and actions, the more you will experience the wonder of his love. His New Covenant replaced the Old Covenant in the Old Testament.

THE THREAT OF A GUN

On November 4, 1970, after a visit with my friend Eleanor Ward, about 7:30 p.m., I headed across New York City's Central Park on 73rd street.

At a stop sign, just inside the park, traffic was stopped and I paused, half thinking of getting a cab and looking around for one (rather hesitantly, for I only had a couple of dollars with me).

Just opposite me was a light colored two-door sedan with two young men in it. One was white with a slight beard and the other black with a large hat. They were waiting for the signal to change, and they asked me if they could give me a lift across the park. I said "Fine" and climbed in the back seat, commenting on the big plastic peace symbol they had hanging above the dashboard. I told them I was just going across the park to the Presbyterian Church on 66th where my car was parked.

As we started up, they took the turn up the park. I immediately said they were headed the wrong way, to which they replied, "Oh, this is wrong. We'll find a place to turn around." Immediately they turned into a desolate parking area, and I found a gun leveled at my forehead. The black man said, "Man, we want your money."

I had no fear that I was conscious of. In fact, I was hardly aware of what happened in the following minutes. It was as if something outside of myself had taken over. I said something about the peace symbol, and that I didn't have any money, and was devoting my life to working for peace.

As I was talking I slowly and deliberately took hold of the barrel of the gun in my left hand and slowly pulled it down, unconsciously twisting it as I did—to my surprise, removing the barrel from the gun! I placed it in my pocket, said I was getting out right there, tilted the seat in front of me, opened the door, and without any hurry walked back to the highway where I headed against the traffic, looking for a taxi.

A few hundred feet down the road, the black man came running up to me. "Hey, Man, give me the barrel." His tone was firm, but not angry or demanding. I thought a moment, and then gave him the barrel. He said he was sorry about what happened and they wouldn't give me any trouble if I wanted a ride over to my car. I said no, I've had enough. I'd get back on my own.

I wished him luck for a better kind of life and headed out of the park.

Later, I felt a little concerned about returning the barrel, but felt that the God who protected me would prevent the gun from ever being used. My wife joined me in prayer for them that night when I returned home.

The experience strengthened my faith and illustrated the main point I have been making for peace: When threatened with violence, most of the world thinks they must fight, or run.

Instead, through the power of God's love, reach out, and take the barrel out of the gun.

21

American History

I N MY READING OF history, the people in the western world who did the most to foster peaceful progress were devout Christians.

JULY 4—ITS HISTORY

In 1776, the Quakers in America and Europe were demonstrating that differences could be resolved better by peaceful methods than by killing. Had their words been heeded, governments would have ended the habit of going to war to settle differences.

"United we stand, divided we fall" is a powerful slogan. But in the long run, it only works when it is applied to a cause that is just and fosters peaceful progress.

History is filled with occasions where people fighting for their homes, or fired by other high purpose, overcame superior odds by ingenious use of what they had. Our own American Revolution is an example.

But even here, one might reflect on whether more patience, fewer inflammatory words, a resort to reason and moral force—aided by spiritual power—might have obtained a just settlement with England without war.

Had the voices of justice and peace been heeded by the Founding Fathers, their differences with England would have been resolved peacefully. Their example would have headed the world toward peaceful progress, tapping the best of religious values and common sense.

There would have been no Civil War, World War I, or World War II.

Today, on July 4th, instead of Peace Bells ringing in celebration of peaceful progress on our planet, we hear the mad clatter of fire-crackers.

DID THE FOUNDING FATHERS FAIL?

Two hundred years ago our Founding Fathers endeavored to establish a society of freedom and justice on these shores dedicated to the highest aspirations of humankind.

Today we know the government they designed provided a greater opportunity for realizing human potentials than any which preceded or has followed. Through the years Americans visiting other countries have often been recognized because even their features reflected an air of openness, confidence, and independence.

Nevertheless, grave mistakes were made in the formation of this Republic which have gradually led to catastrophe, for America and the world. Where our forebears failed, we must, to the best of our ability, strive to succeed. This nation, conceived in liberty, can and must take a lead in creating an Earth society that will fulfill the high hopes of those who gave birth to our own nation.

But first, we must consider our present dilemma. From Hiroshima to acid rain, a garbage crisis, a hole in the ozone layer, and possible space wars, our steps seem bent toward hell instead of heaven. The nation, which has been proclaimed as man's best hope, in a few decades has killed millions of men, women, and children. Our technology, which appeared to be mankind's greatest boon, has destroyed and polluted and wasted irreplaceable resources on such a vast scale that life itself on our planet is threatened. What a sad mockery of Jefferson's dreams!

What has gone wrong? Where did our forebears fail? Among the many things that have gone wrong in our country, three important problems can be traced to the mistakes of the idealists who started our great experiment.

The first was the result of the insufficient thought on the nature of property rights. While it is easy to understand their failure, it would be tragic now to continue their mistakes. They could not easily envision to-day's population. If they had, they might have approached the question of property rights in a more equitable and responsible way.

The right to free property, or land, was taken for granted and later implemented in the Homestead Act. But there was a failure to recognize the nature of the special privileges enjoyed by the original settlers. For example, by staking out the most desirable land in Manhattan (and retaining it in perpetuity), the first settlers deprived future immigrants an equal opportunity for a useful piece of land. Of course, at first, there was always other land, less desirable, perhaps, but still attractive. However, consideration two hundred years ago of our present population growth would have indicated a growing disparity of opportunity.

Now, with our whole planet's best land controlled by a small minority, some better system is required to meet the needs for justice and equal opportunity. Today's unequal opportunity here in the United States would be greatly reduced had each new citizen (by birth or immigration) been able to obtain as his right a stake in the land equal in value to every person's birthright inheritance. There should be no special right of rich parents to bequeath to their offspring more than the offspring's fair share of land, minerals or oil, the raw resources of the Earth, which fundamentally belong equally to all Earth's people. The children of the poor and of the rich have an equal right to the use of planet Earth. Special advantage to one's children should be through legacies of created wealth, not of basic limited resources.

Steps should be taken to assure each person—now or two hundred years from now—a birthright stake in the planet; an unquestioned opportunity for obtaining an apartment, a house, or piece of land as a homestead and an inheritance in the Earth. This can be done without severe disruption of those who have more than their fair share of Earth's raw resources. Special taxes, or "royalty payments," for all uses of nature's bounty (land or minerals) can furnish funds. These funds can then be used to obtain for the deprived a birthright home in new towns and in garden or farming communities. All undeveloped land should now be quarantined and limited to environmentally sound land-use projects, private or public, with special priorities for the above purposes. Legislation and voluntary actions are both needed, to move in this direction with all deliberate speed.

In addition to aiding the cause of social justice, Earth-Rights action of this kind will bring public understanding and support for global conservation, less population growth, and more environmental action—for each person will see in these actions a direct benefit to his home.

A second key mistake two centuries ago was the failure to provide a fair and honest medium of exchange. Efforts in this direction were thwarted, and ever since, manipulation and inflation of money have robbed the honest and the thrifty.

With today's knowledge and computer technology it is possible to provide a stable medium of exchange based on the things to be exchanged and available to individuals and groups with audited credit, for a reasonable service charge, without interest. This could begin a reevaluation on Wall Street about how it too can better serve the public weal.

Correcting these two major problems would do much to reduce our excessive drive for profit and spurious gain.

It has been said that in the final analysis every problem is basically a moral and spiritual problem. At Boston and at Philadelphia there was a great failure of faith, the cause of our third and most urgent problem.

Among the seekers who first came to this land were men like William Penn who demonstrated the enormous power of faith and love. Differences with the Indians were resolved without resort to violence through great respect for their opinions, a dynamic goodwill, and a great strong faith that the Spirit of God would aid those who spoke the truth in love. This was the Colonies' finest heritage.

When violence in Boston threatened, a day of fasting and prayer for a peaceful settlement was called by the Church in Williamsburg. But the voices of faith and love were weak. The efforts to pursue justice and independence through "sweet reason" were soon forgotten in the heat of Patrick Henry's emotional appeals to vanity and violence. As a result, independence was won, not through reason, but through violence and a needless cost of lives. And today William Penn and the Church at Williamsburg are almost forgotten. Our hero is the soldier at Bunker Hill. And on the day when we celebrate our independence we hear, not hymns of praise, but firecrackers.

Throughout the world our major problems are greed and prejudice. But everywhere we find some people who are relatively free of these moral diseases. Strengthening the bonds that link the loving hearts of the world and rallying their faith for Earth's renewal is our most important task. Then the interface of separate institutions will help, rather than hinder, the flow of life-giving energy for Earth's rebirth. Political, economic, cultural, and religious groupings will then aid one another in the pursuit of common goals. Then love will be more contagious than hate, and peace more contagious than war.

In facing the many environmental and social problems in America and the world, the key is a return to conscience and a new kind of commitment, a commitment to the care of Earth. By renouncing our greed, stopping pollution, conserving energy, aiding Nature's systems of material cycling (production, decomposition, and reuse), and by new honest advertising and fair taxes that promote incentives for a no-waste ecology ethic, and by helping the disinherited get their stake in the Earth, we can and will find a new hope for the poor and the rich and all who are in despair.

We can, with boldness, now make the dreams at Philadelphia a reality for the whole Earth. Aware of their mistakes, and virtues, we can now add to their structure of democratic freedom the economic equality, ecological commitment, and spiritual unity needed for the conversion of our country, and our planet, to the fulfillment of its highest destiny. It is our actions that will decide whether the grand endeavor of the Founding Fathers results in failure or a lasting success.

But we cannot do the job, or face our responsibility to our progeny two hundred years hence, without searching our souls and following our conscience as our forefathers sought to do in 1776. As we turn within to our God (or to our highest good), we will certainly find that our duty requires a dedication equal to that of the signers of the Declaration of Independence, and that our new enlightenment requires a great creative love, a love that will transcend Earth's past and usher in its new future.

And to this task we solemnly pledge our lives, our fortunes, and our new sacred love for our planet Earth.

PROCLAIM LIBERTY THROUGHOUT THE EARTH

Despite the missed opportunity in 1776, the Founders of the United States did recognize principles of democratic government and their basis in individual liberty and human dignity. On July 4, 1976, 200 years after the founding, I issued a call for a new proclamation, to be joined by all members of the human family, that recognizes the need for self-regulation as essential for individual liberty, that designates Earth Day as a global celebration of life, and that espouses a new economic order assuring every individual the opportunity for useful training, work, and honest pay. Finally, it calls for a campaign for Earth care and efforts for liberty in peace.

BEHIND THE SCENES

All through history and particularly in our time, there is the surface news of what is being said and done, but then there are deceptive secret things going on underneath that are appalling. What sums it up in a way is this—there was a man who told me, "John, you have such great ideas, but of course you'll never succeed." I said, "Why? Why do you make such a statement?" He said, "Well, you should know by now that the devil is in control of this planet."

There's a sense in which that is true. It's the lust for money and the power of the people who make billions from devilish weapons, and from promoting war, that keeps the world in turmoil. There are many arguments that can be made to support this idea.

We need to understand how our CIA and FBI work, and where the power really is. The corporations rule the world. The people who are running the corporations, the biggest ones, are driven by just one thing, and that is the lust for money and for power. Money is power.

I think that what could help aid in a transformation of the global state of mind, that would be powerful, is if billions of dollars were provided to back daily Earth Minutes to get attention for actions helping to achieve the goal of peace, justice, and the care of Earth, through nonviolent resolution of conflict, and heartfelt love. If we combine joy and hope and the positive things—if we accent the positive—to create a global state of mind that favors peace instead of war, then I believe we might see a new beginning for the human family.

What do I mean by a new beginning? If you look at things positively, we have an amazing planet with a skin of life. The more we learn about it, the more miraculous it is, and the more wonderful it is. With our technology today, we are the deciding factor in what the future will be. If individuals and institutions serve the purpose of the Earth Trustee agenda, that is, peace, justice, and the care of Earth, and if this is motivated by real love (that word is so corrupted we can hardly use it today), if by love we mean creative altruism, if love is the dominant theme of education, and of religion, and of all human efforts, why, we can explore the unknown and come together on what we agree is immediate and important.

The first thing we should do, of course, is for all time to do away with war as the way of settling differences. We can make friends. Jesus taught us how to make friends with our enemies instead of making them skeletons.

We should be realistic and aware of the difficulties we face of moving in that direction. I'm not suggesting that we can achieve a future that will be free of difficulties. But there have been times, historical periods, when there has been relative peace in major parts of the world. On the other hand, there are long periods in which there was conflict and war, from the Crusades onward.

I still get great inspiration from reading the history of St. Francis and his way of peace. And then there are the Quakers. They are a peace organization. Also, I've so admired the Mennonites for much of what their history reveals. They believe in nonviolence. And while some negative things are reported about Martin Luther King, I have enjoyed his book immensely, *Strength to Love*,[1] which shows the ways to peace.

1. King, *Strength to Love*.

22

Economics of Resources

PRINCIPLES FOR THE GLOBAL ECONOMY

IF WE ARE GOING to have a healthy global economy, we must recognize three things. *First, there is an equal claim of every person on our planet to Earth's land and raw materials.* Any fair consideration of these rights will lead to some arrangement that will give each individual the title to an equitable portion of his planet, or compensation for its use by others. Earth Rights, or rights to an Earth Claim, is a basic necessity in building a just society.

Second, we must have a fair and stable medium of exchange, based on the commodities or properties to be exchanged, in the amounts needed to maintain a healthy flow of exchange. The system should encourage fair trade and payment of services, rewarding the workers instead of the drones—the manipulators and schemers seeking unearned profits.

If we are going to build a future, if we are going to shift from "Earth Kill" to "Earth Care," then these two problems—equitable property shares and fair money—must be addressed. They can be solved. In fact we have some actions in mind that can be taken to correct these appalling inequities.

Third, we must solve the problem of nationalism.

In this chapter, I consider the first principle, of every person's claim on the planet. The problem of money is considered in the next chapter, Chapter 23. Finally, the problem of nationalism is considered in Chapter 24 on government.

THE BIG PICTURE

The only way to solve the problems of pollution, poverty, and violence is to be objective and look at the total picture.

To this end, let us imagine that we are beings from another planet, looking at Earth's civilization for the first time. Here is a planet with land and raw materials—oil, minerals, gold, diamonds, a great variety of useful metals, chemicals, and amazing natural resources: oceans, forests, insects, and fish. And there are balanced air and ocean currents to help sustain life.

The visitors from space would also see that Earth's human civilization now has technology which, carefully used, could bring the real benefits enjoyed by the affluent few to all Earth's inhabitants.

This can be accomplished in ways that are just and fair. Earth Day (on nature's March equinox) and the Earth Trustee agenda provided by Earth Day point the way.

To state this simply, we are one human family with a miracle home, called planet Earth. We did not produce the planet, but whether considered a gift of God, or from an unknown source, reason tells us that all members of the human family have equal rights to its bounty and equal responsibility for its care.

RIGHTS TO NATURAL RESOURCES

Most great wealth has been obtained by taking advantage of a corrupt economic system for personal advantage, without fair returns to those whose labor makes profit possible.

All over the world, the working poor know something is wrong. To explain the problem and offer a solution, I wrote an Earth Magna Charta, which explains that to continue the human adventure we must think and act as Earth Trustees, seeking choices in economics, ethics, and the care of the environment that would provide peace, justice, and a sustainable future.

The idea that can best illuminate our understanding is recognition that we are all "Trustees of Earth." We each have equal rights and responsibilities in regard to our planet. Our task is to seek in ecology, economics, and ethics the choices that will encourage initiative, eliminate poverty and pollution, and provide a sustainable future.

There are two levels of effort needed. On the one hand, we must take emergency action to remedy problems using social structures as they presently exist. Many political and economic institutions are unfair and inefficient, but compromises are needed for emergency action. The hungry should be fed. The homeless housed. The worst-case pollution addressed.

At the same time we must restructure socio-economic institutions—on a crash basis—to provide stable currency, free credit based on sound assets, methods of capital flow that maximize distribution of production's capabilities, and "Earthfair" instead of welfare—not charity, but royalties to the disinherited poor from the God-created assets of our planet, including oil, gold, minerals, and other natural resources. The Bible says, "The Earth hath he given to the children of men." It's time for the disinherited poor to benefit from their inheritance as well as have opportunity for work.

People of all creeds and cultures make up the human family. We all have an equal claim to Earth's land, raw materials, and natural resources—and an equal responsibility for Earth's care. Every person should be reminded that he is a part owner of this Earth and has an equal right to nature's bounty. He must be given access to his portion of Earth's raw materials and opportunities. It must be the goal of all countries to make available a minimum inheritance of natural resources to everyone. An individual's benefits will then depend on his ability and industry in the use of his birthright.

The wealth of the planet includes the unused natural resources that each generation inherits. It also includes the improvements resulting from human labor: factories, farms, homes, merchandise, oil wells, and power plants presently in use.

Let me emphasize this point even further—the Earth is the inheritance of the whole human family. There is a sense in which each individual has an equal claim to Earth's raw materials and natural resources—not to the results of other people's labor, but to the natural bounty of Earth which makes work possible. Some means should be provided to assure each individual an opportunity to obtain a stake in the planet.

At present the ownership, control, and use of land—the basic property essential for us all—is totally unfair to the majority of people.

PLANETARY INHERITANCE

At present the children of the wealthy inherit wealth, while the children of the poor inherit poverty. It is time that all children inherit the Earth—our common heritage.

Before proceeding further, I would like to mention an incident in a book called *The Far Pavilions*, by M. M. Kaye.[1] As a child, Akbar, the hero in this historical novel, was told by his father that much of the conflict, violence, and war in the world would be eliminated if people would just learn to be fair with one another. We need to put ourselves in other people's shoes and really consider their point of view and circumstances. In the following I would like us to consider what would truly be fair.

Let's think globally. We have an amazing planet with a web of life that can provide a good life for all. But shortsighted greed and lack of understanding of what is fair has resulted in terrible poverty for most of the human race. This fact is used as an excuse for terrorism against the powerful.

There is no excuse for extreme poverty and unearned extreme wealth. New Earth Trustee economic policies can remedy this. There is growing support for a New Millennium Proposal to cancel the massive debts owed by the poorest countries. This should be followed by vigorous efforts to restructure economic institutions and achieve just and efficient production, trade, and currency exchange.

In 1974, I wrote Sheikh Ahmed Yamani, Saudi Arabia's petroleum minister, proposing that 50 percent of oil royalties be given to help the Earth and its disinherited people. Ten percent of this should go to organizations feeding and housing the hungry and homeless. Another 10 percent would be for specific environmental programs to enrich the Earth's natural resources. The larger portion, 30 percent, would be distributed equally and directly to all adults in any poor area of any community of the world. In allocating that 30 percent, each person would receive a share, as of stock, with periodic dividends, perhaps $100 a year.[2]

Later that year in New York, Sheikh Yamani spoke at the United Nations. I was invited to meet with him. Sheikh Yamani told me that he had received my letter, and we discussed what I had written about planetary rights. In our conversation he said he was taken by my ideas

1. M. M. Kaye, *The Far Pavilions*.
2. Cunniff, "Founders Mission: Change World."

and warmly agreed with me that the natural wealth of the world (land, oil, gold, and other resources) was the common property of the whole human family. And that we should find a way to implement these rights, which would foster economic justice all over the world. I was told that the benefit of the Saudi oil wealth was later shared with many countries in need. But he did not fully implement the ideas. Had he done so, the world would be far better off today.

EARTH RIGHTS

What is needed is a totally new doctrine of property rights. Out of Earth Day and the ensuing thoughts about Earth People and Earth Care, I was led to new concepts of individual rights to the use of the Earth.

Our planet is rich in raw materials—gold, oil, minerals, soil, water, and biological wonders. Since God is no respecter of persons and provides equal justice, every individual on our planet has a claim to an equal benefit from his Earth-Rights inheritance. Moreover, every child on Earth has both an equal claim to natural resources and a responsibility to help take care of them. In the 1970 Earth Day, we used buttons that showed the Earth as seen from space and that said, "Our Inheritance, Our Responsibility."

In the new age facing us we should recognize the need for equal human rights on a global scale. Each person who comes into this world should have a right to his share of our global unearned inheritance. Providence has placed on this planet enough land, water, and other natural resources to provide, with proper development and use, a rich and happy life for every man, woman, and child on Earth. Benefits provided by our planet should be enjoyed, not just by the few, but by everyone.

To pursue this end, a determination should be made of the total value of all the raw land and natural resources on Earth (apart from improvements or buildings). The result, divided among all the Earth's population, would give the amount of each person's rightful planetary inheritance.

To provide this inheritance, governments should assess the value of all real estate less improvements, plus the value of any oil, gold, or other minerals produced each year. It is important to note that improvements (such as houses and factories) are not included in this appraisal of the Earth's value. Each person's prosperity would be the result of the wise and efficient use he makes of his global inheritance. He does not have a right to what others have produced from their inheritance.

Two percent of this appraised Earth value should be distributed each year to every family on Earth. The money would come from a 2 percent tax paid by those who have title to these assets, which, in a sense, belong to the whole human family. A 2 percent annual royalty on assets, paid by present owners, would provide the disinherited poor their needed purchasing power without the stigma of charity, and encourage responsibility in its use. While in many cases they would need help in learning how to use their inheritance wisely, there are altruistic individuals and institutions (churches, non-profit groups, etc.) that would gladly render this service. A just demand could then be met by a fair supply.

This would provide a fair, honest solution to the problem of poverty. People would still benefit most from their labor. But the child in a wealthy family would not be the only one to inherit unearned money. Everyone would have a minimum inheritance from our planet's natural bounty. This would be accompanied by voluntary efforts to be responsible Trustees of Earth and help protect and nurture Earth's amazing web of life.

Each person would receive his portion in a form that would contribute most to his welfare, through provisions for education, training, agricultural facilities, purchase of a home, or a combination of all these. This would be each person's stake, his opportunity, his inheritance.

In principle, nature has provided each man with about two acres of ground (or five acres of ocean fishing), containing an allotment of minerals, trees, flowers, and in the tropics, food. Now it is up to each man what he makes of it. Of course, to be practical we must think in terms of equivalent value and opportunity. In our complex society, not every man can have a two-acre plot of ground, but he is entitled to a place of his own and an opportunity to make it a home. Not many would want to mine their share of copper or drill for their share of oil; but they do want and deserve opportunity for materials and facilities that enable them to benefit from some useful service. They want to enjoy the improvements they provide and pass them on to their children.

To extend this principle further, nations that have more than their share of natural resources (oil, minerals, etc.) would make available, at cost, the resources in excess of their share, to those nations who lack their share. This benefit should be extended to every nation that provides its citizens their planetary birthright. Further, people in over-crowded nations should have the opportunity to emigrate to lands with more room. Nations with friendly arrangements to help one another in the full development of their countries would bring great prosperity and a new, deeper justice in their relationships.

EARTH RIGHTS FUND

I again maintain that each Earth Person has an equal right to an equal share of Earth's raw materials and natural resources. Only as we find effective ways to implement this basic right can society achieve social justice for the whole Earth.

To this end I propose that an Earth Rights Fund be established that will provide each Earth Person in war-torn countries a new stake in his planet. Funded by private, corporate, and government contributions, and channeled through the United Nations, this fund would provide an initial demonstration project of Earth Rights for Earth People. And it would send a ray of hope to the down-trodden of every country, a promise that as we seek justice and work together, we all can inherit the Earth.

If the Earth Rights project can be quickly initiated and rapidly spread (via the Earth Signal; see chapter 27), the powers of the human heart will be tapped, the voice of reason will be heard, and a real and lasting peace will begin.

EARTH UNLIMITED CERTIFICATES

To assist in the promotion of Earth Rights in 1973, members of the 1973 international Earth Day Committee advanced the idea of Earth Unlimited Certificates.

The Earth Unlimited Certificate looked like a stock certificate. It was a unique affirmation of each individual's right to the use of our planet Earth, and his equal responsibility for its care.

The certificates were printed free by the American Bank Note Company. The one dollar contribution for each copy went to the Ecology Department of the South Street Seaport Museum in New York City (16 Fulton Street, New York, NY 10038) where Earth Day had its headquarters, not far from Wall Street.

The main purpose of the certificate was to publicize a totally new concept of the individual's relationship to Earth—that each Earth Person has fundamental rights to the use of the Earth, and equally basic responsibilities for actions that will assure pure air, clean water, safe food, adequate shelter, protected wildlife, natural sanctuaries, good health, and enriched life.

Social justice and environmental action are each essential for the other. A new understanding of both are required if Wall Street and Madison Avenue (and the consumers) are to survive the growing economic upheavals.

I would like to see Earth Unlimited Certificates reissued. Their distribution could raise funds for worthy projects to alleviate poverty, such as by vesting the poor with actual resource ownership. Contributions ($1.00 for each certificate) could be deposited with an Earth Trustee fund.

The broadcast media could help get these projects started by simply initiating the daily Earth Signal (to be described in chapter 27).

LAND DISTRIBUTION

When the settlers first landed in Plymouth Rock, then in Virginia and other colonies, there was great opportunity because good land was easily available. Any industrious person could obtain land, build a home, and provide a living for his family. Some were more energetic and efficient than others and would build a beautiful home while others only managed a shack. Success differed from family to family. But each person could obtain land with good soil, timber, and pure water. This was considered each person's right as later provided in homestead laws. (Unfortunately, slavery deprived many people of these rights.)

But as population increased and people fenced in their claims, people who followed had to go farther and farther away. This led to increasing difficulties for new immigrants, for the landless poor, and for the Indian tribes as the Native Americans. Now, both in this country and throughout most of the world, the majority of people are denied their inheritance in Earth's land and natural bounty. Vast areas of land are controlled and used by a few without any compensation to people who have none.

To those who find help in the Bible in determining what is fair and just, I would mention Ps 115:16, which says "the Earth hath he given to the children of men." Since God is no respecter of persons, it must be assumed he intended an equitable distribution of Earth's land and basic bounties to the whole human family. Every child has an equal inheritance in the Earth as God made it.

Of course, the ever increasing number of people means a diminishing portion of land for each person. Presently, if Earth's land were evenly divided among all Earth's people—children and adults—there would be about five acres of usable land for each person. The average value of this Earth portion is, by some measures, $30,000. This figure would be adjusted in different countries to the cost of equivalent homes and conveniences. This value should be available to those who do not own a home, for purchase or down payment on a homestead in city or country, for an apartment or house. The diversity of needs and preferences could be served via grants or partial grants of land, or by housing, and paid by the state or by taxing for this purpose all land in excess of $30,000 value held by individuals and corporations.

Today the good land, the attractive places, are all taken up. There has been little effort around the world to deal with this problem. Great benefit has come from some of the new land reform programs that have been undertaken. But for the most part, there is no determined effort by humanity to provide each individual his own land or home, "his own vine and fig tree," the Bible's poetic words that express each person's claim to a rightful share of the planet.

Whether an individual is able to obtain an acre of fruitful land, or whether he has a house or apartment, the point is that there is some responsibility on the part of society—of leaders and governments—to see that each individual who sojourns on our planet obtains his claim, his right, his stake in the Earth.

At present we find that instead of land going to those who have none, more and more is going to speculators. They buy land, not because they need to use it, but because they expect to make a profit. We have had a tremendous trillion-dollar surge in the purchase of property by individuals and corporations. While some older people still own their homes, many young families, and the poor, cannot buy because of low income. For decades, prices and interest rates skyrocketed—the result of purchases by wealthy speculators, seeking more wealth by seizing more land in anticipation of new population pressures and demand. They sought their gain, not by rendering useful services to society, but by devious methods and manipulation—by playing the money game. So we have here the wrong approach to property, to its use and control.

If we are stewards of Earth, then in addition to equitable distribution, every effort should be made for the best possible use of land. We shouldn't pave over rich soil when there is a limited amount of good agricultural land in the country. There should be some care taken in the use of all Earth's limited resources, of the land, water, and forests, of the different elements that go to make up the essential combinations of living space and living materials needed for a healthy future. An Earth Care Campaign should work to see that every person who will help the care of Earth will be granted ownership of a just portion of our planet—a few acres of fruitful land, or a house or apartment.

With the spread of existing know-how, and the aid of present equipment and technology, an initial stake, as in a home, job, and education, can be offered all who are lacking it. Nature has provided an abundance. If we will creatively cooperate with one another in using it wisely and peacefully, together we can build a global economic democracy with freedom, justice, and prosperity for all.

DECLARATION OF PLANETARY RIGHTS

All the above ideas about planetary inheritance and its distribution were subsumed in a document that I published in 1969, the Declaration of Planetary Rights (see the Appendix). Based on the inalienable right given each person by a beneficent Creator, and the consequent right of all to an equal share in nature's bounty, it called for a small royalty to be collected from natural resource owners and a distribution of the proceeds to all individuals equally, on an annual basis. It also called for United Nations protection of seabed resources as an inheritance for all members of the human family.

The context for my Declaration was that in 1967 a proposal was introduced by Ambassador Arvid Pardo, of Malta, leading to the passage of a resolution by the United Nations' General Assembly in 1970, declaring the seabed to be the common heritage of mankind. This was especially significant because, since the vast regions of the sea had not been assigned as the property of any one nation, it offered a special opportunity for Earth inheritance claims in behalf of the true owners.

Most people acknowledge the right of individuals to inherit property that they have not earned or purchased. The seabed, with its minerals and oil, should be viewed as an inheritance in which all people on Earth have a share. This inheritance should be made available to them now.

To help bring this about, the Earth Society circulated Earth Rights proposals to various members of the United Nations Raw Materials

Conference in April 1974. The encouragement of some of the delegates led to the formation, by the Earth Society, of a Sea Citizen Organization in December 1974, to claim ownership rights for all who request their share by registering as Sea Citizens (see chapter 33).

EARTH BOUNTY PROGRAM

Eliminating Homelessness Worldwide with Earth Shares

As a child of Earth you have a right to an inheritance in your planet. You should be able to obtain Earth royalties and a territorial claim to a portion of planet Earth. The Earth Bounty Program is a unique, logical plan to make this possible.

Five billion Earth shares would be issued, as needed: one share for each person on Earth who is eighteen years of age or older. These shares would represent each person's claim to an equal portion of Earth's natural bounty and a stake in its future. Shares could not be transferred and would be canceled at the death of the holder. Royalties due shareholders from Earth's natural bounty would initially be used to provide homesteads for every family or person who lacks one. Afterwards, royalties would be distributed equally to shareholders worldwide.

The Earth Bounty Program recognizes that every member of the whole human family has an equal claim to the natural planet (land, less any improvements; raw materials; minerals; and oil). In recognition of individual global inheritance claims, participants in the Earth Bounty Program would agree that a 2 percent Earth Royalty Fee would be paid by them yearly on any Earth Inheritance Assets exceeding $50,000 which they may have or acquire.

Earth Inheritance Royalty Fees

The 2 percent yearly payments would be directed to the Earth Bounty Program.

Raw Earth Assets will include:

Any land (less improvements) owned by the participant;

That portion of any stock or bonds that represents raw Earth assets.

The value of any minerals or oil mined by the participant, or any dividend received from any mining, oil, or gas producing company.

Royalty payments would go to provide homesteads—an apartment, condominium, or house and land free and clear—for participants who lack their basic portion of the planet. They in turn would have to agree to support this arrangement by their payment of the annual 2 percent royalty fees when their Earth Assets exceed the $50,000 listed above, a fair portion of their planet. Participants must be eighteen years or older.

These actions would encourage allegiance to Earth, particularly, to peace and the care of Earth. With an Earth Trustee attitude people would give time and money to Earth Trustee projects of their own choosing and affirm an Earth Trustee way of life—talking with and helping other individuals of like mind. Reports of Earth Trustee activities and plans would rapidly increase participation.

Pilot Projects

Initially, collection and disbursement of Earth Royalty Fees could be independently managed by local municipalities in pilot projects. Then, the idle UN Trusteeship Council could be restructured to integrate local Earth Bounty Programs and adjust differences in Earth assets so that all would have an equal claim and equal benefits from their Earth Inheritance.

How You Would Obtain Your Earth Share

All that would be needed for you to obtain an Earth Share is for you to affirm the Earth Bounty Program and agree to its provisions. Taking the above steps would qualify any person eighteen or over to receive Earth Royalties as they become available, as payments toward a free, clear home for participants who lack this minimal stake in their planet. And eventually, after those who lack their minimal stake have received it, additional royalty payments from their fair portion of planet Earth's natural assets would be given to the rest of those over eighteen. As massive public support is obtained for these equitable objectives, large holders of land and raw materials (individuals or corporations) would be persuaded by moral enlightenment, or government regulation, to participate in this program. This would provide a new vigor in free enterprise as we distinguish the difference between each person's rightful inheritance and on the other hand the profit or benefit from labor and the careful, confident use of that inheritance. It would inspire a new spirit of cooperation and hope. This program would gradually bring a fair re-distribution of Earth's land and raw materials, ushering in the day when every person can "sit under their own vine and fig tree" (Mic 4:4).

23

Economics of Money

WEALTH AND POWER

WITH HALF THE MONEY we spend on wars, we can make our planet a Garden of Eden. As we honestly work together, we will recognize all around us the waste of wealth and its unfair monopolization by those in power. The solution is not to condemn the few in positions of power, but to demonstrate solutions and win their support—not by the power of money or military might, but by the power of truth, of good ideas and good will.

Most great wealth has been obtained by taking advantage of a corrupt economic system for personal advantage, without fair returns to those whose labor makes profit possible.

Lord Acton stated, "Power corrupts."[1] All around us are examples. While motives are mixed and many altruists seek financial success with the idea they will use their wealth for good, they repeatedly push up the amount they need for themselves before they give. There are exceptions. I knew George Pepperdine who practiced what he preached and gave 10 percent when he was poor and kept raising the amount as he prospered. When he sold his auto supply business he formed the Pepperdine Foundation and Pepperdine University.

Most of the time, money-power is misused to obtain more power. The solution is a heartfelt sense of responsibility on the part of the individual and an open, fair economic system that would reward honest

1. Acton, letter to Bishop Mandell Creighton.

service and eliminate the drones who on Wall Street and in the banking business make money without rendering an honest service.

UNJUST MONEY SYSTEMS

In efforts for the rejuvenation of our planet, we not only need to change our personal attitudes and conduct, we need to change the institutions that harm our lives. Part of the problem of injustice in the world is faulty economic policies and institutions.

Chief among these are not only institutions and policies involved with global assets of Earth's raw materials (land, oil, gold, etc.), but also the unfair banking system that rewards the powerful and punishes the poor. The global banking system and the stock market are a terrible mistake. These institutions do not foster fairness.

A basic mistake in history was the development and establishment of unfair, inefficient systems of money and credit. We have a planet with assets in the trillions of dollars, much of it in developing countries. Once we see that money is not wealth, that instead, wealth is land, raw materials, technology, factories, people with skills, etc., then we might provide policies that are fair and that stimulate cooperation. Today, money manipulators make more money than producers and workers.

The money system we have is totally dishonest. An honest medium of exchange is needed that would make loans available without interest where suitable assets are put up as security.

At the same time, our country and its whole financial web is based on making money. And the best way to make money is by loaning it for well-secured property. By a change in monetary policies to fair, free credit based on adequate assets, and by making money an honest medium of exchange backed by assets, and available in the measure needed for stable exchange of goods and services, we could soon bring prosperity to our whole planet. There are solutions being demonstrated in different parts of the world.

In addition, the evils of income tax and unfair property taxes should be addressed. The Henry George Schools (see http://www.henrygeorge. org) advocate honest, fair taxation, and are proving its value in many communities where their land tax program has been adopted. Earth Trustee message boards on the Internet should be provided that will tell of such efforts and report progress and success.

We need to restructure the stock market and the banking system. But until that is done, let us try to invest money in ventures that are aiding the environment and promoting health, education, and home ownership, even though the returns are less than in other types of investments.

MONEY, INFLATION, AND INTEREST

In the creation of money and its use, we find that many people who work hard and save their money are deprived of their hard-earned savings through inflation, while others become wealthy by taking advantage of weaknesses in our money systems. If people can rake in the money by unfair manipulation, and nobody works, nobody creates, and nobody produces, of course we are headed for disaster. And we see more and more people seeking success in this way.

Our problem is that we have institutionalized greed. We must now devise and demonstrate a fair financial system that will provide the greatest reward for the greatest service. In the book *Paper Money*, by Adam Smith,[2] we find the failure of governments and banks to provide a fair medium of exchange. Instead, the banking system, through complex methods and misleading promotion, discourages fairness and efficiency. The fairness doctrine requires full disclosure of pertinent facts, but full page ads promoting bank deposits by offering high interest do not mention anticipated costs of inflation. The public is not informed about bank profits from "float" and "multiplier" procedures—all contributing to unearned increments for those who control the money process.

An example is the case of interest. Interest rates may grow, but accompanied by the devaluation of the dollar and other currencies. It's been demonstrated in different times in history that interest is neither a fair nor necessary ingredient for economic development. Incidentally, the Old Testament was against usury. That means interest of any kind. The idea of interest was rejected in the Old Testament, and also in the New. Jesus made the statement, "Lend, hoping for nothing again [no interest]" (Luke 6:35). Muslim teaching also forbids usury, the taking of any interest.

Now, if an individual is sharing risk with another person or group in a mutual investment of time and money, and if it succeeds, he is entitled to a fair share of the increase, for his participation and help in

2. Smith, *Paper Money*.

providing tools, materials, management, or the money to obtain them. Such an individual is entitled to a gain or return on his investment, but only if it succeeds. He must share the risk as well as the benefit.

However, a bank will require security for a loan in a manner that negates equal risk, and thereby, through its unfair advantage, gradually obtains greater and greater control of property and capital. Where a loan is secure, why should a bank receive any increase or interest? A fair charge for handling the transaction should be all that is needed.

The mechanisms of the banking system can create money and credit without cost to the banks. A loan given a borrower in exchange for the deed to his property, to be held as security for the loan, is an exchange of equal values. If anything, the title to the property is a more real form of capital than the money, which has nothing backing it but the confidence of users. Well-secured loans should not be charged interest. Property is real capital and there should be some way for people to use their real capital as security for exchange certificates (money, credit), without paying a special premium to those who control the medium of exchange. A service charge for the cost of the transaction should suffice.

The course pursued by the banking system is aptly illustrated in *Paper Money*.[3] It shows how the competition of Arab countries, who copied the methods of monopoly practiced by western oil companies, increased the price of oil, and with it our spiraling inflation. The increased money was placed in banks whose "multiplier factor" further increases it, with even greater profit to the bankers, and less to the workers and producers because of inflation.

Because banks are allowed to maintain only a limited "reserve" in their accounts (usually 20 percent), new deposits in the banking system result in the "multiplier" effect, bringing an increase of over 400 percent to total deposits in the system. This type of banking system is called fractional reserve banking. For example, let us say that Mr. Jones deposits $100 in new money—cash, or bonds not taken from another bank—in his local bank. The bank can loan $80 of this money which becomes a new deposit in another bank, or account. This bank then loans 80%, in this case $64, which again becomes a new deposit in the system. Then 80% of $64, which is $51.20, results in another new deposit. By the end of the process, over $400 in new deposits are added to the banking system with new wealth and interest from this unearned increment. This

3. Ibid.

pyramid plan is for the special advantage of the owners and controllers of the banks and banking system.

The difficulty is not only a basic lack of fairness and honestly, but also that the spiraling effect of inflation brings increasing danger of a total loss of confidence, followed by another collapse of the money system and terrible losses by depositors who trusted the banks.

CERTIFIED ASSETS CHECKING ACCOUNTS

"Better than Money"

To eliminate interest (usury) presently charged for the use of money needed in trade and exchange, I have proposed that banks, or other financial institutions, provide checking accounts or "Asset Cards" based on a fixed percentage of the appraised value of any real property. The bank would provide no money, and charge no interest. The only charge would be for the cost of the service. (This should be less than 2 percent of Certified Asset transactions.) Writing a Certified Asset check or using the Asset Card would transfer to the party named a claim for the assets in the amount indicated. This check, or Asset Card claim, could then be deposited in the new owners Certified Asset account.

People would use these Asset checks to pay for products or services. Acceptance and use would spread as the advantages become known. This kind of check would have solid backing, which our present money lacks, and provide a fair, efficient, less expensive means of exchange or barter.

To obtain a Certified Asset checking account, a person would need to provide a clear title of real property to the bank which would hold it in trust. The bank would then provide a Certified Asset Checking Account for 70 percent (or other fixed percentage) of the appraised value of the assets.

The bank (or other approved financial firm using this program) would have a right to a new appraisal every five years, charging the account for any depreciation in value, or increasing the account where there is increase in value. The property could be redeemed at any time by paying back outstanding claims against the assets. If the property is sold, cash or Certified Assets would be paid to the bank for the amount of Certified Assets outstanding. Held in a special trust account, these items would continue the guarantee of any outstanding Certified Assets.

The percentage of appraisal available for Certification should be made equal to the percentage of the National Gross Assets needed for healthy exchange flow (without inflation).

In 1963, I copyrighted the above idea, calling it a "CERTICHECK: An Established Credit Checking System."

A variation on the above idea, born of my concern over unfair and excessive felony convictions for bad check writing (labeled as "insufficient funds" or "non-sufficient funds"—NSF), is the concept of "$ave-T-Checks." They would have the same value and general acceptance as cash, by being based on real assets. Consequently, (1) the bank would guarantee each check. (2) The checks would save clients valuable time, offering a space-age accounting system. No stubs to make out. A duplicate would be made of each check as it is written out. (3) Based on real assets, they would be protected against loss or theft in the same way as Travelers Checks. (4) They would encourage savings, and help the client earn money on a "$pend-and-$ave" plan.

$ave-T-Checks would be purchased in denominations of $10, 20, 50, and 100. You would fill out $ave-T-Checks, just as you would a money order, for any amount up to the face value guaranteed by the bank. When the Check returned to your bank for cancellation, the difference between the amount you have written and the face value would be refunded to your savings account, to earn regular interest, or to a special account of your choosing. With refunding to a savings account, there would be extra savings because of the interest accumulations.

DIVIDENDS INSTEAD OF NATIONAL DEBT

We always have unemployment, except during war. Further, many goods sit on shelves of stores, and factories could produce even more. People want goods, but may lack money to buy. Debt keeps rising. Something is wrong! Money is failing its purpose. Our present system fails to meet the needs of an expanding economy with a suitable increase in the flow of stable money and credit.

The proper increase can be provided through a simple formula and program that would encourage prosperity and at the same time prevent inflation. In addition it would replace the United States Bonds (our national debt) with national stock issued in limited amounts to the public, with special incentives for low income groups. This would require elimination of the present system of the Federal Reserve Board in "monetizing" (creating new money) through its banks. Instead, the American people would be the stockholders who would benefit. And the creation of new money would follow a formula to meet the needs of a growing economy.

The basic formula is quite simple: New money, or credit, would be created each year to equal the increase in the Gross National Product.

The new money is needed to buy the extra goods that have been produced. The amount of money that was spent the previous year is not enough to purchase the products available each new year because our economy—barring severe maladjustment—naturally increases production each year. If the consumer is going to buy the extra production, new money must come from somewhere. This plan would create the money and new consumer credit, in an equitable and effective way through dividends on the proposed American Corporation stock.

The program would involve legislation to provide for the formation of the "American Corporation" by the United States Department of the Treasury. Sale of stock in the corporation would be limited to United States citizens, with a limit of $30,000 to any one person. Special plans for low income groups to purchase would include small payments and payroll deduction arrangements. Money from sale of such stock would be used to retire United States Bonds.

Each year the Treasury Department would check the GNP and any other factors that should be taken into consideration, and then declare a monetized "Prosperity Dividend" which would meet the current need for expansion of consumer credit. These dividends would go to the stockholders of the American Corporation who would be urged to spend the dividends—spend the money wisely, but spend it nevertheless—on consumer goods and services. To further encourage spending, dividends might be declared just prior to Christmas.

This plan could be extended to cover Social Security. There might be an arrangement whereby money paid into Social Security could be used to purchase American stock, bringing more advantages to the individual and a greater feeling of self reliance and pride than the present Social Security system.

After the national debt is paid off, new investments in the future of America could be carefully undertaken with new issues of stock. This would encourage better management and more efficiency in the government sector of our economy. There would be more attention given to wise investment by government in the public works that would bring dividends—by increasing the GNP—and more money for the American Corporation stockholders. Those things that can best be done by government, such as highways and the post office, would be done in a responsible way that would contribute most to the private as well as public sector.

PURSUING MAMMON OR PEACE

One of the great problems now is the nature of our corporations and our banking system and our stock market. These are not designed to invest in the good of the people and the planet. They may have some good in them, but they're mostly there to make money.

They remind me of a man advising his son who was going out into the world. He told him, "Son, make money! Honestly if you can, but make money!" This is the drive of greed and lust, a human fault that only sometimes has been overcome. There have been great examples of overcomers in history. I think of Martin Luther King Jr.—in his last book he argued for the methods that work for peace, and he understood them. His end was tragic when he was killed.

Ten percent of a person's time or money in works of peace should be required of each individual, to do his part in tipping the global scales for peace. Nine percent of each person's income now goes in taxes to works of war.

MONEY AND WORK

The "Battle over the Budget" illustrates how blind our leaders are. They all recognize something is wrong, but ignore the cause of our economic folly, and propose solutions that would in one way or another repeat the mistakes of the past.

The question is not just how much do we owe, but what are our assets, to whom do we owe the money, and how much of the debt is legitimate.

Something is obviously wrong if the poor lack money to buy what they need. If they had the money we could produce the goods they need. Of course, for stable prices we need a balance between supply and demand.

Recourse to the old idea of justice for all would provide a simple solution.

There are two sources of money that people are entitled to—money you earn by rendering a needed service, and money you justly inherit.

In the case of obtaining money through work, communities should and do provide education and jobs for their members. Calling attention to examples of success by both private and public sectors is needed.

When it comes to inheriting money, this is presently limited to the children of the rich. If the poor could obtain their rightful inheritance, they would provide the demand for the increase in production new technology affords.

With less fear of poverty, people would find their prosperity in giving and sharing—in better relationships and time for family, friends, music, and play.

A new look at money, credit, interest, property rights, and obligations would lead the way to "justice for all" and a future for all the people of the world.

24

Government

THE GLOBAL ORGANISM

AN AMAZING TRANSFORMATION IS occurring in Earth's governments, institutions, and individuals. People are beginning to experience a new world view, a new *holistic* way of relating to our planet and to one another.

With our exploding population and ruthless technology, we can quickly destroy the Earth, or by re-direction, slowly improve the delicate web of life that sustains us. Choosing and pursuing the latter is our urgent task.

Poets, mystics, and philosophers have spoken through the centuries of how we are all one—one family, one community, all members one of another. But it is only in the last few years that our mutual dependence and interconnectedness has surfaced in the thinking and actions of governments and institutions. More and more we see the bonds that link man with man, and man with nature.

Society as a whole is beginning to function as a human body with brain, blood, glands, and nervous system. Today, we see the burgeoning of mutual assistance between all the major powers, and joint action in United Nation agencies on pollution, population, and poverty. In these and other institutions throughout the world, the critical problems of our environment, industries, and social structures, and the needs of our personal body and spirit are being recorded, studied, and debated with a new candor and humility.

Within our institutions is a small but growing nucleus of individuals who are thinking globally and beginning to turn our society and technology toward the understanding and care of our Earth, its life, and its people. They offer the hope that man can successfully take the helm of planet Earth, understanding and adapting nature's ancient methods and systems, which through eons of evolution have increased Earth's life and beauty. These individuals are now acting as cells in a global organism.

The individual cell in a human body receives, processes, and returns nutrient products with the aid of nervous impulses from the brain. Each cell contains genes with a blueprint of the whole body, which assists in this task.

We see in our embryonic global social body the growth of similar systems for providing information, materials, and action for improvement of Earth's life potentials, as well as "genes" to communicate the emerging Earth-view in the form of ethical criteria and guidelines.

Of course, people have a much higher level of consciousness than cells, and a greater opportunity for mobility and creativity. People can also perceive and influence trends. Nevertheless, the analogy is useful. Through new links of communication and new bonds of feeling and awareness, now each person can uniquely affect the social and biological evolution of Earth's new global human organism.

Many institutions seek to aid this process. Their purpose is to implement the new eco-view of our Earth-ship through environmental action, social justice, and inner renewal, aiding the "natural depth in man" through silent prayer or meditation, religious worship, art, music, poetry, and love of nature, sky, and sea.

SOCIAL ORGANIZATION

How to organize society for implementing the new eco-view is the problem. We need an organic democracy relating people to one another in a manner that will—

- Encourage their highest spiritual and mental development.
- Communicate the best they each have to the greatest benefit of all the others.
- Provide a mental-spiritual grid for decision-making and communication of values.
- Enable the individual to function as part of the global mind.

NEIGHBORHOOD COOPERATION

One evening on October 10, 1973, I walked with my wife from our apartment in Brooklyn to a meeting about a drug addiction program in our neighborhood. The meeting was conducted by the local planning board and was several blocks away at St. Leonard's Catholic Church. It had probably been over a year since we last walked along this street, and it was encouraging to see the street much cleaner, more growing plants and trees, and several three-story multiple homes newly remodeled and decorated. This was the work of the local block association working against terrible odds in an area of poverty, drug addiction, and despair.

At the meeting there were emotional flare-ups between residents who felt threatened by the location of a drug treatment center on their street and those who were undergoing treatment at the center. I could not help but think of the similar angry words being exchanged at that moment at the United Nations Security Council.

A young man from the drug treatment center stepped to the microphone and said that "This Earth belongs to all the people, and we have got to remember that and work together."

ACHIEVING EARTH CARE

There are two schools of thought concerning how to achieve Earth care, and both should be considered. One is to get society and business to do the right thing, by passing laws and regulations, which is the stick approach. The other is the carrot approach, by giving information and inspiration.

I lean toward the carrot approach. We are taught that the door to action is the mind. What is important is getting people thinking, not just doing what others tell them to do, but instead getting them involved with their own thoughts and ideas. People will then set out to do the right thing, and all they need is encouragement, from what others are doing. They will do the job without so many regulations and rules.

The problem in the world today is the conduct of people. What is needed is a change of heart, and a change in attitude of the mind, so that we listen for the best solutions, dramatize solutions, and report solutions.

The door to the mind today is, unfortunately, television. The garbage that comes out of the tube is not designed to encourage, to educate, or to inspire. There are some wonderful exceptions. We need a change in the way we think.

UNITED NATIONS

The United Nations and its Environment Programme have done some wonderful things. The Mediterranean Sea would be far more polluted if it weren't for the efforts carried out by UNEP. One could cite many more examples.

But in every society, and in the United Nations, people have not learned how to put first things first. Repeatedly things are done to increase the power of the people doing them, compromising the greatest good for the greatest personal benefit. Thus there is a mixture of altruism and greed, and seeking for power found even in the United Nations as well as in the rest of society.

The record of Earth Day and its accomplishments would have been far different if the goal we had been advancing had been picked up enthusiastically by the UN Environment Programme, and by other related UN organizations. If the UNDP, UNICEF, and UNEP would see what we have done, they would see an amazing opportunity to get attention and change attitudes.

The various UN groups as well as private groups such as the Sierra Club are a little blind. If they had the vision of possibilities we have been trying to advance, such as participation in the authentic Earth Day, that would bring global attention and change attitudes all over the world. It would tap the best in peoples' religion and it would provide the motivation. If it were accompanied by reports in the media about what is being done to implement this concept, we might finally achieve the moral equivalent of war in advancing Earth care.

COUNCIL OF WORLD CITIES AND TOWNS

Open Minds, Open Hearts, an Open World

The concept of the Council of World Cities and Towns was first formally presented to Habitat 1 in Vancouver in 1976. But I first broached the idea in 1960 to the new mayor of Mountain View, California, where Erling Toness and I were publishers of *The Mountain View*, a weekly newspaper. In 1963, I wrote a piece titled "Council of World Cities and Towns."

The new mayor of Mountain View, Mort Moore, was asked by our reporter what he liked about the town. He replied, "It's people. We're a mixture of races and creeds and classes and we're getting along fine together. I've always maintained that we have no minorities here because everybody is on an equal footing. You could almost say it's an example for the world to follow. That's always the thing I've liked most about this town."

No greater compliment could be paid to any city.

I thought seriously on this very subject, seriously enough to write the *San Francisco Chronicle* after Mayor Christopher's goodwill trip abroad, "Why not a Council of World Cities to work for peace and good-will?" Sharing information and reports of progress, local municipalities can lead the way.

To Heal the World

Part of the difficulty on our planet is the fixed way nations have of re-acting to a challenge or threat from another nation. This in turn is the result of the nature of our loyalties. We have loyalties to family, town, and state; but our highest loyalty is to our nation-state and the ideology it represents. While the nation-state contributes to the preservation of our values and culture, it is also the final source of power and authority over our lives. (However, in most cases, it derives these powers through some measure of consent and loyalty from its citizens.) It is the structure through which we confront other nation-states with similar powers. In the present balance of terror (i.e., inertia) that exists at the apex of our nation-states,[1] there seems little chance of the great changes needed to heal the spirit of the world and harmonize mankind's deepest aspira-tions, unless something new is done.

While the present use of power by the dominant nation-states provides temporary mutual deterrence, the grave responsibility and ever-increasing danger puts the key nations in a tragic paradox. Military and security responsibilities augment fear and stifle cooperation. They hinder effective action for solving social and environmental problems. The atomic giants are like two men facing each other with pistols cocked and drawn—unable to look together in another direction for even a mo-ment because their opponent might take advantage.

Thus, because of their responsibilities for security and their mili-tary rivalries, the heads of nations are deeply influenced by fear in their deliberations.

A new and effective way to solve this problem would be to give the responsibility for global peace to the cities and towns of the world. This

---

1. Portions of the above were written prior to the end of the bi-polar Cold War.

would have many advantages. An atmosphere of trust could be created by an organization made up of the civil governments of cities joined together apart from their state and national governments. In such a Council of World Cities, limited to aiding fraternal forces, peace could become a powerful aid in building bridges of understanding, goodwill, and cooperation. The Atoms for Peace program, the International Geophysical Year, cultural and student exchanges, and the Winter Olympics, are a few examples of the goodwill potential in this kind of cooperation. A Council of World Cities could obtain massive participation in extending these already existing foundations for world peace.

Mayor Moore's words recalled this idea to me. It is only an idea, and a hope. Yet, there must be many mayors like Mr. Moore, in many cities of the United States, who pride themselves on the fact that their community body is on an equal footing with cities all over the world. Perhaps this idea someday can take hold and broaden out. And perhaps the democratic spirit and goodwill of the people of Mountain View can in Mayor Moore's words become "an example for the world to follow."

Every Town, a Town for Humanity

What I am proposing is not that we be disloyal to our nation, but that we give a higher loyalty to our family and town. Society would benefit from such a change for it would provide more local responsibility and pride in the institutions most directly related to our welfare. Through a "Council of World Cities and Towns," that loyalty can be extended around the world to the whole human family. This would not be a political or ideological alliance, but an alliance of work and friendship. Loyalties to the nation would continue—as would differences in political and ideological views—but these would be tempered by a global network of ever-increasing cooperation and mutual trust.

The Council of World Cities and Towns would direct its efforts to extending the Earth Trustee program throughout the world. A short cut to massive participation would be to work through existing regional organizations (such as the Council of Communities, League of Municipalities, etc.), and through them extend the Earth Trustee program.

Groupings by Common Interest

Activities and groupings of towns would be based, not on national identity, but on natural affinities of trade, industry, climate, and culture. Global subdivisions could be mountain, coastal, plains, tropical, temperate, Arctic, industrial, mining, and agricultural. Cooperation and assistance for this could be sought from the already functioning Sister City Program, which the Earth Trustee program could strengthen and support.

The Council would seek to inspire loyalty through the family and local community to the whole human family.

Earth Trustee Organizations

The Council of World Cities and Towns would seek to have all municipalities form their own independent Earth Trustee Committees with a common allegiance to the Earth Magna Charta. The committees would assist the cities by providing information on what others are doing and where information and help can be obtained.

International Harmonizing Council

The Council of World Cities and Towns would form an International Harmonizing Council, comprised of world humanitarians, scientists, educators, business people, and religious leaders. They would be aided by representatives of national and international public relations and publicity organizations. Others who can assist in the success of this organization would be those in the behavioral sciences concerned with the problems of communications.

The Harmonizing Council would search, in a world of discord, for those ideas and programs that have the support of all nations and that have the best chance of being accepted internationally as world goals. The Council members would seek to obtain headlines with human interest stories about Earth Trustee efforts that dramatize our common humanity and our pursuit of global goals we share.

TERRITORIAL PROBLEM

Many of Earth's problems stem from the lack of any globally accepted basis for individual claims by Earth's people to a fair and equal portion of their planet, of its land and its raw materials. A visitor from space would see things more objectively.

Instead of recognizing the territorial rights of individuals, nations have promoted public support for arbitrary national claims to territory—ignoring the rights of their own citizens and the rest of Earth's people to a fair and equal portion of their planet. As a result the great majority are deprived of a just portion of its land and raw materials.

Barriers between nations are erected and wars fought over them.

False claims, based on arbitrary territorial arrangements of past generations, fuel hatred and conflict. Ties with ancient cultures and the lands where they flourished can be peacefully accommodated when they are approached on a cultural instead of a political basis.

If Israel and all its Arab neighbors joined efforts to provide an equal stake in the Earth for every Arab and Jew in their midst, peaceful relations would quickly ensue. As individuals are given land and aided in obtaining a home, work, and education, they will become responsible custodians of Earth, along with all the other members of the human family. The lesser issues of political boundaries and access to holy places will be peacefully resolved.

NATIONALISM

Nations are social structures with arbitrary boundaries, usually determined in the past by force of arms. They often hinder instead of help cultural integrity and development, which cross their lines or are stunted by denial of their needs.

In the past, the only limit to a nation's power was the threat of another nation's power, a situation which repeatedly resulted in an arms race and war.

The people of the world have assumed that their highest loyalty is to their country. This is nationalism. So long as individuals have no higher loyalty there cannot be real peace. *To achieve real peace and prosperity on Earth, loyalty to our conscience and our planet must transcend loyalty to our country or to political and religious leaders.*

Many of the difficulties of nations would be overcome if society could inspire and encourage a higher loyalty to our planet, a stronger feeling of identity with the whole human family. The "Battle for Earth" will help bring this about. Key decisions will be made, not by the national government, but by local municipalities, working across national boundaries with other cities and towns.

The above proposal for a Council of World Cities and Towns would help solve the problem of nationalism. Let's focus on this problem so that we understand it better. The historic tendency of nationalism is to cause conflict. Nationalism is a major cause of injustice, war, and conflict.

The problem is illustrated in the series of UN conferences on the Law of the Sea that started in 1976. There have now been decades of discussion about the common heritage of the sea and the great benefits to be realized by some arrangement for protection and management of the sea and seabed with equitable benefits for all Earth's people. While noble statements in support of the common heritage were made in public by every nation, frantic behind-the-scenes efforts were made for the advantages of individual states and groups of states. It was obvious that the first loyalty of delegates was not to the Earth, or humanity, but to the power leaders of the sovereign countries and to the increase of their partisan advantage.

The problem of nationalism derives from uninhibited sovereignty, with no higher compelling authority, nor commitment, that would temper the ambition, greed, and selfishness of individual states and of their leaders. The underlying issues are the problem of property, and the problem of money—of finances, exchange, and credit. These issues were discussed in chapters 22 and 23 on the economics of resources and money.

Pervading all three problems is the problem of communications. The control and manipulation of media for partisan advantage hampers real communication of meanings. Words become weapons in exchanges where the goal is victory, not insight.

To really be fair with other individuals, and with other cultures and countries, we must listen to one another. Not just exchange of words, but a real dialogue of meaning is essential if we are going to strengthen the spirit of cooperation that is needed in our global quest for freedom, order, and a happy future for our planet.

Finally, a basic problem is the adversary scenario which is taken for granted, perhaps a result of the old idea of the survival of the fittest, misunderstood and taken to excess by attorneys, business men, politicians, and others. People sue each other, slander and attack each other, and oppose each other, as if there were some special merit in confrontation. "Me, mine, more" is to many people a way of life. Too often we resort to the adversary scenario in marriage, in schools, in societies, and in nations—between teachers, students, and parents, between competing religions, between unions and business, and between nations. It is terrible to see how many people are trying to get ahead by putting someone else down.

As a result of these problems we see fear, violence, and failure in our country, and throughout the world. This very moment, destiny requires a great decision, an epic effort, a grand alliance of people in every country to accept responsibility for the protection and nurture of our planet, its people, and its web of life.

To now take charge and take care of our planet we need a moral equivalent of World War II where individuals and institutions will act as responsible Trustees of Earth in an all-out effort for Earth's rejuvenation. We can replace nationalism with a new "ism"—"Trusteeism," with every person seeking to be a responsible Trustee of planet Earth, in his or her own way. Trusteeism can overcome the mistakes of capitalism, communism, and socialism, with new social structures addressing problems in ecology, economics, and ethics.

GLOBAL GOVERNANCE

Our goal must be a "United World." To accomplish this we must find and affirm where we agree—and leave room for our differences. The United States was a step in this direction. Then we were able to form the United Nations. While both were a step in the right direction, they came far short of what is needed.

While there is a basic appeal in the idea of "One World," there is also an element of threat to the freedom of the individual: the fear that in some way the human spirit will be suffocated unless its loyalty is expressed, as an alternative, to some other loyalty than a global government.

The wisdom of America's Founding Fathers will be needed to provide the flexibility, adaptability, and balance of powers essential for success in the new global economic democracy. It will require understanding and strong support from people in differing cultural, religious, and political traditions. A holistic approach to the urgently needed care and protection of the biosphere will help in tempering our differences.

25

Education and Science

EDUCATION PRINCIPLES

MANY PEOPLE CONTEND THAT religion and government don't mix. It is also true that education and government don't mix.

We want every child to have a good education. Giving our money to government for this purpose is a mistake. We can give our money to a church or other institution that reflects our personal values. This would encourage local understanding and responsibility.

The major universities in this country were established by devout Christians and originally taught the moral values that nurtured justice and peaceful progress. We need to recognize similar values in cultures with other religions—but come together in now pursuing "peace, justice, and the care of Planet Earth."

The manner of teaching, and the ability to truly involve children, are seen as important as content. Good education is to a large extent the fostering of enthusiasm and appreciation. No one can really be forced to pay attention or take responsibility for something he or she doesn't enjoy, need, or love. Education is a process by which children are helped to use their senses and minds, to be aware of what they feel and want, to have a growing confidence in their own worth and usefulness, and to care increasingly about their own unique lives and the life around them.

CURRICULUM

Members of the Earth Society Foundation have great interest in seeing Earth Day and ideas of Earth awareness and custodial care of Earth incorporated into educational curricula. In the late 1970s and 1980s we developed and submitted curriculum proposals to the New York City Board of Education.

While conservation, ecology, and other Earth care sciences are already being given emphasis in educational curricula, I have been told by many teachers and principals that there is something unique and appealing in the global approach. I feel that one of the most important contributions to a child's education can be the understanding of his or her role as a custodian of his or her part of Earth—in his or her block or neighborhood—and the great necessity of the whole human family cooperating in the care of our planet.

Earth Day is our first transnational, trans-sectarian occasion, and it is appropriate that a city as cosmopolitan as New York should mark this event, and help its children not only perceive, enjoy, and feel responsible for the local and national community but for global life as well.

In the outline for curricula submitted by the Earth Society Foundation to the New York Board of Education, a primary aim was to help children begin to explore the systems which are a part and meaning of global scale.

Taking responsibility for our planet begins with taking responsibility for our block, neighborhood, school, business, and city—seeking a happy and effective combination of ecology, technology, and economics. Then the principles of Earth care and the Earth Charter will live in peoples' hearts, deeds, and life-styles.

I believe that as people who share this concern come together they will find a contagious excitement in their new role as custodians and caretakers of Earth.

SCIENCE AND REALITY

Instead of "The End of Science" proclaimed by some,[1] we can now have a new beginning of science. We now know a great deal about the largest and smallest physical items—from quarks to quasars and from solar systems to galaxies. It's time to focus on the metaphysical mysteries, which scientists have neglected.

Is there another dimension of reality that accounts for psychic phenomena, for ESP, and for miracles of healing and answered prayer? Am I

---

1. See Horgan, *The End of Science.*

something more than my body and brain? Is there life after death? Does the human adventure have a purpose?

In the past, conflicting creeds have sought to answer these questions. Can science, with its logical methods of evidence and general acceptance of its major findings, now prove useful, not only in the discovery of physical facts, but also in finding the ultimate cause and reason for our existence? The highest form of life on our planet is its people, who will now decide its future. Let scientists now join the effort for the knowledge needed to make the right choices.

THE COSMOS

We are now at a period in history where humanity's greatest good, greatest awakening, is possible. We have far more information about the world and each other than any generation that preceded us. Added to this is amazing new knowledge of the cosmos.

We probe the universe with our great telescopes. Space vehicles bring dramatic clear pictures of the planets that make up our solar system. We are confronted with ever new mysteries in distant galaxies. We are amazed at the vast emptiness in space, and paradoxically at the fantastic mass of objects in space.

On the other hand, while there are indications that the ingredients necessary for life are scattered through the universe, Earth is the only place where there is proven existence of self-conscious life. Strangest of all, while space can carry electronic signals through light years of distance, we have no message indicating intelligence as we know it from outer space. A great portion of the stars are of a kind that should have planets, and many have been discovered. The potential sources are staggering. As our telescopes reach further and further we discover there are billions of galaxies, each with billions of stars. They exist as far as our telescopes can reach.

The best analogy I can think of is to imagine that each star is represented by a grain of sand. The number of stars, many with planets, could be greater than all the grains of sand on all the beaches of all the oceans on our whole planet. Some stars could be the size of rocks. Grains of sand would be separated by many miles of space.

To go a little further, we realize that our little planet is a minor planet. And our Sun is just an average-sized star. If we consider our planet a microscopic grain of sand with some infinitely small microbes crawling around on it, we would find it hard to imagine that the Creator of all the grains of sand was only interested in our grain of sand—to the exclusion of all the others—remembering that he is the one Creator of the entire cosmos, of all that exists. His infinite wisdom may enable him to deal with us and to appear to us as if he were only interested in our tiny planet, but he certainly has more on his plate than our tiny grain of sand!

When we ponder "What Life Is All About," we are confronted with inexplicable mystery! But the greatest mystery is the mystery of Love in the chaos of the cosmos.

26

Political Leaders

POLITICAL OPPORTUNITY

THE CANDIDATES FOR PRESIDENT in the last two elections thus far have seemed blind to the greatest opportunity in history.

The factors that define this opportunity are numerous and significant. The Cold War has ended; there is new appreciation of Earth that astronomy and space exploration now provide—we are one human family and have only one Earth. Links of mind, feeling, and purpose are now possible with the aid of electronic media—global telephone, TV, fax, and computer networks—and science, technology, and their products now make it possible to eliminate poverty and pollution. All these can help to tip the global balance from destruction to nurture, from "Earth Kill" to "Earth Care."

With all this in our favor, all that is necessary is global communication of the key concept or idea that can unite humanity in vigorous efforts for Earth's rejuvenation, efforts that will benefit planet and people. The key idea, a global challenge, is for individuals and institutions to now think and act as responsible Earth Trustees—to be caretakers and managers of a bountiful planet. With nurture and care the Earth can become a Garden of Eden.

The challenge now is to change from the ignorance and prejudice that has prevailed throughout history, with its war and conflict, to awareness that with our new world view we can direct our aggressiveness to battles for Earth—battles against pollution, poverty, and related problems of hunger, homelessness, and illiteracy.

Let the President proclaim that the first priority of the United States is an Earth Trustee agenda, seeking basic changes in what we do about ecology, economics, and ethics. The role of the President is to inspire with a vision of what is needed and what is possible. Effectively communicated, Congress can then develop and implement the vision.

The general goal is a change of attitude that will make individuals and institutions seek the most practical ways to recycle material goods, nurture nature, reduce pollution, foster fair credit and benefits for entrepreneurs, and provide homes for the homeless—a fair stake for everyone in our bountiful planet and its future.

A program to accomplish this will include:

1. Celebration each year of Earth Day on the March equinox (March 20–21), with participation in global silent prayer or meditation when the United Nations Peace Bell is rung at the moment spring begins. Earth Trusteeship begins in the mind. On this special annual event, people everywhere will identify with the whole human family, recognizing our basic unity in the midst of our diversity and differences.

2. Tapping the best in the love and faith of religious people by providing that all radio and TV stations will program at least one of three daily Earth Minutes—0300, 1100 and 1900 GMT. These minutes, which are to be without words, will provide views of the planet from space, views of children and nature, sounds of bells, and inspirational music. Locally produced, these minutes can be globally exchanged.

    Every group will make Earth Minutes a meeting place for members to reinforce their faith. Whenever an Earth Minute is announced, people will add their silent prayer and deepen their commitment to think and act as Earth Trustees.

3. Every community will be urged to adopt the Earth Magna Charta which sets forth the Earth Trustee vision, policies, and agenda.

CAMPAIGN 2000

In the election campaign of 2000, the candidates failed to grasp the idea, "think globally, act locally."

While Vice President Al Gore and Gov. George W. Bush had wonderful values and proclaimed their Christian faith, their statements did not indicate that either one had an ethical vision and agenda for the country. Their actions and what they supported indicated gross hypocrisy. Jesus, whom they both claim to follow, stated that hypocrites were vipers (small, poisonous serpents).[1] It is ironic how much good and how much misbehavior can be in one man. Al Gore's dedication to public service is an ideal example of virtue. On the other hand his hypocritical actions in regard to the environment and world peace have diminished efforts for a better future.

Al Gore wrote a great book on the environment describing the urgent need to eliminate pollution and protect nature's wondrous bounty. But it was flawed, because it stated the solution was to have the federal government correct the problem. Recently he has been promoting regulation to slow down global warming. This would only bring more bureaucracy, which is a major cause of our problems. Legislation to reward compliance and punish gross indifference should be left to the local community and thereby minimize bureaucracy.

The Bible says, "Where there is no vision the people perish" (Prov 29:18). The real solution to pollution and economic injustice is to educate and inspire people and institutions, families, schools, and businesses to think globally and act locally as trustees of their Earth. President Clinton needed to proclaim the importance of Earth Trustee attitudes and actions. His effective use of the White House "bully pulpit" to inspire and lead would have gotten the attention needed to effect change.

Some things become so obvious we fail to see them. Remember the story of *The Emperor's New Clothes*?[2] Those not involved in the power game and the blindness it causes may see relevance in the solutions suggested here.

If I were president, I would use the "bully pulpit" to wake up America and the world. All that is needed is for people to open their eyes to the incredible opportunities we now have and see what they can do.

Media attention was focused in 2000 on two issues—the elections and the trouble in the Holy Land. Neither Mr. Gore nor Mr. Bush showed understanding of the present state of the world or provided a global solution for the human family.

---

1. Matthew 23:29, 33.

2. Andersen, *The Emperor's New Clothes*.

I would have liked the candidates to say whether they agreed that to save America, and the world, we must all think and act as Trustees of Earth in a campaign to eliminate poverty, pollution, and injustice. This idea came from the original Earth Day. When people think and act as Earth Trustees they will show a reverence for life—and for holy places.

The needed policies and actions were initially conceived in the original concept of Earth Day—first celebrated on March 21, 1970. This event was based on nature's special "moment of equipoise"—the March equinox. The importance of having a great global Earth Day based on this event was recognized by United Nations Secretary-General U Thant and has been celebrated every year since then with a Peace Bell Ceremony at the United Nations in New York City. This occasion has brought together world leaders and representative lay people in dedication to a common cause— peace, justice, and the care of Earth.

The original Earth Day gave birth to the EPA and the UN Environment Programme. However, both have failed to provide understanding of Earth Day and its Earth Trustee vision—the only way to a better future. Earth Day played a key role in ending the Cold War, complementing the efforts of the person most responsible—Pope John Paul II.

Much more would have been achieved if Vice President Gore had not undermined these efforts. He backed the spurious April 22 Earth Day, which had started out as a college demonstration to protest pollution. At the November 1969 UNESCO Conference, the April 22 organizers heard the announcement of plans for the March 21 "Earth Day." Recognizing the power of the name, they confiscated the Earth Day name to promote their political agenda.

While any action celebrating the Earth is to be applauded, we already had an Earth Day date, one which was specifically chosen to occur precisely at the moment of the March equinox when day and night are in balance the world over. By choosing a time and date of world significance, the diverse peoples of the Earth can surmount the barriers of time, geography, language, religion, and culture, and come together with benevolent thoughts for their common ground and sustenance.

The imposter April 22 Earth Day, originally named Environmental Teach-In, used the power of the Earth Day name to gain attention for a political agenda. Many well-intentioned people joined the effort of the promoters and achieved some results. But far more good would have

been done had the event been on the right day and for the larger purpose—to convert individuals and institutions to be Earth Trustees.

Repeated phone calls and letters to Gore and Clinton about Earth
Day were ignored, and Vice President Gore did nothing to acknowledge
or support the real Earth Day and its Earth Trustee agenda. He never
called attention to the real Earth Day, that by then had been celebrated
for thirty years at the United Nations, and the good that has resulted.

In regard to Mr. Gore's flagrant plans during the 2000 campaign
for increasing military programs, more weapons to kill people is not the
way to a peaceful future. It only encourages other countries to do the
same. And with the devilish poisons, germs, and explosives now available around the world, peace by force is not possible. Only education and
understanding can bring peace. When money and media are seriously
devoted to promoting peaceful attitudes and programs that are just and
fair, the rejuvenation of planet Earth and prosperity for all will follow.

Neither Gore nor Bush focused on what is truly important. I pray
that God will open their eyes to the truth. Jesus said that we should love
our enemies, and find common ground. He said that what we do to
other people we do to Him. When soldiers realize they are being asked
to kill Jesus, we will find better ways of settling differences than buying
more bullets.

CONTESTED ELECTION—ARMISTICE OR DISASTER

November 11, 2000 provided a solution to the bitter contest between
Governor Bush and Vice President Al Gore. That day marked the last
Armistice Day before the new millennium. The original Armistice Day
was what ended World War I when leaders decided that hate and conflict
were not the way to settle differences. Focusing on where we agree is the
key to resolution of differences and peaceful progress. "A house divided
against itself cannot stand" (Matt 12:25).

Both candidates claimed to be Christian. The same was true again
in 2004, when Senator John Kerry opposed President Bush. Let them all
do what the Bible commanded. Jesus said, "By this shall all men know
that you are my disciples, if you have love one for another" (John 13:35).
1 Corinthians 13 makes clear that in the eyes of God, intellect, power,
and achievements are nothing—a zero—if you lack divine love.

What is the Bible definition of love? This divine love never tears
down, never divides or hinders charitable efforts by others, never

"vaults itself"—makes a show of itself. Love is not "puffed up." We will not go around with a "holier than thou" demeanor when love reigns in our heart.

"Thinketh no evil." It is the devilish seed of unwarranted suspicion that puts a breach between well-intentioned people.

"The love of God rejoices in the truth." When you have the love of God you will never dodge the truth. Even though it hits you hard and exposes you to the world, you will say Amen!

"Hopeth all things." Love always hopes for the best. Faith works by love and our faith will mount just as high as our love flows deep.

"Charity never fails." You will never fail if you keep in the love of God and keep the love of God in you. The love of God is the biggest thing in all the universe.

To all the candidates in every presidential election—show us your charity and turn your attention to action that will further our common cause—love of God and efforts to heal and nurture people and planet.

Bring the country together by mutual support for the idea that everyone should now think and act as Trustees of Earth, and join in a global effort for Earth's rejuvenation. Let us make each Armistice Day a new beginning, and offer a silent prayer that God will deepen our love and will help us succeed.

CAMPAIGN 2004

I liked President Bush's emphasis of local responsibility in 2004—but found no evidence of attention for the Earth Trustee agenda—now essential for peaceful progress. While recognizing the importance of returning power to the individual and local community, George W. Bush did not address the evils of corporate and institutional power. President Bush and the United States are an enigma. You look at the good they have done and there is much to praise. They advanced freedom and democracy in many parts of the world.

On the other hand, powerful American institutions and corporations are responsible for major causes of injustice, pollution, and violence around the world. While America provided Martin Luther King and his peaceful way of resolving differences, America has spent a major part of its ill-gotten gains in diabolic weapons to settle differences by killing. Had the money spent on arms and given to other countries for military programs been spent on education in peaceful resolution of conflict, we would have no more wars and no terrorists.

In his speech at the Air Force Academy in June, 2004, President Bush said, "The best way to protect America is to stay on the offensive." He certainly did that. The billions of dollars and the military expansion of his administration have made the United States the most powerful military force in the world.

However, this presents an enigma. Bush claimed to be a Christian and said that since his conversion years ago in Texas, he has been a follower of Christ. He said that Jesus Christ has been the greatest influence in his life.

In Matt 26:52, Jesus said, "Put up thy sword . . . for all they that take the sword shall perish by the sword." In the Beatitudes of Matt 5, Jesus said we are to love our enemies. He said, "If you love me, keep my commandments." The 147 commandments that Jesus gave expanded the meaning of his love. "Do good to them that hate you . . . . Agree with your adversary."

Ever since Jesus lived there have been differences about what Jesus taught. There have been "War Christians" and "Peace Christians." The Texas Christians where Bush attended Church were War Christians.

Some War Christians became "Dealers in Death" and made big money by developing and promoting devilish weapons. They promoted war and made millions on the weapons they sold.

Bush and his war makers provided us with World War III—the terrorism war. We have responded to terrorists by becoming the more powerful terrorist.

The ways to end our human addiction to war have been ignored. Jesus, saints, and sages throughout history have pointed the way. A heartfelt dedication to the kind of love Jesus taught and demonstrated can make peace on Earth a reality.

Do what you can to aid and support real peace efforts. To avoid total catastrophe we can, and must, now achieve a global turn toward peace. Pray, and put feet to your prayers by words and actions that foster understanding, cooperation, and the peace that Jesus taught and demonstrated.

On questions of responsibility and reinventing government, Ralph Nader in 2004 had many good ideas—but no chance of winning, and no indication of any understanding and commitment to the Earth Trustee vision and agenda.

None of the major candidates stressed the importance of our Christian heritage, and that good ideas must be backed by prayer and the reverence for life, which is the core ethic of all major religions.

I didn't know who to vote for.

I hope and pray that someone will come forward in future presidential elections who will awaken our country and the world—before it is too late.

CAMPAIGN 2008

Candidates in 2008 should have said whether they agree that to save America and the world we must come together in a common cause—the stewardship of planet Earth. We must think and act as Trustees of Earth.

In the future, let the candidates discuss what they would do to support an Earth Trustee agenda, and people can vote for who is most convincing.

It is tragic that at this critical moment of human destiny we see no leader who understands what is important and has the vision and ability to lead.

27

Mass Media and Communication

BANNERS OF VIOLENCE

NEWS MEDIA CONSISTENTLY HEADLINE the bad in the world. In 1969, the *Oakland Tribune* in California, along with its September 29th editorial condemning violence in TV programming, carried on its front page three banner headlines, "Pair Near Death," "Mad Killer Hunted," and "Kidnapped Girl Sold for $500."

Instead of just talk about condemning violence, why don't newspapers start with their own practices, and actually replace violence with humane stories and headlines? Let the position and length of a story be determined by how much it will help readers improve the quality of life—in themselves, their community, and the world.

Stories of violence, especially where there are some new or unusual features of accident or design, receive immediate attention because of their drama. They help the media obtain more viewers and quicker profits. Some of the results may be good; fear and consternation may lead to new safety regulations. But the constant stimulation of people's fears and anxieties is not a healthy or effective way to improve the human condition.

Today, with instant global communication and the million-fold increase in access to stories of human tragedy, we are constantly bombarded by emotion-packed pictures and words of violence. The result is a terribly distorted view of our world and life.

The dramatic efforts to develop and pursue new solutions are being crowded out by the incessant blaring stories of instant doom. And instead of giving creative support to solutions, people are immobilized by fear and emotional stress.

Birth is slow. Death is sudden. Building takes time; destruction but a moment. If we are to build and grow we must somehow see the meaning and capture the inspiration of life and peace and health.

This requires responsible creativity on the part of news media—a quality sadly lacking today. Instead of devoting 90 percent of their energies to instant mechanical reporting of events resulting from hate, fear, lust, and violence, media should make an all-out effort to creatively bring together the many individuals and groups who are vigorously striving to understand and care for Earth and Earth-life.

Of course we need to be informed about crime and violence in our society. And of course media should not neglect their responsibility to report crime and violence. But their present addiction to "nervous news" must be replaced with responsible journalism that sees the whole picture—erring, if at all, on the side of humanity's hopes instead of its fears. Most important are the causes and successful cures of social disorder. These are more relevant to improving our life. They deserve the headlines. Other programming should seek through dramatic education and inspiring entertainment to aid the individual in his or her quest for love and wisdom. There needs to be a special priority for programs that will help us understand and care for our planet, beginning in our own home and community.

Most newspaper stories of violence trigger fear in the average reader. How much better it would be if those stories were simply recorded in the back pages, perhaps by psychiatric or ministerial students concerned about abnormal behavior. This would leave room on the front pages for the professional reporters to use their special talents for human interest stories of new justice, freedom, and cooperation aimed at building people and rejuvenating the Earth.

All that is needed is to emphasize faith instead of fear. Feature the dreamers, the planners, and the doers who are striving for peaceful progress. Make each newspaper an open market place for ideas and actions that heal, build, and unite.

If there is difficulty, invite some ten-year-old children who are especially sensitive to human values to choose the front page stories. Every one will be surprised and delighted with the result! (Many 10 year olds are less de-humanized than adults.)

Objective reporting requires that news media not only tell what is happening but what is trying to happen—and all in the order of its importance to our future welfare. Newspapers have many gifted writers. Given a strong push in this new direction, they could each day feature front page headlines and stories of real hope. In this time of new searching, they would sell more papers than those who continued the old headlines that cater to and increase man's fear and despair. They could set an example that would excite and benefit their readers—and perhaps the whole world.

MASS MEDIA AND THE EARTH TRUSTEE VISION

Press, radio, TV, and the Internet play a vital role. Actions, good or bad, begin in the mind. Those able to command media attention have a special obligation to speak out about the crisis on Earth and its solution in the Earth Trustee vision and agenda.

Mass media have a sacred obligation as the eyes and ears of the public. The media should:

- Feature solutions as well as problems.
- Headline cases of peaceful progress in the human adventure that replace hate, fear, greed, and lust.
- Give recognition and attention to people and projects that eliminate pollution and poverty, and foster peace, justice, and the care of Earth.

This can best be done by featuring stories about the power of the name "Earth Day" when it is used in its original meaning, and by using the name "Earth Trustee" for all people and projects that aid efforts for a sustainable future.

With the media's cooperation, future observance of Earth Day—on nature's historic annual event, the March equinox—will provide a great global holiday with worldwide participation by people of every creed and culture. This will inspire actions for Earth's rejuvenation in this new millennium—with peace, justice, and prosperity for all.

Money and media power should back Earth Day and its Earth Trustee ideas. This is the best way in this time of trouble to tip the balance from "Earth Kill" to "Earth Care" and provide a new beginning for the human family.

MEDIA MISTAKES AND MISSED OPPORTUNITIES

Most people will agree that our society is negatively affected by mass media. Our actions are largely a result of what we see and hear. Instead of headlining items that heal, build, and unite, the TV, radio, press, and the web feature items of hate, fear, greed, and lust. Television programs are filled with stories about corruption permeating society.

The major media moguls are failing to report the solutions that are working. No wonder there is growing fear we are headed toward global catastrophe. The present media policies will make it happen.

The attitudes and actions of mass media are a major cause of terrorism. Change the negative policies of mass media and instead foster peace, justice, and a better future all over the world. This will eliminate the cause of terrorism.

Media managers, reporters, and advertising salesmen are driven by one motive, to make money. The old easy way is to get attention with stories of violence and all the worst that is happening. They are not interested in news of what is being done to make the world a better, safer, and more peaceful place. What sells papers and TV news programs is ever more shocking and violent stories—with pictures. The media have conditioned and addicted the public to eat garbage. No wonder society is sick!

But how much are stories of violence and immorality helping the efforts that are addressing the problems? In fairness to society, there should be as many, or more, articles about the actions of individuals and institutions that are fostering peace, justice, and the care of Earth. The media could lead the way to a better future for the world.

Attitudes and actions, good or bad, begin in the mind. In today's world the altruism taught by leaders in religion and by studies in ethics is a minor factor in the minds of most people.

It is tragic that the Earth Trustee agenda, provided back in 1970 in the original Earth Day, has been ignored by most public media. In spite of the media failure, Earth Day and its Earth Trustee agenda were a key factor in attention for "peace, justice, and the care of Earth." Look at "Earth Day: Past, Present, Future" at http://www.earthsite.org and you will see it helped get attention for the importance of the environment and helped end the Cold War.

Charlie Rose is a program I sometimes watch. He never mentions Earth Day and is most interested in celebrities that are getting attention. I happened to see his interview of Jude Law—a top writer and actor. The subject was "Artificial Intelligence" and the many things being written about it today. Of course that is fascinating. But at this stage of the human adventure it is far more important to understand the crisis faced by the whole human family and what can be done to avoid disaster.

Jude is an able, confident speaker; well informed, and articulate. He mentioned family, purity, and love. He is interested in who we are and where we're going, and I enjoyed listening to him.

If Charlie and Jude had talked about Earth Day and its Earth Magna Charta, the people in power might get the message and with an all-out global effort save us from global disaster.

Jim Lehrer and his News Hour on PBS is the best news program I know. But the enigma is how our global problems are the result—not only of power-hungry evil doers, but of the good people who are blind to solutions. Were I in charge of the News Hour, every program would include an item about successful efforts that are promoting peace, justice, and the care of Earth.

We need a global effort to report and encourage actions that benefit people and planet. People will differ on what is most important, but we should all seek to find out where we can agree—we should find a common cause and leave room for differences.

We need to take the best of our religious faith and feature it in radio, TV, press, and the Internet. We will then create a global state of mind—and the faith that works by love.

Let the global media report the solutions that are working, and we will have a great future.

Jim Lehrer could lead the way!

MEDIA RESPONSIBILITY

A responsible media would today find more headlines for "Earth Care" than for "Earth Kill." They have at their disposal the facilities and talents that can bring together in one dramatic episode those positive elements years in the making—resulting in exciting solutions to pollution and poverty, and to evoking tenderness, confidence, and healthy curiosity.

Things that take time can be speeded up on TV. A two or three-hour special could through animation and time lapse techniques dramatically show the destruction of America's environment during the last 100 years—disappearance of forests, wildlife, vegetation, fish, clear air, and clean water. The same techniques could show how, with present knowledge and know-how, we could in the next hundred years make America and the whole Earth a Garden of Eden.

Leaders in religion and altruists of all kinds must go all-out to publicize what will heal, build, and unite. All too often, because of the power of mass media, what leaders do is the result of what news programs report.

Press, radio, TV, and websites can save the world if they will feature Earth Trustee efforts and results. Focus on this can be aided by a daily "Earth Signal."

EARTH SIGNAL

I first proposed the Earth Signal in 1972, following the twelve-hour TV special, "EDAY '72," which I co-produced for New York's Channel 9. New conditions and new communications technology make it a powerful idea now, in 2011.

My plan was for TV and radio to broadcast each day an Earth Signal. This would be a sound-bite for worldwide use. It would consist of one ring of the United Nations Peace Bell, and would be heard simultaneously throughout the Earth. It would be programmed as "A Call to Peace," followed by a moment of silent meditation for planet Earth.

The taped sound of the Peace Bell would be broadcast at 1900 GMT (2:00 pm EST), the official time of the signing of the United Nations Charter in 1945. This would be repeated twelve hours later at 0700 GMT for maximum effect.

The Earth Signal would require less than five seconds by TV or radio. It could be included with a station break. When I first proposed the Earth Signal, I indicated that it could also be designed as a ten-second or a sixty-second spot. A ten-second spot would include audio of the Peace Bell, and an announcement of the spot as a daily global event "dedicated to peace and good will." The visual for TV would include a color picture of our blue planet above the words "Minute for Peace." A sixty-second spot might add the lingering reverberation of the Peace Bell, with sounds of happy children playing in the background. There could also be promotional spots broadcast at other times. One promotion spot could say, "19:00 International Time—2 pm in New York—is observed in many parts of the world and by this station as a daily global Minute for Peace. Join your thoughts and your faith with others at the same time, and for the same purpose, during this daily Minute for Peace." Another could say, "Does your thought or prayer have power? Use it, feel it, each day at 2 pm, when this station joins the global Minute for Peace."

The purpose of the Earth Signal would be to encourage a global approach to our problems, to reinforce and unite all enlightened people of thought and vision, who find in their own sovereign conscience the best source of ideas and actions. It would provide a new unity and power to all who believe in prayer and meditation, and in the growing evidence that our thoughts, feelings, and will can affect other minds. The Earth Signal would enable people of faith to unite at the same time, for the same purpose, all over the world. It would also encourage the new ideas of Earth Rights and Earth Care, and spread the new discovery that we are first of all Earth People.

I would like to see participation by radio and TV networks. I urge all who would support this idea to write or phone their station. If those who believe in the power of mind and Spirit will act now, the Earth Signal will quickly spread around the world.

This is a call for new action now that can stop war and save the environment. In 1972, I was seeking to help stop the war in Vietnam. Today, we have another war, in Afghanistan.

If there is sending power in the human mind, if united faith really works, if love can be reinforced, then an Earth Signal experiment could result in dramatic new actions of creative conciliation in efforts for peace.

There is a wave of love rising in the silent world of human consciousness. With the help of the Earth Signal, faith can make it grow until it is more powerful than Hitler's wave of hate. So powerful, it will sweep away the fears in the trouble spots of the world and bring us peace.

The proposed Earth Signal is part of a two-pronged course of action which I contend can bring an end to the war now, and at the same time obtain global support for environmental renewal. The other prong is to initiate the program of Earth Rights in chapter 22.

The task is not impossible. Let us begin with the global Earth Signal and the power of the faith that works by love. (Faith "will move the mountains when we pray.") Earth Trustee/Earth Rights action can spread through the Internet, and we will see action from the grass roots up. And by the grace of God some at the top will act. The important thing is, if you agree, then tell others and any group you belong to. The new millennium can be a new beginning!

COMMUNICATION FOR THE PUBLIC GOOD

How can so many great thinkers and writers take opposite views on important subjects? In the Readers Digest article, "Why Are We So Unhappy When We Have It So Good" (January, 1993), Peggy Noonan stated, "We weren't put here to be happy. Our ancestors believed in two worlds, and understood this to be the 'solitary, poor, nasty, brutish and short' one."

While advocating the moral values of the founders of our country, and the need for appreciation of modern technology and its benefits, her views discourage hope and action for economic and environmental changes needed to improve the here and now.

According to Noonan's argument, faith in God brings satisfaction because the next life (the other world) will make up for the suffering in this one. Others argue that seeking first the rule and reign of God's righteousness in this life will bring peace and prosperity right here on Earth.

This is a tiny sampling of the conflicting views that saturate society today. The situation is aided by mass media, which for the most part find importance only in headlines about conflict. As a result, confusion and despair cover the globe.

This is upside-down thinking. We should give most attention to what we all can agree is most valid and important. Should faith in God inspire acts of compassion, or activate protection and nurture of the environment (bringing benefits to everyone), the results should be applauded by agnostics. Actions of this kind by agnostics should receive a similar response by the religious.

What a great future we can have if we put first things first and accent the positive—affirming key points on which we can agree, without denying our differences. We could turn this world right side up.

As we replace conflict and the works of war with the care of our planet and provide fair benefits for all of its people, more time and thought will be given to exploring the great mysteries of life, of love, of time and eternity.

For now, let's prove our faith by our works. This is the right course for the best of both worlds—the here and now, and the hereafter.

THE PRESS AND PEACE

Newspaper and TV reporters should be like doves looking for olive branches, instead of buzzards looking for carrion.

In the present global danger, media could be a powerful force for peace if they would headline solutions with as much gusto as they give to problems. Solutions deserve equal time and in-depth follow-up.

The most important news is that which encourages better human relations—especially with leaders on the "other side" of the issue. Our attitude toward them may decide the fate of the world. We can reach out to one another with understanding and appreciation for things we approve. We can express our disapproval firmly, but without malice. With a dynamic contagious goodwill, we can be friends in spite of differences, and then find peaceful solutions to our problems. With imagination and faith we can work boldly for peace.

Media can inspire such attitudes by confidently reporting successful examples of peaceful progress. Given encouragement by their employers, reporters could do a sensational job on stories of international cooperation and goodwill, with powerful perception of heroic efforts to help instead of harm life on our planet. Most reporters are idealists at heart.

This does not mean that the media should be less vigilant in reporting problems. They should be wary of optimism built on false premises—witness Munich. But today there are people of faith who are working in creative ways for a better future in this world. Give them the headlines and the media will give the world peace.

What a great thing it would be if there were a special TV program or a movie that would dramatize the kind of world that could be, if we took advantage of the opportunities that we have now, and the solutions that are available. There is no excuse for pollution or poverty on our planet, given what we know today. All that is wrong is in the minds of people. Television and radio and press continue to corrupt the mind, and lack any focus on the solutions that must be addressed if we are going to have a future.

SPACE TECHNOLOGY AND GLOBAL COMMUNICATIONS

The Memorial Service in Houston for the seven heroic Astronauts lost in the 2003 Columbia disaster was a moving tribute to them. From its inception, the space program has attracted our planet's best. The pioneer spirit of 100 years ago is seen in our space pioneers and has resulted in amazing technology to accomplish their task. This in turn has benefited all humanity. The computer revolution is a major example.

Not only that, the communications technology inspired by the space program has been used to benefit all humanity. The Internet and World Wide Web is the main example. (Of course, it has been misused by many people.)

A major mistake was to make the space program a national effort, instead of an international effort. Seeking national advantage impaired the common good of the whole human family.

Now our most important task is to take a look at what we know about people and planet, try to understand our mistakes and our dangers, and determine how we can best use technology to achieve peace, justice, and a sustainable future.

To take advantage of the amazing new communications technology that covers the globe, a vital necessity is to tap the spiritual and emotional resources of our religious faith—in ways that will not compromise our separate creeds and beliefs.

Our new global communications with its information superhighway can bring rapid change to heal, nurture, and improve life on Earth. Global communication and education to foster Earth's care can provide the measure of enlightenment needed to justify and confirm the authority of humanity in the management and care of Earth. To accomplish this requires a radical change in attitudes and policies of mass media. They must seek in every way possible to define and further Earth Trustee goals. While plans and methods for achieving goals will differ, affirming points of accord will increase harmony and accommodation. The new policy will be, "Accent the positive, headline solutions, pursue excellence. Give honest assessment of things as they are, and then with creative vision, aided by computer data, show the better future that intelligent decisions will bring—with follow-up on actions taken and their results."

To this end, every radio, television station, and newspaper that endorses my Earth Magna Charta can join the Campaign for Earth, reporting problems and progress. Radio and television stations will carry daily non-verbal Earth Minutes at designated times—0300, 1100 and 1900 GMT. These non-verbal minutes of inspirational music, views of children, and views of natural wonders will remind us that we are all connected and working for one goal—Earth's rejuvenation. Simultaneous and worldwide, Earth Minutes will deepen our awareness.

With all this in our favor, all that is necessary is global communication of the key concept that can unite humanity in vigorous efforts for Earth's rejuvenation, efforts that will benefit planet and people. The key idea, a global challenge, is for individuals and institutions to now think and act as responsible Earth Trustees—to be caretakers and managers of a bountiful planet. With nurture and care, Earth can become a Garden of Eden.

Gospel Car, Waco, TX, 1912, used in evangelistic travels by John S. McConnell Sr. and his wife Hattie.

Participants at the organizing convention for the Assemblies of God in 1914, in Hot Springs, AK. The group included John S. McConnell and his wife Hattie. *Flower Pentecostal Heritage Center.*

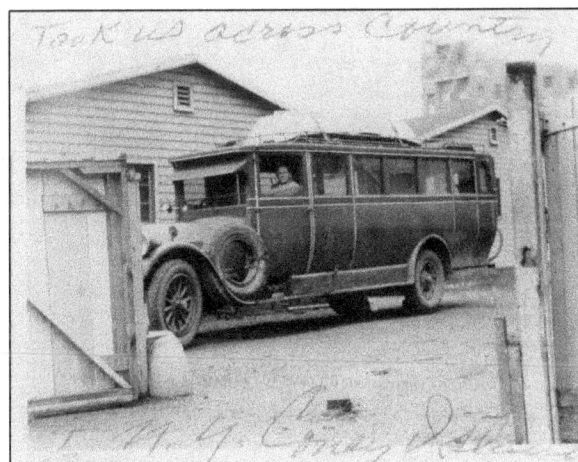

House on wheels (Pierce Arrow Bus) for cross-country travel to Coney Island, NY, where the family lived for three months, 1931.

Left: Evangelist John S. McConnell Sr., father of John McConnell. Right: Theodore W. McConnell, Baptist minister, father of John S. McConnell Sr. and grandfather of John McConnell.

Left: John McConnell, about 2 years old, 1917. Right: John McConnell and his wagon, Walla Walla, WA, about age 8, 1923.

PENTECOSTAL CONVENTION

The Seventeenth Annual Convention of

GLAD TIDINGS TABERNACLE

33rd Street West of Eight Ave., New York City

ROBERT A. BROWN, Pastor

——Will be held——

Beginning Friday, Nov. 14, for 17 Days

J. S. McCONNELL
The Firey Irish Evangelist.

Principal Speaker

BEN COCKERHAN
Singing Evangelist

—and—

MISS MILDRED ANDERSON
of Washington, D. C.

With

The Tabernacle Quartette and Orchestra

Will Sing and Play during the entire Convention

COME AND SEE!

People saved with a glorious salvation
Healed of every disease by the power of God
Filled with the Spirit as on the Day of Pentecost
And hear about the Second Coming of Christ

Two Services Daily: *2:30 and 7:45 p. m.*
Sundays: *10:30 a. m., 3 and 7:30 p. m.*
Missionary Day and Offering, Sunday 23rd.

SPECIAL DIVINE HEALING SERVICES
THROUGHOUT THE CONVENTION *Bring The SICK!*

Other Workers
Evangelist JOSEPH TUNMORE, *Pittsburg, Pa.*
" WILLIAM K. BOUTON, *Flushing, N. Y.*
" EARNEST S. WILLIAMS, *Philadelphia, Pa.*
" WILLIAM I. EVANS, *Newark, N. J.*
and many other ministers and missionaries will be present.

DIRECTIONS. From Jersey or Brooklyn, take Hudson Tubes or B. R. T. to 33rd Street, New York City, walk two blocks West. All elevated and surface car lines stop at 33rd or 34th St. From up or down town New York, take subway to Pennsylvania Station, 33rd St. and 8th Avenue, and walk half block west. For further information as to accommodations, etc., please write *Miss MARIE BURMAN, 311 West 111th St., New York City, Convention Secretary.*

Poster for evangelistic convention in New York featuring John S. McConnell Sr., 1924.
Flower Pentecostal Heritage Center.

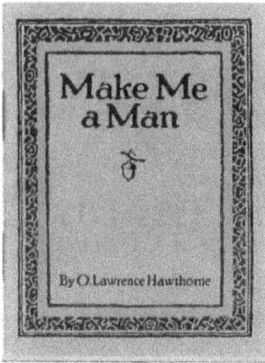

Hawthorne's 1923 poem that John McConnell memorized at age 10, finding it on a scrap of paper on a street in San Diego, CA in 1925. Miniature book publication cover and first 3 pages shown. *University of Iowa Libraries, Iowa City, IA.*

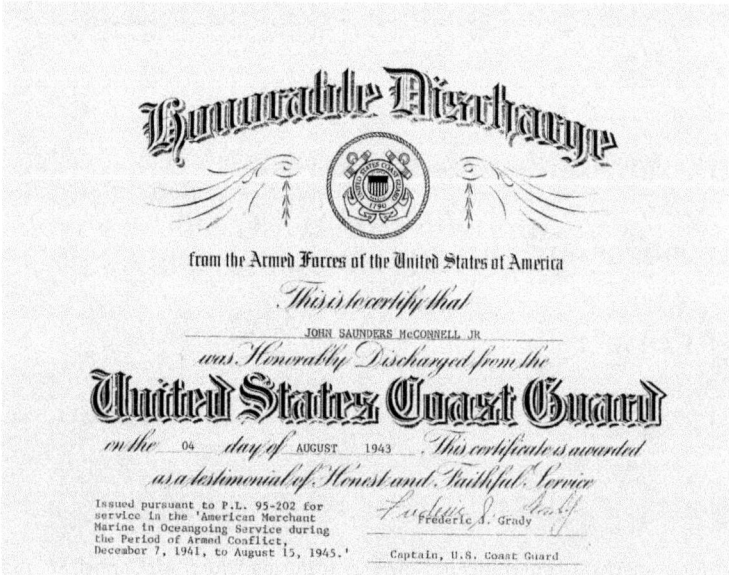

U.S. Coast Guard Honorable Discharge certificate, August, 1943.

Evangelist John S. McConnell Sr. and family, about 1925: Hope, Evan, John Jr. in center rear, Grace, and Hattie.

Evangelist John S. McConnell Sr. and family, 1930: Hattie, Hope, Ruth, John Jr. in center rear at age 15, Evan, Paul, and Grace.

John McConnell (top left) as trombone player in school orchestra, Glendale, CA, 1931. *H. A. Varble, Eagle Rock, CA.*

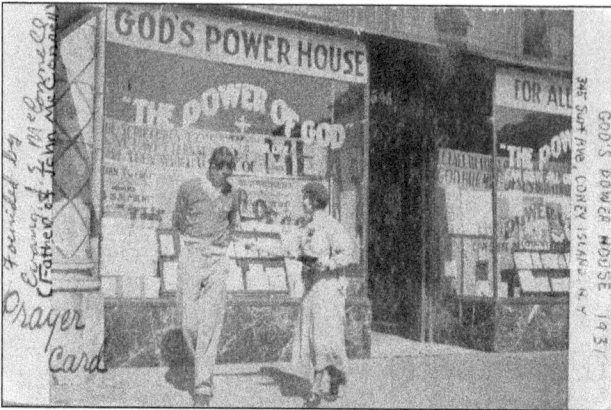

Coney Island storefront church established by John S. McConnell Sr. – "God's Power House," 345 Surf Ave., 1931.

John McConnell as editor of *The Toe Valley View* in Bakersville, NC, from *Life Magazine*, April 29, 1957. *Getty Images, Paul Schutzer.*

John McConnell as a business manager in California in 1940.

John McConnell with his two children by Mary Lou: Constance and Cary, Ashland, OR, 1954.

Anna and John McConnell celebrating their marriage at St. Mark's Lutheran Church in New York City, Christmas Day, 1967.

Mayor Proclaims Earth Day

San Francisco proclaims first Earth Day for March 21, 1970.
— *S.F. Chronicle Sunday Punch* 2/22/70, "Earth Day"
— *S.F. Chronicle* 2/4/70, "Supervisors Unit OKs 'Earth Day'"
— *S.F. Examiner* 2/18/70, "Mayor Proclaims Earth Day" – Mayor Alioto and Krista Lynn Baumhoff (5) admiring an Earth Flag, a day after the Mayor proclaimed March 21 as Earth Day, "a special day to remember Earth's tender seedlings of life and people; a day for planting trees and flowers; a day for cleaning streams and wooded glens." Photo by Seymour Snaer.
— *S.F. Chronicle* 2/19/70, "Mayor Proclaims March 21 'Earth Day'"

STAR OF HOPE

FRIENDSHIP : A FORCE FOR WORLD PEACE.

Today, every man can join in the task of building foundations for world
peace. We, as members of one human family, can show our determination to be friends in spite of our political, religious and racial differences. New ways for cooperation and peaceful progress will be found. The
dismal fear of global suicide will be replaced by hope for tomorrow's
golden age.

COOPERATION : INTERNATIONAL GEOPHYSICAL YEAR

The I. G. Y. is a symbol of cooperation among scientists of all countries. Through their combined efforts the knowledge of earth and space
has been significantly increased and promises many benefits to mankind.

This cooperation can be utilized to provide a dramatic symbol of our
unity with the whole family of man.

A SYMBOL TO RALLY HOPE

In order to aid the will for peace the people of every country are invited to sign the Star of Hope Declaration. To dramatize their determination to be friends and to eliminate the conditions that cause war, the
Declaration and signatures will be microfilmed and presented to the
Secretary General of the International Geophysical Year with the request that they be placed in a satellite that will shine as a brightly visible Star of Hope, launched in joint effort by all the peoples of the world
through the International Geophysical Year Committees.

STAR OF HOPE DECLARATION

I, a citizen of this planet, dedicate my friendship and knowledge to
work for peace among all men. I will aid the efforts that heal, build
and unite mankind.

Add my name to the Star of Hope :

Name	Address
U.R.Krishnan Sept. 9, 1958	National Physical Laboratory New Delhi (INDIA)
Hideki Yukawa Sept. 10, 1958	Kyoto, Japan
P. Grivet 12 Septembre 1958	Paris, France
Ebbe Rasmussen 12. Sept. 1958.	Copenhagen, Denmark
P. Savić, Jugoslavia 12-IX-58	Dorous Sabet Egypt
	A.Hume (USSR)
M.L. Oliphant Australia.	
E. T. S. Walton, Ireland.	
	Argentina. Maria de a Vila de fuéve

Star of Hope Committee, San Francisco, U.S.A.

Star of Hope Declaration, 1958, proposing a satellite carrying names of people dedicated
to working for peace.

by the people of Earth
for the people of Earth

EARTH DAY PROCLAMATION

Whereas; A new world view is emerging; through the eyes of our Astronauts and Cosmonauts we now see our beautiful blue planet as a home for all people, and

Whereas; Planet Earth is facing a grave crisis which only the people of Earth can resolve, and the delicate balances of nature, essential for our survival, can only be saved through a global effort, involving all of us, and

Whereas; In our shortsightedness we have failed to make provisions for the poor, as well as the rich, to inherit the Earth, and our new enlightenment requires that the disinherited be given a just stake in the Earth and its future -- their enthusiastic cooperation is essential if we are to succeed in the great task of Earth renewal, and

Whereas; World equality in economics as well as politics would remove a basic cause of war, and neither Socialism, Communism nor Capitalism in their present forms have realized the potentials of Man for a just society; nor educated Man in the ways of peace and creative love, and

Whereas; Through voluntary action individuals can join with one another in building the Earth in harmony with nature, and promote support thereof by private and government agencies, and

Whereas; Individuals and groups may follow different methods and programs in Earthkeeping and Earthbuilding, nevertheless by constant friendly communication with other groups and daily meditation on the meaning of peace and good will they will tend more and more to be creative, sensitive, experimental, and flexible in resolving differences with others, and

Whereas; An international EARTH DAY each year can provide a special time to draw people together in appreciation of their mutual home, Planet Earth, and bring a global feeling of community through realization of our deepening desire for life, freedom and love, and our mutual dependence on each other,

Be it Therefore Resolved; That each signer of this People Proclamation will seek to help change Man's terrible course toward catastrophe by searching for activities and projects which in the best judgement of the individual signer will:

peacefully end the scourge of war

provide an opportunity for the children of the disinherited poor to obtain their rightful inheritance in the Earth

redirect the energies of industry and society from progress through products... to progress through harmony with Earth's natural systems for improving the quality of life

That each signer (his own conscience being his judge) measure his commitment by how much time and money he gives to these purposes, and realizing the great urgency of the task, he will give freely of his time and money to activities and programs he believes will best further these Earth renewal purposes. (At least nine percent of the world's present income is going to activities that support war and spread pollution. Ten percent can tip the balance for healthy peaceful progress.)

Furthermore, each signer will support and observe EARTH DAY on March 21st, 1971 (Vernal Equinox -- when night and day are equal throughout the Earth) with reflection and actions that will encourage a new respect for Earth with its great potentials for fulfilling Man's highest dreams; and on this day will join at 1900 Universal Time in a global EARTH HOUR-- a silent hour for peace...

* Time changed to moment of the Equinox 1973

(signatures)

Earth Day Proclamation, composed June 21, 1970, with signatures dating to 2000.

Former President Eisenhower greets John McConnell during promotion of the San Francisco Meals for Millions campaign in 1962. *Skelton Photography, San Francisco.*

John with daughter Christa, wife Anna, and mother Hattie, outside their Brooklyn apartment, 1974.

UN Secretary-General U Thant speaking at the international Earth Day Peace Bell ceremony at the United Nations on March 21, 1971. The ceremony has continued each year since then. *UN Photo/T. Chen/Ara.*

Margaret Mead, International Chairman of Earth Day, rang the Peace Bell at the international Earth Day ceremony at the United Nations on the spring equinox, March 20, 1978. Here, she and Mr. Genichi Akatani, Under-Secretary-General for Public Information, address the gathering during the ceremony. *UN Photo/Saw Lwin*

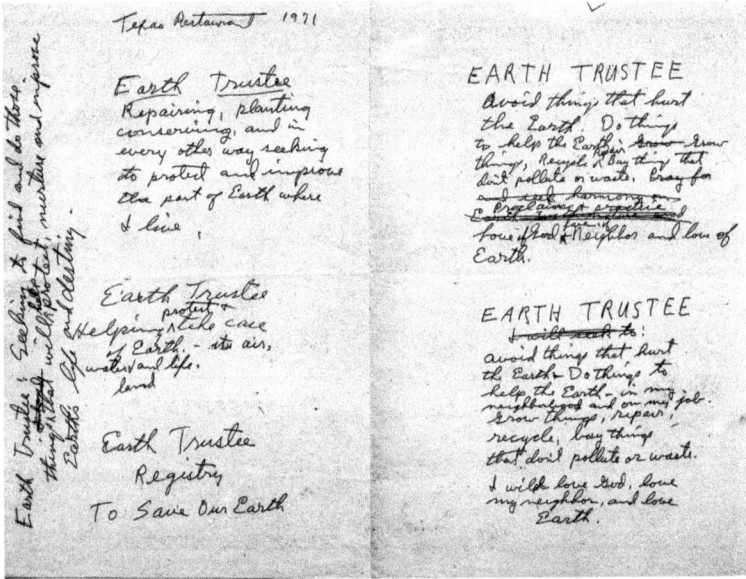

John McConnell's preliminary sketch of the Earth Trustee concept, written on a placemat at a Texas restaurant in 1971.

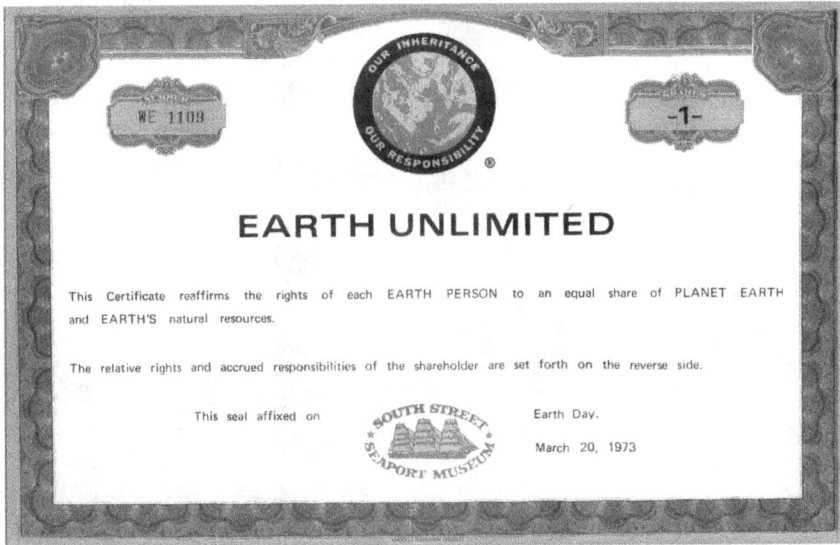

Earth Unlimited Certificate, which "reaffirms the rights of each EARTH PERSON to an equal share of PLANET EARTH and EARTH'S natural resources," advanced in 1973 for educational purposes.

John McConnell speaking in 1990 at an Earth Day ceremony in Ottawa, Canada, on the "other" date for Earth Day of April 22.

Edward Abramson, Majority Whip, NY State Assembly, signer of the Earth Day Proclamation, thanks Stan Lundine, NY Lt. Governor, for signing the Proclamation in 1990, Earth Day's 20th Anniversary. John McConnell and Cynthia Lennon, also a signer, look on.

Audrey McLaughlin, head of the New Democratic Party, House of Commons, Canada, signing the Earth Day Proclamation in Ottawa in 1990.

John McConnell, ca. 1990. *LTI, New York.*

Anna and John McConnell, ca. late 1980s.

American Flag and Earth Flag flying over the Amundsen-Scott South Pole Station, 1983. National Science Foundation, *U.S. Antarctic Program.*

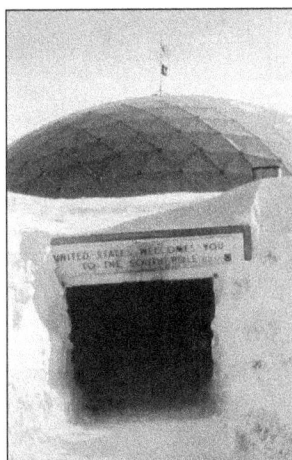

The doorway sign, the Amundsen-Scott South Pole Station is darkened by diesel exhaust from supply tractors, 1983. National Science Foundation, *U.S. Antarctic Program.*

Russian cosmonaut Anatoly Berezovoy, signer of the Earth Day Proclamation. Berezovoy was at the UN Peace Bell ceremony in 1997, and established a similar annual ceremony in Russia in 1998.

Earth Flags at the Earth's Poles, shown by members of the multinational Millennium 2000 Antarctic Expedition, and the Arctic Millennium Expedition. Left: South Pole. Right: North Pole.

Aye Aye Thant, daughter of UN Secretary-General U Thant and President of the U Thant Institute, ready to ring the UN Peace Bell on March 20, 2005, along with Donald MacKay, Ambassador of New Zealand to the UN on the left, and the Acting President of the UN General Assembly, H. E. Edwardo J. Sevilla Somoza, Ambassador of Nicaragua to the UN, in the center. *Ann Charles.*

Anna and John McConnell in New York for Earth Day, 2006. Earth Flag in background. *Ann Charles.*

Anna and John McConnell, with John Munday, outside the McConnell's Denver apartment in 2007.

John McConnell, 2007.

Children of the world, including the young Tarumi Violinists under the direction of Yukako Tarumi, ringing the UN Peace Bell on Earth Day, March 20, 2010. *Noema Chaplin.*

28

Star of Hope

THE STAR OF HOPE began with the launching of Sputnik, the first Earth satellite, put in space by the Soviets in 1957. The Sputnik caused a sensation all over the world. This was one of the great milestones of human history.

It was in that year, 1957, when I first made a global difference—and I'll never forget this experience. I was in North Carolina publishing a little newspaper called *The Toe Valley View* in a wonderful little town called Bakersville near Spruce Pine. Some copies of the paper are at the North Carolina state capital archives.

STOWAWAY ON A SATELLITE

When Sputnik was launched, I was keenly interested because while in California I had visited scientists who worked with the space program in Berkeley. I knew Dr. Teller and other scientists out at Cal Tech in Pasadena. Before that, I had written an article titled "Stowaway on a Satellite." It attracted the attention of the chairman of MGM. His colleagues had me come to see him. They were talking about making it into a motion picture. If they had done that, the world would have gone an entirely different direction.

What I said in the story about the stowaway is as follows:

> The man in the story was a scientist who was very much concerned about the danger of atomic conflict. Back in those days, that was a real fear because both the United States and the U.S.S.R. had atomic weapons. At the same time, we were interested in exploring space. More could be accomplished with a man in space.

So they were going to send a man into space. Before they did that, they were going to send a satellite with everything that the man would need. It would have all the necessities for a three day trip and then return the man to Earth. It would be complete. They wanted to test it before they would put a man in it.

The scientist who was working on the satellite was deeply concerned about the danger of atomic war. He was a Peacenik, if you will. He decided—and he was on the program where he could get away with it—that he would stowaway on this satellite. His motive: to be in a position to speak to the whole world from a vantage point which no man on Earth has ever before occupied, on the necessity of marshalling all of mankind's reason and good-will to stop the plunge toward war and world suicide.

The first phase of his plan worked out. He carried out the substitutions, and the satellite went into orbit. Then, to the amazement of the world, there was a voice from this satellite. He started broadcasting the speech he had very carefully prepared and memorized—mainly an exhortation to think, to use reason, to face all the facts about where the present course of action was leading. His speech was beamed primarily to other scientists and intellectuals. He also stressed the need to summon moral energy to match the physical energy recently released by science. He talked about the danger of war and how people must come together. There must be peace on earth or there would be the end of the human family. He made a big case.

As he talked, his voice was heard by the majority of people all over the world. They recorded it. And they publicized it on the front pages of newspapers everywhere. Stowaway on a Satellite! It was a good story.

Then he discovered that the receiving part of his radio apparatus was not working. He didn't know if he was being heard or not. Then, on top of that, he discovered that the return mechanism didn't work. So he was stuck in space.

So then the end of the story was when he was on his last legs and he wondered whether his message had ever reached the people on earth. He asked that if his message had reached people, they would turn on their lights and keep them on all night in all the cities, so that as his ship circled around the world he would see all these lights and he would know that he had been heard before he died.

Before he died, the lights went on all over the world, and he cried because of the thrill that his message for peace had been heard.

The producers thought that this was a great story. They were going to make a motion picture of it. But that never happened. You never know what happens in Hollywood. I get so disgusted because along comes something that's bad and that pushes away something that's good. A movie based on the story would have been good.

In the Appendix is the work plan I developed for making this story into a movie. The full version of "Stowaway" included there contains the original ending. The ending here is an alternative to the original ending.

SPUTNIK AND THE STAR OF HOPE

My co-publisher Erling Toness at *The Toe Valley View* was a Quaker. We tried to feature items of good news, especially what was happening in the local churches in the community and in that area of the Blue Ridge Mountains.

I had become interested in space exploration. Because of my involvement with scientists of the budding space program, I followed the space program closely. After the first Sputnik satellite was launched on October 4, 1957, I wrote an editorial, "Make Our Satellite a Star of Hope" (see the Appendix). I urged that a bright, visible satellite be launched as a symbol of hope for humanity. We urged that the satellite would be international, and that it would be arranged that when it got into space, it would have a flashing light, so that anyone in the world could look up at night and identify this Star of Hope. The light would be flashing at the rate of a newborn baby's heartbeat.

The idea got terrific attention. It was picked up by the *Asheville Citizen*, and hit the wire services and Associated Press and went all over the world. It got front page attention around the world. Suddenly I was on several TV network programs. I was on the Arlene Francis Show, and the Dave Garroway Show. I talked about how the space program was a great opportunity to bring people together all over the planet. We are one human family, and we have only one Earth. I spoke along those lines.

After the Arlene Francis Show I received over 2,000 letters. I suddenly discovered how many different points of view listeners could have. One letter which made a point in a quaint way came to me by registered mail. The writer said she thought we should launch a satellite that would broadcast a message in space with just one word repeated over and over again, "Help."

Among the letters of support was a telegram of support from Billy Graham, and letters from Eleanor Roosevelt. She thought it was a great idea. She admired the idea tremendously and as a result she had me come and see her. She wrote letters of support. Support also came from Norman Cousins, and various scientists.

We pushed the idea that we should launch this international satellite and people could register in it that they would work for peace. Then they would know that, out there in space, their names would be in this satellite. It was a very ambitious undertaking. I did connect with media. That was a great help. We got some money, a few thousand dollars.

This led to my conversations with key leaders. Dr. Fred Singer, a leading advocate of our venture into space, was in the public eye. He met with me and introduced me and my idea at a special meeting that drew a large crowd.

Werner Von Braun supported my idea. Later I spoke to members of Congress. Then I attended the Atoms for Peace Conference in Geneva in September, 1958. By that time, we had a Star of Hope Committee in San Francisco that raised my airfare for the round trip. As I had very little money for food and lodging, I slept on a park bench several nights.

For the Conference, I got a Star of Hope Proposal typed up on a fancy piece of paper in Geneva. I went there without it, but while there I had the idea—it came out of my soul.

This was during the height of the Cold War. I'll never forget that the Ambassador representing the United States was Glenn Seaborg, from 1958 to 1961 the Chancellor of the University of California. I had met with him in California, and then I met with him over there in Geneva. He thought this was a great idea. He said, "John, what you should do, if you really want this to go somewhere, is to get the Soviet delegate to sign it, and then I'll sign it. Then you'll have something."

So I tried and tried to reach the Soviet delegate. His secret service agents were protecting him. I couldn't get to him. But I got other signatures from the countries of India, Japan, France, Denmark, Egypt, Australia, Yugoslavia, Ireland, Argentina, and Switzerland.

The last day of the Conference, I saw the Russian sitting down by himself. I went over to him, and I had the message in Russian. I don't know what happened to that copy. But I showed it to him, and showed him that other people had signed the proposal, and asked him if he'd sign it. He said he'd be glad to. So he signed it.

And I rushed to reach Dr. Seaborg, but he had left early. Years later, I met him on one of my trips to California, and I told him about this. He said, "I'll be glad to add my name." I didn't have the document with me, and so I said "it wouldn't make any difference now."

Fred Singer, the space scientist, had said that this would be not only a symbolic star, but it could also bring scientific benefit to the planet, because people who are doing survey work could get more accurate survey points.

However, the Star of Hope was not launched, because the military did not approve. Some people in the Pentagon heard about the proposal. They noted the statement of Fred Singer that it would enable us to obtain more accurate property lines on Earth. Somebody in the military read this and said, "Oh. My lord, that's right! That satellite could help us launch our missiles more accurately from our submarines!"

So the military put a satellite in orbit—but it did not have a bright light that all the world could see. Instead, it had a light that could be seen only by a telescope.

So they blocked us from launching our Star of Hope satellite, but they launched their satellite. Instead of a bright Star of Hope that would be as bright as Venus, their satellite was a secret project. You had to have binoculars and know where to look for it.

It wasn't called the Star of Hope. It was called ANNA. (That's my wife's name. We were married in 1967.) It stood for "Air Force Navy NASA Army."

There's a crazy story along with this. It shows how things get turned around. Art Hoppe, a friend of mine who was a reporter with the *San Francisco Chronicle*, wrote a story about the idea of the Star of Hope. I wanted it to be launched on Christmas and promote peace all over the world.

Art Hoppe got a hold of what was happening. You know how some reporters get hold of things that are being covered up. He said that the military didn't launch it on Christmas as I was proposing, to promote peace all over the world. But instead they launched it on Halloween!

GOLDEN ANNIVERSARY OF SPUTNIK

I was on the phone a few years ago with the president of the Institute for Cooperation in Space, Dr. Carol Rosin. ICIS has top astronauts as members. They're trying to get countries to agree that there will be no weapons in space. That would be a great step toward ending wars. Thirty years ago they had made me one of their advisors. They're in Vancouver, BC, and their website is http://www.peaceinspace.com.

I urged that a Peace in Space conference propose and set in motion plans to honor the golden anniversary of Sputnik, which occurred on October 4, 2007. There was enough time before October, they could have easily planned and gotten global attention for launching a satellite that would be a Star of Hope. It would symbolize for all humanity the end of launching weapons of war on planet Earth. Something like this would appeal to all people who look to the heavens as a symbol of peace.

The Star of Hope satellite would be in polar orbit, to be seen every night on every continent. It would have a data bank that could be accessed from everywhere, that would give the latest information on progress in the battle for Earth, on what is being done to nurture our planet and to promote peace, justice, and the care of Earth. It would contain a memory disk containing the name of every person who has committed to being a Trustee of planet Earth.

29

Minute for Peace

ORIGIN OF MINUTE FOR PEACE

MINUTE FOR PEACE LED to Earth Day. My key inspiration for Minute for Peace and Earth Day was the United Nations Peace Bell. I made the first recordings of the bell. We then added the sound of the Mt. Athos Peace Bells.[1] Together, they provided an inspiring preface to the "Minute for Peace" programs which carried a brief thought for peace, followed by an invitation to all listeners to "add your thought, your prayer, with dedication to peace and good will." The first Minute for Peace—which was broadcast worldwide in 1963—got global attention in the press and aided efforts for peace.

In 1963, I was co-publisher of *The Mountain View*, a little weekly paper in Mountain View, California, in the San Francisco area. I discussed with church and business leaders an idea that might halt mankind's plunge into oblivion. I felt that if each person would take one minute a day to think about peace in the best way he knows, we might bring a global victory for peace.

Jules Dundees was vice-president and manager of KCBS, a leading radio station in San Francisco. On Veterans' Day (Armistice Day), November 11 of 1963, I found myself having lunch with Jules. We talked about an idea I had. I said, "You know that people should think and talk and work for peace on our planet. One thing that might help bring about change in attitudes and conduct would be to have a global

1. Mount Athos, on the Halkidiki peninsula in Northern Greece, a monastic republic with twenty monasteries.

minute for peace. It would be just a minute, with thoughts of peace. We could add to it sounds of nature, or beautiful music, or something from Christmastime that would add to the flavor. And we'd announce it every day, and in that minute we would invite the audience to join in a minute for peace with their prayers, with their thoughts, or with their commitment to peace. It would be great if your station would program a daily minute for peace. It could have the sound of a bell and then a brief statement from an outstanding scholar about how we should pursue peace, and then an invitation to join in a thought or prayer, in a commitment to work for world peace."

He liked the idea. He said, "John, that's a great idea. Do you realize that we're having lunch on the old Armistice Day, November 11? They ended World War I at the 11th hour of the 11th day on the 11th month. And for years after that, at 11 o'clock throughout the country and in many parts of the world, it was dedicated to a minute for peace. In fact, in some towns they would stop traffic at that point. When they started that in London, they had a silent minute to remember that moment." Jules thought it was quite a coincidence that we were meeting on the old Armistice Day.

Just eleven days later (remember the number 11) we were shocked by President John F. Kennedy's assassination. His efforts to see peace realized through the United Nations were ended in Dallas on November 22, 1963, at 19:00 GMT, the very moment on the global clock when the United Nations Charter was signed eighteen years earlier. Yet as awful as this tragedy was, it created a kindred feeling around the world. I sensed that it would have been unthinkable at that moment for any major power to make war. Here was further confirmation of the fact that in the right spiritual climate men could live in peace.

I called up Jules the next day and said that this terrible event had gotten world attention. I pointed out that they were going to have a 30-day period of mourning for Kennedy which would end on December 22. I said, "Why don't we end this period of mourning for President Kennedy with a Minute for Peace?" I suggested that such an event would represent a new dedication to peace.

He said, "Absolutely, that's great! Come to my studio and we'll see what we can do." I went to his studio. I felt guided there. The first tape that I found with President Kennedy was his speech at the United Nations two years earlier on September 25, 1961. He said,

> Never have the nations of the world had so much to lose or so much to gain. Together we shall save our planet, or together we shall perish in its flames. Save it we can—and save it we must—and then shall we earn the eternal thanks of mankind and, as peacemakers, the eternal blessing of God.

It was a beautiful statement.

We took Kennedy's voice, those words, and put them on a tape. We added the sound of a bell. And then a marvelous announcer said, "Add your thoughts, your prayers, [and] your efforts for world peace."

Jules knew how to get attention. He sent out a release that we were planning this Minute for Peace. In short order we obtained a proclamation from Mayor George Christopher, a resolution from the San Francisco Board of Supervisors, and public endorsement from Archbishop McGucken, Bishop Pike, Rabbi Fine, and other religious leaders, as well as the Broadcasters' Association. There was a buildup for several weeks. In fact, the *San Francisco Chronicle* had advance stories announcing that there would be a Minute for Peace around the world on December 22.

On Minute for Peace Day, stations across the country carried the voice of President Kennedy saying those marvelous words from his speech at the UN.

Thus, on December 22, just three days before Christmas, the first "Minute for Peace" was broadcast nationwide on radio and TV stations. Wire services featured it in news stories that went around the world. The broadcast included the voice of President Kennedy addressing the United Nations with an urgent plea for peace, and asked each listener to dedicate his thoughts and actions to peace.

During those few weeks, I have never seen anything happen so quickly and spread so fast. I've struggled years to accomplish a fraction of what I did in a week. On another matter, I was trying to get hold of Archbishop McGucken of the Catholic Church, and I had been told to write a letter and they would see if his appointments secretary could get in touch with me, and maybe I could talk with him. On this occasion I called the Archbishop's office, and he answered the phone. And it went on. The chamber of commerce helped; everybody helped. I got a telegram from President Johnson. Minute for Peace went around the world.

The *Pacem in Terris* (Peace on Earth) encyclical of Pope John XXIII had been published a few months earlier, on April 11, 1963. It was followed nearly two years later in February 1965 by the huge *Pacem in Terris* conference in New York (sponsored by an arm of the Ford Foundation, with 2200 attendees).[2] Because of the interest generated by Minute for Peace, I was invited to attend. That event headed me toward Earth Day and the Earth Magna Charta. Soon I knew I had to leave my employment and dedicate all my time to the Minute for Peace project in New York, and work increasingly with the United Nations.

GLOBAL MINUTE FOR PEACE DAY—DECEMBER 22

Thus, the first observance of a global Minute for Peace followed President John F. Kennedy's death in 1963, when December 22 was designated Minute for Peace Day. Although Kennedy's efforts for peace ended in Dallas, the Minute for Peace broadcast with his voice was given at the end of his 30-day mourning period and was broadcast globally—preceded by front page announcements in many newspapers telling when it would occur.

We urge world leaders to speak out for this event now. Efforts by world leaders to speak out for this annual event could result in new hope and a new beginning for the whole human family. The date of December 22 can be designated Global Minute for Peace Day, and celebrated worldwide every year.

Minute for Peace Day occurs on the Winter Solstice (in the Northern Hemisphere). In ancient history the Winter Solstice was a time for rejoicing. The days before the Winter Solstice kept getting shorter. There was fear this would continue and leave the world in darkness. But on the December Solstice they started getting longer. Now people knew the dead leaves on the trees would yield their place to new leaves in the spring.

It's amazing how many different views are expressed about the issues which separate us. Too often we reject those who differ with us. The

---

2. From Steinfels, "Pacem in Terris: A Retrospective": "Two years after the encyclical appeared, in February 1965, the Center for the Study of Democratic Institutions made it the centerpiece of an imposing conference, the International Convocation on Peace in New York City. Twenty two hundred scholars, clergy, statesmen, and peace activists attended, along with hundreds of reporters. Speakers and panelists included U Thant, the Secretary-General of the UN, which had just gone into extended recess, unable to resolve a dispute about payment of dues, Vice-President Hubert Humphrey, Adlai Stevenson, George Kennan, Abba Eban, Eugene McCarthy, the editor of Pravda, and a host of European, Asian, and African leaders whose names were as well known then as Jacques Chirac's and Nelson Mandela's are today." See Reed, *Pacem in Terris*.

message of Christmas was peace and good will—to all people. Everyone can agree that we need peace on Earth, and unite in support of a Minute for Peace Day that will stimulate minutes for peace every day on radio and TV worldwide. This is the way to change the global state of mind from fear to faith, from despair to hope.

Let each individual who believes in the power of prayer, of goodwill, join with others on Minute for Peace Day—December 22, conscious of being linked with others throughout the world on that day, as they pray for peace, talk about the way to peace, and purpose peace in their hearts and minds.

To people of every religion it will be a means to realize the potentials of their faith, that if they agree at the same time, for the same purpose, they can ask what they will and it will be done. On Minute for Peace Day they will ask, in love, for peaceful progress in their lives and throughout the world. To humanists, this will be a time to ponder peace, to celebrate peace with a new awareness of our common humanity.

On this great day of opportunity a new faith, hope, and love can replace the dead leaves of the past millennia with truth, justice, and co-operation for our common good. Together we can provide a new beginning for the human family—a time to forgive, forget, and start anew.

THE UNITED NATIONS AND DAILY MINUTE FOR PEACE

The idea of a daily Minute for Peace on radio and TV was backed by the Mayor and City of San Francisco, who in 1965 sponsored my trip to New York where our Minute for Peace was featured at the 1964–1965 World's Fair. There was a UN Minute for Peace exhibit at the Fair, where 50,000 people signed that they would think and pray for peace for one minute every day.

The Minute for Peace exhibit at the 1965 World's Fair increased interest and resulted in daily Minute for Peace broadcasts on many radio stations. These featured the ringing of the UN Peace Bell, and a statement by a world leader about ways to foster peace and understanding. This was followed by a request that listeners add their prayer and commitment to help foster peaceful progress on our planet.

This resulted in a great deal of interest in other places, particularly at the United Nations. The UN connection developed as follows.

In February, 1965, I was invited to attend the *Pacem in Terris* (Peace on Earth) conference in New York City, where a distinguished group of world leaders considered ways to peace in the context of Pope John XXIII's famous encyclical.

In the final session of the conference, Dr. Jerome Frank spoke out spontaneously for the idea of "Minute for Peace" and urged implementation of the idea as one practical step toward the great goal the conference was discussing. As a result I was invited to the home of Paul V. Hoffman, Director of the UN Special Fund, along with Altheya Youngman, who had come from San Francisco to help advance "Minute for Peace." Hoffman's help enabled us to gain support in the United Nations.

Again my faith was challenged. If the movement was to gain widest acceptance, no one less than UN Secretary-General U Thant would suffice to produce the first of a series of broadcast messages. I was told that such a thing was impossible. A dozen reasons of policy and precedent were cited.

I called the Secretary-General's assistant, Mr. C. V. Narasimhan. He seemed anxious to help. He suggested that since "Minute for Peace" was an official project of San Francisco, and since the Secretary-General was shortly to go there for the twentieth anniversary of the signing of the UN Charter, Narasimhan would get the message from U Thant if I could get Mr. Robert Gros, the chairman of the UN Charter program in San Francisco, to request it.

My heart leapt with joy, for Robert Gros was a cherished friend of long standing and one of the staunch supporters of "Minute for Peace." A phone call got his cooperation and shortly after that, the Secretary-General gave us a message that captured effectively the whole meaning of "Minute for Peace."

Thus it was that, on June 26, 1965, the twentieth anniversary of the signing of the United Nations Charter, UN Secretary-General U Thant proclaimed Minute for Peace Day and issued a Minute for Peace message. The message was broadcast on all major United States radio networks, by United Nations radio, by networks in other countries, and by international short wave radio. Releases went all over the world asking people to join in a Minute for Peace. U Thant's message was as follows:

> We live in a world of noise, yet our conscience is called the still small voice. As Dag Hammarskjold once pointed out, "We all have within us a center of stillness surrounded by silence." Unless we heed our own conscience, we shall continue to be attracted by what is loud and garish and lose our sense of values. If there is

no peace in the world today, it is because there is no peace in the minds of men.

It is important, therefore, that all of us should determine to set aside some time each day to commune with ourselves, to talk with our own still small voices, to devote even one minute for thoughts of peace and goodwill.

The "Minute for Peace" message played in many parts of the world. It was followed by Minute for Peace recordings by many other world leaders—messages from United Nations ambassadors such as Alex Quaison-Sackey of Ghana, Britain's Lord Caradon, Chief Adebo of Nigeria, Dr. Cuevas Cancino of Mexico, Awad El Kony of the United Arab Republic, Michael Comay of Israel, the late Adlai Stevenson and other notables such as Paul V. Hoffman and anthropologist Margaret Mead. With special permission of the Holy See, we broadcast a most compelling "Minute for Peace" containing part of Pope Paul VI's message from his Peace Mass in Yankee Stadium.

A few years ago I woke up one morning with a song going through my mind that I remembered from the past. It was written by a young man who heard me speak in the Las Vegas Chamber of Commerce back in 1965. I was then speaking about our Minute for Peace program which had obtained some global attention. The young man, whose name I don't remember, said he was a song writer and would like to write a Minute for Peace song. I said that would be fine—and the next morning he came to me with the words and music for his Minute for Peace song—". . . a moment of peace will engulf the world, one minute each day of the year."

From nations a wind is rising,
Carrying a message above.
Let's join our voices together,
In a minute of peace and of love.
Together we'll join for the joy of the world,
Our countries will have no fear
A moment of peace will engulf the world,
One minute each day of the year.
Rise up and stand on your feet one and all.
Join with your friends as they answer the call.
One mighty voice, crying aloud . . . for wars to end.
Peace among men!

THE PEACE BELL

The Minute for Peace broadcasts also included messages by the children in the United Nations International School (UNIS) in New York City. This reminds me about the UN Peace Bell.

The Peace Bell is a bell which until a year ago stood under a Japanese pagoda in front of the United Nations Secretariat building (the big tall UN building) in New York City. The Peace Bell has a beautiful history. Before Japan was a member, the Japanese Observer for the UN suggested creating this Peace Bell. A man who had been through Hiroshima wanted to promote world peace and so he collected coins from children all over the world. The Bell was cast from the pennies and coins given by the children of over sixty countries. It was presented by the UN Association of Japan to the UN in June, 1954.

In 1966, I was working in New York City, but not at the UN. I never worked directly for the UN. I had an office across the street in the UN Church Center. But I always sought to give my ideas to UN officials. I obtained a permanent pass to the UN through an application.

One day I was curious about the Peace Bell. Back in those days the UN didn't have the kind of security that they have now. I was standing nearby taking some photographs, and I accidentally touched the striker and clanged the bell. The overtone on it was like "da da da daaah" in Beethoven's 5th Symphony. It had that kind of tone to it. Honestly, the tone was so beautiful it sent a chill up and down my spine! I suddenly thought that people everywhere should hear this bell, more than any other in the world, as it symbolizes peace. Yet no official use had hitherto been made of it.

So I spoke to officials of the United Nations and obtained special permission from the Secretary-General to record it for "Minute for Peace." He arranged for seven of the children from UNIS to ring the bell ceremoniously. He chose October 4th, the anniversary of the Pope's visit to the United Nations, and the Feast Day of St. Francis. Together with Monsignor Giovanetti, Japanese Ambassador Matsui, and other UN officials, the children joined in striking the Peace Bell.

Thus, its first official use was for Minute for Peace, and now this Bell tolls on all our Earth Day programs with our prayer that, wherever it is heard, it will help bring people to thoughts of peace and goodwill.

In the more than fifty years we have had the Peace Bell at the United Nations, it has inspired many successful efforts for peace. The wonderful sound of the Peace Bell speaks to our hearts. It adds meaning to our words and strengthens our cause.

There have been efforts to install a similar peace bell in other locations. I inaugurated the Peace Bell in Austria on March 20, 1996. This Peace Bell, like the one in New York, was given by Japan in 1995. It is located in the Main Plaza of the Vienna International Center, Vienna, Austria.

I have tried to persuade UN leaders that the Peace Bell is their most important public relations tool for peace and the United Nations.

The Peace Bell at the United Nations has contributed more than words to the efforts for peace. It moves our hearts with all the memories that it brings. May each Anniversary of the UN Peace Bell inspire a global turn towards peace. Every time the Peace Bell rings, it signals a silent minute of thought or prayer; a time for people to join in global unity and personal vows for peaceful resolution of conflict, and a time for understanding and good will in all our relationships. Since 1966 the beautiful sound of the Peace Bell has reminded us more than words that the way of peace is the way to a better future.

CONSCIENCE AND PEACE

To help bring peace we must consider the factors of thought and emotion that are common to all humans, recognizing the basic values that are broadly shared throughout the world—the desire for truth, love, equality, and freedom. We all bleed red blood; we all can feel pain and experience joy. Awareness of these shared values can help provide a basic sense of unity, and hope.

The record of great achievements in history would suggest that our growing knowledge of the outer world must be aided by a return to the inner sources of direction, be they God, intuition, or conscience. A quickened conscience with a global view tends to further world unity and cooperation. Long term and enlightened self interest would suggest that each individual follow his own conscience in love and service with wonder and daring, knowing that this will shape his own soul and give it integrity and character; a soul which can, by the grace of God or power of love, finally depart this life with the peace and joy that comes from giving and growing. Saints and sages, and common folk, have proven this true.

While many terrible crimes have been committed in the name of conscience, by far the greatest contribution to human progress has been the result of acts of conscience. There are those who believe that seeking and following their own deepest conviction is the best course, even though it may be distorted by unrecognized factors of prejudice or pride; and that the poorly instructed conscience is better than no conscience, and will improve. Within every community there are men and women of conscience.

Midst the bureaucratic structures of politics, business, and education, there are today a growing host of men and women who, when making decisions, turn unselfishly within to their God, or inner voice, and whose highest authority is their own sovereign conscience. People of conscience who balance intuition and information usually find better answers. Their mostly unofficial and independent actions can lead to essential changes needed in our global society. Let us recognize their value and let them know they are not alone.

As we each share our concerns and commitments let us look for common ground, for what we can honestly approve in those who differ with us. Let us seek to recognize and encourage the quickened conscience in all people.

Now is the time for people to unite. We can and shall bring balance and harmony into our diversity. We can and shall care for our Earth and for one another.

Whenever the Peace Bell is rung, we ask that each person turn to the highest they know in silent prayer, thought, or meditation. Let the ringing of the Peace Bell bring to each person who hears its peal a deep awareness of the ties that bind all living things to one another. This will aid the special ties of love and respect among the many people of conscience who are seeking better ways to help take care of our planet. Together, we can further peace, justice, and a sustainable future.

With the ringing of the Peace Bell let there be a new united dedication to the great task of Earth's renewal, and to the work it requires in our own block or neighborhood.

To succeed, spiritual help is needed. There is documented evidence that great changes for the better have resulted from spiritual awakenings when people prayed. Pray that the Peace Bell message of peace will bring a global change of heart. In this critical moment of danger and opportunity, let's put aside our differences and warmly support what all can agree on. As we turn a global page and move along in the new millennium, here is an idea that all can accept and act upon. We can then end history's long, sad, evil record and realize the age-long hope for the new day "where the lion will lie down with the lamb and the nations will learn war no more."[3]

"As a man thinks, so is he." Awareness and discipline in your unconscious mind is a key to character. Daily prayer or meditation and quiet times for reflection are food for the soul.

"Seek first the kingdom of God." Since God is love, we should seek the rule of his love and wisdom on our planet.

Each year on Earth Day, March 20-21, at the moment of the equinox, the United Nations Peace Bell rings. With simultaneous observances in other countries, this signals two minutes of silent prayer or dedication—a moment in the mind and heart for commitment to peaceful actions that will aid the care of Earth, of its life and its people. This event calls attention to the anxious concern of young and old and their hope for a better future. The only way to eliminate the fears and anxiety of young people is to mend our ways and work through peaceful cooperation to repair the damage we have done to the Earth they will inherit. Many children are saying, "Please save our planet." If we choose now to make the care of Earth a first priority, we can overcome their fears with assurance of a healthy bountiful planet.

To this end, let us begin Earth Day and every new day with silent devotion and love of Earth, seeking what each of us can do to make our children's hope for the future come true.

Our dedication now to this great task is imperative, for tomorrow may be too late. Let us accept the challenge and thereby speed the day when bells all over the world will joyously ring in global peace.

IMPACT ON CHILDREN AND OTHER PEOPLE AROUND THE GLOBE

There are probably 500 children of the delegates and employees in the United Nations International School. There are children from nearly all the countries of Earth. I remember, when recording their voices for Minute for Peace, we heard some heartwarming truths. Let me repeat some of them:

"Peace is when frogs sleep on water lilies"—Perry Fan, Chinese kindergartner.

"Peace is when flowers say hello to the sun"—Debbie Oppenheim, Swedish kindergartner.

---

3. Mixture of verses in Isaiah 2:4 and 11:6-9.

"All people can live together in peace as a family. We here at the United Nations School feel we are a family"—Ahmed El Bouri, Libyan boy.

"Peace starts with yourself, inside yourself. If you are happy, then with your friends you will be happy and will not fight"—Alexandra Pollyea, American girl.

Isn't it wonderful? Out of the mouths of babes . . . .

Many of these thoughts by children were distributed by UNICEF, and have been broadcast in Europe, Cairo, All India Radio, Australia and the U.S.A. Children in the United Nations International School are demonstrating the true potential for all people of every race, color, and creed.

We need to know that peace is contagious, and get excited about the new world that is being born—and joyfully contribute our unifying thought and prayers individually, and in our churches, clubs, civic organizations, and women's groups all over the world.

I believe peace is coming. It is in the air. We can help speed the day when the full purposes of God can be realized in a new age of wonder and beauty.

Working with Minute for Peace at the United Nations led to my idea for a global day for planet Earth. This Earth Day would be celebrated each year on the March equinox. From Earth Day came the Earth Trustee idea and agenda, as discussed in later chapters.

In fact, Minute for Peace became the *centerpiece* of Earth Day, when we invite people worldwide to join in two minutes of silent prayer or reflection, as the Peace Bell at the United Nations is rung to celebrate the beginning of spring.

MINUTE FOR PEACE POEM

by John McConnell

Dedicated to the memory of Yehudi Menuhin:

It was three days before Christmas—And on valley and hill
A Minute for Peace—Joined hearts in good will.
We are one human family—Was the message brought
By the pictures on TV—Where before people fought.
This day then began—A Campaign for Earth
To eliminate poverty—Pollution and dearth.
For when people and groups—Seek a goal all can share
They will treat neighbor and nature—With heartfelt care.

Our planet is suffering—From shortsighted greed
But as Trustees of Earth—We'll meet our Earth's need.

PRAYERS FOR PEACE IN KASHMIR

The idea of Minute for Peace became popular and played a role in ending the war between Pakistan and India in 1965. United Nations Delegates from both sides publicly joined in silent prayer. They were asked to meditate on peace and good will, with determination to overcome hatred and injury with the power and benefit of reconciliation and cooperation. On one night in particular, in a UN Security Council special meeting, they declared peace.

War had broken out between India and Pakistan on August 16, 1965. When the crisis arose over Kashmir, Altheya Youngman, who had once lived in Kashmir, felt we should relate our "Minute for Peace" broadcast to the crisis. Altheya had known Sheikh Abdullah, who was then Governor. His son had often gone swimming from her houseboat. Now the Sheik, known as the "Lion of Kashmir," was in prison in India. His son, now grown, was one of the Pakistani delegates.

Both Altheya and I had many contacts with members of the Pakistani and Indian Missions to the United Nations. We knew the bitterness that existed between the two nations. Knowing members of both UN Missions, Altheya and I felt close to the situation. We obtained a record—a collector's item—which carried the voice of Gandhi with a searching challenge for peace.

A friend of Altheya in the United Nations, Nazri Rashed, agreed to record an introduction to Gandhi's voice. This was most fortunate, for he was both a distinguished poet from Pakistan and the Information Officer for International Cooperation Year at the United Nations.

This "Minute" was a most effective peacemaker. It was featured in several "Minute for Peace" programs in New York City and at the World's Fair on the occasion of Gandhi's birthday. In these programs, citizens of both Pakistan and India joined in singing Gandhi's favorite song, the Ran Duhn.

On the night that the Security Council met to consider a call for a cease-fire, we entered the Council Chamber and remained there until the cease-fire was secured after three in the morning.

The room was charged with tension as Indian and Pakistani delegates maneuvered for advantage. Words of bitter outrage and anger were hurled from one side of the table to the other. I looked around and realized that less than twenty observers were watching this most important meeting. I wondered how many of them were praying, as we were, for those who held the power of decision. I only wished there were others in those empty seats who knew how to pray.

The great decisions in that Chamber are made by people with human passions like you and me. They have their good days and their bad days. They can be influenced by the Holy Spirit as easily as the people you meet in everyday business life.

I realize there are many prayers offered each day, in a general way, that guidance will be given to the people in the United Nations. But we know that the prayers that work are fervent prayers, specific prayers, prayers by people who are close to those who are prayed for, or at least aware of the problems they are facing.

I wonder how many Christians were awake that night, praying for these men, and praying about this grave problem. If there were many, it seems that a few of them who had access to the Council Chamber would have been there.

Now it was after midnight. The men below us faced a crisis that could easily escalate into wide-spread warfare and multiply by a thousand times the deadly carnage that had already taken place. I was deep in intercessory prayer, striving to bring into that room the consciousness of the presence of God. I prayed that wisdom would be given our Ambassador Goldberg, who was Chairman, as well as the British Ambassador Lord Caradon and Soviet Ambassador Federenko in their efforts toward reconciliation— that they would hear the still, small voice.

I do not know how much our prayers contributed to the success of the meeting that night. I do know that Ambassador Goldberg surpassed himself in handling it, that Ambassador Federenko spoke words of understanding and conciliation, that the violence of the disputants was gradually tempered, and that a reluctant but welcome cease-fire was finally obtained. I shall never forget the experience and the conviction it strengthened in me that great power is released whenever people agree in prayer.

IMPACTING THE FUTURE

God has given us a strategy to advance the cause of peace around the world. It is the Minute for Peace. God has led us to work beside the United Nations where representatives of the nations of the world meet to pursue peace. He has given us the wholehearted co-operation of influential public people.

We are taught that the greater the number of people who agree in faith, the greater the power of prayer. If we really believe this, why not link our thoughts around the world in an intensive faith for peace. "Minute for Peace" can provide the vehicle for doing this. Through the use of modern media, the idea can quickly spread around the world.

We have the strategy, and we have the plans to make this work. Every day brings increasing evidence that we can get massive participation by the communications media in every continent. Soon people in all countries will know there is a movement for peace in which each person can participate in ways he can approve. All that is needed is a daily thought for peace shared with neighbors and friends. As this becomes a minute of good will observed in unison around the world, it will move the leaders and those whom they lead in the paths of peace. Then the methods and techniques of understanding and accord will find their rightful place in the great council chambers of nations as well as at the hearth of a humble home.

Can a "Minute for Peace" become a minute of goodwill observed in unison around the world? Will it irresistibly move the leaders of men into paths of peace? Will the hearts and minds of people in all countries be touched by the Holy Spirit with the peace and love that bring men into the Kingdom of God? If Minute for Peace is going to work, it must move at the level of Resurrection. It must be an instrument for the actual coming of the Kingdom. It must be related to events and real issues of history that are now coming into focus.

What has happened so far with Minute for Peace and Earth Day seemed utterly impossible at first. Who knows what may happen if we put our faith to work and use the power of the Spirit to solve the problem of the sword?

The year 2003 was the 40th anniversary of the first Minute for Peace, and the year seemed like an important anniversary. Now in 2011 the need is even more urgent to pray for peaceful reconciliation of conflict. How much can the wars in Iraq and Afghanistan be shortened if we all pray for peace? In 2007, I was praying about the war in Iraq and got the scripture Isa 48:20, which says to "flee Babylon." To me this means "flee Baghdad" (ancient Babylon). President Bush used the power of money and military might to murder his enemies. Jesus commanded his disciples to love their enemies, and the power of his love can convert them and make them our friends.

The actions in Iraq of Bush and Hussein made skeletons of their enemies. Both Washington and Baghdad became like ancient Babylon.

People can honor Minute for Peace in some new way. Actions good and bad begin in the mind, and if we can reach the minds of the people of the world with the truth of thinking and acting the best way we know how to further peace on our planet, then we will have a great future. And remember, by peace we mean non-violent resolution of conflict. We stop the problem without killing the aggressor. I think this would be a wonderful thing.

Sam Shoemaker, co-founder of Alcoholics Anonymous, had the AA group feature the story of how we achieved peace between India and Pakistan in 1966.

DAILY MINUTES FOR PEACE

Every radio and TV station should program a daily "Minute for Peace." A voice would state, "In this *minute for peace* let us join our hearts and minds, each in our own way, with faith and commitment to peaceful actions today and every day." This would be followed by appropriate music or sounds of nature.

Each individual who believes in the power of prayer, of faith, of goodwill, can then join each day at the time of Minute for Peace, conscious of being linked with others throughout the world at that very moment as they pray for peace, or purpose for peace in their hearts and minds.

To humanists, this will be a time to ponder peace, to celebrate peace with a new awareness of our common humanity.

To people of every religion it will be a means to realize the potentials of their faith, that if they agree at the same time, for the same purpose, they can ask what they will and it will be done. Each day during Minute for Peace, they will ask, in love, for peaceful progress in their lives and throughout the world.

These daily Minutes for Peace, or Earth Minutes, will be an opportunity to join in a spirit of love. For adversaries, it will encourage each to take the first step toward reconciliation. It will encourage many to proceed with faith that lasting peace will come, not by the sword, but by the power of the spirit, by the power of love unfeigned for those who appear to be, or may be, enemies. We will then see a change in the global state of mind from conflict and fear to peace and goodwill, from "Earth Kill" to "Earth Care."

To all, Earth's "Minutes for Peace" will be a time for all people, as Earth Trustees, to dedicate and consecrate this ground we call our Earth home to a new birth of freedom and good will, a new promise of peace to our children and to the whole human family. We are one human family and together we can save our planet. Help make the new millennium an Earth Trustee Millennium!

A 33-DAY MINUTE FOR PEACE CAMPAIGN EVERY YEAR

When President Kennedy suddenly died on November 22, 1963, the whole world shared a feeling of compassion at the loss of this one man. This was above and apart from any political consideration of his life and work.

If, through modern communications, an equivalent feeling for peace could be generated, new solutions to global problems would be quickly found. Perhaps we would finally demonstrate that the power of the spirit is greater than the power of the sword.

First in 1967, and again in 2003 (the fortieth anniversary of the death of President Kennedy), I proposed that November 22 should begin a global 33-day campaign for world peace. I now propose that such a campaign be mounted every year. It would lead up to the Christmas season, a time of peace.

During this proposed campaign all the people of the world are asked to join each day in thoughts, words, and deeds of peace. To further this purpose, I propose that the United Nations request leaders of all nations to urge their citizens' participation in an all-out effort to create a global climate for peace. This period would be declared a "season of peace" in which man's best hopes for the future would be proclaimed and aided.

It would be—

a time for deeds of compassion, friendship, and cooperation;

a time for emphasis on governmental and non-governmental activities that heal, build, and unite;

a time to remind ourselves that if we work together in good will, this planet, this nest in the stars, will be a happy home for the whole human family.

It is further proposed that to implement these aims, all communications media assist this campaign with headlines for peace, with human interest stories of the many great endeavors which further understanding and cooperation. And that the United Nations request the people of the world to acclaim as peacemakers all those who, during this period, refrain from condemnation of others and who refrain—even at loss of personal or national advantage—from acts of violence, and whose deeds reflect the pursuit of harmony and accord.

This will be a period to accent the common elements of different points of view. For this purpose all people will be invited to take at least a minute each day to think, each in his own way, about peace and good will.

In this daily Minute for Peace, people of all religions who believe in the power of prayer will be joined together and at the same time joined with others who believe in the power of thought and mind, and also with those humanitarians of no religion who believe in the value of serious reflective thinking about peace. In this way, individual thoughts and prayers for peace will be strengthened by the growing consciousness of being joined by all the others.

This campaign will begin on November 22, and conclude on December 24 with an Hour of Peace, in which the artists of the world will join the children of the world in a global radio and television broadcast of good will.

Christmas Eve will then be the greatest celebration in history, with new faith in the meaning of Christmas, "Peace on Earth, good will to men."

This campaign can bring to the global mind a shift from the present dangerous, mutual fear to a new and growing measure of mutual trust. Then we will begin to truly build the new world of which poets and prophets have dreamed—a world of freedom, order, beauty, and peace.

EARTH MINUTES

On Earth Day at the United Nations in 1991, I proposed that we have three Earth Minutes every day. To provide a better future in the new millennium, radio, websites, and TV in the entire world should broadcast the *daily* ringing of Peace Bells at one or more of the following times: 0300, 1100 and 1900 GMT (converted to local time in each time zone). This will provide daily, global simultaneous silent prayers for peace wherever there is conflict.

This will be a time to thank God for answered prayers—and provide scholars and scientists, as well as the rest of us, evidence that prayer works. "Oh the faith that works by love, will move the mountains when we pray. Oh the faith that works by love, will turn the darkness into day."

The idea would be to have these Earth Minutes without words. Audio would include locally-produced music or bells or sounds of nature. The bells could include the UN Peace Bell, the Liberty Bell, Big Ben, or Tibetan bells. The video would include views of Earth from space, or animals or nature scenes such as mountain scenery, and participation of children. The content could vary, with various images and sounds that inspire reflection and prayer, but the times would be consistent. Message boards on the Internet could post local times around the world, and publicize both support and reports of conflict resolution and results.

Each Earth Minute would make it known that at that minute, if people would turn deep within, and offer prayer for peace, they would be linking their prayer with hundreds of millions around the world. You would know that anytime you heard Earth Minutes announced on radio or TV, your mind and thought would be connected with the whole human family, with people all over the world who were at that moment thinking Earth Minutes, and were thinking about what they could do to be responsible Earth Trustees and caretakers and protectors of our planet. This would help convert us to awareness of our planet. We would think of ourselves as one Earth, one human family. We would be amazed at how many things would then be done to diminish destruction of our planet, and to improve relationships between groups of people, between nation-states, and between religious groups.

To aid inner commitment, I urge all radio and TV stations worldwide to program daily Earth Minutes When you hear an Earth Minute announced, you can link your thought, your prayer, with others all over the world. This can help change the global state of mind—from fear to faith. The daily Minute for Peace on radio and TV programs will foster peaceful thoughts and actions with appropriate music and images.

At other times during the day, there can be reports and features about Earth-care solutions, planned or in progress. This can provide a new sense of Earth Trustee identity that will tap the best of our personal religious convictions, diminish fear, hate, greed, and lust, and assure an era of peaceful progress.

Also, there should be an 800-information number for Earth Trustees, for Earth Day and Minute for Peace, that would direct people to other information resources that would give them specific help in these activities. Libraries should set up exhibits that would feature these approaches. They should be themes in school curricula and in churches. In every institution on our planet there should now be an effort to say and do the things and have the kind of thoughts that would contribute to a new global state of mind and aid in the rejuvenation of our planet.

MINUTE FOR PEACE DAY, 9–11, AND PEARL HARBOR

The horrific event on 9–11 in 2001 showed us the power of hate. But love is more powerful than hate and December 22 provides a special opportunity to prove it.

Each year since then, December 22 provides the opportunity to turn the World Trade Center tragedy into a new beginning in the whole human adventure, and assure a peaceful prosperous future for the whole human family.

Pearl Harbor Day on December 7 reminds us of the terrible tragedy that occurred in most of the world when modern weapons were used to settle differences between powerful nations. Pearl Harbor was followed by World War II and Hiroshima.

On December 7, at the beginning of the Christmas season, we usually are shown vivid horrible images on TV depicting what happened at Pearl Harbor. But today we know that "hatred does not cease by hatred at any time; hatred ceases by love."[4] Gandhi and others have demonstrated non-violent methods of opposing what is wrong.

Martin Luther King Jr. described the power of love in his book, *Strength To Love*[5]—and gave his life to prove it. Now, strength to "kill" is being advocated as the way to stop violence. Hundreds of billions are being spent on armaments. If half as much money were spent on education to eliminate the causes of war, there would be no more wars.

Let's reverse Pearl Harbor.

4. Muller, *Lectures on the Science of Religion.*
5. King, *Strength to Love.*

To settle differences, war is advocated far more than peace. The search engine google.com has 1,310,000,000 items when you type in "war" and only 403,000,000 when you type in "peace."

Actions good or bad begin in the mind. Here is a way to reverse the damage done to people's thinking by what happened at Pearl Harbor and on 9–11. December not only marks Peal Harbor Day, it is also the month we celebrate Christmas. The Minute for Peace Day on December 22 is just three days before Christmas. Since we entered the new millennium, Christmas is of increasing importance, with its message of "peace and good will."

We can also reverse the damage done by media's headlines for violence, and media's silence about the proven benefits of forgiveness, compassion, and cooperation for common goals. One factor in the World Trade Center tragedy was the media's failure to feature the work of the Franciscans and many other groups who are seeking the peaceful nurture of people and planet.

Let's turn the tables on Pearl Harbor and 9–11 by joining worldwide in Minutes for Peace all day on December 22, three days before Christmas, the same day as the first Minute for Peace in 1963. Christmas can then be a turning toward peace with our neighbor and our world. Let every radio and TV station fill the day with minutes of music and words that inspire peaceful actions. Help us unite as one human family in new understanding and care for this wonderful nest in the stars, planet Earth, our home.

A call by Pope Benedict XVI and heads of government could persuade TV networks and others to promote the December 22 Minute for Peace and obtain global participation. Minute for Peace Day can then be a prelude and launch pad for the annual Great Day of Earth—the March 20 Earth Day. We ask the Pope, the leaders of all countries, corporations, and religions to back this initiative with their words and actions.

All that is required for Minute for Peace to succeed is for people to know about it. Talk about it. Pray about it. Spread the word. Then with the power of the words "Love one another" we will reverse Pearl Harbor and 9–11 and welcome the beginning of an era of peaceful progress in this new millennium.

On December 22 (Minute for Peace Day) and on every other day of the year, talk peace, think peace, pray for peace, have faith for peace all over the world—in the home, at work, in corporations, and in global relations of countries—in all human institutions.

30

Earth Day

THE IDEA

IT WAS WHILE WORKING on Minute for Peace that I came up with the idea of Earth Day. Holidays around the world brought people together for partisan purposes. Why not a great global holiday in support of our common desire for "peace, justice, and the care of Earth"?

The concept of Earth Day, which I discussed with Margaret Mead and others at the United Nations in 1968 and 1969, was developed with the objective of providing a global Holy Day that would tap the best in the human heart, and help people identify with the whole human family and our key role as caretakers of Earth.

Throughout the many decades of my life previous to my founding of Earth Day, first observed on March 21, 1970, I pondered how to peacefully resolve the many differences that confront our world, and how we could diminish confrontation. My key solution was to focus attention on the most important common ground and the positive values shared by adversaries.

National holidays, as well as religious ones, are special days and a good example of people coming together to peacefully celebrate. National and religious days will always continue.

However, because of our new technology and our view of Earth provided by our venture into space, we now know we are all one human family and have only one Earth. To aid global unity, we need one annual holiday—observed by all, as a global holiday or holy day.

And so in 1970 we drew attention to a time that is celebrated by the entire world—the first day of spring (the vernal equinox). This is nature's moment of the equinox when the Sun crosses the celestial equator, causing the length of day and night to be equal—a state of equilibrium throughout the Earth. This is the true *Earth Day*, not because I selected it, but because it originates in the Earth's own rotation and revolution. It is nature's choice.

The vernal equinox is a distinct annual astronomical occurrence in our solar system. It is a special moment that affects nature on a grand scale, an event that predates mankind and one that will last for as long as the Earth spins on its axis.

This is nature's inspiring moment of equipoise. At this special time, a six-month-long "day" will begin at the North Pole and a six-month-long "night" at the South Pole. This is the occasion when night and day are equal all over the world.

The first day of spring is a divine symbol and promise of new life. Plants that have died will now be reborn in the seeds they have left. Caterpillars will change into butterflies. Spring is the time for new life and new beginnings.

As our planet progresses in its 365¼ day revolution around the Sun, it passes through two equinoctial points where the length of night and day are equal. In the Northern Hemisphere, where the great land and population masses are located, the March equinox marks the end of winter and the beginning of spring—the time when the days start getting longer in preparation for a season of rebirth. The autumnal equinox begins on or about September 23 and brings longer nights and colder weather.

Thus the ancient vernal equinox is a symbol of Earth equilibrium, renewal, and rebirth. It provides the ideal means for illustrating and dramatizing, in a "new-Earth Day," the new merging ecological worldview. Even before the Druids witnessed the celestial drama of the vernal equinox from their Stonehenge observatory, man's folklore contained records of celebrations that paid homage to nature at springtime. It is exceedingly doubtful that future generations will fail to mark the significance of a vernal equinox Earth Day.

Earth Day means more than just environment—it means "equilibrium in nature, in social systems, and in the minds of men." In taking our cue from nature and using the equinox, a billion-year symbol of unity and balance, we can eventually obtain a world community event uniting our common concern for our Earth home.

The first day of spring, a day that historically has been celebrated by people of every creed and culture, is a day worthy of being a holiday for all of Earth's people.

The first Earth Day was celebrated in the United States on March 21, 1970, primarily in cities in California. The original Earth Day was directed toward achieving peace, justice, and responsible stewardship of the precious web of life that covers the globe.

The term Earth Day was first used for the March 21, 1970 event in California. While the name was an obvious choice at that time, I have never seen a dated document, letter, or printed article that used the term before we published plans for Earth Day in the early fall of 1969—even before our announcement of Earth Day at the November UNESCO Conference on the Environment in San Francisco.

This really puzzles me, for it seemed a simple obvious term. But then I also never understood why no one advocated an Earth Flag before I designed and flew them in 1969.

Earth Day has been celebrated each year thereafter at the United Nations, bringing attention to its original purpose: peace, justice, and the care of Earth. Earth Day at the United Nations has brought together leaders, whose countries were at war with each other, to ring the Peace Bell—and hear great proponents of peaceful methods for conciliation speak at the same ceremony.

The highlight of each ceremony has been the ringing of the Peace Bell, and the inclusion of a Minute for Peace. Indeed, these ceremonies have been a boost for efforts being made for peace. For example, on Earth Day in 1987 the Peace Bell was rung by the representatives of three different cultures and religions. They were Chester Morris, from the United States Mission to the United Nations, Valentine Karymov, from the USSR Mission to the United Nations, and Sheikh Ali Mukhtar, representing the Muslim World League.

In striving for an annual global Earth Day, it is hoped that the unique and beautiful values of the vernal equinox will bring participation by everyone who desires a maximum united effort for a balanced and healthy environment.

THE FOUNDING OF EARTH DAY

I had been working with the United Nations with Minute for Peace. In September of 1969, Anna and I were back in Oakland, California, at my mother's home. We had traveled in August from New York to California by train. We had come for the wedding of Cary, my son from my first marriage. While traveling, I worked on the concept of Earth Day, a day for planet Earth.

I was impressed by the fact that "We set out to explore space and discovered Earth." The view from space set me on my Earth Day/Earth Trustee mission. It is strange how all these things interlink, but I was on the phone recently with the President of the Peace in Space Organization. I love the uniting effect of joining the astronauts in seeing the planet as only one Earth and seeing one human family. If we ever get that concept really understood around the world, we'd have a better future.

I had talked to people at the United Nations about the idea that we should have a global holiday. Holidays are important in every culture. In the United States, we have Christmas and Independence Day. Why not have one day that's for the whole planet, called Earth Day. Everyone I talked to about it thought it was a great idea.

So when we were out in San Francisco, I thought that maybe we could get San Francisco—the city of Saint Francis—to start Earth Day. The Mayor and others there knew me. I called up Peter Tamaris, who was Chairman of the Board of Supervisors. I told him my idea that we should have this annual day—we already had a Minute for Peace—why not have a *day for peace*, call it Earth Day. He said, "Look, John, that's great!" He said, "You write a proclamation for Earth Day and we'll kick it off here in San Francisco, the City of St. Francis. We'll try to get global attention for it. That would be wonderful!"

So, I sat down to write the Proclamation. And I wondered what day Earth Day should be, which was still a question in my mind. I had before me a draft with an open space for the date. I thought of when we landed on the moon, the first Sputnik, St. Francis Day, etc. Nothing jelled, until suddenly I remembered Stonehenge.

I had been reading different things from different parts of history. I remembered that in ancient China their new year was on the March equinox, on the first day of spring. There was a sundial in China. It is constructed to play up that moment, that special moment of their new year. Then, I also discovered that Iran (Persia) and other ancient cultures had special celebrations on the spring equinox—for Iran it is their New Year, called Noruz. These things really came together. Festivals on the March equinox go back to Stonehenge, Persia, the Mayans, and early Chinese history. But what really triggered it was Stonehenge.

Stonehenge has special stones. They're so constructed that when the sunlight comes through the hole of one stone and shines in a certain way, it's the beginning of spring. So way back there, in ancient times, before modern civilization knew anything about it, these ancient people observed the March equinox in some fashion or other. And I thought, the March equinox, why that's the first day of spring. That's nature's symbol of renewal, of new beginnings—that should be Earth Day for the whole planet. And in a flash I said "Earth Day, vernal equinox."

When I realized this, I called my wife, who was washing dishes in the kitchen—I was in the living room—and told her, "I've got it! We're going to have Earth Day on March 21, the first day of spring!"

Exactly when I called her, our house started shaking. We had a minor earthquake at that very moment. I never could get over that. The heavens were responding, or the Earth was responding. It was October 1, 1969.

I then sat down and wrote a Proposed Earth Day Resolution and submitted it to Peter Tamaris on October 3, 1969.

The choice of the spring equinox for Earth Day provides common ground and aids cooperation among people seeking a better future for themselves and others, no matter where they live, and no matter what country they are from.

Earth Day occurs on the first day of spring—nature's moment of equipoise, when night and day are of equal length all over the world. Since early human history, this day has been recognized and observed in different ways as a beautiful symbol of new life and renewal.

The symbolism of Earth Day—the equilibrium and balance of the equinox—encourages and inspires independence and cooperation. The simultaneous global event deepens our sense of unity. It fosters a sense of rights and responsibilities in the protection and care of Earth. From Earth Day has come a growing consensus that every individual and institution should act as Earth Trustees, seeking what can be done in ecology, economics, and ethics to benefit people and planet. This will help us obtain a healthy, peaceful future and speed the day when bells will ring all over the world as we celebrate Earth Day, the Great Day of Earth.

The March Earth Day is the beginning of spring for most of the world's people, who live in the Northern Hemisphere. Those in the Southern Hemisphere observe the autumnal equinox in March. Thus, for everyone on Earth, Earth Day is a special geophysical event.

When I started Earth Day in 1970 I was concerned about this problem. We wanted Earth Day to be once a year and to have it on the first day of spring. To avoid confusion, I decided that, since most land and population is in the Northern Hemisphere, the March equinox would be Earth Day. The September equinox would be "Life Day."

However, our focus was on Earth Day, and as far as I know, not much was ever done with Life Day. I do remember that Richard Register published a pamphlet urging that both be observed. The September equinox was called "World Gratitude Day" by Lester Lindlay. Perhaps it should be called "Heaven Day" or something pertaining to what follows the end of our life.

We always encouraged everyone to celebrate the March equinox as Earth Day. When those in the Southern Hemisphere refer to it, they can mention that Earth Day is the first day of fall—an interesting counterpoint to spring in the Northern Hemisphere. This reflects the balance so eloquently referred to by a correspondent from Australia, who pointed out that

> We live on a round planet, where everything that is allowed to be, is in balance. Day here—night on the other side, summer here, winter there. Wherever we happen to be, the balance is found at the opposite place on the globe. So light balances dark, and death balances life.[1]

Some have said "April is warmer and better for outdoor events." Events to help the environment or other worthy causes can be at any time. But the idea of Earth Day is for a simultaneous global event. As far as weather is concerned, there is no day when weather is more suitable globally than other days.

In the United States weather is usually better in April—even better in June when World Environment Day (sponsored by the UN) occurs. In 1972 at the Stockholm Conference, Japan obtained support for a resolution calling for World Environment Day to be observed on June

1. Only the correspondent's first name is given here—Margaret. She wrote in 2001. Simon Reeves, personal communication.

5, the day the Stockholm Conference began. This happened without consideration or discussion of an equinox Earth Day. But on any given day you will find parts of the world that are freezing while others are too hot. Storms come at different times in different parts of the world. The advantages of the March equinox outweigh these difficulties.

The idea behind the spring date was not local convenience or comfortable weather, which varies from place to place, but a day suitable for international celebration. On this day, night and day are equal. This day is a billion year symbol of the balance of nature and the equilibrium we seek on Earth.

THE FIRST EARTH DAY CELEBRATION

So it was that in 1969 that I persuaded the City of San Francisco, which had supported Minute for Peace, to proclaim March 21, 1970 as Earth Day. San Francisco's Mayor Joseph Alioto issued the first Earth Day Proclamation, a beautiful Proclamation. Swarthmore College has this Proclamation and much more in the John McConnell Peace Archives.

The Earth Day in 1970 on March 21 was a great wonderful warm experience. The City of San Francisco was where Earth Day really began.

We obtained massive support in San Francisco for the 1970 March equinox Earth Day. The object was to mobilize people of every creed and culture to think and act as Trustees of Earth, "Seeking peace, justice, and the care of our planet."

The support that followed included participation by business, schools, churches, the Red Cross, the Sierra Club, the Junior Chamber of Commerce, and ecology organizations, highlighted by the proclamation from the Mayor. Other cities in California such as Oakland joined in observing the day. Places elsewhere in the United States also observed it. The University of California at Berkeley and at Davis had outstanding participation. During preparations for Earth Day in San Francisco, students from the University of California at Davis came to me. They ended up having a massive wonderful event, keeping with purpose and ideas that I put into Earth Day. Streets were closed and there was music, plus speeches and booths with environmental solutions.

The University of California at Davis celebrated the 1970 Earth Day with an all-night 12-hour Vigil of Creation. The program provided dance, theater, and music based on the twelve signs of the Zodiac, and climaxed at the equinox on Earth Day with a one-hour silent prayer vigil attended by over 1500 people of all major religions. The campus had a Global Village including an Avenue of Spring, a Street of Ecology, a Street of Crafts with Earth care products, and a Street of Mysteries. The campus also featured the Earth Flag, a new symbol of loyalty to our planet.

In San Francisco at Golden Gate Park, the city had a Tree Planting Ceremony, and their nursery provided plants which the Red Cross station wagons took to schools throughout the area for children to plant. Earth Day was featured in the papers and on radio and TV. KCBS TV observed a special Earth Hour, Year One, on Earth Day at 1900 UT (11:00 am PST). In this special hour there were views of Earth's wonders of life and resources—the balance of nature. This March 21, 1970 Earth Day was not a protest (as was the April 22, 1970 event), but a celebration focusing on solutions.

Coming right after the dramatic views of Earth from space and our landing on the Moon, Earth Day influenced many people to think about our planet with a totally new view of its problems and possibilities. A fundamental conceptual change began—perhaps as important as the Copernican revolution in thinking—the idea that we must now base all human behavior and future action on the fact of our planetary home and the nature of its interdependent life.

Earth Day is viewed by many as a major turning point in our awareness of our planet and our new responsibility to understand and take care of it.

ST. FRANCIS AND THE BIRTH OF EARTH DAY

The global celebration of Earth Day on March 20-21, the first day of spring, is directly related to St. Francis, the twelfth century mystic, Francis of Assisi, and the amazing results of his vision and life. The first Earth Day was inaugurated, as noted earlier, in San Francisco—The City of St. Francis. The City of San Francisco took its name from St. Francis. Were he here today, he would undoubtedly focus all his prayer and effort on achieving Earth Day's original purpose.

A little more about Earth Day will show the connection.

Earth Day is on the March equinox, which determines the annual date of Easter. Easter is the first Sunday after the first full moon following the March equinox.

Not only that, the March equinox is also the New Year in Iran and other Islamic countries, which makes possible attention for a common purpose—the sustainable care of Earth, with justice and peace for all.

Thus, Earth Day on the spring equinox weaves together the new beginnings of spring, the new beginnings of Easter, the new beginnings of the New Year as celebrated in many countries, and a global vision of peace, justice, and care of Earth. Realizing these connections will help us show real love for our world neighbors and the web of life that covers our globe.

The relation of St. Francis to Earth Day goes even deeper. St. Francis is the patron saint of ecology.[2] St. Francis also had a special passion for peace. I had long been familiar with the "Peace Prayer" of St. Francis: "Lord, make me an instrument of thy peace. Where there is hatred, let me sow love. . . ."[3]

We obtained backing not only of the Mayor, city officials, schools, and businesses, but also churches—a really all-out event with massive coverage in media. The event was backed by Catholic churches and by Franciscans, the Catholic order established by St. Francis. Participation also included synagogues and many other denominations. In succeeding Earth Days at the United Nations, we demonstrated that people of diverse creeds and cultures can leave room for their differences and come together for "peace, justice, and the care of Earth."

Another factor involving St. Francis in the choice of the date was my own history. In 1957 I obtained global attention for an editorial in my weekly North Carolina newspaper, *The Toe Valley View*. The first Sputnik Satellite had just been launched on October 4th. None of the media seemed to note that this date was the "Feast Day of St. Francis." And Sputnik was launched on this Feast Day by the then-Godless USSR! (The person who chose the date must have been a secret Christian.)

My editorial had called for a visible "Star of Hope" satellite. It would be launched as a symbol of hope to further understanding and peace on our planet. It obtained front page attention around the world.

---

2. In 1979, Pope John Paul II proclaimed St. Francis as the patron saint of ecology. See *Apostolic Letter Inter Sanctos*.

3. See http://www.shrinesf.org/prayers.htm#peace for the Peace Prayer of St. Francis, and information about the National Shrine of St. Francis on Vallejo Street near Columbus Avenue in North Beach, San Francisco.

My own study and prayer life led to the conviction that we needed a common purpose that would appeal to people of all creeds and cultures—and a way to get attention for it. We needed something that would end history's terrible record of war and injustice.

These thoughts involving St. Francis and the Star of Hope planted the seeds that eventually led to the first Earth Day being held in the City of St. Francis.

Another factor was my effort in 1963 to get global participation in a daily "Minute for Peace." I was responsible for the Minute for Peace on radio worldwide, which followed the period of mourning for President Kennedy. "Peace begins in the mind." We asked for a one minute radio spot on all stations that would carry the sound of a bell and a thought or prayer for peace. We invited all listeners to join in this special minute—to deepen their commitment and increase their efforts for world peace.

Minute for Peace became the centerpiece of Earth Day. Ever since, on Earth Day when we ring the UN Peace Bell in New York City, we invite people worldwide to join in two minutes of heartfelt prayer that we will overcome "doubt with faith" and strive to be responsible Trustees of Earth.

Please pray that each Earth Day on the March equinox will bring a new sense of identity with the whole human family, and a commitment to seek peace through understanding and love—the love that Jesus revealed. And may we put feet to our prayers with action to help make it happen.

A DISPUTE DEVELOPS

Right after my Earth Day Proclamation was put on the Board of Supervisors' Agenda in the City of San Francisco in October, 1969, there was a UNESCO National Conference on "Man and His Environment" in San Francisco in November, 1969. I was invited and given the opportunity to announce Earth Day.

As I was leaving after my announcement, a couple of young men followed me and said, "Earth Day's a great idea, but you should change your date to April 22. We have been promoting across the country through the colleges an event called 'Environmental Teach-In' on that date." They even had a book called "Environmental Teach-In." They had never before used the term Earth Day anywhere. There is no documentation of the name Earth Day being used by anyone before I proposed it to the City of San Francisco in September, 1969.

I told them, "Absolutely no. Earth Day on the March equinox is too important an event worldwide to change the date. Earth Day is a global event." I told them the equinox is the best basis for a global Earth Day.

A short time later, the Board of Supervisors in San Francisco voted on December 19, 1969 to approve my Earth Day Proclamation. The Proclamation was officially issued by Mayor Alioto on February 11, 1970.

In the meantime, plans for the Environmental Teach-In were in development. The Environmental Teach-In was being organized by Senator Gaylord Nelson and Denis Hayes out of Washington, DC. In January, 1970, Tony Roisman, our lawyer in Washington, called me and said, "John, I did not know that Environmental Teach-In had changed its name to Earth Day. They have a full page ad in the Washington Post and the New York Times." And I was appalled, because I realized that would cause confusion and division. And ever since then there has been a struggle or a fight between the April 22 organizers of their Earth day, and the original Earth Day, which is nature's event. From that moment on there was an effort by them to have their event, their thinking, and their ways. It was a political and financial benefit they were looking for, and it's true that "Earth Day" is an easier name, and a better name, than "Environmental Teach-In."

There's one more caveat on this which is unbelievable. I wondered why they had chosen April 22. Their Earth day just happened to occur on the 100th anniversary of the birth of communism's Lenin, the Russian leader who sought to replace all religions with a secular world-view. The political leaders who decided that their "Environmental Teach-In" should be observed on April 22, 1970 approached the problem of pollution with a secular viewpoint.

The April 22 organizers said their date was for the convenience of students. They said that they just arbitrarily chose the day because it would be convenient on the campuses at that time. It may have been because of the warmer weather, or may have had some connection with Arbor Day in April. It will be noted that Arbor Day was started by J. Sterling Morton in 1872. On his death in 1907, his birth day, April 22, became Arbor Day—a date still recognized as Arbor Day in many countries.

Obviously, their date had been previously decided without any idea of calling it an Earth Day, and without any consideration of the advantages of the vernal equinox.

The spring equinox Earth Day on March 21, 1970 was a celebration, whereas the April 22 event was a protest. In a time of protest, an aroused youth organized clean-ups and teach-ins that dramatized their rejection of technologies' misuse and waste. In a period of tension and uncertainty, media headlined their actions when they cleaned up a river, or buried a car. Newspaper articles published that April showed cars turned over, garbage on corporate carpets, students marching with protest signs, and a car put on a roof. In 1970 there was a terrific protest movement underway. The idea was about protesting pollution, and, to a certain extent that's fine. But if you want to build something really worthwhile, you don't build it on a foundation of lies. They "borrowed" the name "Earth Day" for their event which occurred one month after we observed Earth Day. Then they represented their "Earth Day" as the true Earth Day.

In contrast, the March Earth Day showed the flying of the Earth Flag, exhibits on composting and recycling, children planting flowers and trees, and the ringing of bells—a time of celebration. At the University of California at Davis, on March 21, we had a full hour of silence for meditation and prayer for peace. This hour extended from the moment of the equinox.

Then in 1971 the March equinox Earth Day Peace Bell Ceremonies commenced at the United Nations. Again the focus was on peace and Earth care. These ceremonies brought together leaders of east and west in a common commitment to "think and act as trustees of Earth." The March equinox Earth Day thus promoted conciliation and has been credited with helping end the Cold War and spreading support for environmental action.

This happened in spite of repeated efforts by the April 22 organizers to replace the original Earth Day with their arbitrary date. They renamed their event from "Environmental Teach-In" to "Earth Day," holding it one month after the first true Earth Day. They neglected to mention that the name "Earth Day" was never used by them until after the equinox Earth Day announcement that I made at the UNESCO National Conference on the Environment in San Francisco in November, 1969. Before that, their event was called "Environmental Teach-In."

I want to interject here that I've studied the records over the Internet. With the Internet, you can get all kinds of leads to new records that people don't know about. No one has come up with anyone who proposed a global Earth Day before I announced it.

The April 22 organizers had political and business connections—and massive funding. The public's eager endorsement of the ideals suggested by a day called "Earth Day" attracted the vested interests of politicians and big business, who saw it as a way to capitalize on public empathy. Their backing and the numerous advertisements and editorials in newspapers, including the *New York Times*, repeatedly ignored the authentic Earth Day and promoted the April 22 imposter. The *New York Times* then acted as if Earth Day were April 22—even though the newspaper's biggest front page story and photo of an Earth Day celebration was on March 21, 1971!

Ignoring deception can lead to ignominious mistakes. When Denis Hayes declares that the first "Earth Day" was April 22, when it is well documented that it was March 21, it is a clear signal that the April 22 organizers should not be trusted.

Calling other dates "Earth Day" has hindered suitable attention for the Earth Trustee agenda of the real Earth Day. It also has confused people and somewhat minimized the importance of the true Earth Day, in spite of the fact that the March equinox Earth Day has been sponsored by 33 Nobel Laureates. Leaders such as George Gallup, President Arias of Costa Rica, and the Pope's United Nations representative—Archbishop Renato R. Martino—have stated its importance.

The result of calling April 22 "Earth Day" has been mass confusion. Much good for the environment has been done on April 22, but calling it "Earth Day" has prevented a much larger good. If the equinox Earth Day had been the only Earth Day, focusing on peace, justice, and the care of Earth, the world would now be on its way to a peaceful, prosperous Earth Trustee future.

The truth is that when the Environmental Teach-In hijacked the name Earth Day in 1970 and claimed it was April 22 instead of the March equinox—nature's great icon of new life and renewal—the confusion that was caused succeeded in minimizing participation in the annual event that can do the most for people and planet.

In spite of the confusion, the United Nations has observed Earth Day each year since 1971 on the authentic day, the first day of spring.

While people of all religions, and of no religion, celebrate the real Earth Day on the March equinox, it especially appeals to many Christians—because the centerpiece of Earth Day (the moment of the equinox) provides a powerful moment of opportunity for Christians, as well as others, to join in silent prayer and dedication to the care of Earth.

Calling other dates Earth Day has hindered suitable attention for the Earth Trustee agenda of the real Earth Day. Understanding Earth Day and implementing its Earth Trustee vision of peace, justice, and the care of Earth is now essential for the survival of civilization.

CONTROVERSY OVER THE DATE OF EARTH DAY

Thus, the date that got the most attention in the United States media and various parts of the country was April 22. It was mistakenly called Earth Day, and the people who promoted it have never acknowledged the equinox Earth Day as the first Earth Day.

Public records have many contradictory statements about how Earth Day started, when it is, what it means, and what is the way to observe it. Were the truth about Earth Day more widely known, the world would have a far better future. To clarify the issue and overcome the confusion, major media should provide a calendar that will list dates that have been widely accepted as international holidays. Give their names, purposes, and history.

I was urged to sue. But I just happen to be an evangelical Christian, and I don't believe in trying to settle problems that way. I went to them and talked to them. In fact, Denis Hayes told me he was sorry that they made a mistake on the origin of the name since he didn't really understand the history. He wasn't the one that had heard my original announcement. He said they would come back to our date next year.

But instead of coming back to our day, in 1971 they tried to stop me at the United Nations. One of my friends who assisted UN Secretary-General U Thant told me that he had been in a meeting when an aide from Senator Nelson's office tried to persuade U Thant to declare April 22 as Earth Day—to change the date from March to April. The aide said that the UN has received the hospitality of the United States—and so here was a senator asking him to change the date of the Earth Day observance at the United Nations to April 22. The Secretary-General told him in reply, "John McConnell came to me first and his idea of the equinox Earth Day is a much better idea." I've been told by the top people around the Secretary-General that the equinox Earth Day is the right Earth Day and that it should be given more attention. And that was it. The Secretary-General signed my proclamation.

Nevertheless, in the 1990s, the April event organizers went to UNEP, and so now UNEP has Earth Day on April 22, in addition to promoting an annual World Environment Day on June 5. This is despite the annual UN Peace Bell ceremony for Earth Day on the spring equinox.

There are conspiracy theories out there—but I don't think a conspiracy is involved here. However, there are some people who believe that big corporate powers decide what everybody does. We do live in a media-made world—the corporate world pulls the strings and decides what's in the media. There is an element of truth in that.

If you've read philosophically on the problem of power, there is an explanation. It involves power. Senator Nelson was a powerful senator. He saw power—and the potential of the name "Earth Day." He saw that Earth Day was really going somewhere.

Of course I can't judge what his motives were. But in fact, he had corporations behind him—and he benefited by pushing the idea that his "Earth Day" was the day that corporations needed to identify with. In short, corporations needed to support this in order to stay out of trouble. The matter is filled with conflicting issues.

For years, I tried to reach Senator Nelson by telephone. I would talk to an aide, but the Senator would never return my call. I wrote the Senator in October 1989 (see my letter in the Appendix), and mentioned that I did call Joe Floyd. Floyd told me of his being with the Senator in Florida in the fall of 1969 and suggesting "Earth Day" as a better name than "Environmental Teach-In" for Nelson's planned event. Floyd also said that he had seen something in the paper about "kids in California who were planning an Earth Day." This may have been the students at the University of California in Davis who warmly supported my proposals when I spoke there in October—followed by an outstanding Earth Day event on March 21, 1970.

Confusion persisted, as various groups continued to believe that Earth Day was on April 22. In 1980, I wrote the president of the National Council of Churches to explain Earth Day's true date and history (see the Appendix).

Other people came to me and said, you should praise the good things that are being done on the environment on the April 22 "Earth

Day." Still other people, discouraged by the confusion, said, let's make every day "Earth Day." But they saw the problem with this idea when I countered with, that's fine—forget the day you were born, we'll make every day your birthday. Making every day "Earth Day" would take away from the importance and impact of having one global Earth Day.

I tried and tried to contact Gaylord Nelson. When you have criticism of somebody, you should try to go directly to them.

Finally in 1990 by telephone I connected with Senator Nelson, when he was president of the Wilderness Society. We talked for nearly an hour. Before making the phone call, I told myself to practice what I preach, that if I presented Earth Day and Minute for Peace properly, maybe he would join me in helping it. I told him I knew we had some differences about the history of Earth Day, but since we were both interested in peace and the care of Earth, I wanted to bring to his attention what we were doing with Minute for Peace.

Later in our conversation about Earth Day, he mentioned that a reporter had suggested that "Earth Day" would be a better name than the original name for his event, "Environmental Teach-In," and that the reporter had seen events publicized with the name "Earth Day." Obviously, the reporter had seen publicity about our equinox Earth Day.

Senator Nelson also said his "Earth Day" was more a political event than the equinox Earth Day, and would engage students across the country. That is in fact how his supporters organized it.

After he had heard about the equinox Earth Day, Senator Nelson said he had briefly promoted "Earth Week" in April, but that the idea did not go very far. This is true, because in 1971, he announced Earth Week as the third week in April as an annual event.

I told him it would be great if he would issue a statement acknowledging the two Earth Days, and continue promoting Earth Week in April. He responded, "John, it's wonderful what you have done, but the country has accepted April 22 as Earth Day, and there's nothing I can do to change it. April 22 as Earth Day is so well established, we can't do anything about that." I replied, "If you believe, as you just told me, that the Earth Day celebration on the equinox is of special value, and it has the history of support at the United Nations, you could come out with a statement about it. That would overcome the feeling of friction that exists now when people hear and think that Gaylord Nelson and John McConnell are enemies." He was positive about my suggestion, but of course he didn't do anything about it. And what he said implied that I originated the name and the concept. But he never mentioned that publicly. He kept coming back to the idea that the April "Earth Day" was bigger than the March Earth Day.

I told him that what would give evidence of resolution of the conflict, and of peaceful cooperation, would be if he would come out now in support of our Minute for Peace. He thought it was a great idea. But when I showed him the statement about Minute for Peace, he said, "John, I can't support anything like this—it starts out with 'John McConnell, founder of Earth Day.' I've issued releases all along that I was the founder of Earth Day. I was the founder of the Earth Day that we celebrated, and that's the one that has gotten the most attention around the world."

I replied that we could remove that statement, or mention that I was the founder of the United Nations Earth Day, or the equinox Earth Day, and that he was the founder of the April 22 Earth Day that got so much attention. I told him over and over again that I did not want to deny the great benefit that came from his efforts and his organization. I said if we are interested in the future, in the next one hundred years, and the possibility of unity in our diversity, where we have one global holiday, one day a year, that everybody unites on what every enlightened individual agrees with—the protection and care of our planet—if that is true, and if we are interested in the best for the future, we should find some way to resolve the difference about the two Earth Days. I added that I hoped he would think about it and communicate about any way this could be done.

The meeting ended without any clear-cut change on his part.

But, the fact remains that he stole the name. And I was criticized by a lawyer for not having copyrighted and trademarked the idea. Of course, I never thought such a thing would happen.

My view is well documented. If this ever came up in a court, supporters of Gaylord Nelson would have nothing—absolutely nothing—to stand on.

But I don't want to pursue it. I've got too little time left at age 96. Also, I keep trying to do things without money. We get only minuscule media coverage from our efforts. Hence the financial support is lacking. In short, we live in a media-made world. I have contended that words are not enough. We need examples. We need more people and institutions to demonstrate the Earth Day and Earth Trustee vision and agenda.

EARTH DAY 1971 AND 1972 IN NEW YORK

In early April of 1970, we moved back to New York and started efforts to make Earth Day an international holiday. Many people worked with us and supported our efforts.

Although Margaret Mead had no involvement with the first Earth Day in 1970, she had attended the 1969 UNESCO Conference in San Francisco and had told me it was a good idea. She was not involved in the first UN Earth Day, which was in 1971. But in 1972 she was one of the participants in the twelve-hour Earth Day Special, and showed great interest in the Earth Day concept.

Margaret Mead understood the importance of having Earth Day on the equinox. She helped me form the Earth Society Foundation in 1976. I had earlier formed the Earth Society in June 1973 at a UN Conference on the Environment in Geneva, Switzerland. At an Earth Society Board Meeting on December 8, 1976 (the first Earth Society Foundation meeting), she said,

> You see the conceptualization here is primarily the idea of using the actuality of the planet as the basis of human behavior and transcending national ideological boundaries. That's the basic idea, "Earth Day." All the other ideas flow from that.
>
> That's the conceptualization that we owe to John McConnell. It wasn't conceptualized by anyone else. This is the first real proposal that doesn't have silly dates like BC and AD in it. Or clocks out at Kennedy to tell you what time it is in Tokyo in terms of a twelve-hour clock. This is a basic and important concept which nobody's got. The UN doesn't use any kind of measures that are independent of ideology or national history.
>
> And it is a very basic concept.

On one occasion, Senator Gaylord Nelson and Denis Hayes were in New York, and Denis Hayes was speaking at the auditorium of the American Museum of Natural History. One of the things that he did was to say that Margaret Mead had contributed so much to understanding of the planet and was a great supporter of Earth Day. Of course, he was absolutely right. But she was against their Earth day, absolutely against it, as the above quotation shows.

They have stated more than once that Margaret Mead was a strong supporter of the April 22 Earth Day, which is not true. They don't mention that she would have nothing to do with them, and that she attributed the real Earth Day to me. Let them post what she said in the March 1978 EPA Journal, reprinted in part below (for the full text see the Appendix).

EARTH DAY, BY MARGARET MEAD

EPA Journal, March 1978

Margaret Mead, an internationally recognized anthropologist, educator, and activist in world affairs, is the 1978 Earth Day chairperson.

"Earth Day is the first holy day which transcends all national borders, yet preserves all geographical integrities, spans mountains and oceans and time belts, and yet brings people all over the world into one resonating accord, is devoted to the preservation of the harmony in nature and yet draws upon the triumphs of technology—the measurement of time and instantaneous communication through space. Earth Day draws on astronomical phenomena in a new way; using the vernal equinox, the time when the Sun crosses the equator making night and day of equal length in all parts of the Earth. To this point in the annual calendar, EARTH DAY attaches no local or divisive set of symbols, no statement of the truth or superiority of one way of life over another. But the selection of the March equinox makes planetary observance of a shared event possible . . . ."

My conversations with Margaret Mead and United Nations Ambassadors in 1970 resulted in 1971 participation worldwide. Our first big Earth Day in New York City was in 1971. The International Earth Day Proclamation I had written in June 1970 after the San Francisco event was signed by United Nations Secretary-General U Thant and other world leaders starting in 1971.

When U Thant signed my Earth Day Proclamation, he proclaimed his support and issued a United Nations Release which was featured in the world press designating March 21 as Earth Day. During the UN Earth Day ceremony, when he rang the Peace Bell at the moment of equinox, he said, "Happy Birthday, Planet Earth." The ringing of the Peace Bell at the moment spring began obtained global attention.

Thus, the 1971 Earth Day in New York had the backing of U Thant. He felt Earth Day could become a vital global holiday that would benefit people and planet.

John Lindsay, Mayor of New York in 1971–1972, issued an Earth Day proclamation for New York City. We had a wonderful event in

Central Park with all kinds of groups gathered there. Newspapers reported that over 5,000 people massed in Central Park on that Earth Day. The observance circled the globe.

But it troubled me because some people were doing things I didn't like. It was a mix of good and bad. A good thing that followed, which I think was great, was to promote the idea of block associations. People in the same block would have a piece of ground or something where they would plant things. Somebody even donated trees so that people could plant trees. So we got a little more greenery in the city.

In 1972 the United Nations celebration of Earth Day included the first twelve-hour special on national television. The centerpiece of this remarkable event was the ringing of the Peace Bell by UN Secretary-General Waldheim, calling nations to the Stockholm Conference on the Environment. The event included panels of national and international ecology experts from around the world discussing the growing environmental crisis and what should be done. This was interspersed with music which included Pete Seeger and Odetta.

WOR-TV (Channel 9) provided the twelve-hour E-Day special from 6 a.m. to 6 p.m. The participants at the special at the United Nations included the Secretary-General and the Chairman of PanAm, Najeeb Halaby. He died recently, but I was on the phone with him many times. His daughter is Queen Noor of Jordan. Many stations across the United States carried part of the program, and the United Nations offered the program for global distribution. I was the Associate Producer for the program. We had great music. We had the head of the EPA. It was a wonderful, wonderful program.

How it happened is interesting.

It's the little things that make the big difference. I thought what a great thing it would be if we could have a big all-day special, and I talked to environmental groups and friends of the Red Cross and other places. Nothing happened. Then one day, I got a phone call from some magazine on Wall Street. They wanted a photograph of my Earth Flag for use in a story that they were doing. I didn't have a photo.

I thought to myself about the office building where WOR had its offices. I knew they had a lot of photographers and maybe I could get them to make a photo of the flag.

So, I went over there and when I got to the floor where they're located, I stopped somebody in the hall and I told them who I was and what I was trying to do. He said, "I'm the Public Relations manager of WOR. Come in and let's see what we can do." They photographed my Earth Flag and gave me a copy.

Then he said, "Oh, by the way, are you doing anything for lunch?" So, I joined him for lunch. They were getting criticism because TV stations are supposed to do public service. He had come up with the idea that they should do a special. I said I could give him ideas for a twelve-hour special for Earth Day.

He agreed. He brought in his top people. They decided to call it "E-Day '72." It was a wonderful program. Years later, I tried to get a copy of the tape. Back in those days, they had a different system than they have now. They had reused the tape so it was no longer available.

Over March 19, 20, and 21, along with the Earth Day special on TV, 5,000 people were at the South Street Seaport Museum at 16 Fulton Street, to celebrate life, enjoy films and music, and to see the ecology exhibits. There was a vigil on March 20, and a breakfast for cyclists, who came to the seaport before work on the 20th and 21st.

EFFECT OF EARTH DAY

By 1973, the equinox Earth Day was already being seen as an annual event. Earth Day was proclaimed by UN Secretary-General Waldheim, and observed by many cities and states. The Earth Day observance has continued each year at the United Nations with the ringing of the Peace Bell. The annual UN ceremony has continued now for forty years. It has played a key role in conflict resolution and efforts for the care of Earth.

In Washington, DC in 1973, the thirty-eighth North American Wildlife and Natural Resources Conference featured an Earth Day Program. In Baltimore, an International Earth Day ceremony on board the USS Constellation included a reading of an Earth Month Proclamation by that city's Mayor Schaefer. In Los Angeles, the Survival Research and the Ecology Center of Southern California sponsored an Earth Day program.

In New York City, a five-day celebration took place at the South Street Seaport Museum, with pier exhibits, entertainment, and ecology dialogue groups. Speakers included in the five-day Symposium were Margaret Mead, Russell Peterson (former Governor of Delaware and Chairman of Save Our Seas), Charles D. Hollister, David Sive, Allan Gussow, Miriam Levering, and S. Fred Singer.

In June the same year, 1973, the Earth Society was formed in Geneva during the second UNEP Conference. In December, as the Comet Kohoutek streaked through our solar system, the Earth Society promoted a celebration of welcome to this Space visitor. I called for Earth's people to take Kohoutek's sudden and timely appearance as a signal for the rescue and renewal of planet Earth. Fifty publications from all over the United States, plus radio and TV, heralded the celebration of its visit.

President Sadat of Egypt sent me a telegram for Earth Day 1979, calling it "The Great Day of Earth."

My efforts at the United Nations helped bring attention to the environment and start the environmental movement. The equinox Earth Day at the United Nations had a role in ending the Cold War. The work of Pope John Paul II was a major factor. Archbishop Martino, who represented the Pope at the United Nations, attended our Earth Day Ceremony in 1999 and commended me for my efforts.

In 2000, I told friends I would like to celebrate Earth Day 2000 back in San Francisco where it started. That was the thirtieth anniversary of the first Earth Day and the first in the new millennium. Somebody put up the money for my fare, and I flew back. We had a proclamation from the current Mayor of San Francisco—and we had the ceremony. The daughter of 1970 Mayor Alioto participated. It was such a beautiful event.

RECOGNIZING THE TRUE DATE

It should be recognized that great good cannot come from deception or misdirection. Human history has produced great ideas that were defeated—not by open opposition, but by words that confuse.

Earth Day each year can be "The Great Day of Earth"—only if it taps the energy and Earth Trustee inspiration possible in the March equinox. Massive hype for a lesser date is a betrayal of nature. Make March 20-21 "The Great Day of Earth" and the new millennium will be an Earth Trustee Millennium of great promise and fulfillment.

Regarding conflicting claims about the right date for Earth Day, some have said, "If we are fighting for the same cause, then why should we be fighting each other at the same time?" Indeed, it is tragic that the potential benefit of one great annual holiday for planet Earth has not been achieved—because of the conflict about what Earth Day is and when Earth Day should be observed. It is confusing to go to my website at Earthsite.org and see that Earth Day is March 20–21 and then discover that Earthday.org claims instead that "Earth Day" is April 22.

The records on Earthsite.org, and in my archives at Swarthmore College, clearly prove that no one used the term "Earth Day" before I did. The March 21, 1970 Earth Day was the first "Earth Day." I have the original Earth Day Proclamation. I also have the original proclamation from San Francisco. I have dozens of proclamations, including the most important one signed in 1970 by UN Secretary-General U Thant. He made Earth Day a big event at the UN in 1971—as a result we had attention all over the world.

Still, the *New York Times* publishes big articles about the other Earth Day. Over the years I faxed them and phoned them—and they just ignored the records. No one has ever seen a notice, or a dated letter, or a newspaper article that even mentions the two words Earth Day until I announced it in San Francisco. There are many great statements by world leaders about the March Earth Day. But still, if you read the *New York Times*, or the *Washington Post*, or the average newspaper—or go to the Associated Press—why you wouldn't even know the UN ceremony on Earth Day exists.

With money, political clout, and a different agenda, the April 22 advocates set out to replace the date and purpose of the original Earth Day. The original Earth Day was born in prayer. It used nature's magnificent moment of equipoise—the March equinox—as a global holiday (Holy Day) for a common cause—reverence for life and dedication to the stewardship of Earth.

The confusion about what and when is Earth Day would be ended if scholars and media moguls would look at the records and report the truth. We live in a world of deception and hypocrisy. But it is also a world in search of meaning and peaceful progress. Understanding the nature and importance of the authentic Earth Day could bring a vital common world view and personal inspiration. Then we will make more choices every day that will benefit people and planet.

It is my hope that in this new millennium of new beginnings the truth will get attention. It's great to have different days for special things. There would be no problem if the organizers of the April 22 "Earth Day" would call it by its original name "Environmental Teach-In" or "Eco Day" or any name other than Earth Day.

Nothing should be done to legitimize calling April 22 "Earth Day." When the geophysical, original Earth Day is understood, and celebrated, the global state of mind and the actions of its people will assure a healthy prosperous future.

While people may have events leading up to Earth Day—or events following Earth Day—the object of Earth Day is to have one great annual occasion where the whole human family will forget their differences and celebrate the wonder of our planet—its life and its human family.

PEACEFUL COEXISTENCE

If people want to celebrate April 22 in promotion of environmental action, that's fine. But let them use a name that doesn't infringe on the authentic, original Earth Day. There are many good names they could use. How about "Eco Day," "Environment Day," or their original name, "Environmental Teach-In"? It damages Earth Day when they call April 22 by that name; just as it would damage Christmas to call April 22 "Christmas" and give it a different meaning than the real Christmas.

In today's society too many people ignore the importance of telling the truth. Satan in the Garden of Eden told Eve she could benefit by using deception. The April 22 organizations never mention the true Earth Day—and pretend it doesn't exist.

DIFFERENT CULTURES COME TOGETHER ON EARTH DAY

While I am a devout evangelical Christian, through the years I have brought together leaders of many religions at our UN Earth Day ceremony. I believe people should respect their differences, but come together where they agree.

While I find it impossible to agree with all the many conflicting claims about cultural roots in history, on Earth Day, I join with people of different religious views. I can cooperate with people of differing religious and political views, so long as our cooperation for Earth stewardship is not misused to further partisan beliefs. It is understood that we must honestly recognize our differences. Earth Day avoids matters in which honest people disagree, such as the idea of planetary consciousness and metaphysical mysteries.

We are asking people who in many cases have conflicting views with each other in religious and political matters to celebrate a day dedicated to a common cause—a sustainable future on this physical planet. Earth Day is to celebrate and foster peace, justice, and the care of Earth. Religious groups of all kinds can show the importance of their belief in the Golden Rule, compassion, and faith, by how they care for the environment and support environmental ethics in business and politics.

Part of the problem is the prevalence of syncretism and universalism—the fusion into one of different beliefs, ignoring their differences. Syncretism says in effect that there is no importance in our differences: We all worship the same God; the Earth is God, animals are God, and so on.

While seeking a common cause it is important to do it honestly. Spin doctors twist words to mean something different from what was intended. Repeatedly, there have been efforts by partisan groups to distort the purpose and meaning of Earth Day for their advantage. Earth Day should not be referred to as, for example, "The World Day for Atheism," "World Day for Planetary Consciousness," "World Day for Christianity," or "World Day," that is, for promoting any religion or special interest.

The name "Earth Day" has served well for forty-one years. To also call it "World Day" would confuse the public. While the latter name was intended to be used by the whole world, the word "Earth" is more suitable than "World." The dictionary defines Earth as "the planet we inhabit." While "world" is a synonym for Earth, the term "world" has many meanings and usages making it less suitable as the name for this annual, global, vernal equinox Earth Day celebration. It is hoped that all individuals and organizations will participate in celebration of our common heritage on this day for planet Earth, without diluting its name and purpose.

In recent years, some have integrated an Earth Day celebration into a sunrise celebration devoted to planetary consciousness. One such event was the Planetary Vision Festival 2001, organized in part by the Club of Budapest. I do not think the Festival's integration with Earth Day was a good idea. While the program was excellent, the words and title sought to replace the common ground, provided by the name Earth Day and its Earth Trustee agenda, with a different name, "World Day of Planetary Consciousness," and a different agenda, promotion of pantheism, which is the idea that nature is God. While pantheists have long participated in the Earth Day Celebration at the United Nations, they did not claim it as their exclusive event.

Does the promotion of "planet-conscious actions" mean that we are to be conscious of our planet when we celebrate Earth Day—with which I agree—or does it mean promotion of pantheism (another meaning of "planetary consciousness"), which I strongly reject. Use of "World Day of Planetary Consciousness" is objectionable to many people who have no problem with "Earth Day."

I was flown to Budapest several years ago and was featured in a ceremony where the Dalai Lama and I signed the Club of Budapest document. However, there was never any mention of me, or Earth Day, in their website.

My life has been devoted to conflict resolution and fostering peaceful progress in human affairs. I wish the Club of Budapest Godspeed in its efforts. However, I believe that replacing Earth Day with World Day, or with World Day of Planetary Consciousness, will confuse and detract from the goal of a global Earth Day—a worldwide holiday on nature's March equinox—intended from its 1969 initiation as a worldwide celebration fostering peace, justice, and the care of Earth.

I do hope all our efforts can complement each other without diminishing the power and the purpose of the true Earth Day. I feel very strongly that the name and the accomplishments of the equinox Earth Day make it the only way to a sustainable future on our planet.

Participation in Earth Day by the Club of Budapest is welcome, but I resist any effort to change the name "Earth Day" or its meaning.

I firmly hold to my Christian faith and reject pantheism, shamanism, etc. However, I put our differences aside on Earth Day and join with people of all religions in commitment to "peace, justice, and care of Earth."

Every religion and culture has some record of peaceful solutions of differences. And some records of hate and violence.

While I consider myself an evangelical Christian, I recognize that others who claim this name do not share my thinking about the importance of finding common ground with people of other religions and cultures. I demonstrate the best way to do this in our Peace Bell Ceremony on Earth Day.

A spirit of love can enable one to find common ground without compromising personal convictions. This requires that neither side claim agreement in matters where there are honest differences.

AN INTERVIEW WITH THE EARTH DAY MAN

I was introduced as "Mr. Earth Man" fifteen years ago in Spain. I occupied a special chair standing out on the platform, among other speakers. I spoke to a thousand people or more in an auditorium.

The New York Times carried a feature by David Gonzalez on October 28, 1998 which called me "Mr. Earth Day." It stated the first Earth Day was March 21, 1970.

More recently, I was interviewed by Iranian-American Behrouz Vafa on March 1, 2001. He called me the "Earth Day Man." Here are some things I said in that interview:

In 2001, I read the autobiography of Albert Schweitzer, *My Life and Thought*, which ended by saying that, after all of his study, he had come to the conclusion that the world was inexplicably mysterious and filled with suffering. But the thing that gave him hope was the human impulse for progress, and if people could be given an ethical view, a reverence for life, and apply that at every level, then we might move toward a better future.

The difficulty is that for the last few thousand years the human race has been the problem on this planet. For example, we've destroyed forests. What we have done with our commercial operations is just incredibly terrible.

Recently, I read a book, *Paradise for Sale*,[4] which described Nauru, a tiny island near Australia that had been a paradise for hundreds of years for the natives. But our modern ways of doing things, our exploitation, our methods of producing all kinds of things meant to increase power and make money, were not the way to a better future for the natives. Modern ways had literally destroyed the environment on this little island, and all the natives ended up on welfare. The authors showed that this is where the whole world is headed.

I'm grateful for what the true equinox Earth Day has done. Back in the 1970s, I met with the Ambassador from the Soviet Union in Washington DC. We both agreed that it wouldn't matter whether communism or capitalism won if the planet is destroyed. I stressed that what we need to do is come together where we agree and put aside as much as possible our differences—leave room for them. If we would, for example, cooperate on our space venture and on the environment, we would find

---

4. McDaniel and Gowdy, *Paradise for Sale*.

an amazing thing—that it would reduce tensions and we would make room for our differences without aiming a gun at each other's head.

He agreed with me, and this was followed by actions. A couple of years later I had the ambassador from USSR, the ambassador from the United States, and the head of the world Muslim League together ring the Peace Bell. This was carried in news stories around the world. It was reported in *Pravda*, and afterwards the Soviet delegate told me "You know, I'm not religious, but I was deeply moved by the ceremony."

As noted earlier, actions good or bad begin in the mind. Attitudes have a great deal to do with our actions. If we can get attention that will change attitudes around the world, we have a great future. We're right now at a critical point where if we get enough support and enough people thinking and acting as Earth Trustees, we could have a great future.

We need a great exciting mood—a moral equivalent of war—that will mobilize efforts for peace, justice, and care of Earth, and that will diminish violence, pollution, and injustice. Those are the aims. Let everybody who hears my voice or who reads this statement look to what they can do to help, because there's something for everybody to do.

Find the thing that you feel will help this cause, and recognize that others who are doing different things are also helping. I do believe this cause will succeed when people who catch the vision act upon it. If anybody agrees with these words, the first thing you should do is tell other people about them, talk about what can be done to implement them, because words without action are wasted.

I wish people on the Internet would go to my website, http://www.earthsite.org, where you'll find among other things "Web Way to Save Our Planet." May everyone who agrees with me think of themselves as an Earth Trustee. An Earth Trustee is anyone who is choosing in his/her own way to support a sustainable future, anyone who is choosing peace, justice, and the care of Earth, and who is seeking in ecology and economics and ethics the rejuvenation of our planet—to benefit people and the planet.

In other words, an Earth Trustee is trying to be fair and honest while helping to take care of planet Earth. Everybody has a responsibility to nurture nature—plant a tree, recycle, and so on. This also pertains to what you buy, and what you sell. If you're an Earth Trustee, you're going to have second thoughts against wasting money on something that's going to pollute or damage the Earth. We should even be concerned where the products we buy come from. When you find some big operator is using slave labor in a foreign country to produce something cheap—don't buy it.

So we need to come together in Earth Trustee feeling and emotion. I believe that all those things that I've been describing will come together when we make Earth Day the great event that it should be.[5]

CELEBRATIONS OF EARTH DAY

Earth Day has been celebrated on the March equinox all over the world ever since 1970. Each year Earth Day is celebrated at the UN in New York with the ringing of the Peace Bell. At one of the United Nations Peace Bell Ceremonies on Earth Day, Isaac Asimov said, "When we ring the Peace Bell it is the beginning of spring—nature's moment of new life and new beginnings. And our planet needs a new beginning."

In the 1970s, the Cathedral of St. John the Divine in New York City observed the March equinox Earth Day in a big way.

For the 1971 Earth Day, UN Secretary-General U Thant issued an advance statement that circled the globe, and resulted in media attention and significant global participation by people of every creed and culture. U Thant declared,

> . . . an Earth Day has become suddenly necessary to remind us of the fact our small planet is perishable. All of us, especially the leaders of this world, must have the vision, the courage and a new broadly-based sense of human solidarity to join our thoughts, our hearts and our forces to change the present course of detrimental man-made events and divisions.

The call to Stockholm for the Environmental Conference that resulted in the formation of the UN Environment Programme (UNEP) in 1972 was issued on the March Earth Day at the United Nations by the Secretary-General.

In 1977, on Earth Day at the Peace Bell Ceremony at the United Nations, Margaret Mead said,

> People knew they had to take care of their own meadows, of their own forests or their own rivers. But it was not until we saw the picture of Earth from the moon that we realized how small and

5. See J. McConnell, "Earth Day: Past, Present, Future," on http://www.earthsite .org/mc-lee.htm.

helpless this planet is, something that we must hold in our arms and care for. Earth Day is the first completely international and universal holiday that the world has ever known. Every other holiday was tied to one place, or some political or special event. This Day is tied to Earth itself, and to the place of Earth in the whole solar system.

At this moment, when I climb the steps and ring the Peace Bell, it will be the Equinox in every part of the world, and we can all celebrate it at once on behalf of every part of the world.

That same year, Nobel Laureate Harold Urey stated,

We in the older generation have begun to realize the immense changes on the Earth in our lifetime. Due to trains and airlines, we can travel quickly to all parts of the Earth. Due to atomic bombs people all over the earth are in danger. Due to the success of information and medicine we face the possibility of an overpopulated Earth. All of these things are of great concern to all of us. It is time we began to think in terms of a unified Earth. One of the best ways, it seems to me, is to celebrate EARTH DAY, on March 20, 1977 as well as in all the years to come. In this way the people of the Earth can dedicate themselves to understanding these facts, and to intelligently act on them.[6]

The authentic Earth Day in years past led to new attitudes that helped end communism in Russia. On Earth Day in 1989, the Tass News Service requested an article from me, which was then published in the USSR. In the article I said, "Communism has failed . . . the Cold War is over. We must now recognize the need for a new order of thinking, with actions that will meet the real needs of which we are increasingly aware. Global action, and local action, is needed for protection and improvement of our environment in order to set in motion benefits for all the people on our planet."

Anatoly Berezovoy the Russian Cosmonaut, attended the 1997 Earth Day Ceremony at the UN Peace Bell. This was arranged by Kristina Tomczak of Miracom Partners in Clearwater, Florida. This was followed by efforts since then which resulted in further observance of Earth Day in Russia.

Ms. Tomczak arranged for the Earth Flag to be featured there and on the Mir Space Station in 1998. Outriders of planet Earth thus celebrated Earth Day in space. Cosmonaut Anatoly Berezovoy rang a Peace Bell in

---

6. From 1977 Nobel Laureate statements supporting the equinox Earth Day.

Moscow, accompanied by Elizaveta Matvejeva; these two were President and Vice-President, respectively, of a program called "Earth Flag & Day in Russia." At the Mir Space Station, Russian cosmonauts Talgat Musabaev and Nikolai Budarin held a brief ceremony that included the special moment when the Peace Bell at the United Nations was rung as spring began. Astronauts, Cosmonauts, and people on Earth joined at that time in a brief dedication to be responsible trustees of Earth. This has been followed each year with more and more participation.

We were thrilled when in 1998 Ms. Tomczak also arranged for the Earth Flag to be flown at the South Pole—and in 2000 taken to the North Pole. The wonderful photos she sent us showing the Earth Flag flying at both Poles are now on my website earthsite.org.

Also in 1998, leaders, some from countries in conflict, came together at the United Nations on Earth Day with a profound commitment to the Earth Trustee agenda—"actions to eliminate pollution, poverty, and violence." There was no mention of this in the *New York Times* or the major TV networks. They could have provided advance stories of plans and preparation—and a first time celebration of Earth Day in space. This would have resulted in live coverage and millions of people joining with heart and mind when the United Nations Peace Bell was rung—and would have fostered a change worldwide from "Earth Kill" to "Earth Care."

In 1999, Costa Rica, Austria, and Iran reported Earth Day celebrations. Peace Bells in Moscow, Costa Rica, San Francisco, and at the United Nations Center in Vienna rang simultaneously with the UN Peace Bell in New York. As part of the program in San Francisco, my original "Earth Day" song (see Appendix) and "I Believe" by songwriter Ervin Drake were sung.

In 2000, simultaneous celebrations took place in New York, Vienna, Vilnius (Lithuania), and San Francisco.

In 2001, there were sunrise Earth Day ceremonies in twenty-five major cities across the globe. Bells rang all over the world, in, for example, London, Vienna, Rome, Moscow, Beijing, Shanghai, Hong Kong, Manila, Tokyo, and Sydney.

Some leaders in India led the way. At Bal Bhavan Public School in New Delhi, the Lt. Governor of Delhi hoisted the Earth Flag, and inaugurated a ceremony with the motto, "Save Our Earth—Save Our Progeny." The ceremony included the reading of a statement I submitted. Attendees included 5000 children from eleven schools of New Delhi, their parents, 265 National Service Corps (NCC) Cadets, and other specially invited distinguished guests. The school children took this pledge:

> I am a trustee of Planet Earth. I agree that I will nurture and work for the renewal of Earth. Singly and with the help of others I will act as an Earth Trustee. I will seek in my job, buying-habit, travel, land use and other activities at home, work and play to respect and protect Earth's Amazing Web of Life—Its soil, water, air, plants and living creatures. I will strive to make our planet a Garden of Eden, our home in space, a nest surrounded by beckoning stars.

The ceremony included addresses by several governmental dignitaries. A member of the Planning Commission of India in his address declared that "this is the First officially celebrated Earth Day in India."

This ceremony in India was scheduled for April 21 owing to their confusion about the correct date for Earth Day, which is often the case. I often receive notice of Earth Day celebrations that honor me as the founder of Earth Day but in ignorance represent its date as in April rather than the correct date in March.

The 2001 Earth Day ceremony in New York featured Mayor Rudolph W. Giuliani ringing the Peace Bell. I spoke at the ceremony and my message that day is reprinted in the Appendix. I said,

> I was thinking of a song we used to sing—"Que Sera, Sera, whatever will be, will be. The future's not mine to see, Que Sera, Sera." Too long have we thought that we couldn't make a difference. Earth Trustee vision and action is the key to a better future. Leonardo da Vinci said, "Oh wretched mortals, open your eyes." Earth Day is an event that can help the blind to see. "Amazing Grace, how sweet the sound, that saved a wretch like me. I once was lost, but now I'm found; was blind, but now I see." When the Peace Bell rings, may its sound open our eyes and our heart.

Peace Bells were also rung that year at the UN in Vienna, in Vilnius, the capital of Lithuania, in Alameda, California, and in Newport, Kentucky, the location of the largest free-swinging bell in the world, weighing 66,000 pounds.

In 2003, the newswire story about Earth Day noted its celebration in San Francisco (where the first Earth Day was centered in 1970) and other locations such as New York City at the UN and in Vienna at the UN Plaza.

> RICHMOND, Calif., March 7 (AScribe Newswire)—On March 20, at 5 p.m., Bells of Peace will ring in San Francisco at the National Shrine of Saint Francis of Assisi and throughout the world in order to mark the arrival of the Vernal Equinox signaling the beginning of Earth Day, a time for reflection on peace and mending our planet Earth from ravages of war and pollution. An inter-religious ceremony to proclaim our common hope for peace and healing will begin at 4:30 p.m. at the Shrine.
>
> Simultaneous Peace Bell ringings will take place worldwide under the auspices of the United Nations, the Conventual Franciscans, Artists Embassy International, the Earth Society Foundation and scores of religious and secular organizations who support the worldwide call to peace. The ceremony in San Francisco takes place at the Shrine located at 610 Vallejo Street at the corner of Columbus Avenue.

In 2005, the cities of Denver, Colorado, and Berkeley, California, issued Earth Day Proclamations. In 2006 and 2007, proclamations were issued by Laguna Beach and San Francisco, California.

Through the years a few people have referred to Earth Day as World Day. Some people feel more important if they choose their own special name for the event. It is still Earth Day and in reporting Earth Day events it can be mentioned that it is also called World Day by some.

EARTH DAY—SPECIAL FOR PLANET AND PEOPLE

Earth Day focuses attention on human responsibility for Earth. On this special day of nature's equipoise—the March equinox, when day and night are equal all over the world—the whole human family is invited to join in a common commitment to peace, justice, and the care of Earth. It's the perfect time for global dedication to the stewardship of our planet.

The day that spring begins provides a special opportunity to deepen awareness of nature and our commitment to think and act as trustees of Earth. Then when we buy, when we invest, and in our daily conduct, let us seek choices that will nurture life and eliminate pollution and poverty.

While all people cannot meet at the same place, on Earth Day we can all meet with one another and with God at the same time. Let Earth Day be a time of awareness of people and planet—of our personal family and our global family, of the nearest tree and the worldwide forests, of God's love and our responsibility to think and act as Trustees of Earth.

Christopher Chase in Japan suggested a few years ago that Earth Day be celebrated by a wave proceeding around the globe. Perhaps the wave he suggests could begin 24 hours before the moment of equipoise in New York—and climax with the ringing of the Peace Bell at the United Nations back in New York at the moment equipoise occurs. People worldwide would at that moment have the opportunity for simultaneous prayer, meditation, and commitment to care for one another and care for our planet. Simultaneous prayer worldwide could bring a deep sense of our common identity. The 24-hour wave preceding it would have a powerful climax.

On Earth Day, we focus on where we agree, and seek participation by people of every creed and culture. This can stimulate responsible stewardship of planet Earth. Let's make our new millennium an Earth Trustee Millennium, where the words and actions of individuals and institutions will provide a sustainable future.

Earth Day is an essential element of a culture of peace, agreement, and cooperation. Earth Day starts from the most fundamental thing, our relation to the planet, and spans to the highest aspiration of a cooperative planetary civilization.

It does so by connecting the natural cycles of the planet to the spiral of human evolution, creating common ground for actions that benefit people and planet. Since no one owns Earth Day, Earth Day is open for every one to step into this constructive perspective and use its symbolic power for transforming the seemingly limited abilities of cultural understanding into a common cause. The symbol cannot be "used up," because it is real and not a cultural icon.

CITIES AND EARTH DAY

It was the city of San Francisco that originally brought Earth Day to life. Cities are the environments where most of us inhabit our planet, and the shape of the cities is the human face of the planet, visible from outer space at night.

Unlike nation-states, cities do not wage wars. They are constructed around life's essential problems and life-support systems. They are the melting pot of cultures, the place where humans meet and, as visionary architect Paolo Soleri has expressed it, they prepare the next steps in human evolution.

The features of cities make them the ideal points for initiating and disseminating ideas and actions to promote global peace. This is why in 1960 I proposed a Council of World Cities and Towns (see chapter 24 on government).

Earth Day helps people and their cities "think globally and act locally." Ever since the first Earth Day, with activities in San Francisco, Oakland, Berkeley, Davis and elsewhere, various cities have been the significant sites for celebrating Earth Day.

And of course New York City is the site of the annual Earth Day / Peace Bell ceremony at the UN. Given that priority, New York City, for example, could become a pillar of light, a beacon of hope for all humanity. With the world's greatest engineers, planners, financiers, and communicators, and an already great commitment to the fragile and vital life in our parks, rivers, and wetlands, and with the United Nations and its global awareness and resources at our doorstep, the city can, if it chooses, lead the way in Earth's rejuvenation. New York City can maximize soft energy and solar energy in building, planning, and remodeling; cover the city with neighborhood gardens; provide Earth Care Centers with tools, instruction, and guidance for self-help projects, consumer education, and citizen-care of parks and trees; provide no-interest loans for massive Earth Care development of disaster areas, with jobs for everyone who will work; and undertake massive improvements of public transportation with safe bikeways covering the city. With the cooperation of government, industry, and other private sectors, the people of New York have more than enough assets to carry out such a project. And if backed by the enthusiasm and support of the whole city, its financial success would be assured.

New York could, in ten year's time, be transformed into a city of gardens, with production, marketing, consumption, and communications that would nurture all its children—an exemplary model which could serve as an inspiration to all the nations represented there. Then every New York citizen would stand ten feet tall, and together take its children by the hand and lead them away from the present appalling dangers of violence, pollution, and catastrophes, to a world of hope and promise. New York, and other cities that will go all-out for Earth Care, can lead the way.

THE FUTURE FOR EARTH DAY

Springfield, Ohio is the heartland of America. Since every field experiences spring, the name Springfield is an appropriate name!

We need such words and images. A word, spoken in love, can work miracles. And a great picture or painting can touch our heart.

But what we do depends on connecting our words and emotions with action—positive action to bring about better life for ourselves and others.

A real understanding of Earth Day will inspire us to think and act as Trustees of Earth—joining with friends in efforts and projects that benefit people and planet.

This means that when you buy, sell, invest, travel, or study, you will think and act as a Trustee of Earth, seeking choices in ecology, economics, and ethics that will nurture the amazing skin of life that covers our planet.

It helps me to think about these things each morning when I pray for guidance in what I do that day. Do everything with faith and love. Then each day you will have a positive attitude and find satisfaction in what you do.

Global understanding of the contribution of the March equinox Earth Day to a better future can bring great good to people and planet. It can shift the negative to the positive worldwide. That contribution is the Earth Trustee vision and agenda.

The Space Age, which began 40 some years ago with the launching of the first Sputnik on October 4, 1957, sparked a larger awareness of our planet and its people. This set in motion altruistic efforts in collaboration for "peace, justice, and the care of Earth." In fact, those words were used in the initial announcement of the first Earth Day celebrated on the March equinox.

Social change is always difficult. But now propitious events make this possible. We have amazing global communication possibilities through the Internet.

The centerpiece of Earth Day is people of every creed and culture joining in heartfelt dedication to Earth's rejuvenation when the United Nations Peace Bell is rung as spring begins. In this special moment, people can prove the power of their heart-felt faith by their silent prayer and commitment to think and act as Trustees of Earth. During every day people can share (in person and on the Internet) what they have done and will do to eliminate pollution, poverty, and economic injustice.

Begin now, talking about and doing what is needed. Report plans and solutions to "20/20" and other TV programs—with a request that they act as Earth Trustees and feature solutions in their programs.

In this way we can see a global change of heart and conduct with growing promise for our future.

Let's all work for and expect a miracle as we seek to make the new millennium a time of peaceful progress by thinking and acting as Earth Trustees—the way to peace, justice, and prosperity for the whole human family!

New technology and global communications now make it possible to spread good ideas and actions worldwide. Now is the time to mobilize the whole world in a Moral Equivalent of War that will reduce and eventually eliminate the hate, fear, and ignorance that causes injustice, strife, poverty, and pollution.

Via the Internet, websites can offer QuickTime movies of the Earth Day events including the Peace bell ringing at the UN in New York, Vienna, and elsewhere.

Spread the word. Prepare to celebrate. Now is the time to put the past behind us. May we humble ourselves, repent of past sins, and clear the way for vigorous actions to rejuvenate our planet and invigorate its people. Here is a chance for people of faith to prove the value of their belief in a future life by what they do in this life.

Report your plans and actions to media and your friends. Cover the world with Earth Trustee pages and websites. Together we can save our planet and make the new millennium a new beginning!

Earth Day and its Earth Trustee agenda puts the Golden Rule to work—do unto others as you would have them do unto you. Here is a chance for people of all religions to show their ethical values by being Earth Trustees and practicing reverence for life in word and deed.

Think globally—not just as an American, or British subject, or German, etc. The greatest unity comes from thinking globally.

On March 20 at the United Nations we sang:

> On the first Day of Spring,
> Let the bells of Earth ring
> As together we silently pray
> Sun and Stars will rejoice,

> As we make our sacred choice
> To care for our planet every day.

In Australia, in the Southern Hemisphere, they joined with us and sang:

> On the first Day of Fall
> Let us heed our planet's call.

By featuring Earth Day as The Great Day of Earth and adopting the Earth Trustee idea, the global balance of good and evil will change more and more to what is best.

While we live in the midst of a crumbling civilization, overwhelmed with grave problems, Earth Day provides an event and agenda that given global attention can save civilization and provide a new beginning for the human family.

As we progress further in this new millennium, we must choose whether we will live or die. Let us choose life on every momentous Earth Day. As the Peace Bell rings at the United Nations, at the moment spring begins, let us join in silent prayer and dedication to be responsible Trustees of Earth. Strengthened by awareness of the whole human family and of our beautiful planet, our heart will tell our feet to walk each day in the path of peaceful progress. Then every day we will think and act as responsible Trustees of Earth.

31

Signers of the Earth Day Proclamation

GORBACHEV, FORMER PRESIDENT OF the former USSR, was the thirty-sixth and last signer of the Earth Day Proclamation, in 2000. There was only so much room on the page. When I put it together, I made one mistake. I didn't leave room for names of signers to be printed under their signatures. Some people have terrible signatures. You'd never dream that the last signature is Gorbachev's.

1.   The first person I got to sign the Proclamation was Alexander B. Grannis, in 1970. He was with the New York State Assembly in Albany.

2.   Judith Hollister—she was a wonderful person. She set up the program for understanding among all the world's religions, the Temple of Understanding in New York City. Repeatedly she brought together leaders of the world's religions and aided efforts for peace.

3.   Luther Evans, former Director General of UNESCO, was also Director of the Legislative Reference Service at the Library of Congress, a very distinguished scholar for many, many reasons.

4.   Estelle Feldman was chair of a group from Ireland called the Commission on Man and the Environment, representing the youth of the world. In 1970 a World Youth Assembly was held at the United Nations.

5.   David Brower, founder of the Sierra Club, went on to found Friends of the Earth.

6. Dr. Arvid Pardo, a wonderful man, was Ambassador of Malta to the United Nations. He took the initiative in 1967 to address the United Nations about rights to the wealth of the seas and seabeds, and preservation of the life of the seas. Arvid Pardo, Senator Mark Hatfield, and Frank Braynard joined me in forming the Earth Society's "Sea Citizens" program.

7. Margaret Mead, the anthropologist, strongly endorsed Earth Day and helped found the Earth Society Foundation.

8. Eugene McCarthy, United States Senator from Minnesota. I was on the phone with him on many occasions.

9. John W. Gardner, President of Common Cause. He was a wonderful man who promoted the great idea of a "common cause." I was in touch with him repeatedly.

10. Mike Gravel, United States Senator from Alaska.

11. Hugh Scott, United States Senator from Pennsylvania. We had great conversations.

12. Buzz Aldrin, astronaut.

13. Chief S. O. Adebo, United Nations Under-Secretary-General at that time. He was the Ambassador from Nigeria. I'll never forget, he had gold toothpicks. When we had dinner, he'd pull out his gold toothpick. Anyway, he was really open to our coming together on matters like peace, justice, and care of Earth. Everybody was. I always approached potential signers concerning peace and Earth care; they all claimed to support it. But getting them to follow through was another matter.

14. U Thant of Burma/Myanmar, United Nations Secretary-General. I considered it a great achievement when I got him to sign it. He issued a release about his signing the Earth Day Proclamation.

15. Maurice Strong, UN Environment Programme. He's the one that disappointed me. At first he spoke so warmly and signed the Proclamation. He was a multimillionaire. He didn't back the equinox Earth Day—he signed the Proclamation, but he didn't provide any money to help our efforts. Instead, he went back to Canada, and backed the April 22 "Earth Day," giving its organizers a million dollars!

16. Prof. Yasuhiro Fukushima—this wonderful man from Japan, an environmental scientist. He thought all the countries of the world should come together on the care of the environment.

17. René J. Dubos, one of the best thinkers of our time. I so enjoyed him. He and Lady Jackson (Barbara Ward) and Maurice Strong wrote a book called *Only One Earth*. I was in the Dubos home up in New England.

18. Lubos Kohoutek, astronomer from Czechoslovakia. I remember that we went out on the Queen Elizabeth 2 to see the Comet Kohoutek, named for him. He signed my Earth Day Proclamation on the Queen Elizabeth 2. Before we sailed, we had a comet watch breakfast on December 8, 1974 at the South Street Seaport. The breakfast and the subsequent comet expeditions on the Queen Elizabeth 2 helped us get attention for Earth Care ideas and actions.

19. Buckminster Fuller, one of the real leaders in common sense in our century. He was an inventor, scientist, and scholar. He thought the idea of Earth Day was great. I was on a TV program with him.

20. Mark Hatfield, United States Senator from Oregon, helped me start Sea Citizens in 1974, and helped me get to Iran in 1980. Incidentally, he is a very dedicated Christian, and liked where I was coming from as far as my religion is concerned.

21. John Denver, singer. I was very fortunate in getting him to sign just before his death.

22. Robert Muller, Assistant Secretary-General of the United Nations, and later Chancellor Emeritus of the University of Peace in Costa Rica. He was from Alsace-Lorraine, the part of France where there were German people. He did many things for peace. His support for my efforts over the years has meant much to me.

23. Edward Abramson, the chairman of Earth Day in 1990. He was one of the leaders in the state government in New York, serving as Majority Whip, New York State Assembly.

24. Isaac Asimov, leading writer of science fiction. I was really thrilled to get his signature and was in his home many times. I'll never forget what he said at one Peace Bell ceremony—"When we ring the Peace Bell, it's the beginning of spring. And spring is nature's symbol of new life and new beginnings. And our planet needs a new beginning."

25. Aly Teymour of Egypt was Chief of Protocol at the United Nations. Do you know how he happened to sign the Proclamation? They had a special event at the United Nations. And the Proclamation was out on a special table for people to look at. Guests came there and saw it, and I happened to be away from the table. He came up and saw it, and signed it. Because he was from Egypt, that brought in another dimension. At one time I had a telegram from Nasser. He wanted to see me but was afraid he couldn't make it.

26. Anatoly Berezovoy, cosmonaut from Russia.

27. Cynthia Lennon, first wife of John Lennon, was an artist from England.

28. Stan Lundine, Lieutenant Governor of New York. The addition of his signature was a kind of mixup. I was invited to go up to Albany to meet the Governor who had said he would sign the Proclamation. When I got there his aides said, "Oh, he was called out." But the man I met with said "I'll sign it in his stead." He didn't write that he was signing in the Governor's stead.

29. David Dinkins, Mayor of New York. I had wonderful conversations with him.

30. Oscar Arias, President of Costa Rica. I connected with him through Robert Muller.

31. Audrey McLaughlin, head of the New Democratic Party, House of Commons. I went all the way to Ottawa, the capital of Canada, to meet the Prime Minister of Canada. He signed it, and then somebody must have gotten to him. I don't know who it was. Perhaps it was someone from the April 22 group. When I came to pick up the Proclamation in the Prime Minister's office (of course, I had left it there for him to sign), the Prime Minister had obviously signed it, but the signature had been whited out.

So I took the Proclamation with the white-out. I was furious. Later, I happened to be having a wonderful conversation with Audrey. I asked her would she sign it, and she said she'd be glad to. I didn't want my trip to Canada to be for nothing, so I had her sign it.

32. George Fernandes of India. I was thrilled to get his signature. He was Minister of Transportation and almost became head of India. Hans Janitschek was responsible for my meeting him when he came to New York.

33. Carlos Salinas, President of Mexico. I made a trip to Mexico City, because we had been told that he would add his name to my Proclamation, which he did. Shortly after he signed it, he was turned out of office.

34. Yasser Arafat, Chairman of the Palestine Liberation Organization and President of the Palestinian National Authority. Getting his signature was an amazing miracle. I had a wonderful talk with him. At the time, I hoped to get a Jew to sign it, along with somebody from Palestine. Arafat thought the Proclamation was great and he added his signature.

35. Yehudi Menuhin, violinist. Shortly before he died, I received an invitation to meet with him at a party for him, where he signed the Proclamation. At his suggestion, I added a statement to my Earth Magna Charta stressing the importance of children learning music.

36. Then the finale was when Hans Janitschek arranged for me to meet Mikhail Gorbachev, when Gorbachev visited the United States in 2000. His is the last signature. He made a line under his signature, which I like.

32

Earth Flag

The Earth Flag is my symbol of the task before us all. Only in the last quarter of my life have we come to know what it means to be custodians of the future of the Earth—to know that unless we care, unless we check the rapacious exploitations of our Earth and protect it, we are endangering the future of our children and our children's children. We did not know this before, except in little pieces. People knew that they had to take care of their own . . . , but it was not until we saw the picture of the Earth, from the Moon, that we realized how small and how helpless this planet is—something that we must hold in our arms and care for.

—Margaret Mead, March 21, 1977

HISTORY OF THE EARTH FLAG[1]

I DESIGNED THE EARTH Flag in 1969. The first Earth Flags were produced by screen printing and sold at the July 1969 Moon Watch in Central Park, New York City, celebrating the first astronaut landing on the Moon. Strangely, the two colors were accidentally reversed by the producer—clouds were blue, oceans were white. (Flags produced later had the correct colors.) These original flags with colors reversed are now a collectors' prize.

I copyrighted the Earth Flag in 1969. A year later a registered trade mark was obtained. In both cases the copyright for the Earth Flag was under the name of WE, Inc. (World Equality, Inc.). I had formed WE,

1. Parts of this chapter were presented in a lecture at the 9th International Congress of Vexillology, 1981.

Inc. to promote the idea that this planet belongs to all of us. "WE" was a simple concept, a person-to-person global communication plan incorporating a Minute for Peace, Planetary Inheritance (see the Appendix), and a Global Network. Through expanding links with other members (which were to reach around the world), the members could obtain maximum exposure and evaluation of their ideas and experiences. WE was a non-profit organization. It was not connected with or in support of any particular political, religious, or ideological organization or program. Earth Day activities were under WE, Inc. from 1969 through 1974.

Later, when I started Earth Society, Inc. in 1973, I naturally used the Earth Flag. It was subsequently used by the Earth Society Foundation, which we formed in 1976. The Earth Flag copyright and trademark were never under Earth Society, Inc. or Earth Society Foundation, Inc. I renewed the copyright in 1978, but I ignorantly failed to renew the trademark. I didn't realize that trademarks have to be renewed every five years.

The Earth Flag design was adapted from a 1969 photo of Earth, taken by the astronauts and published in *Life Magazine*. It was considered the first photo of Earth from outer space (Apollo 10 Earth photo 69-HC-487, May 18, 1969), at a distance of 250,000 miles.

When the photo appeared, I was deeply stirred—as were many other people—by what I saw. My own special interest was the result of years of effort to promote international cooperation in space. The efforts went back to 1957, when a "Star of Hope" editorial in my weekly newspaper in North Carolina attracted national attention. As I looked at the *Life* photo in 1969 it occurred to me that an Earth flag could symbolize and encourage our new world view, and that the Earth as seen from space was the best possible symbol for this purpose.

The Copernican revolution back in the sixteenth century had enlarged our perspective of the human race. We became more aware of our planet and its relation to our solar system and to the universe. However, in viewing the first photo from space, thereby sharing in part the experience of the astronauts, we experienced in a deep and emotional way a brand new awareness of our planet. In fact, our venture into space resulted in a new conceptual revolution that gave us a more generalist approach to our problems, and new and reverent wonder about the nature of the human adventure.

I called the National Aeronautics and Space Administration and spoke to the head of public relations, who sent me a transparency of the photo used in *Life*. When I told him what it was for, he said, "What a wonderful idea." In talking to friends, many suggestions were made for adding other elements to the flag—for example, the figure of a person. Nevertheless, I proceeded with the simple design of the Earth centered on a dark blue background.

The photo showed only white clouds and blue ocean—no land, and the image was not quite round. My design was also just clouds and water—with the shape of the image slightly changed to make it completely round, like the Earth. This original design enabled me to obtain the copyright and trademark.

In the rush to make these first flags, the colors in the screening of the Earth were reversed. The Earth view consisted mostly of clouds and oceans, the only land being a small part of Lower California and Central America. For simplicity we had combined the bit of land with the sea. But on these first Earth Flags, due to the color reversal, the ocean is white and the clouds are blue. We saved a small supply of these color-reversed flags, for posterity.

We had 500 12x18" (31.5x47 cm) Earth Flags produced by the American Flag Co. in New Jersey. In Geneva in 1973 I showed the Earth flag to Denis de Rougemont, the Swiss historian. On seeing it, he said "You've got the right one." I said, "What do you mean?" He said, "Well, there have been arguments about which was the first photo of Earth. I contend that the first one used from the many photos they took at that time should be considered the first photo of Earth, and that's the one you used." There had been differences about which photo was the first high resolution photo of Earth. The astronauts didn't know which photo they had taken first. Denis felt the first one published should be considered the first photo of Earth.

Our first 500 flags were produced in a hurry, in order to use them at the Moon Watch at Central Park in New York City. This was the big event where we watched and celebrated the first landing on the Moon on 20 July 1969. Prominent at the ceremony was a large Earth Flag specially made by volunteers. Several hundred of the small flags were sold and some were given away.

Right after this I went to California and initiated the first efforts for Earth Day, another idea that had grown out of my thinking and efforts.

On the first Earth Day, 21 March 1970, the City of San Francisco flew the Earth Flag. Schools, churches, ecology groups, businesses, and youth organizations flew and used the Earth Flag. In one interesting case, when students in Hayward, California, draped a steam roller with Earth Flags and flowers while singing "Where Have All the Flowers Gone?," they managed to stop the paving of their schoolyard.

The *Whole Earth Catalogue* featured the Earth Flag in 1969. After the first production of the Earth Flag, the artist Norman Laliberte contacted me with the suggestion that the Earth Flag have the figure of a person along with the Earth on the flag. I rejected this suggestion. I did not meet with Laliberte before the first Earth Flag production. Hence, the *Whole Earth Catalogue* reference to Laliberte is misleading.

After the Apollo 17 mission in 1972 obtained a better image of the Earth on the way to the Moon, a new Earth Flag was created using an image from December 7 (an anniversary of Pearl Harbor)(Apollo 17, AS17-148-22727).[2]

In the 1980s, I gave John Drysdale permission to put the flag in the Earth Day-Earth Trustee Logo he designed. Also, Ed Brennan formed an Earth Flag company and produced and sold the Earth Flags with my permission. Later (unknown to me), he changed the design and obtained his own copyright.

Since that time requests for Earth Flags have come from all over the world. Meeting the requests was in the early days a poorly-run operation carried on with a few Earth Day volunteers. Efforts to obtain financing and promotion were unsuccessful. We also had repeated difficulty in obtaining a satisfactory product from flag companies due to the unusual nature of our requirements for a photo-like representation of the Earth. Lack of capital resulted in our having to order small quantities of flags at expensive prices.

This "extracurricular activity," in the midst of deep involvement in global problems, was not conducive to a successful undertaking. Nevertheless, by the 1980s, since our first Earth Day, we had distributed over 15,000 Earth Flags—all in response to requests and contributions unsolicited by us. Many of these were the result of free mention in the *Whole Earth Catalogue* and other articles about the flag.

2. The image can be downloaded from http://eol.jsc.nasa.gov/scripts/sseop/photo .pl?mission=AS17&roll=148&frame=22727. The image shows Africa, and the south polar ice cap for the first time.

Still, one woman criticized me. She said, "John, you claim to be a Christian. You should make your contribution for a better world free to all the people, rather than just make money for yourself." The funny part about it is, I've never made money on the Earth Flag. Now, Earth Flags are sold on the Internet by many different companies.

Earth Day 1979 was observed at the New York headquarters of the United Nations in cooperation with the Year of the Child. Several hundred children streamed across the street into the United Nations grounds, carrying and waving small (12″ x 18″) Earth Flags.

At the last minute a volunteer had come up with the idea of distributing Earth Flags to the children, who were participating in the Earth Day program. By the time I learned of this they all had their flags. Knowing the stiff protocol at the United Nations, I asked the guards if it would be all right for them to carry the flags and was informed that they might carry them up to the gate, but that they would have to leave the flags there and pick them up as they left. Yet when they came through the gate, no guard had the heart to ask for a flag and so the Earth Flags added to our joyous celebration.

You will find photos on my website earthsite.org showing that the Earth Flag was planted at the South Pole and the North Pole, and also taken by the Russians into Earth orbit in 1998 aboard the Mir Space Station. In 2001, the Bhoovigyan Vikas Foundation in India hoisted the Earth Flag in an Earth Day Awareness Campaign. The Campaign was publicized by ceremonies with 5,000 children participating from eleven schools in New Delhi.

The Earth Flag has been used each year in Earth Day Ceremonies around the world. It has been presented to many world leaders.

One time I used the Earth Flag in a personal way. This was my own doing. I was invited to speak at some gathering. I knew the value to the media of an interesting picture. So I took two Earth Flags, and pinned them together, and put my head through the middle, so that my costume was the Earth Flag. I wish I could find where that was photographed. I remember it got attention.

We live in a strange world where what's important isn't what gets attention, but what's dramatic gets attention.

IMPACT OF THE EARTH FLAG

Our experience with the Earth Flag has been inspiring. One young man in the Shetland Islands wrote, "I received the large flag in beautiful condition and I love it. It is now serving as a curtain in my room. The first morning I woke up with it, there the sunrise was shining through it and it was fantastic. The Earth seemed to glow and I could imagine the exhilaration the astronauts must experience when they see the beautiful planet, Mother Earth, in its full."

I have unexpectedly found Earth Flags in business offices, newsrooms, schools, and churches. The Earth Flag has been officially flown in many cities. It has been displayed at UN conferences and was featured in an Earth Day essay by Margaret Mead for UPI. She stated ". . . the selection of the March equinox for Earth Day makes planetary observance of a shared event possible. And a flag which shows the Earth as seen from space is appropriate."

When the City of New York celebrated the city's ethnic diversity in a program at Central Park, they ordered 30 large Earth Flags. A Park Department aide confided later, "It solved a problem. All you'd have to do is leave out one ethnic flag and you'd have a crisis. This covers everybody."

Pete Seeger said that the best symbol for Earth was a flag with the Earth on it, and he flew the Earth Flag on the Hudson River Sloop Clearwater. The Queen Elizabeth 2 flew the Earth Flag in 1973 on a two-week Earth Society cruise in the Caribbean with Isaac Asimov, Carl Sagan, Burl Ives, and other Earth patriots.

Through the years we have said many things to try and express the meaning and purpose of the Earth Flag. Initially we stated that the Earth flag was created to remind us that each person has a basic right to use the Earth and an equal responsibility to build the Earth. All nations have flags. The UN has a flag, states have flags, and businesses have flags. There ought to be a flag that's just for people.

On another occasion we said, "The Earth Flag is a non-government flag for all Earth people. Its purpose is to encourage equilibrium in nature, in social systems, and in the minds of men." Another purpose is to foster loyalty to Earth that will transcend national loyalties and differences.

The most beautiful thing is that many people find their own words to express the meaning of the Earth Flag. Several have sent us pledges of allegiance to the Earth Flag. A prisoner who had several years to serve sent for an Earth Flag; he stated that he felt it would give him hope for a better life and a better world when he was released.

Flags have inspired heroic actions in war campaigns. The Earth Flag is inspiring heroic actions for peace and the care and rejuvenation of Earth. Blowing in the wind, the Earth Flag speaks in silence. In rhythm, metaphor, and color it tells us our most important task is to take care of our planet.

Can the Earth Flag give clear meaning and purpose to foster a global community of conscience, free of partisan coercion and control, and dedicated to the care of Earth? Flags have been used for centuries to communicate and encourage values and loyalties, but national flags have been divisive. While many depict the Sun, Moon, and stars, none depicts our home planet. Not one has a symbol or representation of the Earth, to which all are indebted for their very existence.

Action by any government to place the Earth in a corner of its flag, and to initiate a global effort to halt the degradation of Earth and foster its nurture and care, would be welcome. To repeat my statement at an Earth Flag Ceremony in New York City in 1978:

Earth Flag Pledge

We raise the Earth Flag, to encourage and inspire love of Earth.

We raise the Earth Flag to enlist and unite young and old in courageous actions for our planet's protection—for cautious nurture of its life and care of its resources in every city and neighborhood.

We raise the Earth Flag as a promise to all who work to help our planet that they and their children will obtain a fair stake in Earth and its future, with equitable access to its beauty and bounty.

We raise the Earth Flag with a firm conviction that together we can save our planet; that our actions now and in future years will encourage people of every creed and culture to help make Earth a healthy, peaceful planet.

Then on each succeeding Earth Day we will report our Earth Trustee efforts to better life on our planet and celebrate the growing benefits to all.

33

Earth Society and The Earth Society Foundation

EARTH SOCIETY HISTORY

To further the Earth Day concept and activities, and encourage like-minded people to join in supporting Earth Day, in 1973 I formed the Earth Society.

The initial organizing meeting of the Earth Society was held in Geneva, Switzerland, under the large tree by the "golden globe," near the La Palais des Nations-Unies et la Sphere Manship, United Nations in Geneva, at noon on June 19, 1973.

I wrote the following about the Society in September of 1973:

Earth Day Office
September 24, 1973
16 Fulton St.
New York, NY 11206

EARTH SOCIETY: Potentials and Prospects

All over the world people are engaged in trying to understand and care for Earth and its life potentials.

THE NEW WORLD VIEW

An amazing transformation is occurring in Earth's governments, institutions and individuals. People are beginning to experience a new world view, a new whole way of relating to our planet and to one another. The Earth Society is a non-governmental program to aid this process.

EARTH IS ONE

The visit of Comet Kohoutek to our Solar System, like Sputnik, Apollo, and Sky Lab, reminds us that Earth is also a space voyager. It is our one and only Earth. We're all on it together.

HUMANKIND DEPENDENT ON NATURE AND EACH OTHER

Poets, mystics and philosophers have spoken through the centuries of how we are all one: one family, one community, all members one of another. It is only in the last few years that our mutual dependence and interconnectedness has surfaced in the thinking and action of governments and institutions. More and more we see the bonds that link man with man, and man with nature.

BIOLOGY PROVIDES EXAMPLES FOR SOCIAL EVOLUTION

Society as a whole is beginning to function as a human body with brain, blood, glands and nervous system. Today, we see the burgeoning of mutual assistance between all the major powers, and joint action in United Nations agencies on pollution, population and poverty. In these and other institutions throughout the world the critical problems of our environment, industries, social structures, and the needs of our personal body and spirit are being recorded, studied and debated with a new candor and humility.

HARMONY WITH NATURE

Within Earth's institutions is a small but growing nucleus of individuals who are thinking globally and beginning to turn our society and technology toward the understanding and care of our Earth, its life and its people. They offer the hope that Man can successfully take the helm of planet Earth; understanding and adapting nature's ancient methods and systems, which through eons of evolution have increased Earth's life and beauty. These individuals are now acting as cells in a global organism.

THE INFINITE INDIVIDUAL

The individual cell in a human body receives, processes and returns nutrient products with the aid of nervous impulses from the brain. Each cell contains genes with a blueprint of the whole body, which assists in this task.

HUMANITY BECOMING AS ONE GLOBAL BEING

We see in our embryonic global social body the growth of similar systems for providing information, material and action, and "genes" to communicate the emerging Earth-view (ethics, criteria, guidelines) for improvement of Earth's life potentials.

UNIQUENESS AND UNIVERSALITY

Of course people have a much higher level of consciousness than cells and greater opportunity for mobility and creativity. And they can perceive and influence trends. Nevertheless, the analogy is useful. Through new links of communication and new bonds of feeling and awareness, now each person can uniquely affect the social and biological evolution of Earth's new global human organism.

The Earth Society will seek to aid this process.

THE EARTH SOCIETY'S MESSAGE

The Earth Society came into being during a period when I was developing my ideas about Earth Rights. In 1972 I had recognized that it was time to distinguish between the portion of wealth that is the result of labor and skill, and the portion that is obtained by depriving the poor of their inheritance in the Earth.

The new "spaceship Earth" concept, I realized, not only requires global responsibility for the environment, but also awareness of the fundamental right of each person to Earth's natural bounty. Recognizing this right and implementing it would (1) aid efforts for peace, and (2) begin a new era of social justice that could spread around the world.

There are justified complaints in developing countries about the resources of minerals, oil, and other Earth materials which have been taken away and used mainly to improve life in affluent countries. Some compensation is needed for the injustice of the past. New steps should be taken to assure equity in the future. It is time to affirm that in our small "Earth nest" every person has an equal right to an equal share in all the Earth's resources, and to the increment of technology benefits that have accrued from past generations.

While the efforts of labor and management are essential to create goods and services, even more important factors in the creation of wealth are the Earth materials, which, in all fairness, must be considered the common heritage of all mankind.

The prosperous minority should recognize that a major part of their riches are the result, not of their work, but of their status. It is time for this inequity to be corrected. All passengers on "spaceship Earth" should enjoy first-class privileges.

Implementing our new Earth-view with Earth Rights could win the support and voluntary assistance of the poor, which is essential for the crucial actions needed to save the environment. Whether through guaranteed income, royalties on resources, or a $1,000 basic minimum, Earth Rights, divorced from ignominious welfare concepts and attitudes, could change the despair of the deprived to new hope and unity in building the future. The poor in this country, and in the world, would lose their resentment of the rich.

The following spring, in April of 1974, I represented the Earth Society in making the following "Proposal on Earth Rights" to the UN's Ad Hoc Committee on Raw Materials and Development. I focused on three necessary global objectives that would further establish and apply Earth Rights principles that had been in development in the UN and elsewhere for many years:

1. Earth Care: Education and action that will convert our desire and practice to the care of Earth; the preservation and enhancement of its marvelous eco-systems.

2. Justice: Equal individual rights to the use of Earth and its raw materials, and equal responsibility for the care and preservation of Earth's natural bounty.

3. Love: Encouragement and reward for the attributes, values, and actions which, in spite of limiting dogmas and institutional barriers, have nourished the great religions and all humanitarian endeavors.

In proposing these objectives, I pointed out that Earth Society members speak, not for one country, nor for any partisan ideology, creed, or vested interest. We speak for Earth, its life, and its unborn children.

To aid the efforts that were already moving in this direction, we urged the UN delegates to include in their forthcoming declaration on Earth Rights a reference to these objectives, with guidelines for action that would further their purposes.

SEA CITIZEN PROGRAM

A few months later, in August of 1974, I wrote Earth Society members that "After years of search, I believe we have discovered a plan that can spark global cooperation for the care of Earth. . . . [W]e have found an effective way to begin, through a grand initiative to protect, save, and harvest the Sea. We will register supporters as Sea Citizens."

Members of the organizing committee for this initiative included: Arvid Pardo, former chairman of the UN Seabed Committee; Harold Taylor, former president of Sarah Lawrence College and chairman of the United States Committee for the United Nations University; Frank Braynard, General Manager of Operation Sail '76 and author of eleven books on the sea; Louise Eggleston, former president of the International Literacy Foundation; Senator Mark Hatfield of Oregon; and myself, as president of the Earth Society and founder of Earth Day.

The Sea Citizen Program was the first Earth Care Campaign initiative. Since the sea is the physical and biological source of all life, we stressed that it is appropriate that mankind begin his new task of Earth stewardship by careful and productive management of the sea—the new territory in which all people can have a common citizenship and common economic benefit.

The Sea Citizen Organization aimed to register the poor both in this and other countries, obtain for them dividends from their ownership of the sea, and describe the responsibilities inherent in ownership.

To aid these efforts for economic justice, the Sea Citizen Organization planned to establish a Sea Heritage Trust Fund. Financing for the Trust Fund was to come from individuals and institutions interested in perpetuating the life and bounty of the Sea. The Sea Heritage Trust Fund was to seek and accept royalties from sea ventures that acknowledge Sea Citizen claims, and distribute them equally to all registered Sea Citizens.

Along the way it was envisioned that the emphasis of the Earth Society would be "land" and the Sea Citizen Organization would emphasize the sea. The Sea Citizen Organization was to publicize and promote the products of sea ventures, so long as they met environmental criteria. Initial efforts were to obtain ownership royalties on crude oil taken from the seabed.

It was hoped that corporations and governments interested in long-term exploitation of the sea would acknowledge and pay these royalties as they came to understand the great advantage of the resulting strong Sea Citizen program—a program effectively working for uniform rules and regulations to maintain and increase the life and wealth of the sea. Officials in some off-shore oil companies stated at the time that they would prefer paying royalties to the Sea Citizen Organization instead of to separate governments—if the organization could obtain agreement of governments and support for an International Sea Authority with stable global rules and regulations.

Leaders of landlocked and other countries without oil prospects told us our Sea Citizen plan would benefit them and their people more than alternative plans for separate national economic zones in the sea.

MANAGEMENT OF THE SEA

The management of the sea requires the combined efforts of scientists, governments, and industry. Environmentalists and oceanographers must provide the guidelines. Governments, through an International Sea Authority, must aid the enforcement of regulations. Industry must carefully divide and organize the work, which will require their best management skills. In addition, we must recognize that the sea is in fact a sixth continent, as I emphasized in a news release in 1975 (see the Appendix).

But best of all, involving people directly as individuals in a new relationship with the sea, to give to its care and to receive its bounty, can assure public support and provide real protection and cautious harvesting and management of the sea. This would be the task of Sea Citizens.

Efforts were made to strengthen and enlarge the Sea Citizen Organization by recruiting individuals from international institutions representing science, art, culture, religion, economics, and business management (ICSU, World Bank, Red Cross, etc.). Alfred van der Essen, Chairman of the Belgium Delegation to the UN Law of the Sea Conference, was the first delegate to register his name as a Sea Citizen. This was in response to a letter of invitation circulated at the close of the conference. The letter was from Dr. Arvid Pardo, the father of the idea that the seabed is the common heritage of mankind.

Others in Geneva who registered and expressed support of the idea were Henrik Beer, Sec. Gen. of the League of Red Cross Societies, and Dr. Hassan Ahmed, Legal Adviser to the UN Environment Programme. Additional support for Sea Citizen objectives was sought in the United

States Congress, the United Nations, environmental organizations, and multinational corporations. We hoped for participation by major oil producing countries and companies. They, along with all of us, have much to gain.

Leaders of the Sea Citizen and Earth Care Campaign sought by imaginative actions to obtain corporate, government, and public support that would capture the headlines of the world. We knew that yesterday's impossible stories are today's headlines: "Man on the Moon," "President Resigns," etc. Perhaps the following headlines are not impossible dreams for tomorrow: "Japan Approves Sea Citizen Claims," "India Helps Register Sea Citizens in Bangladesh," "IBM Data Bank to Serve Sea Citizen Information Center," "HEW Computerizes Sea Citizen Dividends," "QE2 Joins Sea Citizen Fleet," "New York Times Advertising Converted to Earth Care Catalogue."

Our planet is dying. The Earth is weak and dirty but still beautiful. Man has the scientific knowledge to save her. It has been his unknowing neglect and estrangement that has brought her to death's door. Will he be moved by new appreciation and love to act in time?

You will decide.

THE EARTH SOCIETY FOUNDATION FORMED IN 1976

Because of Margaret Mead's interest, she urged me to change the Earth Society, Inc. (of which she was never a member) to The Earth Society Foundation for tax purposes. In 1976, The Earth Society Foundation was formed by John McConnell, Capt. Anthony Keasby and Frank Braynard. Margaret Mead became a Member of the Board and strongly supported the goals of the Society. Capt. Keasby had made the first recording of the humpback whale. Frank Braynard founded Op-Sail.

Margaret Mead was just brilliant. Concerning our Earth Society Foundation, she said, "John, we don't want to become the awesome Earth Society Foundation. We want to communicate the great ideas that will help other people to do powerful organizations." I thought that was a very Christian attitude. We stressed getting Earth Day understood and accepted by different governments.

The goals below were incorporated into The Earth Society Foundation at its first Board Meeting, on December 8, 1976:

A Program for Earth's Rejuvenation.

The Earth Society believes technology has given us the new modes for production, distribution, consumption, travel, and land use that can preserve and restore the Earth. What is needed is a coalition of people making a massive effort equal to the task.

The Earth Society believes the global Sea belongs to the people of Earth, and the Society has formed a Sea Citizen Organization to claim these rights for all who register as Sea Citizens. The Sea Citizen Organization is especially seeking to register the poor, both in this country and elsewhere, and will work to obtain for them dividends from their partial ownership of the Sea. Participation and support for Sea Citizen objectives are being sought in the United Nations, the United States Congress, environmental organizations, and multi-national corporations. The Earth Society's conceptions of the continuation of the freedom of the seas, responsible resource management, and universal ownership must be a part of the consciousness of those attending the Law of the Sea Conference in New York, March 27, 1976.

The Earth Society believes the entire Earth Family should have a day of celebration. In initiating Earth Day, marking the March equinox and Earth's rebirth, the Earth Society has provided an occasion and symbol for uniting, rejoicing, and giving thanks for our Earth home. Earth Day is the first, and as yet the only, multinational, nonsectarian holiday the globe celebrates. The theme for Earth Day 1976 is "Share the Sea," to acknowledge universal ownership of the seas.

The Earth Society believes that planet Earth belongs to each of us, that every individual's inheritance includes a share in the Earth's natural resources and that the preservation and care of the Earth is the responsibility of individuals as well as of governments and other institutions.

The Earth Society is seeking through communication to obtain a grand alliance of producers and consumers in a program for Earth's rejuvenation.

Here we have defined our major concepts and goals. Now we need your participation. . . . with ideas, time, money, to design, organize and together demonstrate a program that will work.

JOIN US NOW . . .

SINCE 1976

In 1977, I met Claes Nobel, the Founder-President of an organization named Earth Aid Society promoting "Equilibrium Between Man & Nature." We found we had very common interests and goals, and therefore discussed a possible merger of the Earth Aid Society and The Earth Society Foundation. At first, the boards of the two organizations believed a merger would multiply all our common efforts, and we aimed to develop and disseminate materials for use in New York's Earth Day celebration in 1978. However, after further discussion, the merger fell through.

The activities of The Earth Society Foundation since then have focused on organizing the annual Earth Day celebration at the UN in New York City. The website for the Foundation is http://www.earthsocietyfoundation.org.

34

Earth Charter

IN 1979 I BEGAN promoting the Earth Care Campaign, drawing together various themes including Earth Day and efforts for peace. As
part of this Campaign, in 1979 I wrote an Earth Charter. Later, in 1985,
I wrote the "77 Theses." In 1995, I produced the Earth Magna Charta,
which is much longer than the Earth Charter. All three documents are
included in the Appendix.

The original Earth Charter was featured in a large-sized illustrated
poster designed by John Drysdale. Beautiful copies of this poster were
placed on every floor of the United Nations building and circulated at
the United Nations. On December, 1982, I spoke at Princeton University.
My subject was the Earth Care Campaign. This address is reproduced
in the Appendix.

It is unfortunate that we didn't push to get resolutions through the
General Assembly adopting the Earth Charter. Later, in the later 1990s,
the United Nations backed a different version of an Earth Charter. As far
as I am concerned, their version wasn't as simple and wasn't as good as
the one I originally wrote. The substitute was pushed by Maurice Strong.
Those that take credit for that version of an Earth Charter don't mention that my original Earth Charter was all over the UN building long
before the new one was composed. Of course, they also don't mention
the March equinox Earth Day or the Earth Trustee agenda.

You'll find all sorts of confusion at the United Nations. One time I
was meeting with a small group studying dreams. A dream that I shared
with the group involved a balloon that was high in the heavens. As part
of the dream, I was speaking to people that over the years I had met at

the United Nations. I asked a member of the study group what did he think of the dream. And he said, "The only thing I can get out of it is that the UN is like a balloon, a place full of hot air."

35

Earth Trustees

THE STATE OF THE PLANET

HUMAN GREED, INJUSTICE, AND folly have almost ruined our planet. People worldwide know we have a serious problem with pollution, poverty, and violence. But with the aid of new technology a vigorous global effort can repair the damage. Until now, Earth Caretakers have been a sad minority. The most powerful institutions (global corporations and rich governments) have usually put profit and power first. The resulting social and environmental damage is disastrous. But Earth Trustee vision and action can change our present course of conflict. The Earth Trustee vision provides a way for each one of us to tap the best in his thinking and faith.

ENVISION OUR RESPONSIBILITY

A new idea that came from Minute for Peace and Earth Day was the idea that we can now all think of ourselves as Trustees of Earth. In this age of space exploration we know—more than former generations—that we are one human family and have only one Earth home. With care and use of new technology we can now eliminate poverty, pollution, and violence. All we need is a clear vision of our goal, and spread of reports on the Internet and other media of every successful effort to think and act as Trustees of Earth—in ecology, economics, and ethics. Then a new spirit of cooperation will engulf the world.

As soon as you read this message, take action. Pray, and plan what you will do. Call your friends. Contact media, churches, and colleges.

Act now—with faith that accents the positive and negates the negative. "Oh the faith that works by love."

THE TERM EARTH TRUSTEE

While many terms have been used to indicate social and environmental responsibility, the term which came from the original Earth Day and offers the most advantage is the term "Earth Trustee." The reason I chose the term "Earth Trustee" was that it came from the word "trust." And what we need in our program of taking care of planet Earth is something we can really trust. I started using the term in the early 1970s.

In actions at the United Nations and among its member states, the term has come to mean "Individuals and institutions that are devoted to peace, justice, and the care of Earth." Any action that is helping eliminate poverty, pollution, and violence can be considered Earth Trustee action.

"Earth Trustee" is also considered a new designation of an individual's identity. While in regard to my national identity, I am referred to as an American, more important is to accept the Earth Trustee designation and conduct my life as a responsible "Earth Trustee."

If we can get the term "Earth Trustee" defined and communicated effectively, then this will be a catalyst for all of the efforts being made to improve the environment and to promote harmony and peace on our planet, and be very important in achieving our goal.

EARTH CARE CAMPAIGN

In December of 1999, as Anna and I were organizing our voluminous records, we came across a copy of a speech I had given almost 20 years earlier at Princeton University to the Youth Environmental Society. The title is "Earth Care Campaign." I found it interesting that it reflects my views today. One thing I would add is that the term Earth Trustee provides a name for people engaged in Earth Care. Also, the Earth Magna Charta, which was written some years after the speech, is a better document.

The Earth Care message is long, and therefore it is printed as part of the Appendix. A central idea in the message is that "What is needed today is a great unifying purpose, a strong bonding idea that can interlink all of society. I believe the only thing that can bring this about is the recognition of our planet and a commitment to be Earth Trustees, to accept our role as the caretakers of this marvelous planet."

HELPING THE MOST—ACTING AS EARTH TRUSTEES

What would most help the people of this planet? I keep coming back to this: We all should think and act as Earth Trustees and pursue peace, justice, and a sustainable future. Or, in other words, peace, justice, and the care of the Earth. If this were taught from grammar school through the college years, and if everyone wanted to be an Earth Trustee, why we would see every city and every business making decisions and choices that would achieve this goal.

We have an amazing planet. I refer to it as "Our Nest in the Stars."

We are now at a critical point. At one time, we were in danger from the population explosion but that has been reduced in all kinds of ways—birth control and so on. And then we have technology today that could eliminate a great many problems.

We must all think and act as Earth Trustees.

Now is the time to mobilize our faith and our institutions in an Earth Trustee Campaign for Earth. Now is the time, especially, for a new sense of purpose and responsibility by public media. Let them sponsor a Media Blitz for Earth's rejuvenation, with features and headlines for the many solutions that are working and need attention. Call attention to places where Earth Trustee words are being followed by Earth Trustee actions.

The people of Earth have the raw materials and technology for all to enjoy a life of quality. Individuals and institutions can now be Trustees of the Earth, seeking in ecology, economics, and ethics, policies and decisions that will benefit people and planet. In the present state of the world, this space age Earth Trustee concept has a chance of tapping the best in human hopes and aspirations, and providing a healthy, innovative, and fulfilling future for our planet and its people. In this new future, deeds will demonstrate what is best in all creeds.

EARTH TRUSTEE SOLUTION

Environment, Economics, and Ethics

As Earth Trustees, we must give priority to three things that will decide our future: environment, economics, and ethics. Environmental actions must be a chief concern of individuals and institutions. This means doing things needed to make our economic systems work fairly with incentives for Earth Care. We must also address the need for ethics, for integrity, for achieving a balance of freedom and order as we pursue our task.

We may have different cultural values and use different methods, but as long as we keep the goal of Earth Trusteeship as a guiding star for all humanity, we will solve our problems. Our diversity will find harmony and strength through its united purpose. More and more, we will move to better understanding and cooperation in managing and taking care of our planet.

This will bring the rejuvenation of our planet and fair benefits for everyone.

We will see a change of attitude and conduct worldwide from fear and despair to hope and faith. People will act, each in their own way, as responsible Trustees of Earth. They will sincerely act as Trustees of Earth because they know it will be best for them as well as for others. This will provide a moral equivalent of war—a *Peace Blitz for a Better World*. Instead of wealth being spent for war, it will be devoted to projects that heal, build, and unite.

Earth Day gave birth to the Earth Trustee idea and agenda. The following is the Earth Trustee solution—a simple, practical, formula that will appeal to the most people and do the most good for people and planet:

Let every individual and institution now think and act as an Earth Trustee, seeking in ecology, economics, and ethics to foster a sustainable future and eliminate poverty, pollution, and violence on our planet.

How this idea can be applied in very specific ways is described in the Earth Magna Charta, which is reprinted later in this book, and available in electronic form on the Internet at earthsite.org.

Earth Day, Earth Trustees, and related topics have obtained endorsement and praise from many people, including some world leaders. But many people misunderstand and misapply its tenets. What is needed is more attention for Earth Trustee actions and results. In this book I cover as much relevant material as possible. My purpose here is to provide ideas and information that will show the possibilities and inspire individuals and institutions to apply the formula in their own way. Only when you are moved emotionally as well as intellectually, will you act effectively.

THE EARTH TRUSTEE WAY TO EARTH CARE AND PEACE

The Power of Earth Care Thinking and Doing

All that is needed to provide a healthy, prosperous future for our planet and its people is for all to act as Trustees of Earth—to do those things that will nurture and improve Earth's amazing web of life, seeking fair benefits for each person who works for this goal.

After such a sweeping generalization, is their any practical way to bring this about?

Becoming an Earth Trustee is a simple formula which anyone can use. One person's action might seem to accomplish little—other than a good feeling for doing one's part. But confident, enthusiastic action can bring a contagious multiplication of Earth Trustees that will cover the Earth and rejuvenate our planet.

EARTH TRUSTEE OBJECTIVES

The key concept is for everyone to be a Trustee of planet Earth—each in his or her own way. The objectives of Earth Trustees will be to:

1. Make an inner commitment—through prayer, meditation, or reflection—to be a Trustee of planet Earth, seeking each day to combine love of God, love of neighbor and love of Earth. Join each year on Earth Day, March 20–21, in global dedication to this task.

2. Protect and nurture Earth's life and natural resources by Earth Care choices in buying, selling, and giving, choices that diminish pollution and increase Earth's natural equilibrium and bounty.

3. Support efforts to provide the disinherited poor a stake in their planet—a secure homestead in city or country. Seek stable money and fair credit for everyone.

4. Join some group with a project for the care of Earth that meets some or all of the above criteria. Be a connecting link between two or more groups pursuing these purposes.

5. Tell your friends what you are doing and invite them to do the same. Most people know we have a global crisis and want to do the right thing—something that will help.

SLOGAN FOR GLOBAL EARTH TRUSTEE ACCEPTANCE

Sometimes a slogan repeated often can bring about the needed change in thinking. A slogan suggested for advancing the Earth Trustee concept is the following:

By the Power of Truth, Peaceful Progress on Our Planet.

Given the focus and effort that put a man on the moon, the Earth Trustee agenda can rapidly change attitudes and conduct—enough that we in the new millennium will replace despair with hope for the future.

EARTH TRUSTEE MISSION STATEMENT

The Earth Trustee idea is embodied in the following Earth Trustee Mission Statement, which includes an enhanced version of the formula from above:

To proclaim the truth that can appeal to the most people and convert tragedy into triumph on our planet: Every individual and institution can now think and act as a Trustee of Earth, seeking choices in ecology, economics, and ethics that will provide a sustainable future, eliminate pollution, poverty, and violence, and awaken the wonder of life and foster peaceful progress in the human adventure.

CHILDREN AS EARTH TRUSTEES

We believe the world belongs to the children.

A few years ago we had children at our Earth Day Ceremony chanting the words from Ps 115:16, "The Earth hath he given to the children of men." Even before the first Earth Day, I arranged for seven children from the United Nations International School to ring the bell in 1966 on October 4, the Feast Day of St. Francis.

In this time of great fear and anxiety, every child should think about the love they have known and felt. We feel better when there is love in what we say and hear. When we are helped, we feel good and say "Thank you"—which makes the person who helped us feel good too.

Many children think and act as Trustees of Earth—which means that they avoid things that waste or pollute, and love to plant things and take care of pets. In many cases, grown-ups also become Earth Trustees because of what a child has said and done.

Children of the world have ways of loving nature and people that can give hope to the grown-ups, that we will overcome the despair caused by polluters and war-makers.

Children of the world can plan now how to celebrate Earth Day on March 20, the first day of spring. We ring the Peace Bell at the United Nations at the moment spring begins. This is nature's symbol of new life and new beginnings. Our planet needs a new beginning. Children can take the lead in making it happen.

Fred Burrous was one of my oldest friends. He was PR Director for the Red Cross in San Francisco, and later in Geneva. He helped start Minute for Peace and Earth Day. He suggested we stress "Young Earth Trustees" in the Earth Magna Charta. He also provided a Young Earth Trustee Exhibit on Earth Day at the United Nations, and formed a Young Earth Trustee organization. He visited the Institute of Noetic Sciences—started by astronaut Edgar Mitchell—and briefly represented them in Florida. They back his Young Earth Trustee program.

Young Earth Trustees will lead the way. This was recognized in the Earth Magna Charta. It was Lord Menuhin that provided the statement about Young Earth Trustees which was made a part of the Earth Magna Charta. The text is as follows:

Young Earth Trustees: Arts and Crafts

The exercise of arts and crafts—especially in the form of singing, dancing, mime acting and music-making—is the most effective antidote to violence and crime. Let us ensure that every child from the very first year will NEVER be deprived of the aural and physical experience on which its whole life and the future of humanity depends.

Yehudi Menuhin thus added music to the purpose of Earth Day.

When I was in the Merchant Marine during World War II, Yehudi Menuhin played his violin at a USO in Trinidad. I was there, and after his wonderful music, I got his autograph.

On August 11, 1996, I attended the Yehudi Menuhin Tribute at Avery Fisher Hall. At that event Lord Menuhin added his signature to the original 1970 Earth Day Proclamation, which I had brought for him to sign. Throughout his life Lord Menuhin effectively contributed to efforts for peace and understanding, by his words and with his music.

EARTH TRUSTEE OPPORTUNITY

A Time to Test the Power of Faith and Love

Two thousand years ago a drama of tragedy and triumph planted new seeds of hope in human minds. Hope for brotherhood, freedom, and love. Hope that the spirit could be more powerful than the sword.

Two hundred years ago, the hope had evolved into a world-view that made possible great experiments in democracy. But still the sword seemed more powerful than the spirit: The soldier who fought was more a hero than the man of reason who persuaded by reason and good will. People were not yet ready or able to use the great powers of the spirit for good will and peace.

Today we have an opportunity to prove the power of that ancient hope and the possibility of its earthly fulfillment. Circumstances are propitious for a global test of its validity.

Today, a disillusioned world is groping for eternal verities. New potentials of the mind and spirit are being discovered. A new world-view is emerging—a view of our planet as a nest in the stars, a home for "earthlings" who are beginning the great adventure of exploring the deep skies of space.

There is a new awareness of the importance of each individual and, at the same time, a realization that we share with all people a need for water and food, for beauty, and for one another.

In the past, people were disconnected by space and time. Now, an event can transcend distances, and can speed to every part of the world in a few seconds.

Now, in this great moment of opportunity, let us prove the power of faith and prayer to change attitudes and actions—to end wars and violence. Let us demonstrate that the power of the spirit can defeat the power of the sword. Let all who believe in the power of the Spirit, of thought or prayer, prove the power of their faith by the vigor of their daily Earth Trustee actions.

IMPLEMENTING THE EARTH TRUSTEE SOLUTION

In different ways every Earth Trustee should seek to engage in some action or project that is helping the care of Earth. As an example, a person who becomes concerned with the destruction of rainforests, or the killing of whales, and seeks to do something to solve the problem through publicity, education, legislation, or personal moral persuasion, is engaged in an effort that can appropriately be called an Earth Care Project. Every Earth Trustee should have an Earth Care Project.

We may be doing different things and at times using conflicting methods in different approaches to solving the same kind of problems. But more and more we will move in the right direction. The idea of Earth Trusteeship can change the world. It can save our planet.

To accomplish these purposes—literally the conversion of Earth to a peaceful, prosperous planet—will require a deep contagious commitment and a practical plan to spread participation worldwide. Many individuals, groups, and organizations are already moving in this direction. An Earth Trustee Plan should appeal to all of them and greatly assist their endeavors where these endeavors are consistent with Earth Trustee goals. The name Earth Trustee, and its goals, can unify and strengthen these efforts and encourage participation of some kind by all the benevolent institutions on Earth.

A basic premise of an Earth Trustee Plan is that peaceful progress is mainly the result of finding urgent matters in which there is honest accord and then building on that accord. Society, mainly because of irresponsible media seeking quick profits, tends to focus on discord— aggravating it by neglecting or ignoring areas of agreement and creative possibilities of peace.

It is well in the beginning to consider the difficulties that may be encountered and how to avoid them or surmount them. In many trouble spots around the world, both parties in a conflict feel they are the injured ones. In the present terrible state of affairs, hate and violence are rampant in many parts of the world. The Earth Trustee agenda can help bring sanity to our troubled planet.

In this new millennium, given the information explosion with its confusion and contradictions, let us use the key that will peacefully unlock the door to the future. The key is to combine faith and works in Earth Trustee vision and action. What is needed cannot be done in a day, or in a year. But a firm commitment can be made now with ever increasing faith and action in the coming days. Think about, pray about, talk about what you will do, and you will make a difference.

This task is fraught with great difficulties. We are all products of our personal and cultural history. In fact, the words and images we use often mean different things to different people. A Christian may experience warm feelings about the Cross of Christ, while many (not all) Muslims are offended by attention given to it. They prefer the image of the Crescent—which calls attention to their different view of things. This is just one example of the different views of what is important.

Elsewhere in this book I discuss the problem of our differences, but here let me mention that there are more and more people who now recognize that the future depends on our coming together in the vital matters in which we agree. Successful efforts for conciliation and cooperation around the world have been based on this premise.

If Arab and Jew, or any other adversaries, know there is a worldwide program that convincingly offers a chance for each family to have their own homestead with fair opportunities for employment, and a share, through royalties, in Earth's natural bounty, and that crisscrossing political and religious boundaries there is a new idea, "We Are All Trustees of Planet Earth," there will be a new acceptance of diversity, with more cooperation for mutual goals (at a distance from one another when necessary!).

In this new way of thinking we will respect the right of others to follow a religious creed or political belief different from ours—so long as it does not intrude on our similar right to follow our own belief. And we will agree that the merit that all should acknowledge and accept in people of different creeds or beliefs, is the honesty, virtue, fairness, and charity demonstrated by their followers. This is the unity that must complement our diversity. This can result in each culture and group finding its own place "in the Sun."

The object here is to win acceptance of the Earth Trustee concept by different competing groups, or groups in conflict, aiding cooperation in vital matters in which they agree while avoiding in this program conflicting partisan views.

We are not saying to a conservative charismatic Christian (or to a Muslim or Jew) that all religions are the same, or even that one must approve of other religions, or worship with people of a different faith. One can pursue the goals of Trusteeship independently—but now with the constraint of awareness that people of different beliefs share our love of Earth and its people, and they will seek in their own way to be Trustees of Earth.

This unity will be dramatized each Earth Day when people of different religions and political views pray or meditate in their separate ways at the same time and for the same purpose all over the world. Earth Day would be a great time for a "Global Roll Call" of nations and major cities to find those willing to make a commitment to think and act as responsible Earth Trustees.

HOW TO COMMUNICATE THE IDEA

American citizens of every political and religious persuasion are united in loyalty to their country. Now we must find a way to demonstrate loyalty to our planet that will transcend and accommodate our global differences.

The question then is, "How can we win global attention and acceptance?" There are two ways we can proceed. One, we can spur participation in a grass roots movement. I believe in the trickle-up theory. From the grass roots we can develop Earth Trusteeship—how it will work, and the most effective way to communicate it and get people involved. We can begin with ourselves. This is a contagious idea. We and our friends can plant the seeds locally and globally. It can quickly spread around the world.

I also believe in the trickle-down theory. If the door opens for someone to meet a president of this or that nation, I believe such a president will be attracted to the idea. Clearly presented, the Earth Trustee idea would appeal to the leaders of many major countries, and they would do something about it. Gorbachev, former president of the former USSR, responded to the concept of Earth Day and signed the Earth Day Proclamation. Other public leaders could speed the spread of the idea by supporting it with their words and deeds.

Let's plan to persuade individuals and groups all over the world to have this one guiding star—they are all going to be Trustees of planet Earth and make of our planet a Garden of Eden. Soon the great majority of human activity and effort will be to heal and build, to conserve, to rejuvenate the Earth and creatively to expand human potentials.

The role of press and all public media is essential. They must report Earth Trustee actions and their results. We will then rapidly see more good news than bad news in the media. The media will feature the Earth Trustee efforts of individuals, churches, service clubs, and businesses.

I ask radio, TV stations, and newspapers to start an "Earth Trustee Media Blitz." We have the raw materials, the technology, and instant global communications—and there are people ready and willing around the world.

All that is needed is to get their attention. The ideas presented here can then bring the needed Earth Trustee choices in words and actions—and peaceful progress will prevail.

SPECIFIC ACTIONS FOR IMPLEMENTING THE EARTH TRUSTEE SOLUTION

The Earth Trustee Solution is the key that can bring us all together. Here are specific actions for its implementation:

1. *Earth Trustee Communities—Pattern for Global Rejuvenation*
    Verbal response to the Earth Trustee proposals has been positive. We have received many strong statements of support by leaders in environmental and peace organizations. What is needed now is attention for examples. What is meant in words needs to be effectively illustrated by action.

    To accomplish this, there needs to be warm-hearted support and action by entire communities. We need communities that will firmly apply the Earth Trustee formula and adopt the Earth Magna Charta. To succeed there is need for every local institution to join the effort and apply the Earth Trustee policies in what they do. They can each do this in their own way and at the same time get ideas from others and help one another.

    Participation, led by a Mayor or other official, should include schools, churches, stores, banks, service clubs, libraries, newspapers, radio, TV, and any other local institutions. We need to invite all of them to become "Earth Trustee Communities."

2. *Maximized Use of the Internet to Spread the Earth Trustee Mission*
    The Internet has provided WWW—a World Without Walls. The Internet provides a means for spreading the Earth Trustee mission worldwide. Every website can be an Earth Trustee site and do its part to help people and planet. Make every Earth Day an Internet Earth Day.

    Precede Earth Day with reports of Earth Trustee solutions on the Internet. Reports of Earth Trustee solutions on Internet message boards could be promoted by colleges or other responsible institutions.

    Webmasters should provide web pages with rosters of Earth Trustee websites, designating the physical location of the providers and their statements of purpose. Some university or think tank should find and list every institution that supports the Earth Trustee Mission and approves the Earth Magna Charta.

Earth Trustee forums can be formed—especially by Earth Trustee universities. They can seek links with other websites, assisting and advising one another. While recognizing and rejecting matters in which they differ, they can focus on areas of accord. This can be done without approval of political or religious views which one rejects. Cooperation will be on common ground, for common goals and a common agenda. The Earth Trustee agenda and the global celebration of Earth Day each year on nature's special day, the March equinox, can provide a future for our planet.

This should all be coordinated in a way that will maximize connections. Outstanding examples of Earth Trustee policies and actions should be posted on the Internet. Earth Trustee websites can post a notice of adoption of the Earth Magna Charta by cities, states, and nations, and any similar actions that implement the Earth Trustee agenda. Earth Trustee message boards and prayer lines should follow.

3. *Actions by Individuals*
    As an individual you can make a difference by your words and actions. You who have a voice in some profit or non-profit institution can seek changes in policies that will favor Earth Trustee purposes. When churches and religious institutions, universities, banks, corporations, and local and national governments all seek to apply Earth Trustee thinking in their policies and actions, the whole world will have a great future.

Use of the name Earth Trustee by everyone whose actions are helping Earth Trustee goals can increase our sense of identity with the whole human family, and bring to our diversity the needed measure of global unity and cooperation.

All we need to do is make a heartfelt decision to think and act as an Earth Trustee, striving each day to do things that will help people and planet. Share this idea with your closest friends and any organization of which you are a member. More ideas for pursuing this goal are at the Earth Trustee website, earthsite.org.

Help the Earth Trustee effort. There is no special Earth Trustee organization to join—any organizations can adopt and advocate the Earth Trustee policies and agenda.

Report your suggestions and solutions to message boards or forums. Forward this page to friends and ask them to do the same. As they in turn share this good news it will soon spread through the Internet and bring the changes needed to provide a peaceful, prosperous future on our planet.

On Earth Day join with your friends and family at home, church, school or work to mark this day with attention for the wonder of life and what we can do for people and planet. Let's have bells ring all over the world when the Peace Bells are rung on Earth Day. Explorers in space will share their inspiring views of our beautiful planet as they join in the celebration.

Our key job in the new millennium is to all help make it an Earth Trustee Millennium, where peace, love and care of Earth will reign supreme.

There are many non-profit voluntary projects which can be described as Earth Trustee projects. They are to be found in environmental, conservation, neighborhood, gardening, urban homestead, solar energy, and consumer information organizations; in schools, churches, unions, businesses, fraternal clubs, and youth programs. Increasing them a hundredfold will dramatically demonstrate our willingness and ability to live in harmony with nature and one another, to take charge and take care of Earth.

We can make the care of Earth fashionable. Every person can support at least one Earth Trustee project with time and money. If we double Earth Trustee actions each year for five years—an easy goal if we get our priorities straight—we will save our planet.

Examples of Earth Trustee projects include the following: conservation, insulation, alternative energy, recycling, and appropriate technology; products that are energy efficient with minimal pollution in production and use; travel habits that save energy, such as public transportation and bicycles; neighborhood gardens, industries, crafts, and urban homesteads.

In addition to voluntary non-profit projects, we need to see publicity about people and programs that apply the Earth Trustee precepts in business and industry. Investing in, or producing Earth

Trustee products and services, will provide better jobs and a better tomorrow for everyone.

As campaigns for Earth Trustee actions spread worldwide, they will bring new love for our planet: a global change of attitude— a new way of thinking—common objectives—mutual trust—a chance to prove religious faith or ethical belief—money made and used in ways that foster Earth's care—disarmament—with peaceful alternatives for freedom and order in the human adventure.

4. *Earth Trustee Registry*
To confirm and strengthen your resolve to act as an Earth Trustee, you can add your name to the Earth Trustee Registry at earthsite. org. Webmasters who support the Earth Trustee agenda on earthsite. org are invited to link their own Earth Trustee pages to earthsite.org to further the Earth Trustee goals. There will be differences in approach, but one common purpose and one annual coming together in heart and mind in the celebration of the equinox Earth Day.

5. *Earth Trustee Campaign*
The purpose of the Earth Trustee Campaign will be to demonstrate awareness of our amazing planet and its need for our care, beginning in our own backyard.

All communities in all countries are invited to initiate their own Earth Trustee efforts. With effective use of the Internet we can rapidly bring about a global change of attitude and conduct and see a solution to the terrible problems we face.

It has been my dream that universities around the world would adopt the Earth Trustee agenda and the equinox Earth Day as a common priority around the world. And I have repeatedly sought for individual cities to adopt the Earth Trustee agenda.

Heartfelt Earth Trustee vision and vigorous Earth Trustee action is the best cure for the global cancer of terrorism—and the way to a peaceful, prosperous future on our planet.

6. *Earth Trustee Institutions*
Individual Earth Trustee actions can improve conditions in institutions as they presently exist. Far more benefits will result as we restructure institutions to conform to Earth Trustee policies and purposes. Businesses, banks, churches and temples, clubs, and towns and cities, are all invited to help implement the Earth Trustee

agenda. They can adopt the Earth Magna Charta and implement its Earth Trustee ideas in their own way. Adoption by all altruistic institutions of the Earth Trustee idea is needed, seeking in their own way to implement its purposes.

7.   *Earth Trustee Adoption by States and Provinces*
Large political units can also act as Earth Trustees. All it takes is a few key people to promote the Earth Trustee idea. Gerry Coffey has been an associate and colleague of mine since October 1991. We were introduced when I appeared as a guest on a radio program where she was the volunteer host, at WAJF in Decatur, Alabama.

Since that time, Ms. Coffey and I have worked on a number of environmental projects with schools and city officials in Huntsville and Decatur, Alabama, as well as with the Governor, who signed a proclamation making Alabama an Earth Trustee State.

Over the years Ms. Coffey has assisted me on numerous occasions, and she was also instrumental in recognizing the contribution of children working with the First Lady of Alabama to bring environmental awareness to the public. This resulted in a pictorial exhibition that was displayed at the United Nations on Earth Day 1998. In 1999 Ms. Coffey helped *The Huntsville Times* win the first award for Media Excellence in Environmental Reporting for their series called "The River Defiled."

8.   *Accenting Positive Efforts and Adopting the Earth Trustee Label*
While people may use different words to describe their efforts, here and there around the world are success stories of efforts to eliminate pollution, poverty, and violence—to educate, cooperate, and achieve worthwhile community goals. Giving these success stories a common Earth Trustee label will strengthen these efforts and foster support. These are the stories that should be featured in media—TV, radio, press—and supported by all individuals and institutions. These efforts would help foster non-violent resolution of conflict.

9. *Measuring Success by Earth Day Celebrations*
    The icon of global harmony and pursuit of the Earth Trustee agenda
    will be the celebration of Earth Day on every March equinox, and
    the ringing of bells all over the world at the moment spring begins
    in the Northern Hemisphere.

EARTH TRUSTEE PROGRAM ORGANIZATION AND DEVELOPMENT

Earth Trustee Agenda—Organization and Development

To accomplish Earth Trustee goals, the following items should be included in the organization and development of an Earth Trustee program:

1. Develop a simple brochure asking people to be Trustees of planet
    Earth. Combine a Star of Hope with the Earth Trustee agenda, and
    provide a means for Trustees to register their names with the Star of
    Hope. The goal would be to seek to have all names in a visible Star
    of Hope satellite by the Year 2012. A contribution of $5 or more will
    be suggested, though not required. This will help fund the collec-
    tion of signatures and promotion of the Star of Hope satellite.

2. Approach different organizations to be Star of Hope affiliates, to
    approve the Earth Trustee concept and collect signatures for the
    Star of Hope satellite. They would bear the cost of recording sig-
    natures they collect. But contributions would be to their own or-
    ganization, and should be stimulated by the dramatic appeal of the
    Earth Trustee/Star of Hope idea. They would also plan their own
    observances of Earth Day.

3. Obtain an 800 number that will carry taped messages, with prog-
    ress reports and where to send names for the Star of Hope. Later,
    a switchboard with Earth Trustee experts could be available to an-
    swer questions.

4. Organize and promote Star of Hope telephone prayer lines, talk
    lines (for action reports and discussion), and Earth lines—with
    taped top Earth care items from around the world (900 #).

5. Expand the Earth Trustee program. Invite leaders in science, edu-
    cation, religion, business, and the arts to be Trustees. Find a suit-
    able Trustee chairman who will obtain helpful statements and ac-
    tion by Trustees.

6. Line up bells to be rung around the world next Earth Day, to be covered by radio and TV. Ask NGOs to be Star of Hope affiliates and plan observances of Earth Day.

7. Make the Sunday preceding Earth Day a special day of prayer in churches, synagogues, temples, and other places of worship, praying for a global change of heart to occur on Earth Day, March 20.

8. Produce Earth Day videotapes, making available both 3-minute and 30-minute videos for fundraising and promotion.

9. Encourage several independent Earth Trustee clearinghouses, such as with UNESCO, the Ford Foundation, the Catholic House of Bishops, etc. While independent and probably different in approach, they would share information with each other and the public about Earth Trustee projects and progress.

10. Develop a program for telephone company participation. Star of Hope affiliates would obtain contributions by having supporters dial their special 900#. The telephone company would mail Star of Hope certificates to callers.

11. Publish and make available the 77 Theses, Earth Bounty Program, and Certified Assets Checking Account proposal. These would be described as some of the possible options to implement the Earth Trustee program. Report other examples of alternatives and their success.

ENVISIONING THE FUTURE

By these Earth Trustee actions we can honor peace. With vision and fervor we can now make our planet blossom. The best potentials of our children can now be encouraged and realized on a planet of peaceful progress and new hope for the future.

To proceed, all that is needed is global attention for this dynamic world view, which is one all can accept and support. Science, technology, and the best in our religions—love of neighbor and love of our planet—have prepared us for this moment of opportunity. We've ended the cold war, are less threatened by bandit states, and through efforts in the United Nations are improving communications, understanding, and cooperation.

The new world view sees humanity as one family and Earth as our home. It requires that we now choose to be Trustees of Earth, seeking the protection and care of our planet, with fair benefits for all. Recognizing our diversity, we may pursue this goal in different ways, but we will learn from each other. With our common goal we will find and define points of common accord as we strive to act as responsible Trustees of Earth in every home, business, school, neighborhood, and municipality.

There are three parts to our Earth Trustee responsibility:

1. Ecology—care of the eco-systems that cover our globe via protection and nurture of soil, air, water, trees, and creatures great and small. The use of technology in ways that extend instead of destroy nature's natural bounty. Lifestyles and conduct that favor nature's needs.

2. Economics—business and financial structures and programs must be devised that provide fair opportunity for everyone—including the disinherited poor—and incentives for nurturing instead of polluting the environment. Any honest worldwide examination of the inequity in present tax programs, credit policies, and property rights will result in adoption of Earth Trustee economic policies that are based on justice, that eliminate waste, and that promote fair opportunities.

3. Ethics—growing awareness of the importance of ethics in our conduct. People are creatures of habit and civilization is fraught with conflicting basic assumptions (mostly unexamined) about the purpose and meaning of life, resulting in confrontation which sometimes provokes violence and war. While differences about the mysteries of life and consciousness will continue, there is now a possibility of a basic unity in our diversity, a single goal that people of all religions and no religion can accept: the rejuvenation and enjoyment of planet Earth. Focusing on this goal can break the habit of focusing on our differences.

To accomplish this requires a deep heartfelt motivation that will tap the best in our spiritual roots. The best proof—here and now—of ethical value in our religious faith is our compassion, sense of responsibility, and our practice of the Golden Rule, with love of neighbor, love of our planet, and love of God (or of the mystery that is the source of life).

Now is the time to mobilize our faith and our institutions in a global "Campaign for Earth." Now is the time, especially, for a new sense of purpose and responsibility by public media. What is needed are features and headlines for the many solutions that are working and that need attention. *Let there be a media blitz for earth's rejuvenation.*

What can the individual do? There are hundreds of organizations and programs that need help. How do you decide what to do?

Determine that you are going to be an Earth Trustee and do what you can. Actions, good or bad, begin in the mind. Many are putting their faith in practice by the habit of prayer as they go to sleep—with faith that in their first waking thoughts they will sense God's presence with new ideas and inspiration for Earth Trustee action. Others, who do not believe in God, will be aided in their Earth Trustee choices by the power of positive thinking.

Can the future be prosperous, where an Earth Trustee peace agenda will enable people to realize their human potentials? What you do will help decide. We're all in this together. Action now will halt history's long sad record and provide a continuation of the human adventure with more answers to our questions about the mystery of life. Do what you can with faith and vigor—and you will make a difference.

36

Earth Magna Charta

THE VISION

THE PEOPLE OF PLANET Earth have the raw materials, natural resources, and the technology for all to enjoy a life of quality. But they are still restricted by the evil that has dominated history. They lack the vision of the great future now possible and how to attain it. As a result, the world is filled with confusion and conflict.

The Earth Magna Charta (see the Appendix) provides the needed vision and the way. Individuals and institutions can now be Trustees of Earth, seeking in ecology, economics, and ethics, policies and decisions that will benefit people and planet. In the present state of the world, this space age Earth Trustee concept has a chance of tapping the best in human hopes and aspirations and providing a healthy, innovative, and fulfilling future for our planet and its people. In this new future, deeds will demonstrate what is best in creeds.

Here is a pathway out of the tragedies on our planet. Earth Trustees will lead the way.

PROCLAMATIONS

Throughout recorded history there have been proclamations, declarations, charters, and essays. Their ideas reflect humanity's search for a better future. We especially remember the Declaration of Independence, and the United Nations Charter, which begins, "We the people . . . ."

My first effort in this direction was the "Star of Hope Declaration," which was used in my failed attempt in 1957, right after the first Sputnik, to obtain global cooperation in space; and to dramatize this with the launching of a visible Star of Hope satellite, containing signatures of all who would "seek to work for things that heal, build, and unite."

Later, I felt there was a need for an Earth Charter—a document that would set forth the key items that humanity should address in order to achieve a viable future. In 1979 I wrote "The Earth Charter." John Drysdale persuaded Primary Metal & Mineral Corp. to print and donate several thousand posters with the Earth Charter on one side and on the other side the beautiful image by William Blake showing God reaching down to Earth. The Earth was portrayed as seen from space. Below it were the words: *Earth Day: Work with Earth in Peace.*

The Earth Charter poster was featured at the United Nations each year on Earth Day.

EARTH MAGNA CHARTA

England's Magna Charta was in my mind when I wrote the Earth Magna Charta in 1995. The heart of my statement is the simple idea of being an Earth Trustee (see the formula in the previous chapter). Elements of the Earth Charter were incorporated in the Earth Magna Charta.

Words do have an effect, even though they seldom fully accomplish their purpose. Today the information explosion seems to blur what is true and important. A way to set things right is to make the international equinox Earth Day an Internet Earth Day.

On this day email and websites can report what they are doing, and what they plan to do, that will implement the Earth Trustee idea. The goal will be to change attitudes and conduct worldwide, from "Earth Kill" to "Earth Care."

Websites can give excitement and breakthrough-attention to the values that are shared by people of every creed—resulting in powerful peaceful actions for the rejuvenation of our planet. Make every website an Earth Trustee website. Set up Earth Trustee message boards and forums to report actions and their results. Repeatedly bringing attention to the Earth Magna Charta via the Internet can provoke new efforts in peace, justice, and Earth care.

37

Peace on Earth

PEACE STARTS WITH EACH INDIVIDUAL

THE THEME OF THE United Nations is, "Peace through understanding." Every one of us has assumptions, many of them unexamined, that affect our understanding of what is said. For real communication we must constantly ask ourselves, "What does the speaker mean?" Our individual experiences have led to word usage and meaning that often differs from that of other people—especially if they are of a different race, religion, or culture.

In addition, modern life has produced short attention spans, and many listeners allow other things on their mind to distract them from what is said. I would like to interject here, our character and attitudes are shaped by what we think. Actions good or bad begin in the mind. It is a good idea to occasionally stop and think of what may be going on in the subconscious mind. There can be two or more tracks of thought going on at the same time. Young people, especially, know how erotic and other unspoken thoughts—good or bad—influence our lives. "As a man thinks, so is he." Awareness and discipline in the subconscious mind is a key to character. Daily prayer or meditation and quiet times for reflection are food for the soul.

GLOBAL PEACE BLITZ

The war-makers must be stopped before they end the human adventure. Throughout history, love of power has caused wars in every generation and every part of the world. We must now replace the love of power with the power of love, and end our war habits—or face extinction.

Today the United States military spends billions of dollars for devilish weapons and for war-making. Had even half of the money spent on ways to make skeletons of our enemies been spent on ways to make them our friends, through the proven methods of non-violence, we would have no more wars. We could then focus our efforts on providing a sustainable future for people and planet.

On August 28, 1963, I finished the following plan for a world blitz for peace:

WORLD PEACE BLITZ

A global strategy for waging peace which provides a way for all men of good will to participate.

Contents in Brief

I. Strategy

The ingredients needed to tap the positive energies of war in a campaign to wage peace.

II. Peace Blitz Pilot Campaigns

To demonstrate feasibility of massive attack by a town or city against global enemies of FEAR, HUNGER, ILLITERACY, POVERTY, and BARRIERS (to information, trade, and travel).

III. Council of World Cities and Towns

An appropriate structure to represent all the regional organizations concerned with government of communities (the Council of Communities in Paris, the League of Municipalities in the United States, etc.). This organization would extend the community Peace Blitz campaigns globally. They would be aided by formation of an International Public Relations Committee.

IV. Sharing, International

To provide a volunteer organization for financial support of the Peace Blitz campaigns through Share projects.

V. Tactics

A suggested plan of action for achieving success in the World Peace Blitz.

The following are the first two chapters of the World Peace Blitz:

Chapter I. Strategy

The program presented herein will require very little to start and in the present world situation there is a possibility of success.

It will encourage the pursuit of the highest good. Properly implemented, it will create the necessary conditions for a lasting peace.

This is predicated on the idea that the way to achieve and maintain world peace is for people in all countries to work together for worldwide goals they can conscientiously support. Periodically (every fifteen or twenty years), they would do this in a special three-year global ritual or game that will demonstrate a moral equivalent to war. This can in a very real way channel the combativeness of man in a new surge of creative services for the welfare of mankind. It will require the same amount of vigor and sacrifice that would be given to a major war. The thought here is not to just "do away" with war, but find a substitute for it.

In conducting this new kind of warfare—or peacefare—simple terms would be used that have rather universal acceptance; war on fear, hunger, misery, mental and physical barriers, etc. These then would become "The Enemy." All possible structures for successfully conducting this war against the causes of war would be used—so long as the method enabled men to work together for global goals. The important thing would be to get the job done. Both government and the private sector would participate in every way possible. Voluntary, church, business, national and United Nations agencies would all be used by those who supported them to achieve the great goals of the World Peace Blitz. Of course, some will take advantage of the extended hand of friendship for political reasons, but these risks can be recognized and faced, and are far less than those to be experienced in a continuing arms race. In fact, properly understood, the risks of cooperation on the road to peace will result in a healthy and creative "Brinkmanship."

There must be a few over-arching goals for which men of all nations can in some sense join hands and work together in spite of their differences. When this is done, greed and ambition, as well as competing ideas and interests, will be dealt with, not so much as emotion-packed threats and conflicts, but more and more as problems to be better understood and solved. We must repeatedly define and support the areas of unity and at the same time recognize the extent and nature of worldwide diversity. In such a context, individual, economic, political, religious and cultural systems can pursue their goals in an experimental and creative way.

To overcome the apathy and inertia which today exists in waging peace, several ingredients are needed:

1. The individual must face the global crisis. Efforts through the communications media can make this real, but at the same time, the individual must see a total strategy that offers a chance of success and the importance of the minute but specific contribution he can make.

2. There must be an effort in the publicity and public relations activities to make the individual feel a connection between his efforts and the efforts of people everywhere so that a sense of identity with the whole human family is generated. What is needed here is a global in-group feeling, where "The Enemy" is the dramatized figure of Fear, Hunger, etc., and where "The Enemy" is War itself, instead of other groups of people or lesser enemies, such as current threatening ideologies. For example, various devices could be used through suitable posters to connect the volunteer's service or money in a Freedom from Hunger project with similar efforts of people of good will in all countries who are working for the same goal.

3. A demonstration project within one or more towns is needed that will provide a forceful example to overcome the negative feeling, "It can't be done."

Experts such as the Rand Corporation, through their "Gaming Technique," could then describe what would happen if 100,000 towns and cities around the world were to follow the example with campaigns of their own. Discussions with leading behavioral scientists have indicated that this would produce a climate of world public opinion so strong that national leaders would be forced to take the necessary steps—in world law, strengthening the United Nations, global disarmament—that are needed for creating a world of freedom and order.

In the strategy of the World Peace Blitz there are no plans for political actions. This does not mean they are unimportant. Those who participated in the Peace Blitz would be urged to support the political actions of their nation which they felt would best aid the cause of peace, but this would not be the responsibility of the Peace Blitz or the Council of World Cities and Towns. While the Council would coordinate its world service projects with UN Agencies, and, depending on local wishes, channel much of its efforts through these agencies, there would be a definite separation between the Council, which would represent local communities in a carefully limited sphere of action, and the UN, which represents nations and is primarily concerned with political problems. The separation here would be comparable to that of church and state in our own government.

The only exception to this would be in matters pertaining to the "Barriers" hindering freedom of information, trade and travel. In this field the Council would use the strength of its position to influence local and United Nations policies and laws that would bring about a more and more open world.

The function of the World Peace Blitz is not to directly restrain nations in making war, but to remove the causes and create the climate in which this can easily and safely be done. The Council of World Cities and Towns could urge the UN to have a great Peace Conference in the third and final year of the Peace Blitz. With the support of a successful 3 year campaign to create the conditions for peace, the United Nations would have an excellent chance of achieving the great goal for which it was created.

The proposals that follow offer the advantage of strengthening one another and together providing sufficient strength to spark the positive aspects of war (common purpose, loyalty, crisis, heroism) and channel them into a dynamic campaign for waging peace throughout the world.

Chapter II. Peace Blitz Pilot Campaigns

PURPOSE

To change the climate and activities in one or more towns in a way that will provide an appropriate definition of waging peace—one which could be expanded throughout the country and around the world.

A SUBSTITUTE FOR WAR

In order to do away with war, we hereby pledge our wholehearted effort in an attack against the enemies of man that down through the centuries have caused war.

These principal enemies we name for worldwide destruction:

FEAR—We will strike down fear with faith. We will prepare for a world without war.

HUNGER—Our efforts will replace the cries of hungry children with songs of joy!

ILLITERACY—We will help build schools and provide teachers and scholarships, that all may learn.

POVERTY—We will use our resources and knowledge to help those who toil for a better life.

BARRIERS—We will seek an Open World with freedom of information, trade and travel; where any are free to meet and work together.

We realize that the measure of our achievement will be judged, not by our words, but by how successfully we convert our words into action. We therefore seek those changes within ourselves that will increase our self-reliance and personal responsibility, and make us effective in working for world peace.

Let there be peace on earth, and let it begin with me.

*****

PEACEMAKERS OF THE WORLD UNITE!

The only hope for the future is an all-out Peace Blitz such as the above—a moral equivalent of World War II—that will provide a contagious spread of peacemaking words and actions. We must make effective use of all we know regarding the power of positive thinking, prayer, and the faith that works by love.

A key factor will be our success in getting attention in mass media. A Peace Blitz policy in major newspapers and TV news programs would assure a global change in thinking and actions.

UNITING EFFORTS FOR PEACE

Many scholars agree human history will soon come to an end—unless we end our addiction to war. New diabolical weapons make it possible for a few individuals to inflict massive death and destruction.

How can the many, who seek peace, justice, and a sustainable future through understanding and good will, come together and have a greater impact than those who use the power of their big money and military might to achieve their evil ends?

Scattered around the world are wonderful programs for peaceful resolution of conflict—Franciscans, churches, service clubs, Fellowship of Reconciliation, World Neighbors, and others.

But most people do not appreciate this because the mass media do not feature actions for peaceful progress. Media are the source of most public opinion and they make more money by features and headlines for violence and conflict. Public opinion is media-made. Whether intentional or not, the fact is that media accent the negative and give more attention to hate, fear, greed, and lust than to the many actions of understanding and good will. As a result major nations are addicted to war.

The only way to avoid global catastrophe is for all who support the ways of peace to now come together in a moral equivalent of war. United, we can change the global war mentality to a global state of mind dedicated to positive actions for peaceful resolution of conflict.

Our problem is the "Dealers in Death" who make billions from the production of weapons. Their lust for money and power blinds them to peaceful policies that would destroy the causes of violence. Their only way is to "kill the killers."

Years ago there was a saying, "I discovered who the enemy was, and it is US." I don't think the author meant the United States, but now it seems to be the case. If President Bush had been a follower of Jesus, whom he claimed to serve, he would have known that love for your enemy will bring understanding of the cause of hate, fear, and violence, and eliminate its source.

The key message of Jesus is found in the Sermon on the Mount in Matthew 5. He said, "Love your enemies . . . . Do good to them that hate you." What this meant and its contribution to peace was demonstrated through the ages by his followers. From St. Francis to Martin Luther King, we find opposition to the ways of war and the power of nonviolent resolution of conflict when hearts are filled with the love of Christ.

It's amazing how Bush and his spin doctors changed the plain meaning of words.

Our greatest problem is the problem of power. In reality, we are ruled by the military-industrial complex and the war profiteers. These corporations and their million dollar lobbyists are adept at deceiving the public.

The corrupting influence of power increases the desire for power. As a result, efforts to make the most money lead many to invest in the stock that brings the greatest return—instead of the stock that does the most good. Long ago the war-maker dealers in death discovered the greatest financial profit and power came from producing weapons of war. The more diabolical, the greater the profit.

Can the power of the love of Christ bring peace on Earth?

That now seems impossible. But I believe in miracles. Join with me today in helping bring a global turn toward peace.

I invite people of faith to spread the word that war is evil, that you don't overcome evil with evil. Killing is not the right way to stop killing.

There are cases in history where the most evil people have been converted. It was a converted slave trader who wrote "Amazing Grace." We should act immediately, but at the same time pray with faith and love for the conversion of war-making presidents and terrorists. We need a miracle, and that would certainly be a miracle. Instead of making skeletons of their enemies, our leaders would make their enemies their friends.

38

An EarthView Equation

REDEMPTION OF EARTH—
SPIRITUAL, ECONOMICAL, AND PHYSICAL

IN ORDER TO MOVE effectively toward the redemption of Earth, an EarthView Equation is needed. This equation should include the factors presently known, their relation to one another, and their relation to the goal of a healthy, peaceful, and creative planet. Three major factors are the spiritual, the economic, and the physical aspects of life on Earth.

We are here seeking key concepts that can find wide acceptance and help us take care of our planet, that will help us save our planet from catastrophe and provide a future of peaceful progress. The following items can serve this purpose:

1. In the realm of the physical world, the point on which we can agree is that our planet exists, and that it now requires our understanding, protection, and care. In order to obtain the support of people worldwide, this must be done in a way that provides equitable benefit for everyone. A firm priority on which we all can agree is the physical rejuvenation and care of our planet with fair benefits for its people. Accepting trusteeship of our planet is a vital necessity. Understanding and celebrating the March equinox Earth Day will further this purpose.

2. As far as our conduct and relationship with each other in material matters is concerned, we must consider that we are dealing with elements of property, credit, money, and politics. In each of

these areas we should seek an understanding that will be recognized worldwide as fair for everyone. This involves a recognition that our planet, particularly its natural land and raw materials, are the inheritance of every person and every family, and that we must find some mechanism that will provide every person a claim or stake in the planet. Everyone must have a homestead, a habitable place of his own, and a means for livelihood. This will encourage free enterprise.

For exchange and trade there must be currency and credit that are fair to everyone. To nourish freedom, industry, and cooperation, free credit in exchange for ample security should be provided. Given these provisions, we can have an economy based, not on scarcity, but on Earth's plentiful bounty. Political power can then shift from the nation state to the local community—the nation acting as a public utility in managing the larger mechanisms of money, communications, and travel.

3. To accomplish all this, we must deal with the mind and spirit. The greatest changes have often occurred just with an idea whose time has come, and that stirred the hearts of people. To capture the imagination of the world we must appeal to conscience—to our global consciousness. We must find agreement about the important things that pertain to the mind, to the spirit, and to the deepest emotions, that will be a core concept—an Earth-life world view that is accepted by all. Now, as we extend, develop, and use it, we of course will have many different efforts that complement each other more and more as we seek the same ultimate goal—the care and protection of planet Earth in ways that will assure equitable benefits for all people.

In seeking via the realm of the spirit a better world, and a better life for everyone, we must think first in terms of love—creative altruism, the Golden Rule, Divine Love, the virtue that grows from love within aided by prayer and faith—love of people and planet. Second, we must think of peace. Peace, "pachem," means to agree. Finding what is most important in which we can all agree, is an important key to a great future. Finally, we must seek wisdom. Wisdom is the practical application of the knowledge and experience of love and peace, making it work in every situation for the highest good we can visualize. In these three elements

I believe we have the formula which is true to the best in every religion or ideology, and the best way to build a better tomorrow. The test of any philosophy, of any ideology, of any religion, or of any effort to save our planet, is how successfully it generates these three things—love, peace, and wisdom.

THE SPIRITUAL FACTOR

For the most part, the scientific community has avoided questions that cannot be measured, analyzed, and evaluated by their present tools and procedures. An example of this is the scientist who stated that she would consider the possible existence of a soul—as soon as they determined the part of the brain that provided communication with the soul.

Most people on our planet believe they have a soul and are concerned with questions about life after death, the existence and nature of God, and the meaning of life. Religious beliefs and values have enabled them to relate to the unknown with benefit to their personal values, conduct, and happiness.

However, most scientists by their indifference and skepticism have tended to undermine the value of faith and treat it as superstition. In these matters, hypotheses that cannot be proven or disproved should be judged, or at least acknowledged of value, by the results in the lives of individuals who practice their faith or hypothesis.

The one belief that science has mathematically proven is the existence and benefit of love.[1] Love can thus provide the test of hypotheses about phenomena of mind and spirit that presently defy explanation. Thus, ultimate questions about reality, which remain profound mysteries that cannot be approached by scientific measurements or methods, can nevertheless be recognized and pursued through articles of faith and practice.

If reality is consistent, then the truth and the value of a faith or belief can be judged by the increase and depth of love—or creative altruism—in the lives of those who practice their beliefs. Prayer to a personal God and practice of the Sermon on the Mount have inspired personal love and courage and led to great peaceful changes for social freedom and justice.[2] Let critics of faith be challenged to show better evidence of love in those who reject faith.

1. See Von Foerster, "Logical Structure of Environment and Its Internal Representation."
2. See Bready, *This Freedom—Whence?* and Lowry, *Communism and Christ.*

Science must no longer negate the values of religious belief, but rather strengthen and support the importance of faith—of using the personal metaphor that increases the well-being of the individual, that deepens relationships with people and kinship with life on Earth.

The scientific approach can at the same time diminish religious intolerance by calling attention to the nature of metaphor or hypothesis. An hypothesis can be exciting and useful, and produce confidence in its supporters who may believe totally in its validity. Nevertheless, by its nature there must be, and can be, recognition and respect for people with different hypotheses about reality.

Where approval for a different religious or philosophical doctrine may be impossible, there still can be deep approval of the love that is motivated and demonstrated in connection with it. The scientific community should also give importance to any phenomena that greatly affect human values and potentials, even though scientific explanation eludes their grasp.

There is overwhelming evidence of answered prayer in the lives of many people. The frequency of favorable coincidence in deeply dedicated people who pray with fervor and faith should be studied and compared with other people who practice a purely psychological approach to needs.

The nature and extent of coincidences that run contrary to probability theory should be more thoroughly explored. Perhaps there is no satisfactory explanation possible. But this should not cause science to ignore the phenomenon of answered prayer, and its causes and effects in the lives of people.

Of course, on the one hand, scientists would make a careful distinction between a phenomenon and its effects, and on the other hand, explaining what it is and how it works. Great benefit could come from more attention to phenomenology and the many instances of its effects in the lives of people.

For example, the nature and extent of spiritual healing should be more critically examined. While success may seem to some people to be a random effect that is rare, many proven cases defy medical explanation. And people of faith are never in doubt about God's response in faith-based healing.

By its very nature, any effort to make Earth a healthy, peaceful planet can only be achieved through a great spiritual awakening of a kind that will foster the nurture and care of Earth and a creative happy life for all its people.

39

My Dream for the Future

ON THE EDGE OF TRANSITION

THE 9-11 DESTRUCTION OF the World Trade Center has resulted in people all over the world asking the question, "What will the future bring?" The following is for those who believe in the power of faith, and who welcome records of the past that point the way to a better future.

Earth Day promoted the openness, awareness, and attitudes that helped end the Cold War. It brought together capitalists and communists, and people of almost every religion. It helped create the conditions that made possible the historic handshake between PLO Chief Yasser Arafat and Israel's Yitzhak Rabin. (Arafat signed the Earth Day Proclamation, and Shimon Peres rang the Peace Bell.)

Earth Day affirms that we can disagree on creeds and still cooperate in deeds for our mutual benefit, deeds that will benefit the wonderful skin of life on our planet on which our own life depends.

With this generation's increasing longevity I expect a few more years before it's my time to go. (I turned 96 on March 22, 2011.) I hope to live a few more years and see a breakthrough to a world view that will bring the global changes in attitude and conduct that are needed.

I do believe we can be idealistic in our visions of the future. One of the great things scientists have discovered over and over again is that when they were trying to come up with a theory that would fit the facts they found that the most beautiful theory was invariably the right one. Once we consider all the factors, we can have a hope that our truly ideal expectations will be finally realized.

It seems that we are at a point in history where the human family is going through the rites of passage, going from one period to another period. I hope and pray that the period we are going into will be a time of peace, and fulfillment—a wonderful time when human beings will have a chance to realize their potentials. I think this is a great possibility. And the more we visualize it and the more we work for it, the more we have faith for it, why the more certain it is that it will be experienced.

MY DREAM AND VISION

Here is my dream:

I believe the "Battle for Earth" that I have advocated could in the coming decades win the support needed to defeat the enemies of humanity—pollution, poverty, ignorance, and strife.

Following are the key actions that have been started and the difficulties that can and must be overcome in order for this dream to come true: In 1957, in the midst of the Cold War and right after the first Sputnik satellite was launched, a beautiful idea came to me. Why not launch a bright visible Star of Hope as a symbol of understanding and good will? The editorial I then wrote in my weekly newspaper in North Carolina (*The Toe Valley View*) brought global attention and support from world leaders. But the funding to make it happen was never provided and the satellite was never launched.

In 1960 I wrote a proposal for a World Peace Blitz that was distributed in San Francisco at a World Industrial Conference. It urged municipalities to step in where nations had failed and vigorously engage in joint ventures across national boundaries to heal, unite, and build the future. The President of Stanford University and the Chairman of the Conference Board both expressed strong support for the idea, but action did not follow.

In 1962 I became the Northern California director of the Meals for Millions office in San Francisco and worked to stem the hunger problem in China and other places. We sent multi-purpose food to Hong Kong refugees. Again, the program was in place that could help solve the hunger problem worldwide, but while much good was done the effort fell far short, despite our best efforts. Lester Pearson, former Prime Minister of Canada, once said, "When it comes to war we're precocious giants. When it comes to peace we're stunted pygmies." The same could be said when it comes to hunger.

In 1963 we ended the period of mourning for President Kennedy on December 22 with a global "Minute for Peace." This was initiated at my behest. We had the sound of a bell and then the voice of Kennedy on radio worldwide. In this "Minute for Peace" we heard his voice in a speech he had given at the United Nations before his death: "Never have the nations of the world had so much to gain or so much to lose. Together we can save our planet, or together perish in its flames. Save it we can and save it we must . . . ." Then people were invited to join with silent prayer and a renewed commitment to work for peace.

In 1965, "Minute for Peace" played a role in ending the war between Pakistan and India. A Minute for Peace musical program across the street from the United Nations was provided for UN Delegates from India and Pakistan. It featured the voice of Ghandi speaking for peace. They then joined in singing Ghandi's favorite song and that evening at the United Nations the two nations came together and agreed to end the war.

It was while working with Minute for Peace that I became aware of the need for a global holiday that would celebrate the wonder of life on our planet and deepen commitment to the peaceful care of Earth. I spoke to friends about the idea of an "Earth Day," and finally in 1969 at San Francisco, my former home, I was able to launch the first Earth Day, which was held on March 21, 1970.

In 1971, UN Secretary-General U Thant signed an International Earth Day Proclamation and obtained global participation. The Earth Day celebration has continued at the UN every year since 1971 with the ringing of the Peace Bell at the moment spring begins. This is the global moment of nature's equipoise and the appropriate time for joining our hearts and minds in commitment to peaceful relations and mutual efforts for the care of Earth. When the Peace Bell rings, people of different religious beliefs and political views join in silent prayer, meditation, or reflection, and manage to forget their differences for a moment, and to discover what they have in common: a beautiful planet that needs our care, and that together, helping each other, we can use our amazing technology in production and communication to eliminate pollution and poverty, and diminish misunderstanding and discord.

From Earth Day has sprung the Earth Trustee concept, that everyone and every institution can and should now act as a Trustee of Earth—in ecology, economics, and ethics—seeking the benefit of people and planet.

To add vigor to these efforts we are urging institutions and individuals to now join in a "Battle for Earth," a war against pollution, poverty, hate, and greed. Mass media—TV, radio, press—can help by changing their definition of important news from "conflict and change" to "change without conflict"—the moral war.

These are dreams, the vision of the future I see. They reflect the dreams of many others who hope for a better tomorrow.

Are they idle dreams? It is true that civilization is in a crisis of turmoil, violence, danger, and confusion. Every phase of my effort has met with disappointment. The Star of Hope was never launched. Meals for Millions was never adequately backed. Minute for Peace dwindled and almost disappeared. The World Peace Blitz was applauded but not mobilized.

As for Earth Day, the authentic original Earth Day was based on the scientific and historic meaning of the March equinox. Earth Day deals with the whole: people, freedom, justice, the environment, the whole planet—peace, justice, and the care of Earth. There should be a singular date for Earth Day. April 22 and other dates that are being called "Earth Day" defeat the original purpose of Earth Day. They should use other names for events that are not on nature's day, and seek to complement instead of undermine the real Earth Day.

It is my dream that eventually we will have a singular Earth Day where bells will ring all over the world—in some places trumpets will sound and drums will roll—when the Peace Bell at the United Nations is rung at the moment spring begins. It is my dream that the Battle for Earth will bring a rapid transition from polluting fuel to clean energy; composting and recycling in every community; and new villages where interactive communication by computer enables people to work in their homes or neighborhood for offices in other cities.

The goal will be for every person to be a home owner—able to buy a computer if they wish! Art and music of every culture will be encouraged. There will be freedom to choose a community that features a chosen religion and culture, or one where they are diverse. But there will be a common bond and toleration of differences because all will recognize we are members of one human family. It is my dream there will be a global sense of unity as people everywhere join in observance of the Earth Day Minute for Peace.

Cooperation in the care of Earth will also increase, as radio, web, and TV programs provide daily "Earth Minutes," using their best talent to keep them interesting and effective symbols of our common identity—a human family with a great future. These simultaneous Minutes (at 0300, 1100 and 1900 GMT) will speak without words using sounds of music, bells, and nature, with pictures of Earth, trees, whales, elephants, humming birds, and children—a heartbeat of hope for humanity—replacing our addiction to war.

COMMUNITY NEEDS

The Peace Corps usually divides community needs into felt and real needs. Felt needs are determined by finding the kinds of symbols or projects that can bring the community to action. Felt needs are those needs which the community will express by concerted action. Real needs can be determined by surveys and studies of suspected problems. Often, the community will express little interest in them. The term real refers to the perception of the social scientist or community developer rather than that of the mass. Of the two kinds of needs, the felt needs are the more important because the community can be mobilized into action to fulfill the felt need. Once mobilized, the community can be led to facing the "real" and often more difficult needs. Of course felt needs can be real needs and real needs can be turned into felt needs.

When modern urban man pushes his way down a major New York street looking at our visible air, life can seem like a journey of quiet desperation. Some try to escape their environment by moving to the suburbs or to the woods. Still others try to escape from their own bodies with drugs or mysticism. When all these escapes prove only partially satisfying, the call to nature, for equilibrium, for peace, provided by a project like Earth Day, touches the feelings of the community deeply. The project becomes a felt need.

The hope of planetary and personal regeneration brought thousands of people to Central Park, New York City, on March 21, 1971. Ecology programs were riding the crest of a deeply felt public need for an improved life style. This has been amply demonstrated by the numbers of people participating then, in 1971, and over the years since. We feel that the community need for this type of program expressing feelings has intensified over the years.

We know, however, that the intense public feeling that Earth Day will play upon and generate is not enough. The people must begin to associate their felt need for environmental purity with the hard personal and political decisions needed to actualize their new feelings of one-ness with the Earth. They must be shown not only the hope of regenera-tion, but also the political and economic implications of their feelings. International Earth Day will try to strike a balance between the felt need for regeneration and the real needs for hard political and economic deci-sions within individuals and society.

To combine hope and reality, our Earth Day "celebration" includes music, dance, and recreation, and yet invites scientists and ecology groups to explain through lectures, exhibits, and film, the real needs of the community. By giving cognitive information to those who exhibit the felt need, and a spirit of hope and joy to those who know but do not act on real needs, our program will serve the total needs of our community.

A CALL TO LOVE

The meanings we give to words are in a measure affected by our feelings and attitudes. When I began writing this book I thought "A Call to Arms" could use the sense of power that military terms suggest, and direct it to non-violent action. This was effective in the essay by William James, "The Moral Equivalent of War." However, in thinking of Martin Luther King Jr. and his wonderful book, *Power to Love*, I believe a strong appeal can be "A Call to Love." Jesus said, "Love thy neighbor as thyself."

At this important juncture in history there are leaders and laymen in every major religion who believe in the power of divine love, the kind of love Dr. King talked about. What I have described here is "A Call to Love." It provides a way to come together in a global effort that will not compromise our separate beliefs. Here is a way to effectively demonstrate our common identity with the human family: to join with heart, hand, and mind for our mutual goal—harmony with nature and neighbor. This is the way to a peaceful prosperous future.

Some say the trouble is that we're all a bunch of sinners. If we look at what is happening on our planet, and we have the objective view of someone from another planet, we could certainly agree. At the same time, the evidence of love and compassion and real sympathy, that are to be found in people of every culture and clime, is a real basis for hope.

We can focus more attention on what enlightened people of every culture and race and persuasion can agree. Every religion at some point teaches the Golden Rule, teaches love instead of hate, and teaches justice instead of inequality. If we start thinking about these things, and giving headlines and features to solutions and to the hope that exists in the human drama, we can turn things around.

I dream of the time when, as stewards and trustees of planet Earth, we recognize the link between the slaughter of animals and our health: physical, mental, emotional, spiritual, financial, and environmental. In the Bible, Adam was told to sustain all the living things of Earth, and his food was to be the fruit of the tree and the grain of the soil. Vegetarians have demonstrated the benefits to health and peace of mind that come from reverence for life.

I dream of a global attitude of mind where individuals and groups are not trapped in the mistakes of the past; where complicated, inefficient taxes and credit policies will be replaced by simple, fair mechanisms as they are tested and proven of value; where ancient rules, values, and customs that have stood the test of time are revered and applied whenever they can improve life today. I dream of a time when mistakes will not be repeated, nor magnified more than records and achievements of human integrity, progress, and success. I dream of the time when everyone will know that change in individuals and situations can always be better achieved by the power of reason and good ideas than by the power of weapons. Once we learn the ways of honest love, we will demonstrate that in a world of interactive communication the power of good is greater than the power of guns.

Our task is to increase our understanding of the past, recognize what is best in every place and culture, preserve the records and artifacts so that people in this and future generations can find in their roots the basis to define their unique role in cultures that complement and enrich one another. Then the profit-seeking imposition of multi-national images and products—soda, food, garish foreign hotels, etc.—will be replaced (aided by new technology) with architecture and products that reflect distinct cultures and roots.

I dream of the time when the value of creeds will be judged by deeds. And people of different religions and with different ideas about the great mysteries of life can firmly hold to their beliefs and reject other beliefs without rejecting the people who hold them, when they too show honesty, fairness, and mutual respect in their actions.

I dream of the time, which may be rapidly approaching, when we will discover that there are other beings in our galaxy, whose life adventure has brought them to an understanding, probably better than ours, of the mysteries of life and love.

I dream of the time when a Star of Hope will circle our planet. A bright symbol of understanding and goodwill, its radio beams will report progress on planet Earth worldwide. A child looking up at night will say, "That's the Star of Hope. My name's in it. I'm a Trustee of planet Earth."

Appendix

John McConnell Biography—Summary
The Boy Evangelist—J. S. McConnell 1911
Address by Evangelist John S. McConnell 1925
The Commandments of Jesus—J. S. McConnell 1925
Earth Day Proclamation 1970
Earth Day by Margaret Mead 1978
United Nations Press Release 1971
U.S. Earth Day Proclamation 1975
Earth Day Message 2001
Statement by Ambassador Nejad Hosseinian of Iran on Earth Day, 1998
Proclamation—Denver, Colorado 2004
Letter of Honor from Denver 2003
Letter from Eleanor Roosevelt 1958
Letter to Senator Nelson 1989
Letter to National Council of Churches 1980
Letter to Mr. Gamaroody, Assistant to Bani-Sadr 1980
Statement in Tehran, Iran 1980
Declaration of Planetary Rights 1969
The Global Seabed—A Sixth Continent 1975
Earth Charter 1979
77 Theses on the Care of the Earth 1985
Earth Magna Charta 1995
Earth's Resurrection #1 1974
Earth's Resurrection #2 2005
Message to President Bush 2003
Proclaim Liberty throughout the Earth 1976
Proposal for Ringing the Peace Bell 1966
A Daring Strategy for World Peace 1961

Stowaway on a Satellite 1957
Make Our Satellite a Symbol of Hope! 1957
Invitation to the Cities of the World 2003
Proclamation: Earth Care Campaign 1982
Joint Agenda for the Care of Earth 1983
Earth Changes—Metamorphous for a Golden Age 1971
Poetry

John McConnell Biography—Summary

4924 East Kentucky Circle

4924 East Kentucky Circle
Denver, CO 80246
303–758–7687
trusteeone@aol.com

JOHN MCCONNELL (JOHN SAUNDERS McConnell, Jr.) was born in Davis City, Iowa on March 22, 1915, the son of an independent evangelist. As a child and as a teenager, John McConnell accompanied his family during his father's evangelistic tours around the United States.

Mr. McConnell's concern for peace in the world, and his interest in human affairs, religion, and science, have resulted in a number of projects and organizational initiatives to promote peace, relieve human suffering, and promote care of the Earth. He has sought to understand human potentials and to seek solutions to the crucial problems facing civilization.

RESEARCH LABORATORY—1939

In 1939 John McConnell met Albert Nobell (no relation to Albert Nobel), a chemist with whom he founded the Nobell Research Foundation in Los Angeles. Mr. McConnell served as Vice-President and business manager of the Foundation. Their laboratory developed a thermosetting plastic, and designed the first plastic plant on the west coast for its manufacture. Thinking about conservation of nature led to development of a plastic manufactured from walnut shells. Through other research in the laboratory, seeking uses for waste products, Mr. McConnell's concern for ecology grew.

WORLD WAR II—1943

During World War II, Mr. McConnell joined the Merchant Marine. Taking the position that prayer and love could be more powerful than bombs, he conducted services aboard Merchant Marine vessels, on which he worked as a seaman. Inducted into the United States Army, Mr. McConnell as a pacifist and pastor eventually fled to Honduras, for which he briefly went to prison upon his return. After World War II, Mr. McConnell worked as Registrar at Lincoln Law School in San Francisco, California, and as a representative of the American Correspondence School.

WEEKLY NEWSPAPERS—1956

Mr. McConnell joined Erling Toness, an editor in North Carolina, in publishing a weekly newspaper, *The Toe Valley View*. *Life Magazine* carried a feature story, "Trouble in the Toe Valley," about their efforts against local violence and corruption. On October 31, 1957, after the first Sputnik, Mr. McConnell wrote an editorial entitled, "Make Our Satellite A Symbol Of Hope," calling for peaceful cooperation in the exploration of Space with a visible "Star of Hope" Satellite. This editorial was picked up by the wire services and reprinted in hundreds of newspapers. Mr. McConnell appeared on the Arlene Francis Show, the Today Show and other TV Network programs. This led Mr. McConnell to form a Star of Hope organization to foster International Cooperation in Space. In pursuit of this goal, Mr. McConnell in 1958 obtained support in Geneva from the President of the Atoms for Peace Conference and other leaders, including Dr. Glen Seaborg of the United States and Professor A. P. Alexandrov of the USSR.

In 1959, Mr. McConnell moved to Mountain View, California (Silicon Valley), where he and co-publisher Erling Toness founded the weekly *The Mountain View*. An editorial in this paper on April 19, 1961 urged a joint venture in space with American Astronauts and Soviet Cosmonauts. The editorial was circulated in the White House, and given to Soviet officials. President Kennedy supported the idea, and later President Nixon obtained agreement for a joint venture.

MEALS FOR MILLIONS—1962

As Northern California Director of "Meals for Millions," John McConnell formulated and organized a successful campaign in San Francisco to feed thousands of Hong Kong refugees.

MINUTE FOR PEACE—1963

For several years after the Meals for Millions campaign, Mr. McConnell worked on a "Minute for Peace" program. This began with his obtaining global attention and participation in a Minute for Peace broadcast, which on December 22, 1963 ended the period of mourning for President Kennedy.

On June 26, 1965, the twentieth anniversary of the signing of the United Nations Charter, Secretary-General U Thant spoke for Minute for Peace on worldwide radio. At that time, Mr. McConnell spoke at the National Education Association Convention in Madison Square Garden where the participants joined in a silent "Minute for Peace." Later, in conversations with NEA officials, he urged silent prayer in schools.

Also in 1965, the New York World's Fair featured a Minute for Peace Pledge. Over 50,000 visitors signed the pledge.

WORLD EQUALITY—1968

In 1968, Mr. McConnell incorporated "World Equality" (WE, Inc.) to foster the idea of equilibrium in nature and human society. In 1969, he began circulating his ideas on "Planetary Inheritance," the rights of all Earth's people to an equal share of Earth's natural resources.

EARTH FLAG—1969

The Earth Flag was designed by Mr. McConnell after he saw the first space photo of Earth in *Life Magazine*. The Earth Flag was featured in the "Whole Earth Catalogue." The Earth Flag is still being sold and used around the world, to show support of efforts to help people and planet. In 1983 the Earth Flag was flown at the South Pole, and in 2000 at the North Pole, and later on the Mir Space Station. The Earth Flag is a part of the Earth Day Ceremony each year at the United Nations. In 1997 the Smithsonian Institution in Washington, DC requested an original Earth Flag plus records.

EARTH DAY AND THE EARTH DAY PROCLAMATION—1969

In September of 1969, Mr. McConnell proposed Earth Day to the San Francisco Board of Supervisors. The proposal won strong support and was followed by Earth Day Proclamations issued by Mayor Joseph L. Alioto of the City of San Francisco and other Northern California cities.

To promote individual and international support for stewardship of Earth, Mr. McConnell at the November 1969 National UNESCO Conference in San Francisco announced the plans for the first Earth Day on the following spring equinox. The purpose of this day was to celebrate Earth's life and beauty, and to alert people to the need for preserving and renewing the threatened ecological balances upon which all life on Earth depends.

The first Earth Day celebration was held on March 21, 1970 with participation in San Francisco, Davis, Berkeley, and other cities in tree planting, recycling exhibits, music, and silent meditation at the time of the equinox.

On his return to New York, a former residence, John McConnell wrote an Earth Day Proclamation in June 1970. It incorporated rights and responsibilities of Earth's people in the care of their planet. It was signed by United Nations Secretary-General U Thant, Margaret Mead, John Gardner, and other concerned world leaders.

In 1971 Secretary-General U Thant gave his support to the UN Celebration of the March equinox Earth Day. U Thant rang the Peace Bell and obtained global attention. The ringing of the United Nations Peace Bell at the moment of the March equinox on Earth Day has become a tradition, celebrated annually.

Since then, others have added their signatures to the Earth Day Proclamation to show support for its objectives. The last few signatures, added in the 1990s, were those of Yasser Arafat, Yehudi Menuhin, Cosmonaut Anatoly Berezovoy, and in 2000 Mikhail Gorbachev. These completed the 36 signatures on the Earth Day Proclamation.

E-DAY TV SPECIAL—1972

In 1972, Mr. McConnell instigated and was co-producer of a twelve-hour Special on WOR-TV, called E-Day '72. Carried whole or in part by over sixty stations, the program was an extensive study of environment, featuring national and international ecology experts, and won many awards. At that time Mr. McConnell started using the term "Earth Trustee" to define people who were seeking to make choices in their daily life that would benefit nature and society.

EARTH SOCIETY—1973

The Earth Society was formed by John McConnell while attending the 1973 UNEP Conference in Geneva. In 1976, with Dr. Margaret Mead, Frank Braynard of the U. S. Bicentennial "Operation Sail," and Capt. Anthony Keasby, McConnell incorporated the Earth Society as the Earth Society Foundation, which later obtained thirty-three Nobel Laureates as Sponsors. The Earth Society Foundation seeks to make the care of Earth humanity's first objective, aiding this purpose through Earth Day, Earth Rights, Sea Citizens, and silent prayer or meditation.

In 1973, Dr. Margaret Mead wrote an Earth Day Essay, featured by the International News Service.

EARTH RIGHTS—1974

In 1974, Mr. McConnell personally discussed his Earth Rights proposals with Sheikh Yamani of Saudi Arabia, and other leading delegates at the United Nations Raw Materials Conference. In an address at the United Nations Church Center on "Earth's Resurrection," McConnell stated, "Underlying property rights and sovereignty rights is the fundamental right of every person on Earth to an equal share in Earth's raw materials and natural resources."

SEA CITIZENS—1974

To foster Earth Care and Earth Right principles dealing with the Sea, Mr. McConnell organized a "Sea Citizens" program advocating protection and equal shares in the bounty of the sea. The organizing committee, headed by John McConnell, included United Nations Ambassador Dr. Arvid Pardo of Malta, Senator Mark Hatfield of Oregon, and Frank O. Braynard, Founder of Operation Sail. To obtain support, McConnell attended the Geneva "Law of the Sea" Conference.

EARTH CHARTER—1979

This document, written by John McConnell in 1979, was featured in a large-sized illustrated poster designed by J. Drysdale. The poster was placed on every floor of the United Nations building and circulated at the United Nations.

TRIP TO IRAN—1980

Mr. McConnell met with Secretary of State Cyrus Vance in 1980 to discuss the Iran hostage crisis. McConnell felt that because Iran's New Year (Noruz) is on the March equinox Earth Day, he might negotiate the release of the hostages. McConnell traveled to Iran, and met with Mr Gamaroodi, Assistant to the President of Iran, to discuss release of the hostages.

77 THESES—1985

In 1985, Mr. McConnell published "75 Theses on the Care of Earth." About a year later, two theses were added, and now "77 Theses" can be seen at Mr. McConnell's website: http://www.earthsite.org.

EARTH MAGNA CHARTA—1995

Mr. McConnell wrote the Earth Magna Charta in 1995, in which he stated the goals and policies needed for "peace, justice, and the care of Earth."

This document emerged from his previous efforts, experiences and thinking. It describes the actions needed and how they can be achieved by the following Earth Trustee Formula:

> *Let every individual and institution now think and act as an Earth Trustee, seeking choices in ecology, economics and ethics that will provide a sustainable future, eliminate pollution, poverty and violence, awaken the wonder of life and foster peaceful progress in the human adventure.*

EARTH DAY WEBSITE—

In the late 1990s, Mr. McConnell learned the use of the computer, and with help from friends a website was born, http://www.earthsite.org. Website pages were developed describing his initiatives and efforts over the years. Mr. McConnell has continued his efforts for peace, justice, and Earth care in the new millennium by maintaining and adding to the website, and actively using phone contacts to promote Earth Day and Earth Trustee efforts.

The Boy Evangelist—J. S. McConnell

THE STORY BELOW ABOUT my father was in material sent to me by Wayne Warner, Assembly of God Archives, in October, 2000. Dad was nineteen when this was written and was called by some, "The Boy Evangelist." I remember him telling about this. As a boy, I was witness to many miracles of healing and answered prayer. I remember Dad talking about the Stone Church where he got the call to "evangelize new fields." This article helps explain the 1912 photo of the Gospel Car.

THE LATTER RAIN EVANGEL
Stone Church, Chicago
November 1911
Sowing the Seed

Our young brother, J. S. McConnell, who attended our ministry for several months at the Stone Church, has responded to the call of God to sow the Gospel seed in out of the way places, and God has been blessing him. He writes as follows, under date of August 25th.

> I traded a note I had for an auto express car and built a Gospel car on it. I asked the Lord to provide me with the means to carry the Gospel away from the railroads, and he has enabled me to fit up the car in a very handy and comfortable way, and has supplied all our needs. We traveled through Nebraska, part of Wyoming, Colorado, and into Kansas, with a small house built on the car that has only 20 horse power, and went through places where big machines got stuck. One evening we had a slight accident to the machinery and in the morning it refused to run. After I had worked with it for about two hours I came to the conclusion that

I could do nothing, so we got down on our knees and asked God to make it go. We got up and it started right off and didn't bother us any more. Another time I was driving up a steep hill: There had been a heavy rain and there had washed large holes in the wagon tracks. In spite of my efforts the wheels sank into these holes and, try as we would, we could not get the car out. Finally, we went to God and asked Him to get it out, and as I got upon the seat and started the machine, it moved right off.

God has been with us along the way: generally we have just stopped on the street and preached, and then started on, but God is pouring out His blessing in a wonderful way in this place (Pierceville, Kansas). There have been eight conversions up to this time, and the people are interested.

God performed a miracle of healing a few days ago. My little nephew, who is traveling with me, fell off the car and bent his arm between the elbow and the wrist, almost double. When I picked him up I thought it was broken, but it bent the arm in a sick L shape. The pain was so intense that he could hardly stand it, and the first thing we did was ask God to take away the pain, and it wasn't fifteen minutes until he was sound asleep. Then we asked God to straighten the arm out and heal it, and when we arose from our knees it was almost straight, but God did not straighten it perfectly then, for if He had, the people would not have believed the boy was badly hurt, but he went to the meeting that evening, and from that time, the arm has not hurt him, and is now perfectly straight. He wrote a letter with it two days ago, and he is a living witness to the loving kindness and goodness of God.

Address by Evangelist John S. McConnell

THE ASSEMBLIES OF GOD Archives sent me this 1925 sermon by my father. I think you will enjoy it. It brings back a lot of memories. Dad was called "The Fiery Irishman."

Its key points need to be heard by American leaders who profess to be Christians.

Published in the PENTECOSTAL EVANGEL
Springfield, Mo., October 10, 1925
The Latter Rain Outpouring
Elder W. T. Gaston, Chairman of the General Council
(Page 5) A Remarkable Address

Evangelist John S. McConnell asked for the privilege of speaking a few words before the Council went to prayer. The following are some of the thoughts the Lord gave our brother. We will never forget the fervency that was back of this address. It gripped everyone to the heart. We give full space to this message because it was the keynote for the whole Council session. Brother McConnell read Col. 3:1–17 and said:

> I want you to notice that expression in verse 14, "And above all things put on charity, which is the bond of perfectness." Notice, God puts charity, or divine love, above all these things. That is, it is the greatest and most important of all.
>
> I do not know whether this has ever struck you forcibly or not, but after fourteen years of evangelistic work, going through all kinds of places and conditions, I have been forced by experience to recognize there is one eternal principle upon which salvation is based; both as to our part, and also as to God's part,

and that principle is charity, or divine love. To get away from that principle is to get away from salvation.

My Bible tells me that God is love, therefore to be in harmony with God you must be in harmony with divine love. If you fail to have this attribute of divine love—no matter what you profess— you are out of harmony with God. Because God is love, His part in the plan of salvation is based upon that one principle—LOVE. "For God so loved the world that He gave His only begotten Son." God cannot save us without our cooperation. Therefore to cooperate with Him we must build on the same principle of divine love. Jesus laid down two phases of that principle as to our part in salvation: "Thou shalt love the Lord thy God with all thy heart, and with all thy soul, and with all thy strength,' and 'thou shalt love thy neighbor as thyself.'" Notice, He not only requires us to love God supremely, but demands that we love our neighbor as ourselves. If we fail to love our neighbor, we fail to harmonize with God, fail to cooperate with God, and thus separate ourselves from God. This is a vital thing.

We have a great many blessing recorded in the Scriptures, but there is one thing alone by which we know we are the children of God. "We KNOW we have passed from death unto life, BECAUSE WE LOVE THE BRETHREN. He that loveth not his brother abideth in death." Christ speaks of those who will say in that day, "Lord, Lord, have we not prophesied in Thy name? and in thy name have cast out devils? and in Thy name done many wonderful works?" and yet He will profess unto them, "I never knew you." Many are taking feelings and blessings as an evidence of salvation, and resting upon the things they have done in the name of the Lord; but, after all, there is only one standard by which we can judge a tree, and that is by its fruits, and where the fruit of love is missing, the tree is bad, regardless of the beautiful leaves it may adorn itself with. The only way we can know by actual experience we are right with God is if we really love the brethren.

Not only is that the Bible evidence to the individual, that he is right with God, but it is the only evidence that will convince the world that we are God's true children. Jesus declared, "By this shall all men KNOW that ye are My disciples, if ye have love one for another." No wonder we cannot convince the world we are the true children of God when we fail to manifest real love toward one another. You can contend for Bible truths, and be as zealous for God as you please, but you will never be able to convince the world that you are following Jesus Christ except you love the brethren. That is the great thing that marks you as being in harmony with Christ.

It is important that we should hold up a Bible standard. Well, this is the greatest standard. It is above all things. It is the bond of perfectness. While other things are important, this is so much more important than anything else that Paul declares in 1 Cor. 13:1–3, "Though I speak with the tongues of men and of angels, and have not charity, I am become as sounding brass, or a tinkling cymbal." Think of that, brethren! We are very careful to hold up the Bible evidence of tongues, but according to God's Word we might as well beat on a brass pan as to speak with tongues while we lack divine love.

Again he says, "And though I have the gift of prophecy, and understand all mysteries, and all knowledge; and though I have all faith, so that I could remove mountains, and have not charity, I am nothing." Did you get that? I did not put it in the Bible. We boast of our gifts, and our knowledge, and our faith, but we may possess and be exercised in all these things, and yet be nothing; just a zero mark in God's sight, because we lack divine love.

Brethren, in the face of God's eternal Word, I declare unto you it is more important that we retain the spirit of divine love than any and all other things put together. "Above all things put on charity." What a sad thing it will be after we have had the gift of prophecy, and have learned the Bible from cover to cover, and have had such faith we have seen great miracles wrought, and then come before the judgment bar of God and have the angel step out and mark a zero on our life—NOTHING—because we lacked divine love when the brethren were in controversy, when the testing was on, while we were contending for our rights, or even for the truth of God, or when our brethren got out of the Spirit, or made mistakes, or misunderstood us. We will all be nothing but a zero mark in God's sight if we do not keep in the love of God during this Council.

Again, "And though I bestow all my goods to feed the poor, and though I give my body to be burned, and have not charity it profiteth me nothing." You can surely see from this that nothing will profit you unless it is done in love. Your preaching, your zeal, your loyalty are all a failure unless they come from a heart of love. I cannot help but take the stand that if you have divine love according to the word of God you will have the others, but on the other hand, if you lack divine love you lack everything. The time will come when tongues will cease, and knowledge will vanish away, but faith, hope and charity shall abide, and the greatest of these is charity.

Notice again in Rev. 2:1–5, the importance of divine love. Jesus Christ, writing to the church in Ephesus, commends them for their labor, and patience, and works, and their absence from evil, and their stand upon the Word, and how they had borne and labored for His name's sake and had not fainted. Surely that was a wonderful church, and you would have to hunt a good while to find one that would measure up to it today, but in spite of all their good points, He declares "Nevertheless, I have somewhat against thee, because thou hast LEFT THY FIRST LOVE." You would think that was not very serious in the face of all their faithfulness. But it was just serious enough that it knocked the bottom clear out of their salvation and put them completely out of harmony with God. "Remember therefore from whence thou art FALLEN, and repent, and do the first works, or else I will come unto thee quickly, and I will REMOVE THY CANDLESTICK OUT OF HIS PLACE, EXCEPT THOU REPENT." To leave their first love had not only put them in a FALLEN state but they were in terrible danger of losing their place in God, and nothing but real repentance could save them. Surely love is the most important thing in all the world. You might possess all the good attributes that church had and yet if you lose the love of God you are fallen— separated from God.

If we believe the words of our Master we will have to face this matter. Brother, how do you stand in the light of the eternal Word of God? Is that burning, consuming, tender, compassionate, flaming love of God burning in your soul like it was when you first got saved? Or have you allowed bitterness, and fault-finding, and talebearing and strife to rob you of the love of God? If so, no matter what you profess, or how you seem to get blessed, you need to repent and do the first works, yea, until you love all the brethren and your heart is tender, until you can weep over sinners and have compassion and mercy toward your erring brethren.

When we realize the importance of keeping ourselves in the love of God, then let us begin to realize what love is. What is the fruit of love? God wants us to get a proper position of ourselves on the point.

"Knowledge puffeth up, but charity edifieth." We all claim a little knowledge. God says it puffeth up. Everybody thinks he is right, and the more knowledge you have the more you puff up, and unless you keep under the blood and in the love of Jesus your knowledge will wreck you.

But love edifieth, that is, buildeth up. If love buildeth up then it never tears down. It will never divide nor hinder the work of God anywhere. We can tell by the fruit whether we have love or not. If we do not build up we are clear off the track. Any issue that seems to be truth that will divide God's real people and tear down the work of God is lacking the essence of salvation—divine love. As long as we keep in the love of God we will edify—build up. Those who claim to love God and are causing divisions and strife among God's true people are impostors. "Mark them that cause divisions."

Let us look at God's definition of divine love in 1 Cor. 13. "Charity suffereth long and is kind." No matter how long it suffers it still remains kind. Remember if we have God's love in our heart, no matter how long it suffers it still remains kind. Remember if we have God's love in our heart, no matter how long we suffer from someone we will still remain kind to them.

"Charity envieth not." In the very best of God's people there is danger of getting envious. And oh, what devilish sins spring from the poisonous fangs of envy! You will never feel bad when somebody else gets the praise or is blessed or is exalted if you keep the love of God in your heart.

"Charity vaunteth not itself." The margin says, "Is not rash." It is not hasty to judge or act. It thinks twice before it speaks. It does not vaunt itself, make a show of itself. I am one of you in this Pentecostal movement, but it grieves me the way some Pentecostal people vaunt themselves, push themselves forward and try to make a show of themselves. Try to show off that they have the baptism or speak in tongues! We are told to follow Jesus, imitate Him but I cannot imagine Him acting as some people do. I believe in manifestations of the Spirit, but if it is the Spirit, it will be in harmony with love, and love "doth not behave itself unseemly." "Love is not puffed up" and we will never go around with a 'holier than thou' demeanor when love reigns within. Love will make us esteem the least of the brethren better than ourselves.

"Charity seeketh not her own." Here is the essence of love. It is the exact opposite to selfishness. Love never puts self first. Never seeks to gratify self, satisfy self, serve self, obey self, protect self, exalt self, justify self, excuse self, or trust in self. Any such are manifestations of selfishness and selfishness is the root of all sin. Sin proceeds from a motive. There are two motives from which an action can proceed. A selfish motive, or an unselfish motive, which is a motive of divine love. If your motive is selfish your action will be selfish. Love is the exact opposite of selfishness, therefore it seeks not her own. It never puts self first.

This is the test of divine love. Whenever you put self before God's will and the good of His kingdom you can know that your motive is selfish and you are void of the love of God. I wonder if we have tried our motives in this Council. There must be a motive before an act can proceed. Brethren, what is your motive? Is it selfishness or is it charity? Are you seeking your own? "He that seeketh to save his life shall lose it." Anything that tries to put self first is nothing more or less than selfishness, and if you act from love you cannot put self first. If we would have God's smile upon us we must purify our motives and seek not our own.

"Charity is not easily provoked." The Greek says, "Is not provoked." No matter what the other fellow does either.

"Thinketh no evil." Love does not suspicion the brethren. It trusts until they have proven themselves false. Let us have confidence in one another, and believe that our brother is just as honest and conscientious as we are. It is the devilish seed of suspicion unwarranted that has put a breach between the best of brethren and wrought havoc in God's work. Brother, cleanse your mind of those evil thoughts.

"Rejoiceth not in iniquity." Love does not compromise with sin. It hates sin, because sin injures God's creatures. This mushy stuff they call love that can take sin in its bosom is not God's love. God's love stands as a wall against sin, but at the same time has tender compassion and mercy to the sinner.

"But rejoiceth in the truth." Brother, when you have the love of God you will never dodge the truth. Even though it hits you hard and exposes you to the world you will say Amen. You will never be ashamed of tongues or any other part of God's word as long as you retain the love of God.

"Beareth all things." ALL THINGS! Persecution, misunderstanding, insults, injustice, being ignored, and so forth. Yes, from your wife, husband, children, even your best friends. Honestly, brother, do you measure up? Yes, and it not only bears them, but "endureth all things." Endures those obnoxious persons whom we would naturally detest. Endures the fleshly foolishness of the shallow professor. Endures the nerve-wracking noise of the loud-praying brother.

"Hopeth all things." Praise God! Love never loses faith, never becomes pessimistic. It believes God. You will never have the blues, nor fret and worry as long as love reigns in your heart. To say I expect everything to go wrong shows a lack of divine love in the heart, for love hopeth all things. One thing that has helped me in all places of church affairs is the promise of Jesus, "Upon this rock I will build my church and the gates of hell shall not prevail against it." Oh Glory to God! He is on the throne, and has the keys of hell and death. All power is in His hands, what have we to fear. Love trusts unto death and always hopes for the best. Faith worketh by love and our faith will mount just as high as our love flows deep. Our God is leading this battle, let us hope in Him.

And last of all, God declares that "Charity never faileth." Brother, there is no chance for you to fail if you will keep in the love of God and keep the love of God in you. You will be a tremendous success. All the devils in the world cannot down you. People can backslide in revivals and they can backslide in the midst of blessings. They can backslide from the new birth and from the Baptism. But there is no power in Earth or hell can make you backslide if you keep the love of God. Charity never faileth. It will stick through thick and thin, it will carry you through every trial and test, yes, in all these things you will be more than conqueror through the love of God. It is the biggest thing in all the universe. Above all things put on charity. Brother, have you got it? Is it burning in your breast now as it once did? If you have left your first love get it back if you have to come to this altar and stay here until this Council is over. Let us—each of us—get back to our first love—get converted anew this afternoon. If we do, this Council will go over the top for Jesus.

At the close of Brother McConnell's message, the space around the altar was soon filled up, and men and women all over the tent were kneeling in prayer. Many were weeping before the Lord. A great volume of prayer ascended to heaven and it was like the sound of many waters. It was certainly a remarkable scene.

The Commandments of Jesus

Compiled and published by Evangelist J. S. McConnell in 1925.
This copy is made available by his son,
John McConnell, founder of Earth Day.

My father, evangelist J. S. McConnell, compiled "The Commandments of Jesus" following a vision of Christ in 1921 in Walla
Walla, Washington. For several weeks, each time he prayed he
would see verses of Scripture slowly drifting down a ray of light,
with illumination on their meaning and the meaning of the New
Covenant. Further weeks and months of searching the Scriptures resulted in a book called *The New Covenant*, which ended
with "The Commandments of Jesus." About 1934, a tract was
published containing only "The Commandments of Jesus." In
later years my father expanded and expressed his thoughts about
Christ in more universal terms, seeing in all religions, and in all
honest, fervent love, the grace of God at work in human life.

JESUS, IN THE GOSPELS, laid down the great foundational principles
and laws to govern the children of God during the entire church age—
"even unto the end of the world"—as we see from His great commission
as recorded in Matt 28:18–20. Our great duty and privilege is to do as
He said, "Follow Me."

We see the practical results which followed the keeping of His commandments in the great revivals as recorded in the book of Acts. Further
explanations and application of the commandments of Jesus are given
by the Lord through the writers of the epistles, but the foundational
principles and the final authority rests in the words of Jesus Himself. In
the book of Revelation Jesus gives His final warnings, reproofs, instructions and encouragements to the Church.

An outline of the Commandments of Jesus under twenty-one principles is given below. Examine yourself by these. Read over these words of our Lord and take an inventory often. See if you are, in truth, pleasing God, or if you are deceiving yourself. God, the heavenly Father, loved you so much that He gave His Son, Jesus, to die for you (see John 3:16). He will help you if you humble yourself, are willing to follow Jesus, and will earnestly seek HIM.

Ask God to help you understand the teachings of Jesus, and to live them out in your life. Salvation and the true Christian life is a gigantic love affair. It is not by merely keeping the letter of the Word that we will please God; we must keep the spirit of the two great commandments all through our lives, and remember that these two great principles are given to guide us in knowing just how God would have us apply the teachings of His Holy Word. Here are the two great foundational commandments: "Jesus said . . . Thou shalt love the Lord thy God with all thy heart, and with all thy soul, and with all thy mind. This is the first and great commandment. And the second is like unto it, Thou shalt love thy neighbor as thyself. On these two commandments hang all the law and the prophets." Matt 22:37–40.

THE COMMANDMENTS OF JESUS

I. REPENTANCE
1. "Repent" Matt 4:17; Rev 2:5
2. "Come unto Me" Matt 11:28
3. "Seek first God and His righteousness" Matt 6:33
4. "Forgive if ye have ought against any" Mark 11:25
5. "Deny Yourself" Matt 16:24
6. "Ask . . . seek . . . knock" Matt 7:7
7. "Strive to enter in at the strait gate" Luke 13:24

II. BELIEF
1. "Believe the Gospel" Mark 1:15
2. "Ye believe in God, believe also in Me" John 14:1
3. "Believe on Him who He (God) hath sent" John 6:28–29
4. "Believe Me that I am in the Father and the Father in Me" John 14:11

5. "Believe the works . . . I do" John 10:37–38
6. "While ye have light believe in the light" John 12:36
7. "Believe that ye receive" Mark 11:24

III. THE NEW BIRTH

1. "Ye must be born again" John 3:7
2. "Cleanse first that which is within" Matt 23:26
3. "Make the tree good, and his fruit good" Matt 12:33
4. "Abide in Me and I in you" John 15:4
5. "Have salt in yourselves" Mark 9:50
6. "Labor . . . for that meat which endureth unto everlasting life" John 6:27
7. "Rejoice, because your names are written in heaven" Luke 10:20

IV. RECEIVING THE HOLY SPIRIT

1. "Receive ye the Holy Ghost" John 20:23
2. "Let the children first be filled" Mark 7:27
3. "If any man thirst, let him come unto Me and drink" John 7:37–39
4. "Keep my commandments and . . . the Father . . . shall give you another Comforter" John 14:15–17
5. "Ask . . . with importunity" John 16:24; Luke11:5–13
6. "Tarry . . . until ye be endued with power from on high" Luke 24:49
7. "When the Comforter is come . . . He shall testify of Me: and ye also shall bear witness" John 15:26–27

V. FOLLOWING JESUS

1. "Follow Me" John 12:26
2. "Be baptized" Matt 3:13–15; Matt 28:19
3. "Take this . . . (communion) in remembrance of Me" Luke 22:17–19
4. "Ye also ought to wash one another's feet" John 13:14–15
5. "If any man will come after Me . . . let him take up his cross daily" Luke 9:23
6. "Learn of Me" Matt 11:29
7. "Continue ye in My love" John 15:9

VI. PRAYER

1. "Pray always" Luke 21:36
2. "Pray that ye enter not into temptation" Luke 22:40, 46

3. "Pray . . . the Lord of the harvest, that He would send forth labourers" Luke 10:2
4. "Pray for them which despitefully use you" Luke 6:28
5. "Pray to the Father . . . in my name" Matt 6:6; John16:24, 26
6. "After this manner therefore pray ye: Our Father, which art in heaven . . . " Matt 6:9–13
7. "When ye pray, use not vain repetitions" Matt 6:7–8

VII. FAITH
1. "Have faith in God" Mark 11:22
2. "Be not faithless" John 20:27
3. "Neither be ye of doubtful mind" Luke 12:29
4. "Take no thought for your life" Matt 6:25–34
5. "Let not your heart be troubled" John 14:1, 27
6. "Be of good cheer" Matt 14:27
7. "Be not afraid" Mark 5:36; Luke 12:4–7

VIII. SEARCHING THE SCRIPTURES
1. "Search the scriptures" John 5:39
2. "Remember the word that I said" John 15:20
3. "Let these sayings sink down into your ears" Luke 9:44
4. "Take heed therefore how ye hear" Luke 8:18
5. "Take heed what ye hear" Mark 4:24
6. "Beware of the leaven (doctrine) of the Pharisees" Matt 16:6, 12
7. "Beware of false prophets" Matt 7:15–17

IX. LETTING YOUR LIGHT SHINE
1. "Let your light so shine before men, that they may see your good works" Matt 5:16
2. "Take heed therefore that the light which is in thee be not darkness" Luke 11:35
3. "Go and bring forth fruit, and . . . bear much fruit" John 15:16, 8
4. "Be ye therefore merciful, as your Father" Luke 6:36
5. "Tell . . . how great things the Lord hath done for thee" Mark 5:19
6. "Lift up you eyes, and look on the fields" John 4:35
7. "Walk while you have the light" John 12:35

X. THE SECOND COMING OF CHRIST

1. "Hold fast till I come" Rev 2:25; Rev 3:2–3
2. "Be ye therefore ready also: for the Son of man cometh" Luke 12:40
3. "Let your loins be girded about, and your lights burning; and ye yourselves like unto men that wait for their Lord" Luke 12:35–36
4. "Take heed . . . lest . . . your hearts be overcharged with surfeiting, and drunkenness, and cares of this life" Luke 21:34
5. "Remember Lot's wife" Luke 17:31–32
6. "Take heed that ye be not deceived" Luke 21:8; Mark 13:5–6
7. "Watch" Mark 13:34–37

XI. SUPREME LOVE TO GOD

1. "Thou shalt love the Lord thy God with all thy heart . . . soul . . . mind . . . strength" Mark 12:30
2. "God, and Him only shalt thou serve" Matt 4:10
3. "Worship the Father in spirit and in truth" John 4:23–24
4. "Call no man your father upon the Earth" Matt 23:9
5. "Thou shalt not tempt the Lord thy God" Matt 4:7
6. "Fear Him (God) which . . . hath power to cast into hell" Luke 12:5
7. "All men should honor the Son" John 5:22–23

XII. OUR DUTY TO GOD AND MAN

1. "Render to Caesar the things that are Caesar's, and to God the things that are God's" Mark 12:17
2. "Swear not at all" Matt 5:34–37; Mark 4:22
3. "What therefore God hath joined together, let not man put asunder" Matt 19:5–6
4. "Agree with thine adversary quickly" Matt 5:25
5. "We saw one casting out devils in thy name . . . Forbid him not" Mark 9:38–40
6. "Eat such things as are set before you" Luke 10:8
7. "Gather up the fragments that remain, that nothing be lost" John 6:12

XIII. OUR DUTY TO OUR NEIGHBOR

1. "Thou shalt love thy neighbor as thyself" Matt 19:17–19
2. "Thou shalt do no murder" Matt 19:18
3. "Thou shalt not commit adultery" Matt 19:18

4. "Thou shalt not steal" Matt 19:18
5. "Thou shalt not bear false witness" Matt 19:18
6. "Honor thy father and thy mother" Matt 19:19
7. "As ye would that men should do to you, do ye also to them likewise" Luke 6:31

XIV. COVETOUSNESS

1. "Take heed and beware of covetousness" Luke 12:15
2. "Lay not up for yourselves treasures upon earth . . . but lay up for yourselves treasures in heaven" Matt 6:19–20
3. "Ye pay tithe . . . and not leave (them) undone" Matt 23:23
4. "Give to him that asketh thee, and from him that would borrow of thee turn not thou away" Matt 5:42
5. "Give alms of such things as ye have" Luke 11:41
6. "When thou makest a dinner . . . call not thy friends, nor thy brethren . . . but . . . call the poor" Luke 14:12–13
7. "Make yourselves friends of the mammon . . . " Luke 16:9

XV. HYPOCRISY

1. "Beware ye of the leaven of the Pharisees, which is hypocrisy" Luke 12:1
2. "Beware of the scribes, which desire to walk in long robes" Luke 20:46–47
3. "Do not ye after their works" Matt 23:2–3
4. "Make not My Father's house an house of merchandise" John 2:16
5. "Do not your alms before men, to be seen of them" Matt 6:1–4
6. "When thou prayest thou shalt not be as the hypocrites . . . to be seen of men . . . enter into thy closet and pray . . . in secret" Matt 6:5–6
7. "When thou fastest, anoint thine head, and wash thy face; that thou appear not unto men to fast" Matt 6:16–18

XVI. MEEKNESS

1. "Take my yoke upon you . . . for I am meek and lowly in heart" Matt 11:29
2. "The princes of the Gentiles exercise dominion over them . . . but it shall not be so among you" Matt 20:25–26
3. "Whosoever of you will be the chiefest, shall be servant of all" Mark 10:43–44

4. "Be not ye called Rabbi" Matt 23:8
5. "Sit not down in the highest room" Luke 14:8–11
6. "Rejoice not, that the spirits are subject unto you" Luke 10:20
7. "Say, we are unprofitable servants" Luke 17:10

XVII. OUR LOVE TO THE BRETHREN

1. "Love one another as I have loved you" John 15:12
2. "Despise not one of these little ones" Matt 18:10–14
3. "Have peace one with another . . . and be reconciled to thy brother" Mark 9:50; Matt 5:23–24
4. "If thy brother . . . trespass against thee go and tell him his fault between thee and him alone" Matt 18:15–17
5. "If thy brother trespass against thee seven times a day . . . thou shalt forgive him" Luke 17:3–4; Matt 18:21–22
6. "Judge not according to appearance . . . first cast the beam out of thine own eye" John 7:24; Matt 7:1–5
7. "Condemn not" Luke 6:37

XVIII. PERFECT LOVE

1. "Be ye therefore perfect" Matt 5:48
2. "Sell that ye have and give alms" Matt 19:21; Luke 12:32–33
3. "Love your enemies" Matt 5:44; Matt 26:52
4. "Do good to them which hate you" Luke 6:27–28
5. "Lend, hoping for nothing again" Luke 6:35
6. "Resist not evil" Matt 5:39–41
7. "In your patience possess ye your souls" Luke 21:19

XIX. FAITHFUL UNTO DEATH

1. "Be thou faithful unto death" Rev 2:10
2. "Hold that fast which thou hast" Rev 3:11
3. "When men shall revile you, and persecute you, . . . rejoice, and be exceeding glad" Matt 5:11–12; Luke 6:23
4. "When they persecute you in this city, flee ye into another" Matt 10:23
5. "When they deliver you up, take no thought how or what you shall speak" Matt 10:19
6. "Murmur not among yourselves" John 6:41–43
7. "Look up and lift up your hands" Luke 21:28

XX. PREACHING THE GOSPEL

1. "Preach the gospel to every creature" Mark 16:15; Matt 10:7
2. "Repentance and remission of sins should be preached in His (Christ's) name" Luke 24:46–47
3. "Baptize disciples, in the name of the Father, and of the Son, and the Holy Ghost" Matt 28:19
4. "Teach them to observe all things whatsoever I have commanded" Matt 28:20
5. "What I tell you . . . that speak" Matt 10:27; Mark 4:22
6. "Feed my sheep" John 21:15–17
7. "Heal the sick" Matt 10:8

XXI. WISDOM

1. "Be ye therefore wise as serpents, and harmless as doves" Matt 10:16
2. "Beware of men" Matt 10:17
3. "Let (the blind leaders) alone" Matt 15:12–14
4. "Give not that which is holy unto the dogs, neither cast ye your pearls before swine" Matt 7:6
5. "Consider the lilies . . . how they grow" Matt 6:28
6. "Whatsoever city . . . ye shall enter, inquire who is worthy; and there abide . . . Go not from house to house" Matt 10:11–13; Luke 10:5–7
7. "Whosoever will not receive you . . . shake off the very dust from your feet for a testimony against them" Luke 9:5; Luke 10:10–11

"IF A MAN LOVE ME, HE WILL KEEP MY WORDS."
John 14:23

Earth Day Proclamation

by
John McConnell
June 21, 1970

by the people of Earth
for the people of Earth

Whereas: A new world view is emerging; through the eyes of our Astronauts and Cosmonauts we now see our beautiful blue planet as a home for all people, and

Whereas: Planet Earth is facing a grave crisis which only the people of Earth can resolve, and the delicate balances of nature, essential for our survival, can only be saved through a global effort, involving all of us, and

Whereas: In our shortsightedness we have failed to make provisions for the poor, as well as the rich, to inherit the Earth, and our new enlightenment requires that the disinherited be given a just stake in the Earth and its future—their enthusiastic cooperation is essential if we are to succeed in the great task of Earth renewal, and

Whereas: World equality in economics as well as politics would remove a basic cause of war, and neither Socialism, Communism nor Capitalism in their present forms have realized the potentials of Man for a just society, nor educated Man in the ways of peace and creative love, and

Whereas: Through voluntary action individuals can join with one another in building the Earth in harmony with nature, and promote support thereof by private and government agencies, and

Whereas: Individuals and groups may follow different methods and programmes in Earthkeeping and Earthbuilding, nevertheless by constant friendly communication with other groups and daily meditation on the meaning of peace and goodwill they will tend more and more to be creative, sensitive, experimental, and flexible in resolving differences with others, and

Whereas: An international EARTH DAY each year can provide a special time to draw people together in appreciation of their mutual home, Planet Earth, and bring a global feeling of community through realization of our deepening desire for life, freedom and love, and our mutual dependence on each other,

Be it Therefore Resolved: That each signer of this People Proclamation will seek to help change Man's terrible course toward catastrophe by searching for activities and projects which in the best judgment of the individual signer will:

peacefully end the scourge of war

provide an opportunity for the children of the disinherited poor to obtain their rightful inheritance in the Earth

redirect the energies of industry and society from progress through products . . . to progress through harmony with Earth's natural systems for improving the quality of life

That each signer will (his own conscience being his judge) measure his commitment by how much time and money he gives to these purposes, and realizing the great urgency of the task, he will give freely of his time and money to activities and programs he believes will best further these Earth renewal purposes. (At least nine percent of the world's present income is going to activities that support war and spread pollution. Ten percent can tip the balance for healthy peaceful progress.)

Furthermore, each signer will support and observe EARTH DAY on March 21st 1971 (Vernal Equinox—when night and day are equal throughout the Earth) with reflection and actions that encourage a new respect for Earth with its great potentials for fulfilling Man's highest dreams; and on this day will join at 1900* Universal Time in a global EARTH HOUR—a silent hour for peace . . .

*Time changed to moment of the Equinox 1973

ORIGINAL SIGNERS OF THE EARTH DAY
PROCLAMATION—1970-71

1. Alexander B. Grannis—New York Assembly;
2. Judith Hollister—Temple of Understanding;
3. Luther Evans—former Director General of UNESCO;
4. Estelle Feldman (Ireland)—1970 World Youth Assembly;
5. David R. Brower—Friends of the Earth;
6. Arvid Pardo—Ambassador of Malta to the United Nations;
7. Margaret Mead—anthropologist;
8. Eugene McCarthy—United States Senator from Minnesota;
9. John Gardner—Common Cause;
10. Mike Gravel—United States Senator from Alaska;
11. Hugh Scott—United States Senator from Pennsylvania;
12. Buzz Aldrin—American astronaut;
13. S. O. Adebo (Nigeria)—United Nations Under-Secretary-General;
14. U Thant (Burma/Myanmar)—United Nations Secretary-General;
15. Maurice Strong (Canada)—UN Environment Programme;
16. Yasuhiro Fukushima (Japan)—environmental scientist;
17. René J. Dubos—environmental scientist;
18. Lubos Kohoutek (Czechoslovakia)—astronomer;
19. Buckminster Fuller—inventor, scientist, scholar;
20. Mark Hatfield—United States Senator from Oregon.

In the years between 1990–1996, as more people had become aware of the observance of Earth Day; they wanted to be involved. They familiarized themselves with the Earth Day Proclamation. To demonstrate their agreement with all the concerns and issues set forth they placed their signatures on the Proclamation joining that of the Secretary-General and those that had signed in the previous years; they are:

21. John Denver—singer;
22. Robert Muller (France)—Assistant Secretary-General, United Nations;
23. Isaac Asimov—author;
24. Edward Abramson—Majority Whip, New York State Assembly;
25. Aly Teymour (Egypt)—Chief of Protocol, United Nations;
26. Anatoly N. Berezovoy (Russia)—cosmonaut;

27. Cynthia Lennon (England)—artist;

28. Stan Lundine—Lieutenant Governor, New York;

29. David Dinkins—Mayor of New York City;

30. Oscar Arias—President of Costa Rica;

31. Audrey McLaughlin—Leader, NDP, Canada;

32. George Fernandes—Minister of Transportation, India;

33. Carlos Salinas—President of Mexico;

34. Yasser Arafat—President of Palestinian National Authority;

35. Yehudi Menuhin—musician, violinist;

36. Mikhail Gorbachev—former President of USSR.

The last signature was added on September 7, 2000.

Earth Day
by Margaret Mead

Broadcast on WQXR radio and printed in the EPA Journal March 1978. Margaret Mead, an internationally recognized anthropologist, educator, and activist in world affairs, was the 1978 Earth Day chairperson.

EARTH DAY IS THE first holy day which transcends all national borders, yet preserves all geographical integrities, spans mountains and oceans and time belts, and yet brings people all over the world into one resonating accord, is devoted to the preservation of the harmony in nature and yet draws upon the triumphs of technology, the measurement of time and instantaneous communication through space.

EARTH DAY draws on astronomical phenomena in a new way; using the vernal equinox, the time when the Sun crosses the equator making night and day of equal length in all parts of the Earth. To this point in the annual calendar, EARTH DAY attaches no local or divisive set of symbols, no statement of the truth or superiority of one way of life over another.

But the selection of the March equinox makes planetary observance of a shared event possible, and a flag which shows the Earth as seen from space appropriate. The choice has been made of one of two equinoxes, the springtime of one hemisphere, the autumn of the other, making the rhythmic relationship between the two capable of being shared by all the peoples of the Earth, translated into any language, marked on any calendar, destroying no historical calendar, yet transcending them all. Where men have fought over calendrical differences in the past and invested particular days like May Day or Christmas with desperate partisanship, invoking their God with enthusiasms which excluded others, the prayers for EARTH DAY are silence, where there is no confusion of tongues and the peal of the peace bell ringing around the Earth, as now satellites transform distance into communication.

EARTH DAY celebrates the interdependence within the natural world of all living things, humanity's utter dependence upon Earth, man's only home, and in turn the vulnerability of this Earth of ours to the ravages of irresponsible technological exploitation. It celebrates our long past in which we have learned so much of the ways of the universe, and our long future, if only we apply what we know responsibly and wisely. It celebrates the importance of the air and the oceans to life and to peace. On the blue and white wastes of the picture of Earth from space, there are no boundary lines except those made by water and mountains. Yet in this picture of the Earth, the harsh impersonal structures of world politik disappear; there are no zones of influences, political satellites, international blocs, only people who live in lands, on land, that they cherish.

EARTH DAY is a great idea, well founded in our present scientific knowledge, tied specifically to our solar universe. But the protection of the Earth is also a matter of day-to-day decisions, of how a field is to be fertilized, a dam built, a crop planted, how some technical process is to be used to enrich or deplete the soil. It is a matter of whether the conveniences of the moment are to override provision for our children's future. All this involves decisions, some taken by individuals, some by national governments, some by multinational corporations, and some by the United Nations. Planetary housekeeping is not, as men's work has been said to be, just from sun to sun, but, as has been said, like women's work that is never done. Earth Day lends itself to ceremony, to purple passages of glowing rhetoric, to a catch in the throat and a tear in the eye, easily evoked, but also too easily wiped away.

EARTH DAY uses one of humanity's great discoveries, the discovery of anniversaries by which, throughout time, human beings have kept their sorrows and their joys, their victories, their revelations and their obligations alive, for re-celebration and re-dedication another year, another decade, another century, another aeon. But the noblest anniversary, devoted to the vastest enterprise now in our power, the preservation of this planet could easily become an empty observance if our hearts are not in it.

EARTH DAY reminds the people of the world of the continuing care which is vital to Earth's safety.

Margaret Mead

United Nations Press Release
SG/1749—26 February 1971

SECRETARY-GENERAL SIGNS EARTH DAY PROCLAMATION

THE SECRETARY-GENERAL, U THANT, signed today an Earth Day Proclamation for the celebration of Earth Day on 21 March 1971— the vernal equinox, or first day of spring in the Northern Hemisphere.

The observance of Earth Day was initiated last year by the City of San Francisco. The Proclamation has already been signed by a number of eminent personalities, including Col. Buzz Aldrin, United States astronaut; Luther H. Evans, former Director-General of the United Nations Educational, Scientific and Cultural Organization; Miss Margaret Mead, anthropologist; Miss Estelle Feldman, Chairman of the Commission on Man and Environment of the 1970 World Youth Assembly, and Chief S. O. Adebo, Executive Director of the United Nations Institute for Training and Research.

The Secretary-General has also agreed to issue a message in connection with the observance of Earth Day, and to attend a private ceremony at United Nations Headquarters at which the Peace Bell will be rung. The ceremony will take place at 2 p.m. on Sunday, 21 March (1900 GMT), the hour of the signing of the United Nations Charter at San Francisco on 26 June 1945.

U.S. Earth Day Proclamation

FOR IMMEDIATE RELEASE

MARCH 20, 1975

OFFICE OF THE WHITE HOUSE PRESS SECRETARY

THE WHITE HOUSE

EARTH DAY 1975

BY THE PRESIDENT OF THE UNITED STATES OF AMERICA

A PROCLAMATION

The earth will continue to regenerate its life sources only as long as we and all the peoples of the world do our part to conserve its natural resources. It is a responsibility which every human being shares.

Energy problems have heightened our growing awareness of the interdependence of our natural resources. We must work together to solve the environmental issues associated with the proper use and preservation of those resources.

Through voluntary action, each of us can join in building a productive land in harmony with nature.

By a joint resolution, the Congress has pointed out the need to continue our environmental education and to promote a greater understanding of the environmental problems facing America.

NOW, THEREFORE, I, GERALD R. FORD, President of the United States of America, do hereby proclaim Friday, March 21, 1975, as Earth Day. I call upon all concerned citizens and government officials to observe this day with appropriate ceremonies and activities. I ask that special attention be given to personal voluntary activities and educational efforts directed toward protecting and enhancing our life-giving environment.

IN WITNESS WHEREOF, I have hereunto set my hand this twentieth day of March, in the year of our Lord nineteen hundred seventy-five, and of the Independence of the United States of America the one hundred ninety-ninth.

—GERALD R. FORD

Earth Day Message

John McConnell
UN Peace Bell Ceremony
New York City
March 20, 2001

A S WE LOOK AROUND the world today we see a global crisis, with hate and fury in so many people. We ask ourselves, is there any hope for the future?

We have a simple idea, a concept that needs to be known worldwide. As it spreads we will see a global change of attitude, a global change of heart. This will bring a future for ourselves and our children.

That concept is simply that each one of us, in our own way, must think and act as responsible Trustees of Earth.

When the Peace Bell rings on Earth Day, we can use that moment to join in global commitment to work for the protection and care of our planet, and to do it with great love—love of our planet and its people.

Regardless of what our religious faith is, we can deepen it by recognizing that in the care of Earth we are showing our love of God's creation.

I pray that as we experience this Earth Day moment of consecration, we will commit ourselves to do everything with love.

When we ring the Peace Bell, let there be a commitment that in this coming year we will foster resolution of conflict and fair opportunities for all—in our local and global affairs.

May Peaceful Progress Prevail on Earth!

Statement by Ambassador Nejad Hosseinian of Iran on Earth Day, 1998

Permanent Mission of the Islamic Republic of Iran to the United Nations
No. 154
March 20, 1998

Statement by

H.E. Hadi Nejad Hosseinian,
Ambassador and Permanent Representative
of the Islamic Republic of Iran

on Earth Day ceremony
at the United Nations Headquarters

Dear friends and earth trustees,

It is a pleasure for me, as a new comer to the United Nations, to be part of this Earth Day-1998 Celebration. This celebration focusing on prayer for peace and prosperity for all and the care of earth by all irrespective of national boundaries, race or creed has been observed in Iran and the greater region surrounding it since the time immemorial.

At this very moment peoples of Iran and many other nations are celebrating "Noruz," the "New Day," the first day of spring and the new year in Iranian calendar; they renew their pledge to earth, its god-given bounty and harmony, and to each other in a solemn and deeply personal way to set aside differences and pray for peace on our only earth.

Let us hope and pray that from this "New Day" forward, we, as individuals and as groups, undertake to plan for the care of the earth, restoration of harmony on our planet, and for the care of our fellow citizens on earth aiming for justice, peace and prosperity for all.

Proclamation—Denver, Colorado

Celebrate Earth Day—March 20, 2004

WHEREAS: THE HUMAN FAMILY has inherited a beautiful planet and our future depends on our actions, and

Whereas: The human family is made up of many creeds and cultures, and

Whereas: Emphasis on our differences has repeatedly resulted in hate, fear, violence and war, and

Whereas: New technology has provided diabolic weapons of mass destruction—available to the weak as well as the strong, and

Whereas: The present global crisis can soon bring the end of civilization, and

Whereas: The only hope for the future is for those who believe in peaceful resolution of conflict to unite in a global moral equivalent of war, and

Whereas: A great global Earth Day on the first day of Spring—nature's symbol of renewal and new life—can unite and motivate people in vigorous efforts for peace, justice and a sustainable future, and

Whereas: People of faith can prove the power of their love and creative altruism and its benefits in the here and now by support of Earth Day and its Earth Trustee Agenda, and

Whereas: Earth Day on the first day of Spring—nature's symbol of renewal and new life—can unite people in vigorous efforts for peace, justice and a sustainable future, and

Whereas: Denver is a mile high city with high aspirations and will circulate this Earth Day Proclamation worldwide—inviting all cities to celebrate the Great Day of Earth,

Be it Therefore Resolved:

That the people of Denver will celebrate Earth Day on March 20, 2004—choosing as best we can the actions that will benefit people and planet,

That on Earth Day we will dedicate our lives to peaceful cooperation in pursuing the mutual goals that will nurture the wonderful skin of life that covers our globe.

To help unite the human family in heart and mind, bells all over the world will ring around the time that Spring begins. This moment of nature's equipoise is a special time for all to join in silent prayer and heartfelt dedication to peace, justice and the care of Earth.

Wellington E. Webb
Mayor
City and County of Denver
Denver CO 80202
Phone: 720–865–9000

Letter of Honor from Denver

July 1, 2003

Mr. John McConnell
4924 East Kentucky Circle
Denver, CO 80246

Dear Mr. McConnell:

As Mayor of the City and County of Denver, I take great pride in honoring our diverse citizens, history and culture. Although impossible to discern everthing and everyone deserving of special recognition, it is with great pleasure that I write this letter to inform you that you have been chosen to be honored as one of this year's "Mile High Legend–Unsung Heroes".

A "Mile High Legend–Unsung Hero" is an individual that has displayed outstanding commitment and dedication to the "Mile High" City of Denver through volunteerism and community involvement. Mr. McConnell, you have undoubtedly justified your worthiness of this honor.

The 2003 "Mile High Legend–Unsung Hero" Reception will be held on July 15, 2003, at the City Hall, Second Floor Rotunda, 1437 Bannock Street, Denver, CO, 5:30 p.m.–7:30 p.m.

Please submit, no later than July 8, 2003, a copy of your bio, a color photograph, and a copy of your guest list with mailing addresses, with a maximum of 15 guests to:

Office of the Mayor
C/O 2003 "Mile High Mile Legend-Unsung Hero"
1437 Bannock Street, Room 350
Denver, CO 80202

If you have any questions, concerns or need any additional information, please contact my Special Assistant, Denice Edwards, or LaTonya Lane Becton, Special Projects Coordinator at 720–865–9025. CONGRATULATIONS! I look forward to seeing you on July 15, 2003.

Yours truly,

Wellington E. Webb
Mayor

Letter from Eleanor Roosevelt

John McConnell Archives
American Association for the United Nations, Inc.
Commission to Study the Organization of Peace
National Headquarters
343 E. 40th St.
New York, NY

Mr. John McConnell
2260 B. Market St.
San Francisco 14, Calif.

July 2, 1958

Dear Mr. McConnell,

I read your letter and the attached material with great interest and would like to thank you very much for keeping me informed about your plans.

I am delighted to see how encouraging the response to the Star of Hope has been, and I would like to use this opportunity to send you my best wishes for success for all your future campaigns.

With kindest regards,
yours very sincerely,

Eleanor Roosevelt
Mrs. F. D. Roosevelt.

Letter to Senator Nelson

October 11, 1989

Dear Senator Nelson,

Thank you for taking the time on the phone to discuss at length the difficulty of two different dates being promoted as Earth Day.

If the original Earth Day, which has the unique advantage of being on the equinox, can be recognized and supported by all groups, then the April 22 event can strengthen, rather than weaken by dissension, the goal we all share—to be trustees and caretakers of Planet Earth.

I do hope the misunderstandings of the past can be put behind us. I did call Joe Floyd and he told me of his being with you in Florida in the fall of 1969, and suggesting "Earth Day" as a better name than Environmental Teach-In for your planned event. He did tell me that he had seen something in the paper about "kids in California who were planning an Earth Day." This may have been the students at the University of California in Davis who warmly supported my proposals when I spoke there in October—followed by an outstanding Earth Day event on March 21, 1970.

Since your initial idea was to obtain support for an "Environmental Teach-In" but the name Earth Day was adopted without your knowledge of our prior announcements and plans, it seems to me the solution to the present difficulty would be to add a word and call your event "Earth Day Teach-In." If this were accompanied by warm support and publicity for Earth Day at the United Nations on March 20—with bells ringing in the capitals of the world when the United Nations Peace Bell rings at the moment of equinox—I'm sure the April 22 event will be a great success. The whole year will see a global change of attitude.

To accomplish this I would be happy to join you in a joint statement and Press Conference.

Sincerely,

John McConnell

Senator Gaylord Nelson
Wilderness Society
1400 Eye Street N.W.
Washington, D.C. 20005

Letter to National Council of Churches

February 3, 1980

Dr. William Howard, President
National Council of Churches
475 Riverside Drive
New York, N.Y. 10027

Dear Dr. Howard,

A vital question of ethics is involved in the present conflict over the date of Earth Day. It is important for you to know the facts and take immediate action to correct the wrong that is being done.

Dr. Margaret Mead eloquently stated the case for a global Earth Day on the equinox in the essay which is enclosed. She also stated that I was responsible for the conceptualization of Earth Day. The original Earth Day was celebrated on March 21, 1970, not April 22 as stated in President Carter's Proclamation on January 2nd of this year.

In 1970 the Environmental Teach-In changed their name to Earth Day—usurping the name announced in San Francisco at the UN Conference of UNESCO (Nov. 23, 1969) by our organizing committee. Several of their people were present when we announced that there were plans, which already had the support of San Francisco and other cities, to celebrate March 21, the equinox, as Earth Day. But on January 20th the Environmental Teach-In placed a full page ad in the New York Times announcing Earth Day would be on April 22.

Confronted with these unethical actions Denis Hayes, the National Coordinator, stated that he personally was ignorant of what happened in San Francisco and that it was now too late to do anything. He did issue a statement that they had learned we "were already out on deck with Earth Day . . . John McConnell announced some months ago in San Francisco that it wished to make March 21 'Earth Day'" and apologized for any confusion which this had caused.

The news release they said they issued received no attention. We had an Earth Day on March 21—the equinox—in San Francisco and a few other cities; a spectacular event at the University of California at Davis. But millions of people celebrated Earth Day on April 22, not knowing that the date was based on a lie—the oft repeated statement that the organizers of the April 22 event were the originators of Earth Day and that it was the first Earth Day.

At first glance it seems inconsequential what day is celebrated as Earth Day. But the tiny lie about the date can affect the course of history.

The best strategy for global peace is to find some point of deep felt agreement—to dramatize and increase this common feeling and then vigorously cooperate in the common objectives that follow, regardless of differences in other areas.

Such action is possible with Earth Day on the equinox. We can unite at the moment of the equinox with silent prayer or meditation—in a great simultaneous dedication to our most important task, the care of Earth. Global TV and the ringing of bells worldwide can stir humanity with its dramatization of our one common ground, our Earth. This can bring a turnabout in values and thinking and be implemented everywhere by pursuit of the Earth Care Guidelines outlined in the Earth Charter. Each Earth Day will then begin a new Earth Year of effort to save, restore and enhance life on our planet.

On the other hand, April 22, 1970 was the centennial of Lenin's birthday. My conversations with ambassadors from other countries make it clear that April 22nd can never be a global Earth Day. The fact that the choice of the date was possibly an accident on the part of organizers does not mitigate the problem. To foster an Earth Day that cannot become global is a disservice to humanity.

As agreed, Earth Day on April 22 has not been repeated for the past ten years. But now it appears that in order to increase their control over information and funding, the organizers have revived April 22 as Earth Day, causing great confusion among schools and churches planning to celebrate March 20 as Earth Day, which never obtained federal funding.

I admire and approve of many efforts by Denis Hayes and his associates to call attention to the urgent need for alternative energy. But I do not believe their methods are in accord with their goals. Perhaps excessive drive for power to control budgets, information and regulations causes them to deny and undermine our efforts, rather than cooperate. We are seeking to achieve Earth care goals by education and a change of heart, by stressing individual responsibility and free, open, local efforts as the key to needed change.

Any activity at any time and any place that calls attention to the need of Earth care is a good activity. But it should not usurp the name "Earth Day" to the detriment of global unity on the equinox.

We must be loyal to the Earth Day that has been celebrated for the last ten years at the United Nations. U Thant, Waldheim, Margaret Mead and last year six children representing the Year of the Child were among those who rang the Peace Bell on Earth Day—March 20 or 21, the day of the equinox. In the face of these facts we cannot change and celebrate Earth Day on April 22. No amount of money spent by government agencies can change the fact that Earth Day is on the equinox, when the Sun first crosses the Equator—symbolizing equilibrium: harmony between Sun, Earth and life.

On Earth Day, March 20 at 6:10 a.m. in New York, the moment of the equinox, the United Nations Peace Bell will be rung, signaling two minutes of silent prayer for Earth—its people, its life, its future. A whole-hearted effort now by you could help lift this moment to a higher perspective that can save our planet. All that is needed is a touch of the grace and love of God. This will be freely given when with one heart and one mind, we respond to His call and decide to take charge and take care of our planet. Our other problems will then gradually diminish as we make the care of Earth our first priority.

19 Troutman St., Brooklyn, New York 11206 (212) 574-3059

Letter to Mr. Gamaroody,
Assistant to Bani-Sadr

John McConnell in Iran—1980

WHEN WE MET ON Noruz I felt a kindred spirit and had high hopes for understanding and support for my mission here.

I realize the great burdens you carry, but I am greatly disappointed that in these two weeks you could not find time to see me again. Now I must return to New York.

As expressed in the material I gave Mr. Toghavi—which he said he would give you—my only purpose is to save our planet, which is in great danger of total catastrophe. Recognizing this need could give added life and direction to your new government. Building on the traditions and values of Noruz with support of Earth Day and the Earth Charter could unite the different segments of your country in a high common goal that would command respect and loyal support.

After talking with you I felt your openness and imagination might be fired by a bold idea . . . for which I could make a very strong case given the opportunity to explain more fully. In fact if I could meet with Eman Houghmani I believe he would understand and support such a plan.

The idea is to quickly return the hostages—not to President Carter, but to me—for their return to the United States. To do this for the sake of Earth—for Noruz, Earth Day and an Earth Care Revolution to save our planet Earth.

I know TV. This would make heroes of your country and of me. (The more you see what I stand for the less you will mind.) Support in countries around the world would follow. I believe that even the United States and Soviet Union would finally see the abject folly of their pres-

460

ent policies as the world mobilized to protect and save our planet. Next year—or the year after—a billion people would join on Earth Day (Noruz in Iran), alone with their families and their God, with a firm resolve to help take charge and take care of their planet.

Such a course of action would accomplish more in one year than could be done in 20 years by other means. and I don't think we have 20 years.

Now you may disagree, or have another suggestion. One way or another I hope the meanings and purposes of Noruz will be given the highest possible support in your country and that everything about it will be shared with the rest of the world. This will inspire many countries to resurrect similar practices for their own history and culture.

I have had many enjoyable talks with your friend Ackbar at the Embassy. Enclosed is a tape I recorded at home. If you find it interesting you might borrow a different tape I gave to Ackbar—which he liked.

Also enclosed is a poem I wrote. Not a very good poem—but some good ideas.

I do want you to know meeting you was a special pleasure, and I have made many friends in Iran.

I return to New York now. But if you decide you would like me to come back—to explain further how we can work together for our planet—please let me know.

My home address is: 19 Troutman St. New York

With fond memories and warm regards,
John McConnell

The above was typed on 4-3-02 from a handwritten rough draft we found in my papers. I do not have a copy of the actual letter that was given to Mr. Gamaroody.

Statement in Tehran, Iran

John McConnell, Founder of Earth Day
March 22, 1980

A S THE FOUNDER OF Earth Day, I have directed my thought to a global view, seeking a strategy that might avoid total destruction of life on our planet.

It does little good to solve a crisis in Iran, or South Africa, the U.S.A., or any other place, if in spite of local success the whole world goes down the drain—an ever increasing danger that frightens many of the most thoughtful and informed people in the world.

In Iran there exists a unique opportunity to save our planet. It is this possibility that I want to discuss. But first I must set forth some basic facts that go to the heart of our global problem.

Whether it is inflation, pollution, poverty, or clashes of group against group and nation against nation, efforts to solve the problem ignore the basic cause of the problem.

The reason for our difficulty is greed and selfishness. Many people recognize this but there seems to be a total disinterest in doing anything about it. It is assumed that nothing can be done, that in the "real" world of business and politics, greed and gain will decide the future.

The cause of this corrupt world-view is a false basic assumption —sinister, secret and taken for granted—that in the hard world of reality, stimulating greed and selfishness is the dynamic that will bring the greatest prosperity—an ingenious lie that must be exposed.

Basing an economy on the stimulation of greed and acquisitiveness does bring material wealth and affluence—but with it a loss of morality, meaning and integrity which are essential for the well-being of the body, mind and spirit in the total person, and for the healthy functioning of a community or society—which is also determined by the degree of morality and integrity.

By morality is meant the honest pursuit of what is good and the rejection of what is evil; the practice of the Golden Rule, love of neighbor. Now, with our new awareness of our whole planet and the vital necessity to understand its man-made problems—to act as custodians for its protection and care —the best definition of morality is: To seek the well-being of our planet and its people.

The United States is a prime example of what has gone wrong. The irresponsible drive for "me, mine, more," has dramatically increased production, affluence, superficial pleasures and creature comforts. But while these people say they are "increased with goods and have need of nothing," inside they are "wretched, miserable, poor, blind and naked." Inflation, crime and corruption is a part of the terrible toll they must pay. Worst of all the house of the future in which their children must dwell is poisoned, polluted and crumbling. The spacious skies are filled with smog, the amber grain with chemicals, the purple mountains scarred by ill-planned roads and houses have lost their majesty—and their forests. The fruited plain is paved. The next generation will never know the natural bounty of the once beautiful land called America.

Any plans to save our planet must include a return to morality. There must be a massive mobilization of science, psychology and religion to achieve this goal. Major guidelines for this purpose are given in the Earth Charter—which, while broad in its approach, can obtain universal support and provide direction for global efforts.

However, to achieve the massive changes needed in attitudes, values and conduct, it is vital that we make the challenge clear and evoke the same energetic response that has fueled support for wars and revolutions.

In the United States, in 1941, Pearl Harbor triggered an energetic response. Citizens from every walk of life stopped their greed and selfishness to help save their country. A clear effective challenge today could obtain a similar response to save our planet and avoid catastrophe for our children. It must be made clear that the threat to our planet is such that we cannot wait for the catastrophe to trigger our response for then it will be too late. There can be no response to atomic war, the death of the oceans, or the destruction of the ozone layer that protects us from the Sun's radioactivity, just a few of the dangers we face because of our short-sighted greed and selfishness and our misdirected technology.

To escape the ultimate catastrophe, I suggest we turn to the world of theatre, of imagination for the answer. Napoleon said, "Imagination rules the world." While the world is made of mind and matter, it's mind that matters most.

Shakespeare told us, "All the world's a stage." At present the playwrights and producers of our global drama are the world leaders who are masters of money, guns and communications. They call the shots and keep the players puppets to their passions and pride—all for lucrative profits and with amazing ability to rationalize their actions. The play is a bad play, a terrible play.

But we can change all that. Following is a way we can close the show and provide in its place a grand epic, a heroic epic, in which people who love their fellow man—who want to save their planet—will be the producers, playwrights and principal actors.

The conjunction of Earth Day, Iran's New Year, the hostages at the American Embassy, and the meetings of the Revolutionary Council, provide an unprecedented opportunity.

Let the hostages be freed now. Connect their release with Earth Day and Iran's New Year. Announce support of the Earth Charter and plans to implement the Charter in the new government. (This need not all be done at one time.) State your commitment to make your revolution an Earth Care Revolution; to be the first country dedicated to the care of our planet as described in the Earth Charter—that in striving to obey the moral law, choosing the good and refusing the evil, you will seek the well-being of our planet and all its people.

By your example you will let the people of the world know they can be the producers instead of the puppets. More and more the seekers and doers, the people who love their fellow man, will take action in their own way to further the Earth Care Revolution. Succeed in this grand endeavor and future generations will sing your praises. You can succeed. After all, this world is made for music, not for madness.

Without the unique circumstances regarding the hostages, the kind of action I suggest would be largely ignored by media. But given the present situation it will create a media shock wave with continuing coverage of efforts and results.

Why not end the bad play? Ring down the curtain! LET A NEW PLAY BEGIN!

Declaration of Planetary Rights

By John McConnell
(Copyrighted 1969 WE, Inc. Anyone may quote or print this article
so long as they indicate the author, John McConnell.)
Concerning the rights of all people to Earth's land, sea,
minerals, oil and other natural resources.

1. That all men are created equally free and independent and have among their inalienable rights certain fundamental property rights during their sojourn on this planet.

2. That a beneficent Creator has provided this Earth-home, this nest in the stars, with an abundance of land and natural resources; enough that with care and cooperation a good life can be enjoyed by all members of the family of man.

3. That among the equal rights of men is the right to an equal share in nature's bounty; a right of each person to his planetary inheritance—his share of land, water, minerals or an appropriate equivalent in food, housing or other benefits. No one can, by any compact, deprive or divest their posterity, or any other man's posterity, of the right to his portion of Earth. All natural resources belong equally to every living person.

4. That steps should be taken to compensate for, or other wise adjust the differences in the present unequal ownership of the gifts of nature. To this end each nation should collect a two percent royalty each year for all use (including its own) of any land or other natural resources. These royalties would be above and apart from taxation for government needs, and be distributed equally to all citizens through quarterly payments, or other appropriate measures. In this way within a

fifty year life span there will be full and just compensation to each person for the use of his portion of Earth's natural riches.

5.   That since the benefits of nature's bounty can only be realized through man's constructive effort and the wise use of his accumulated knowledge, each person's learning and labor should be encouraged and rewarded. Therefore, no individual, or group should be deprived of any just benefits obtained from Earth's available resources—so long as fair payment for its use is made to the rest of mankind.

6.   That the basic raw materials of the Earth should be made available to all on an equal basis, with due regard for the requirements of conservation; that the United Nations should seek agreements to serve this purpose.

7.   That steps be taken by the United Nations to assure that the use and exploitation of the sea and sea floor will be equally available to people of all nations, subject to careful conservation regulations and supervision; and that in addition to fees for its services, the United Nations will collect royalties for the use of the sea and sea floor to be distributed equally among the ultimate owners—all the people of this Earth.

8.   That as these steps toward social justice and cooperation demonstrate their advantage, all nations should seek to adjust the remaining differences among them in natural resources benefits through participation in a natural resource Royalties pool, whereby equal royalty payments would be paid each and every member of the whole human family. These steps toward realization of global property rights will encourage cooperation, individual initiative, and responsibility; they will make feasible full production with ever-growing peaceful progress as we explore the nature of man and his place in the universe, and find new ways to encourage and inspire his highest potentials.

The Global Seabed—A Sixth Continent

From John McConnell
19 Troutman St.
Brooklyn, N.Y. 11206

NEWS RELEASE
APRIL 19, 1975

IN 1975 THE WHOLE world is in a crisis of pollution, diminishing resources, increasing crime and violence. While the big power nations
have finally begun peaceful accommodation, still the institutions and
policies of business and government are based on greed and mindless
growth. The wise and thoughtful see the possibilities of a global disaster.

Efforts to create a world community of freedom and order seem
doomed to failure. The creation of world government and the rule of law
in international affairs seems no closer than twenty years ago. Chaotic
shifts in economic power benefit a few at the expense of the poor and
increase an already dangerous inflation. Leaders in business and government cling to their power and property with little regard for the rights
and needs of the people. And still most everyone is looking for an answer that will stop the headlong plunge toward disaster and bring a sane
program of care for Earth and its people.

In the midst of increasing confusion and panic, a great discovery
has been made that can change the world.

For centuries children have been taught that Planet Earth contains
five continents: North America, South America, Africa, Europe and
Asia, and some islands. The rest was Ocean, or Sea; a place to sail or
fish. But man's institutions, governments and division of property were
of the land.

However, in the last few decades Mankind has begun to seriously
explore the bed of the Sea, and now is finding oil, and mineral in great
quantities with the promise of much more to come.

Moreover, in 1970 the United Nations declared the Seabed to be the common heritage of Mankind. Of course the whole Earth is the common heritage of mankind, but through a lack of just laws and policies, the land, and mineral heritage of Earth's people has been taken over for the most part, by a privileged few who "own" and control vast properties in democratic countries, or "control" vast raw materials in communist or socialist countries. Changing the distribution system on land will require the powerful to relinquish their advantage through great changes in established ways of doing things. Not so in the Sea.

For in 1975 a few individuals believe the Sea can be considered a new continent, unrecognized until now, where the past mistakes and injustices in the use of raw materials on land can be avoided. By recognizing all the seas as constituting one Sea Continent, with an equal claim of every Earth person to a share in this valuable property, a demonstration of economic justice can be initiated that will bring the people of Earth together in a growing venture for their common good. A new place and basis for global harmony and cooperation has been found. The seas that nurtured the beginnings of life can now nurture our renewal of Earth's global web of life.

EARTH SOCIETY
1047 AMSTERDAM AVENUE
NEW YORK, N.Y. 10025
212 864–5424

Earth Charter

History of original Earth Charter—1979

This document, written by John McConnell, was featured in a large sized illustrated poster. The poster was posted at key places at the United Nations. It was circulated and used by many UN Offices.

John McConnell, founder of Earth Day, felt there was a need for an Earth Charter—a document that would set forth the key items humanity should address in order to achieve a viable future. In 1979 he wrote "The Earth Charter." John Drysdale persuaded Primary Metal & Mineral Corp. to print and donate to Earth Day several thousand posters with The Earth Charter on one side and on the other side the beautiful image by William Blake showing God reaching down to Earth. Earth was portrayed as seen from Space and below it:

The Earth Charter poster was featured at the United Nations each year on Earth Day.

[Elements of this document were incorporated in the "Earth Magna Charta" written in 1995.]

EARTH CHARTER INTRODUCTION

A Key to Earth's Survival

HERE IS A WORLD view with incentives for our Earth's physical and spiritual regeneration. It calls for heroic efforts to achieve a critical common goal: To save our planet. Genuine cooperation to save Earth will lead to mutual understanding and trust—a true basis upon which to forge lasting peacekeeping accords.

Disarmament can become a reality, economic order and opportunity can spread, and a spirit of cooperation can grow as we work together. The power of these ideals will make our Earth a healthy, peaceful planet—a harmonious home for all our children to enjoy.

We can begin now, with a major effort this year and in each succeeding year, to become responsible custodians and benefactors of Earth's amazing web of life. With progress reported each year on Earth Day, we can, by the year 2000, observe a two year Bi-millennium to celebrate our triumph over fear and greed, graduating to a larger, richer destiny for our planet and its people.

In this year 1979 many people around the world realize that we are the first generation to determine the life or death of the planet we have inherited.

This Earth Charter is intended to help define our new role and responsibility and to strengthen the many efforts that are moving in this direction. It is intended to inspire unity and cooperation in our task that we may preserve, restore and increase Earth's beauty and bounty for our own and future generations.

People of all ideologies and religions can, and must, unite in pursuing this vital purpose. To many religious people, stewardship is a divine obligation: subjecting oneself to the will of God creatively and comprehensively. To humanitarians, stewardship is a moral imperative.

Every community on Earth is invited to ratify this Earth Charter and support it by their words and deeds.

EARTH CHARTER

Preamble

In order for us as one human family to effectively assume our new role as the custodians of Earth, and as people who care about Earth's future, we will strive to act in accordance with the following principles and guidelines.

We are the first generation to determine the life or death of the planet we have inherited. The care of Earth is now our most important task. The Earth Charter defines our new role and responsibility and strengthens our efforts. It inspires unity and cooperation in our task so that we may preserve, restore and increase Earth's beauty and bounty for our own and future generations. People of all ideologies and religions can, and must, unite in pursuing this vital purpose.

A massive communications effort is needed to publicize every program or product that improves the care of Earth. We must no longer condemn others, but each seek what we can honestly praise. In this way we can obtain public support and enthusiasm for Earth care action and motivate people everywhere to practice Earth care.

We believe that a vigorous united effort to understand, protect and revive our planet will at the same time promote mutual trust and accommodations needed for creating a peaceful future. The signers urge individuals and communities throughout the world to endorse and ratify this Earth Charter. Together we can save our planet.

Principles

Article 1. Earth Care

The natural bounty of land and sea is the inheritance and responsibility of all Earth's people. Each person's help is now needed for the care of Earth and each person can benefit from that care. We must each act responsibly to help nurture and care for our planet—in our block, our neighborhood, our vocation and in the new policies, formulated within all institutions and governments, that affect the future of Earth. The fact of Earth's existence, and the nature of the live web of life, of which we are all a part, should form the basis for all future actions.

Article 2. Earth Rights

We hereby determine that in pursuing the goal of Earth's renewal, opportunity will be provided every person on Earth to share in its future. More important than property rights and the rights of sovereignty is the fundamental right of each person's claim to a portion of our planet: and opportunity for every person, who will contribute to the care of Earth, to have a portion of land, a home, a job and the means to learn the skills needed to live a wholesome life.

Article 3. The Human Spirit

The greatest contributions to human progress—whether in art, music, science, religion or philosophy—have come from tapping the inner resources of the human spirit. To many religious people stewardship is a divine obligation: subjecting oneself to the will of God creatively and comprehensively. To humanitarians, stewardship is a moral imperative. To foster a global spirit of cooperation it is essential that we recognize our common desires for love, truth, beauty, justice and freedom, and that we are all inter-dependent members of one human family.

Article 4. Education

In order to carry out our responsibility as custodians of Earth, we must all learn how to produce, trade, consume and create without damaging the delicate fabric of life; to practice an Earth Care Ethic. An Earth Care Curriculum is now the first requisite for a good education.

Article 5. Production

We must walk the soft path that meets human needs without endangering the many interdependent Earth life forms that exist throughout our biosphere. So urgent is this task that we must now achieve the same kind of massive innovation that nations have demonstrated in time of war. Decentralism and self-help programs are urged for grass roots participation everywhere. Eventually, all mass-produced products must conform to Earth care criteria: (1) long life; (2) easy repair; (3) non-polluting in production and use; (4) energy efficient; and (5) recyclable.

Article 6. Trade-Marketing/Advertising

Our goal in Earth's renewal is to provide fair and equal access to credit, raw materials, exchange and trade. Economic policies and incentives must reward those who provide basic human needs instead of those who, out of mindless shortsighted greed, unfairly exploit their neighbors. For this purpose a stable medium of exchange can and must be created, as well as an accessible means of mass transportation. Advertising should inform, not deceive.

Article 7. Consumption

Every consumer should realize each product he buys and uses can affect Earth for good or bad. An Earth Care Ethic will foster in our buying habits and personal conduct, choices that will avoid pollution and waste. Each person will be an educated consumer. The present practice of Earth Kill will be supplanted by Earth Care.

Article 8. Renewable Resources

The preservation, improvement and renewal of soil, water, air, wild life and vegetation must be a primary goal in our research and planning.

All the basic physical needs of society must be obtained in ways that will increase rather than destroy Earth's renewable bounty. To this end a rapid transition is needed to greater conservation and use of renewable resources: to tracking and recycling scarce non-renewable raw materials, to new land use policies for clean water, healthy soil, parks, gardens and creative humane settlements. Sustainable population goals and sustainable solar energy are all essential for our survival.

Article 9. Communications

The new Earth Care Ethic is best communicated person-to-person. Each individual who makes Earth care a major goal can contagiously spread the excitement and adventure to be enjoyed as caretakers of our planet. Communicators in all media can also make a vital difference. Headlines for heroes who are caring for Earth and about Earth care alternatives can create a sense of high purpose and adventure in young and old.

Article 10. Earth Day

A yearly Celebration to unite the World in the Care of Earth.

To strengthen the efforts described in this Earth Charter, and to call attention to yearly progress in these efforts, we will celebrate Earth Day each year on the day of the March Equinox. In the week preceding Earth Day, we will help give an accounting of the state of the Earth—in every part and as a whole. Earth Day will then be a time to celebrate Earth's life and progress, a time to come together in renewed dedication to its care, a time to rejoice, sing, dance and play, a public holiday shared by all people of Earth. Every community, city, state and nation is invited and urged to plan their own special ceremonies and participation in this annual event.

To forever commemorate our task and our challenge we will in the year 2000 begin a two-year Bi-Millennium celebration, graduating to a larger, richer destiny for our planet and its people.

77 Theses on the Care of the Earth

A Guide for Earth Trustees
Principles and Policies that will foster the peaceful nurture and care of
the planet Earth.
Written by John McConnell, the Founder of Earth Day
1985

> The world of tomorrow is not foreordained to be either good or
> bad . . . rather it will be what we make it. In these 77 theses I
> have tried to present the essential ideas needed to achieve a his-
> toric global change—from mindless exploitation, with increasing
> danger of worldwide catastrophe, to the peaceful nurture of our
> home, Planet Earth.

John McConnell

PROLOGUE—EARTH TRUSTEESHIP

THE 77 THESES ARE especially for people who will think of themselves
as Trustees of Earth and who seek to do the things about ecology,
economics and ethics that foster peaceful progress on our planet.

Earth's rejuvenation can best be realized by individuals and small
groups of people (preferably 5 to 15 each) who will make their own
special commitment to projects for the care of Earth. And, who at the
same time, affirm a common world view about the protection and care
of Earth—which they share with other Earth Trustee groups—a view and
commitment which hopefully will soon spread to include all, or practically
all, of Earth's people. The Earth-Trustee concept can provide the measure
of unity in our diversity needed for achieving Earth's rejuvenation.

A useful analogy is the way each cell in the body has its specific task, but has within it the genetic code—or pattern—for the whole body.

The problem is to determine the items in the Earth Trustee world view that can be accepted and shared voluntarily by people of every clime and culture, of every ideology, religious belief and temperament.

To accomplish this it is important to separate the vital facts on which most people can agree (2+2=4, etc.) from the items of belief that deal with uncertainties or differing viewpoints—in politics, religion, economics, education, social justice, etc.

The 77 THESES can obtain general support for a broad Earth Trustee world view. With this as a common template all approve—not in details of implementation, but in general purpose—rapport and appropriate bonds between groups can be established. Earth Trustees will recognize their independence and points of difference. The purpose they will share is the care of Earth.

The object then in each group will be to obtain information that will assist their choices and the pursuit of their Earth Care project, or projects, computer networks, data banks and flow of communication about what others are doing will serve this purpose.

With the above in mind, Earth Care Handbooks* in every language will provide an Earth Trustee world view and orientation, plus guidelines for finding and choosing Earth Care projects—carefully avoiding the partisan issues that cause disagreement. Our goal is a global consensus on the care of Earth.

*Handbooks can be produced independently, with common guidelines.

Part of the program—and basis of eventual success—will be a practical determined effort by each person and group to share their enthusiastic interest with friends and thereby bring about a rapid doubling—each month if possible—of individuals joining or organizing Earth Care projects.

In these efforts a key to success will be the sense of community, or spirit of cooperation that is engendered. Special emphasis on reverent prayer, worship, dedication to and emphasis of moral and ethical values in the terms acceptable to each group will make a vital contribution.

The most important inner point of unity in the care of Earth is our love of Earth, its life and its people—especially our nearest neighbors.

The most important outer point of unity is the simultaneous celebration of and dedication to the care of Earth on each EARTH DAY, March 20–21 and will be aided by observance each day on radio and TV of global Earth Minutes. Religious groups are especially invited to participate—each in its own way. In this there is no compromise or watering down of their particular faith or belief. The point of unity is not doctrinal or ideological belief, but dedication to the care of Earth and inner love of our planet and its people.

I can engage in this united action in spite of strong differences with people of other religions or political beliefs. Loyalty to country, which exists in spite of differences with other citizens, must now be equaled and transcended by loyalty to our planet and dedication to its care.

A sign of participation can be the flying of the Earth Flag . . .

> Dear John, I have read and reread your 77 Theses. They are wonderful and so much to the point.
>
> > Robert Muller, Chancellor of the
> > University of Peace, Costa Rica.

Along with the Secretary-General U Thant and other world leaders, Robert Muller signed the 1971 UN Earth Day Proclamation designating the March 20–21 equinox to be Earth Day. The Proclamation was written by John McConnell.

Be a Trustee of Planet Earth
Fly the Earth Flag
Order the Earth Flag Online

77 Theses on the Care of the Earth

EARTH DANGER

1. Recognizing: That ignorance and neglect of our planet, combined with the folly of international rivalries, has now endangered all life on Earth;

2. That our planet's life is threatened by policies and actions that cause massive pollution of air, water and soil and dangers of chemical, biological and nuclear disaster;

3. That mutual trust is necessary in order to counter these threats;

MUTUAL TRUST

4. That only by open communication and joint action, for a great common good, can mutual trust develop;

5. That the one thing we have in common is our planet;

CAMPAIGN FOR EARTH

6. That a campaign for the care of Earth will create relationships leading to mutual trust and ultimately to reciprocal disarmament and stable peace;

7. That in pursuing peace it is important to identify and emphasize vital matters and the extent and nature of our accord, and to build on this accord;

8. That peaceful actions beget peace;

9. That in a world of instant global communications a strong, informed public opinion in all nations dedicated to peace and care of Earth, could become the greatest deterrent to war and to local violence;

10. That the greatest challenge in history is the present challenge of destiny involving all humanity; a challenge to reclaim the Earth for all peoples and to free them from the fear of war and want;

11. That accepting this challenge will bring the measure of trust needed to achieve these goals;

WHOLEHEARTED DEDICATION NEEDED

12. That the peaceful care of our planet cannot be accomplished through half-hearted or insincere efforts, but will require the dedication of all humanity;

13. That in seeking the basic change in the conduct of governments and their peoples, we acknowledge the failures of all previous efforts to achieve a peaceful world;

14. That investments worldwide in instruments of destruction endangers the human race;

15. That excessive destruction of trees, vegetation, and wildlife, from ancient times to the present, has decimated or destroyed numerous

species and degraded Earth's potential for nurturing life, and that the current acceleration of this process will bring global catastrophe if it is not soon brought to a halt;

HUMANITY'S SPACE AGE CHOICE

16. That world peace requires a basic long-term commitment to change attitudes and conduct, and to develop structures and programs that will foster peaceful progress in the care of Earth and in our relationships with each other;

17. That new factors in the quest for peace are Space Age global awareness and deep concern everywhere that something must be done;

18. That we owe to untold generations in our past and future a firm decision for peace and care of Earth;

19. That it is time for humanity to take charge and take care of their planet;

NURTURE OF EARTH

20. That the campaign for Earth requires ideas and attitudes conducive to the nurture and care of Earth;

21. That loyalty to community, bioregion, and planet is essential for the healing of our planet and people;

22. That a patriotism embracing people and planet as well as nations is necessary now;

23. That loyalty to our planet will not hurt, but instead will help our lesser loyalties;

ALLEGIANCE TO EARTH

24. That while national governments use police force to coerce allegiance when needed, their long-term strength depends on voluntary support by their citizens;

25. That loyalty to our planet can best be achieved through voluntary efforts to understand its life systems and processes, and then with love for our planet to help nurture and sustain the amazing web of life that covers our globe;

26. That global communication and education to foster Earth's care can

provide the measure of enlightenment needed to justify and assert the authority of humanity in the management and care of Earth;

GLOBAL COMMUNITY OF CONSCIENCE

27. That voluntary support of Earth care and person-to-person communication about Earth care can provide a global communication of conscience dedicated to Earth's protection. This will bring inner peace and global peace;

28. That constraints and requirements for Earth care will then permeate society and provide our global conscience with moral authority and influence greater than that of national governments;

29. That as we develop a strong community commitment of individuals and governments to the care of Earth and to one another, and are aided by world public opinion filled with hope instead of fear, we will establish peaceful relationships and make any war unthinkable and impossible;

30. That the management and care of Earth by the people of Earth can only be achieved by their willing support;

31. That the willing support of people throughout our world can only be obtained by providing equitable, fair benefits in return for their services;

32. That it is necessary to determine the rights and responsibility of individuals in the care of Earth;

RIGHTS TO THE USE OF EARTH

33. That religions teach, and philosophers aver that the Earth is for all people. The Psalms state, "The Earth hath He given to the children of men";

34. That, whether considered the gift of God, or the bounty of Nature, every individual has an equal claim, or right to Earth's natural bounty; to a portion or benefit from their share of Earth's land, raw materials and natural resources;

35. That every country should provide a free homestead for each family that lacks one, or the means to obtain one. Every person who wishes to receive this basic inheritance in their planet should be

given a secure habitable shelter, or be provided the purchasing capacity or land and materials;

FAIR BENEFITS FROM EARTH

36. That expenses of government and public needs they serve can best be met by land use fees, or single tax, based on the value of the land (not on improvements or labor);

37. That every individual, regardless of circumstances or lack of resources, should be assured an opportunity for basic nutritious food, or practical means for procuring it;

38. That raw materials—oil, coal, minerals—are the inheritance of all Earth's people. As they are mined, sold, or used, at least 2 percent of their value should be equally distributed as royalties to everyone. These unearned assets in the ground, the inheritance of all Earth's people, should be carefully mined, conserved and recycled by the owners or managers, and used by consumers in ways that will increase the Earth's natural bounty and benefit Earth's people;

RESPONSIBILITY FOR THE CARE OF EARTH

39. That rights to the bounty of Earth must be equaled by responsibility for its care;

40. That every individual should be taught from childhood the requirements for Earth care by instruction and experience in caring for gardens, animals, and birds. Later instruction should include Earth Care criteria and guidelines for land use, manufacturing, recycling, energy, design of homes and communities with sustainable goals in population and development; preservation of wildlife and wilderness areas, ways to diminish pollution of air, soil and water;

MONEY AND TRADE

41. That equitable trade and development requires a fair honest medium of exchange;

42. That money should not be a product, controlled by special interests and sold to the highest bidder, but instead should be a free medium of exchange, based on things to be exchanged, and made available

through collateral loans in percentages needed to facilitate trade
and exchange without inflation;

43. That amply secured loans should not require payment of interest,
only the cost of paper work. Usury (interest) is condemned by major religions. It can cause inflation and results in unearned and un-
necessary income by manipulators;

44. That in high risk loans to individuals or firms, security provided by
the borrower should be of equal value to money provided by the
bank. And both should share equally in any losses or profits; in this
case money is actually an investment instead of a loan;

PRODUCERS AND CONSUMERS

45. That control of capital should be widely dispersed and prevented
from being used to take unfair advantages of individuals or corporations with legitimate need for money;

46. That public disclosure should be required in the management of
any business or the sale of any stock setting forth the company's
adherence to Earth Care criteria:

    Such as what is being done to avoid pollution in production and
use of products or services; energy efficiency; design for easy repair, service and recycling of products; fair wages and benefits to
employees. Reports of standards adopted and adherence should be
provided by appropriate independent authorities;

47. That leaders in church, state and entertainment should urge support of Earth Trustee efforts and provide examples of an Earth
Trustee conscience in investments, purchases and life style;

48. That individuals who invest for greatest profit with no regard for
how the money is made—bombs for poor misguided countries,
production lacking environmental safeguards, unfair poverty wages
for employees—should be made aware of the harm they are causing. Companies responsible for such Earth Kill practices should be
exposed, penalized and their products shunned until they convert
to Earth Trustee conduct;

49. That the media should be the guardian of the public's long-term interest and could serve this purpose by exposing gross Earth Kill examples, and by headlining Earth Trustee solutions and programs;

GREED AND WHAT TO DO ABOUT IT

50. That a major cause of injustice, of crimes against Nature and people, is the way we have accepted and institutionalized greed, particularly greed for private profit from the land and natural resources of the Earth;

51. That most success in selling products is presently achieved by advertising and promotion that increases greed, lust and vanity. Subtle motivational techniques are used to deceive and corrupt and thereby make greater profits: for example, in the promotion and sale of cigarettes;

52. That to attain a viable Earth Trustee future it is essential that designers, inventors, planners, producers, consumers and advertising executives, all learn the necessity of Earth Trustee constraints. A massive educational program in schools, churches and voluntary agencies is needed to expose Earth Kill kinds of promotion and products and instead promote public awareness of Earth Trustee values and choices;

EDUCATION

53. That an Earth Trustee curriculum in schools is urgently needed. Earth Trustee studies can provide the best unifying purpose for education;

54. That it is essential for children to learn more about the wonders of Earth and that our generation can become trustees, custodians and caretakers of our beautiful planet;

55. That to accomplish these goals effective use must be made of every means of communication—print, fax, radio, TV, telephone, satellite, computer networks;

MEDIA

56. That the general knowledge about how the world works should be constantly presented by media—in news and special programs. For example, the role of light, soil, water, air and living organisms in nurturing the thin skin of life that covers our globe; the diversity of plants, trees, animals, birds, insects—all necessary to the delicate balance of life-giving nutrients on our planet;

TECHNOLOGY

57. That technology must be used to foster Earth's care. The present mindless use of technology in ways that poison, pollute and disrupt Nature's ecosystems must be halted. Instead of a destroyer, technology can and must become a harmonious extender of Nature's bounty;

RIGHT SIZE FOR EVERYTHING

58. That there is a right and wrong size for everything. Finding the right size is essential to the lasting success of any product, system, arrangement, institution or endeavor;

59. That everything should be as small as possible, unless there is a good reason for it to be larger. In many cases communities and businesses should be smaller—providing more intimate, humane services to smaller groups of people;

60. That constant growth of a city or a business will eventually lead to disaster. Exponential factors decree this. Cities and towns can avoid this by providing laws that only allow new construction which replaces old structures. New Earth communities using interactive technologies can relieve congestion;

61. That once a community or business reaches an optimum size, progress should be sought, not through an increase in size or profits, but through improved quality of services and products. In a small business where the employees are close to owners with a personal interest in each employee, a shared understanding of the operation and its purpose brings better give and take, the pursuit of excellence and efficiency. Given a level playing field of competition, when a business gets too big, its smaller competitors will be the ones to increase sales. Also, cooperatives will be given a better chance to prove their worth;

ETHICS OF RELIGION

62. That a sense of responsibility and the practice of Earth Trustee ethics is an essential requirement for the future;

63. That major religions, philosophies and ideologies teach the "Golden Rule"—to do unto others as you would have them do unto you;

64. That while some people of faith are engaged in works of peace and works of charity, many religious people show in their actions bigotry and hypocrisy;

65. That the majority of people fail miserably to live up to their intentions;

66. That moral responsibility and ethical behavior is for the most part found in people of deep, religious faith—reflected in their compassion, fairness and charity;

67. That most conflict over religious and ideological beliefs have their roots in different hypotheses about the unknown. Does God exist? What is the nature or purpose of reality?;

KEY TO BASIC ACCORD

68. That in the question of what life is all about, we face profound mysteries and unanswerable questions. Who can imagine the Universe never having a beginning or ever having an end?;

69. That there is in the human spirit a desire for meaning in life. Religious belief, especially belief in a loving God, provides a more promising hypothesis about the unknown. While belief in God or life after death cannot be scientifically proven, there are phenomena that suggests its possibility; for example, answers to prayer, and reports by people who were briefly dead;

70. That the value and test in the here and now of religious faith or philosophical belief is its good effect on the believer: the measure of confidence, virtue, integrity and the practice of the Golden Rule;

VIRTUE

71. That in the present crisis of our planet the greatest virtue or moral imperative is the care and rejuvenation of Earth and securing the right of all people to its natural bounty;

A NEW GOLDEN AGE

72. That every adherent of ethics or religious faith should act as a responsible Trustee of Planet Earth: join the global Earth Trustee Effort and assist some Earth Care project;

73. That every municipality or community should form an independent Earth Trustee Committee, which will discuss the 77 Theses and then form their own program to help the Earth Campaign: initiating or assisting projects that eliminate poverty and pollution and benefit humanity;

74. That radio stations and TV need to program one or more daily Earth Minutes—at 0300, 1100 or 1900 GMT.* These simultaneous global "minutes without words" can be produced independently by any radio or TV station, with views and sounds of nature, children, music, bells, our planet;

75. That to foster the vital unity needed in our diversity, all individuals and institutions will celebrate Earth Day each year on the March Equinox—Nature's Day, March 20 or 21; the first day of Spring (Fall in the Southern Hemisphere);

76. That global acceptance of responsibility for the protection and care of Earth can usher in a new golden age of opportunity for all humanity;

77. THEREFORE, LET US PLEDGE OUR LIVES AND FORTUNES TO AID THE GREAT TASK OF EARTH'S REJUVENATION, AND WITH CONFIDENCE AND FAITH, EACH DO OUR PART AS A TRUSTEE OF EARTH TO TAKE CHARGE AND TAKE CARE OF OUR PLANET.

*Whenever people hear an Earth Minute on radio or TV, they will add their thought or silent prayer. A growing multitude are praying and working for Earth's rejuvenation: for the prosperity that harmony with nature and neighbors will bring.

Earth Magna Charta

By John McConnell
Founder of Earth Day
A world view, goal and agenda for the people of Earth
that will provide a healthy, sustainable future.

1995

John McConnell's inspiring and carefully crafted document, the
Earth Magna Charta, could serve as a vital global rallying cry at
this moment in history.

George Gallup, Jr.

PRELUDE

THE PEOPLE OF PLANET Earth possess the raw materials, natural resources, and the technology for all to enjoy a life of quality. But they
are still restricted by the evil that has dominated history. They lack the
vision of the great future now possible and how to attain it. As a result,
the world is filled with confusion and conflict.

This Earth Magna Charta provides the needed vision and the way.
Individuals and institutions can now be trustees of Earth, seeking in
ecology, economics and ethics, policies and decisions that will benefit
people and planet. In the present state of the world, this Space Age trustee
concept has a chance of tapping the best in human hopes and aspirations
and providing a healthy, innovative and fulfilling future for our planet
and its people. In this new future, deeds will demonstrate what is best in
creeds. Young Earth Trustees will lead the way.

OUR MIRACLE PLANET

In this Magna Charta we will consider what we have, as a human family, on this miracle planet we call Earth. To understand the possibilities and how we can each participate in realizing them we need to think about basics. Actions good or bad begin in the mind.

To plan and achieve the best future we must look at our assets and liabilities. Experts will confirm the abundance of raw materials and natural resources on our planet. (They have a value of hundreds of trillions of dollars.) There is more than enough to provide and maintain a healthy life-style for everyone, with more for those with greater ability and initiative.

This is possible now because of our advanced technology. A major problem is how to restructure the social institutions of money, credit and property rights so that there will be a level playing field where rights and responsibilities will be recognized and realized. The Earth Magna Charta provides guidelines to achieve these goals—recognizing that people with different cultures and creeds will apply them in different ways. But all can warmly support the goals presented here. Aided by the sense of connectedness and the spirit of cooperation engendered by thinking of themselves as Trustees of Earth—all benefit.

HARMONY WITH NEIGHBOR AND NATURE

The people of Earth can have a great future by working together for a global goal all can approve. Here is a basic goal that most enlightened people of every religion, clime and culture will support. Here is a principled purpose that will quickly reduce the terrible chaos and conflict that troubles civilization. Here is an idea that will bring ever increasing harmony with neighbor and nature and bring peaceful progress in the human adventure.

The Earth Magna Charta describes the most important points of general agreement about the physical world—and the common view of human rights and responsibilities that naturally follow.

RIGHTS AND RESPONSIBILITIES

We are all members of one human family that has inherited a planet rich in resources. We each have an equal claim to its land, minerals and raw materials. None of us produced them. We all need them or what they provide. We all have need for their sustainable development and use. To assure equitable benefits every individual and institution should seek to balance rights and responsibilities.

The long term goal must be to restructure social institutions so that there is equitable return for services, efficient balance of supply and demand, and fair benefits from our mutual claims to Earth's natural bounty.

One possible way to equitable benefits is for those who own land, oil, gold or other minerals to pay a 2% royalty each year on their income from these resources to a fund that will then provide the homeless their inheritance or stake in their planet. All will then join in responsible care of Earth.

The digital economy will make it possible to eventually replace money and credit as we know it with new, fair methods of trade and exchange.

GLOBAL GOAL: EVERY PERSON A TRUSTEE OF EARTH

In regard to the physical world we all can agree that we have only one Earth—a miracle planet teeming with life. With our amazing new technology and awareness of Earth's raw materials and natural resources we know that poverty and pollution, the breeding ground of crime and corruption, can quickly be eliminated. All that is needed is the will.

Here is the way: First, as Earth Trustees, leaders will focus on the many solutions that are being found around the world. At present, too many accent the negative and have no clear objective. You cannot be objective without an object. The object is now the rejuvenation of Earth.

Then we must rally and inspire a grand Effort for Earth, an Earth Campaign that will eliminate poverty and pollution and bring new freedom, order and opportunity. This will happen as every individual and institution chooses to act as a responsible Trustee of Earth.

ETHICS AND MORAL VALUES

While there are many differences about race, religion, money control and power—and conspiracy theories throughout history—we can agree that institutional policies and actions of greed and deception are unfair, defeat the common good and should be corrected. While laws are needed and passed, without a strong spirit of community and cooperation their measure of success is limited. The Earth Campaign will meet this need.

The great periods of progress in history have resulted from religious fervor for universal ideals of honesty, freedom, justice and creative altruism or divine love. A recent example was the Civil Rights Movement of Martin Luther King Jr. Its essence is described in his book, *Strength to Love*.[1] The Campaign for Earth needs to tap the deepest and the best in our religious faith or inner feelings.

METAPHYSICAL MYSTERIES

People of different cultures can agree on basic moral values and deeds though they may differ on creeds that relate to the great mysteries of life. For honest agreement and cooperation we need to separate our creeds and their claims about life and death from the ideas and actions in which we can all agree. We can agree on the need for deeds that nurture people and planet though we differ on creeds warmly held about mind and spirit and the ultimate mysteries of the cosmos and its Creator. Of course the best evidence of the value of our creed is the love it produces in our lives. Common to every major religion is the Golden Rule—treat others as you would like to be treated. Now we have a new common ground: Awareness of our planet and our responsibility to take care of it.

HOW TO BE AN EARTH TRUSTEE

"Actions good or bad begin in the mind." Think, pray, talk and write about how you can be an Earth Trustee. Help your neighborhood or town to be an Earth Trustee community. Spread the word about recycling, planting trees, neighborhood gardens, composting and saving energy, healthy diet, sleep and exercise. When you buy or invest, make choices that diminish pollution and poverty—that increase sustainable development. Join or form a group that will further these purposes. As a start, register with the EarthSite and become an Earth Trustee.

YOUNG EARTH TRUSTEES: ARTS AND CRAFTS

The exercise of arts and crafts—especially in the form of singing, dancing, mime acting and music-making—is an effective antidote to violence

1   King, *Strength to Love*.

and crime. It is important for each child to experience some form of arts and crafts.

ORGANIZATION

There is no official Earth Trustee authorizing organization. Anyone is welcome to use the name as long as they base their effort on the principles set forth in this document. Any existing organization that adopts these purposes can be an Earth Trustee business, school, church or mosque. Any neighborhood, city or state can form an independent Earth Trustee Committee to further these purposes in their own way. All are invited to share what they are doing with others.

COMMUNICATIONS

Our new global communications with its Information Superhighway can under this Charter bring rapid change to heal, nurture and improve life on Earth. To accomplish this requires a radical change in attitudes and policies of mass media. They must seek in every way possible to define and further Earth Trustee goals. While plans and methods for achieving goals will differ, affirming points of accord will increase harmony and accommodation. The new policy will be, "Accent the positive, headline solutions, pursue excellence. Give honest assessment of things as they are and then with creative vision, aided by computer data, show the better future that intelligent decisions will bring—with follow-up on actions taken and their results."

EARTH CAMPAIGN: A GLOBAL "EFFORT FOR EARTH"

To this end, every radio, television station and newspaper who endorses this Earth Magna Charta will join the Campaign for Earth, reporting problems and progress; radio and television stations will carry daily non-verbal Earth Minutes at designated times—0300, 1100 and 1900 GMT. These non-verbal minutes of inspirational music, views of children and natural wonders, will remind us we are all connected and working for one goal—Earth's rejuvenation. Simultaneous and worldwide, they will deepen our awareness.

EARTH DAY

Each year on Earth Day, March 20–21, the Peace Bell at the United Nations will ring at the moment spring begins. As this occurs, a celebration of life will cover our globe as bells ring in every community and people join in heartfelt love and devotion to the care of this nest in the stars: Earth, our wonderful home.

Earth's Resurrection
(#1 - 1974)

Address by John McConnell
President of Earth Society
777 United Nations Plaza
New York, New York
Easter Sunday 4/14/74
From:
EARTH SOCIETY
1047 Amsterdam Avenue
New York, N.Y. 10025
(212) 864–5424

THE CONJUNCTION OF EASTER and the United Nations raw materials conference provides a perfect opportunity to set forth the spiritual and material sickness of our planet and the possibility of its cure.

I believe this can be done without offending those who celebrate the resurrection of Christ on this day, for nothing would please Him more than a practical application of The Golden Rule, which He, and all the great religions, have taught.

Nor will I offend seekers of truth in other religions, or no religion, for in all, the search for a peaceable loving life is aided by symbols of transcendence, rebirth and resurrection, and their application to our institutions and actions.

I join all those who find in this beautiful Spring day Nature's promise of Earth's rebirth.

But globally, we are in a night of Nature's despair. For after more than a billion years of her constant improvement of life on our planet, suddenly, in a few brief decades, man has wrested from her the control of Earth's global life support system and is mindlessly destroying the delicate web of life that sustains us. Ignorant of Nature's laws and the interacting systems of living organisms that process and renew our global environment, man has polluted and poisoned Earth's air, water, land and vegetation, and recklessly wasted her finite supply of oil and strategic minerals. With the global demand for products that waste and pollute rapidly spreading like a cancer, and with ever-more manufacturing plants and systems of the kind that destroy Nature's vital checks and balances, many able scientists see no way to prevent a global catastrophe.

Is there a way out? Can we convert our industries and institutions to the care and preservation of Earth in time to avoid disaster?

I would like to suggest, especially to the United Nations Delegates meeting across the street, a course of action which I believe can now bring about a global change of direction and transform our dismal night of despair into the dawning of peaceful cooperation in a new and challenging adventure—the care of our planet and the exploration of its life potentials, in harmony with nature and our finest human values.

To this end I propose three goals, which already commend themselves to most thoughtful and informed individuals, with, however, a possible plan for their implementation.

The three necessary global objectives are: (1) Ecology: education and action that will convert our desire and practice to the care of Earth; the preservation and enhancement of its marvelous eco-systems. (2) Justice: equal individual rights to the use of Earth and its raw materials, and equal responsibility for the care and preservation of Earth's natural bounty. (3) Love: encouragement and reward for the attributes and values and actions which in spite of limiting dogmas and institutional barriers, have nourished the great religions, and all humanitarian endeavors.

In proposing these goals I speak, not for one country, nor for any partisan ideology, creed, or vested interest. I speak for Earth, its life and its unborn children.

To aid the efforts that are already moving in this direction, I would urge the delegates at the UN Special Session to include in their forthcoming declaration reference to these goals, with guidelines for action that will further these purposes.

Ecology and justice must go hand in hand. A basic principle on which to build is the "fundamental right of each Earth person to an equal share in Earth's raw materials and natural resources, and his equal responsibility for the care and preservation of Earth's natural bounty." Establishing guidelines now can lead to implementation in the forthcoming Law of the Sea Conference, and in the later World Food and also Water Conferences.

The countries that recognize the seabed is truly "the common heritage of mankind" could coalesce and give to all their citizens certificates extending to them a special "Citizenship of the Seas," with shares (only one share per person) in the bounty of the seas. Then ocean-bed capital ventures (public or private) which contributed 50% of their profits (or a percentage of their gross receipts) to a common fund representing Sea Citizens, and who at the same time observed UN requirements and submitted to monitoring by the UN, would receive a preferential treatment, and avoid boycott by Sea Citizen countries. Shares and dividends to individuals could be accompanied by ecology and ocean lore education.

Other similar steps could be taken by oil and mineral ventures on land to spread participation in dividends to the greatest number of people (especially poor people) and combine it with ecology education. Computers could handle periodic dividends for "only one per person" shares. Provision could be made for people without money to get their share through voluntary work for environmental projects. It is not suggested that corporations in general convert to one share per person operations, but in ventures such as oil, energy and minerals this Earth-right program would be an effective means for providing the disinherited a stake in the Earth, in its raw materials and its future.

There is today a growing realization that all children have a right to food and shelter. Starving the poor does not increase incentives for useful work. A stake in the Earth—a home, apartment, land, and access to tools and training for a useful life—are the keys to renewal of a community or a country. It is possible, and essential, that in the World Food Conference this Fall, the rights to and means for minimal existence be extended globally. Earth-care shares and dividends could serve this purpose. This could best be done by several separate and independent organizations committed to guidelines and monitoring by the UN.

It is true that anthropologists find self-interest and conflict a major factor in evolution. But animals and man evidence a growing capacity for love, mutual interest and even self-denial. While history abounds with war, and crimes of violence prevail today, nevertheless there are many examples in history, and today, of a better way. There were not only

Nero, and Hitler, there were also Buddha, Jesus, Mohammed, Gandhi, Martin Luther King and many more. Strong, loving hearts are everywhere today—especially among the young. And over and over again we find the worst of men capable of conversion. The main difficulty is the lack of a unifying world view, a plan and a demonstration that it works.

It may be that now by great vision and bold actions the latent potential of humankind for love can be awakened and our fears transformed to a new courage and hope.

This is beginning to happen. Not just through the spoken and written word, but through the mysterious power of the spirit, through meditation, prayer and true worship, through contemplation of nature, music, people and distant stars, and through quiet commitment to deeds of conscience, a new breed of evolution is emerging dedicated to the peaceful loving care of planet Earth, and to its cosmic search for identity and for harmony with the Universe. In the spreading death that circles our globe there are signs of life, of global renewal. Let us reject death and choose life. We can now be a part of Earth's resurrection.

Earth's Resurrection
(#2 - 2005)

EARTH DAY AND PALM Sunday were both on March 20 in the year 2005. This was an amazing coincidence. Earth Day is always on the first day of Spring. Palm Sunday usually follows Earth Day. But in 2005 they were on the same day. They both call attention to the beauty and bounty of Nature.

Palm Sunday is a prelude to Easter, which celebrates the Resurrection of Christ. Earth Day (First Day of Spring) celebrates the annual Resurrection of life in Nature.

We call on all to help make the annual Earth Day a global day of dedication to peace, justice, and the care of Earth. Continue the celebration through Easter, which celebrates the resurrection of Jesus Christ. This will bring new hope and faith for a future of peaceful progress on our planet.

> Oh the faith that works by love. It will move the mountains when we pray.
> Oh the faith that works by love. It will turn the darkness into day.

EARTH TRUSTEE AGENDA

From the original 1970 Earth Day came the Earth Trustee idea:

> Let every individual and institution now think and act as a responsible trustee of Earth, seeking choices in ecology, economics and ethics that will provide a sustainable future, eliminate pollution, poverty and violence, awaken the wonder of life and foster peaceful progress in the human adventure.

To succeed we must combine heart and mind in effective action. If this article moves you emotionally and you now know what to do, you will act.

In order to come together in care for our planet we must respect and care about one another. People of all creeds and persuasions find agreement in the three most important words in human history, "Love One Another." They were uttered by Jesus, the man most recognized in history as wise and good. Heartfelt love, faith and prayer is increasing around the world. While great differences exist in creeds and social issues, more and more people are finding common ground. There is growing awareness that we are one human family and must now take charge and take care of our planet. We can and must now come together where we agree—leaving room for differences on matters where we don't agree.

SPACE AGE WORLD VIEW

"We set out to explore space and discovered Earth."

Now we know Planet Earth has amazing raw materials (land, water, gold, oil—etc., and organic life). With proper use of our new technologies, with logical economic policies and fair benefits for services, everyone could join in the rejuvenation of Earth. In this New Millennium we can make our planet a Garden of Eden.

There is no excuse for extreme poverty and unearned extreme wealth. New Earth Trustee economic policies can remedy this. Let all institutions now report how much their policies and programs accomplish Earth Trustee goals. A growing flood of Earth Trustee solutions will follow.

FACING THE DIFFICULTIES

While it is good to accent the positive and focus on solutions, we also need to honestly face the difficulties. Whether it is the result of sinful nature, childhood neglect or bad genes, humanity today is crippled by hate, fear, greed, sickness, crime and misuse of money and power. Fortunately, many people believe in the golden rule and try to be honest. They can support the vision and actions that will bring a positive, global, state of mind. This will better enable efforts and their values to reach the minds and hearts of those engaged in evil acts—who in truth "know not what they do." Earth Trustee vision and action will replace enmity with harmony.

The best of our science and logic provide no answers all can agree on. Our beliefs are based on faith. While we may differ on the nature of

God and life after death, we can commend actions that nurture people and planet—regardless of the person's creed.

The Earth Trustee Agenda should not be a stumbling block to people of any creed—who want to help "peace, justice and the care of Earth."

To continue our quest to understand the great mysteries of life we must avoid the death of nature and the collapse of civilization—a real present danger. Let us now convert "Earth Kill" to "Earth Care" and make this new millennium an Earth Trustee Millennium.

EARTH DAY

This is the day that Spring begins and provides a powerful time for people worldwide to celebrate and join in dedication to be responsible Trustees of Earth. On this day, there is a moment that is special to the whole human family—the March Equinox.

The March Equinox was chosen for Earth Day in 1970—the first Earth Day. The idea was not local convenience or comfortable weather—which varies from place to place, but a day suitable for international celebration. On this day, night and day are equal. This day is a million year symbol of the balance of Nature and the equilibrium we seek on Earth. Earth Day is also the First Day of Spring—Nature's symbol of New Life and New Beginnings.

Each year since then the Peace Bell at the United Nations has been rung on Earth Day at the moment Spring begins. This is followed by silent prayer—a time for heartfelt commitment to think and act as Earth Trustees.

WHAT INDIVIDUALS CAN DO

If you agree in principle with this Earth Trustee way to a sustainable future, then decide you will help make it work.

First, adopt an Earth Trustee attitude. That means an Earth Trustee way of looking at everything. You want your daily choices in work, travel, shopping and other activities to naturally reflect your Earth Trustee values. Individuals will differ to what they pay most attention. You may get interested in composting, planting trees, or volunteering for some project that is bringing peace and justice with understanding and action to better your neighborhood.

If you have not already done so, join some group that you feel will assist Earth Trustee goals. Where possible get them to use the name "Earth Trustee" for their efforts. All who seek to further peace, justice and the care of our planet can foster mutual understanding and cooperation by labeling their effort an "Earth Trustee" effort. The Earth Day/ Earth Trustee Agenda in the Earth Magna Charta can help any worthwhile project. Your church, club, school or business can adopt the Earth Magna Charta and in its own way implement its policies and agenda.

EARTH TRUSTEE INSTITUTIONS

Individual Earth Trustee actions can improve conditions in institutions as they presently exist. Far more will result as we restructure institutions to conform with Earth Trustee policies and purposes. Businesses, banks, churches and temples, clubs, towns and cities, are all invited to help implement the Earth Trustee Agenda. They can adopt the Earth Magna Charta (http://www.earthsite.org) and implement its Earth Trustee ideas in their own way. Every website can be an Earth Trustee site and do their part to help people and planet.

WORLD WIDE WEB

Make every day an Earth Trustee Day and do something that will benefit people and planet.

Then on every Earth Day (March 20) join with your friends and family at home, church, school or work to mark this day with attention for the wonder of life and what we can do for people and planet. Let's have bells ring all over the world when the Peace Bells are rung on Earth Day. Explorers in Space will share their inspiring views of our beautiful planet as they join in the celebration. This new Earth Trustee Millennium can be a new beginning of promise and hope.

The important thing is to act—and document honest reports of results. Together, with faith and love, we can participate in Earth's Resurrection.

Message to President Bush

Published in *Christian News*, July 7, 2003, p. 20.
From John McConnell, founder of Earth Day

DEAR MR. PRESIDENT:
Your efforts to kill terrorists are exactly opposite to what we expected from a "born again Christian."

I was delighted when you invited Christian leaders to the White House to pray for you and your leadership. I was glad I had voted for you.

But Jesus said, "Love your enemies . . . Do good to them that hate you . . . Agree with your adversary" (Matt 5).

Jesus said, "If you love me, keep my commandments." The commandments of Jesus point the way to peaceful progress on our planet.

I found that with prayer and the love of God you can always find something in your enemy that you can applaud and support. This will lead to cooperation where you agree—and the benefit of a common cause.

We don't need to kill the killers. We need to kill the cause of their actions. "Peace through Understanding" is the key.

Through the ages followers of Jesus have found this true. Many organizations that foster "peace, justice and the care of Earth" have demonstrated the benefit of what he taught. William Penn and the Quakers are an example. The followers of St. Francis are another.

We now need all the individuals and institutions devoted to peace to now join in fervent prayer and action. A new global state of mind that favors peace would result.

Earth Day (on the March Equinox) and its Earth Trustee Agenda was a major factor in fostering environmental education and ending the

Cold War. (See Earth Day: Past, Present, Future.) With your backing and the support of world leaders—which you could obtain, we would move toward a world of understanding and peace.

Sincerely,

John McConnell

Proclaim Liberty throughout the Earth

JULY 4, 1976

TWO HUNDRED YEARS AGO a small group of men set forth in the Declaration of Independence new concepts of democratic government which aided the growth and global spread of individual liberty and human dignity.

Now, a mindless industrial production and communications technology, misused in different ways by East and West, has resulted in new tyrannies with explosive population, waste, pollution and destruction of human liberties. License and anarchy in many cases have replaced freedom and order as a basis for conduct, with liberty the loser. A global crisis now endangers all Earth's people, as well as whales, eagles, trees and plants. It is incumbent on all informed and concerned individuals to seek, practice and proclaim those actions which can best break the chains in mind and circumstance binding the spirit of humanity. These informed and concerned individuals should reconstitute private and public institutions.

To this end, we, as individual members of the human family, do hereby:

PROCLAIM liberty in 1976 for all Earth's people: a time of jubilee, a time for every individual and community to join in commitment and actions which we believe will promote life and liberty for all.

PROCLAIM self-regulation as essential for individual liberty, and determine that we will begin each day with a quiet time of gratitude, worship or reflection, to seek through conscience and faith the inner fire, to set the inner compass for discipline, freedom and love.

PROCLAIM Earth Day, March 20, 1976 (equinox) as a time to join with people of all religions and ideologies in a global celebration of life, assessing progress in the care and protection of nature's vital nutrients and joining together at the time of the equinox on that day in a silent minute of prayer, unity and thanksgiving.

PROCLAIM protection of nature. We seek to stop the pollution and waste that is endangering our whole planet, and will take positive, strong actions to change technology from destroying to nurturing Earth's thin skin of life. To this end we urge that all mass produced products be tested for environmental effects in production and use, with regulations and controls to prevent reckless waste and pollution. We also urge and seek that individuals in labor and management (ourselves included) limit their drive for wages and profit and only produce or buy and sell useful products.

PROCLAIM and urge a new policy and program for all mass media. Since the larger world most of us see and relate to is now that portrayed by TV, radio and press, the media has a special responsibility to convey and portray every possible aid to Earth's rejuvenation. We urge each TV, and radio station, each newspaper and magazine to provide and advance a plan for the coming year that will achieve this purpose. Let them submit this plan to community leaders of their choice, plus all their viewers, readers or listeners for their comments. At least fifty percent of all programs, including news and advertising, should be devoted to ideas, information and actions that will aid Earth's care.

PROCLAIM liberty for victims chained by poverty and debt to hopelessness and despair. We urge a new economic order that will assure every individual opportunity for useful training, work and honest pay. We urge a democratic Ocean Regime, composed of all nations, to protect and manage the oceans for the benefit of all people. We further urge that governments provide an honest global medium of exchange, based on the things to be exchanged, that will assure with measured flow a non-inflatable stable currency: that governments seek in every way to provide systems of trade and credit where profit will only accrue to those who render a real service to the common good.

PROCLAIM peaceful liberty. To end the scourge of mass conflict and war and provide a healthy global village where liberty and love can flower and grow, we urge a great campaign of individuals, institutions and nations in a moral equivalent of war. This all-out effort can fully engage the nations of East and West, Muslim and Jew, Capitalist and Socialist in the great task of Earth's renewal. It will overwhelm angry partisans engaged in conflict by providing new alternatives for healthy prosperous lives. The conspiring forces of political and economic aggression will be constantly thrown off balance by the faith and force of a mighty multitude demonstrating that cooperation with nature and one another in the care of our fragile Earth home is the only way to a good life, and right now the only way of survival.

We appeal to all lovers of liberty to join now in a grand alliance for the care and renewal of Earth, that life may continue and liberty may grow. To this end we will strive to the best of our ability to accomplish the goals set forth in this Liberty Proclamation.

The Earth Society

Proposal for Ringing the Peace Bell

Proposal for Ringing the Peace Bell
Before the Opening of the UN General Assembly Session

John McConnell—History
Copy of letter—dated 19th September, 1966
His Excellency U Thant
Secretary-General
United Nations Secretariat
New York

Excellency,

I am sure you know Mr. McConnell of the "Minute for Peace" Movement. He has been to see me with a suggestion which appears to me to be deserving of consideration.

Mr. McConnell's idea is that, a few minutes before the opening of this General Assembly session, there should be a symbolic ringing of the Peace Bell. The ringing would be done by a selected group of children from the United Nations International School, and it would be done in your presence. Following that you would proceed to the General Assembly for the opening ceremony.

Mr. McConnell feels that the ringing ceremony would encourage people all over the world to pause and reflect for one minute on how peace might be attained through their own personal thoughts and actions and that this would create renewed interest in your own often-expressed thought that "Peace begins in the minds of men."

I respectfully submit this proposal for your consideration.

Accept, Excellency, the assurances of my highest consideration,

S. O. Adebo
Permanent Representative of Nigeria
cc: Mr. J. McConnell,
Minute for Peace

A Daring Strategy for World Peace

1961

W E SHOULD BE AS realistic about what is necessary to achieve world peace as we are about the necessities for success in a great military campaign. In the latter, an effort is made to clearly define the goals, to assess the resources that can be used and then to develop a strategy for success. Something of this kind can and should be done if we are going to bring about the great changes needed to achieve a world of freedom and order without the threat of war.

An understanding of a total strategy fiat offers a chance of success which could enable the individual to see the importance of the small but specific contribution he can make. An experiment showing it could work would inspire him to act

At Pearl Harbor, the war was made real. This was followed by unity, purpose and fervor in our efforts to defeat our enemies. Millions of men were recruited; the giant strength of our industrial complex was quickly converted to meet the needs of war. Shortly there were thousands of trucks, tanks, planes, ships, manned by quickly trained men, moving toward battle fronts that would bring the greatest destruction the world has ever known.

An equally dramatic impact for peace is needed that will catch the attention of people throughout our country and give a sense of unity, purpose and fervor in waging peace. If we are going to seriously meet the challenge of our time and do away with the threat of war, we must activate our industrial might, our technical know-how and our best humanitarian concerns in a mighty effort to build schools, plants, roads, dams, modernize agriculture — in short, work together with our neighbors around the world, for global goals in research, education, health and welfare. What we can do for war, we can do even better for Peace.

Instead of thousands of machines to destroy, we must provide and use thousands of machines to build a better world. Of course we must use the techniques of cooperation that meet real desire and need. We should now mobilize for a massive Peace Blitz! (This term was used by Norman Corwin in his 1949 radio-play "Could Be.")

There is no reason why we cannot wage peace with a vigor that will demonstrate a moral equivalent to war. A forceful example is needed to overcome the negative feeling "It can't be done." IT HAS NEVER BEEN TRIED!

PEACE BLITZ CAMPAIGNS

Purpose

To change the climate and activities in one or more towns in a way that will provide an appropriate definition of waging peace—which could be expanded throughout the country and perhaps throughout the world. This could be an instrument for bringing about a profound change in national policies on disarmament and peace.

The Peace Blitz Declaration defines waging peace in general terms which need to be made specific through democratic planning and action in the local community. It calls for an attack against the causes of war, such as fear, hunger, illiteracy, poverty, barriers. The local community would choose five or more projects for this purpose.

In order to effectively defeat the apathy and complacency which is at the heart of the problem, help should be obtained from the best possible source. A brief outline of the local plan can be sent to organizations such as CARE, American Friends Service Committee, UNESCO, Peace Corps, etc., requesting suggestions for the project section of the campaign.

Program

Objective of the campaign is to rally all the fraternal resources of the community in a twofold program. The first part of this would be a great discourse on the problems of peace.

Discussion

Discussion and study would cover the whole spectrum from the inner peace taught by religion and psychology to such problems as disarmament and world law. Able speakers would be invited to speak

in local service clubs, churches, schools and in house meetings conducted throughout the town. Every possible aspect of peace and disarmament would be discussed and publicized, but the leaders of the
campaign would not give formal support to any political solutions for
peace. However, the results of the discourse would be shown in an
opinion survey conducted at the close of the campaign.

Projects

The second part of the campaign would be devoted to projects for peace.
The purpose of these projects would not be political action (although such
action might be discussed in a "World Affairs Forum" project), but participation in activities that would further understanding, good will and
cooperation for worldwide goals that can sincerely be aided. (The activities of Communists would have been openly discussed along with other
issues, and where they conflicted with the concept of democracy, firmly
resisted, but in areas of agreement—science, space, medicine, student exchange, etc.—communication and cooperation would be encouraged.)

These projects would be designed to attract people at different levels of concern. They could include a student exchange program, Peace
Corps Project, Volunteers for UN projects, Food for Peace, Books for
Peace, Equipment for Peace, etc. Using the concept of the Peace Blitz in
publicity and promotion would redirect feelings of hostility into positive
peace action.

To give the feeling and the reality of strength to the program, it
would be important to obtain large scale participation by the industries
and businesses of the town. These are the organizations with which the
average man is mostly involved. American industry was a major factor
in winning our wars. Their contribution can be a tremendous advantage
in winning a lasting peace. In this bold experiment they would be asked
to provide help from the best of their personnel along with funds and
encouragement of their employees to aid the campaign projects. Their
participation should be obtained in the initial planning of the campaign.
This should also apply to all the important organization leaders in the
community—Service Clubs, Churches, Schools, etc.

Peace Blitz Headquarters

This headquarters would be managed by an executive director and secretary with an office and minimum budget. Its function would be to develop a suitable program structure, and support for the campaign. It would also function as a pubic relations organization to prepare the way of operations however they may develop.

Coordinating Group

Envisioned to be comprised of responsible leaders in the community representing the best insights of sociology, psychology, economics, political science, religion, etc., this body would serve as an experimental, detached group who would watch carefully the total development, make suggestions as to the ongoing local program and be alert to the broad outreach of possibilities related to the nation and the world.

This would be strictly an idea and consulting group and not responsible for the conduct of the program, but it would at the same time see that ideas of merit were picked up and carried out. They would also watch for breakdowns in any part of the program and seek to remedy this.

A working committee of this group could consult with other similar groups to develop appropriate steps toward the formation of an international council (patterned, in part, after their own function). This International Council could create a council of World Cities and with the help of an International Public Relations Committee provide a structure for encouraging world friendship and cooperation. (Proposals for these organizations are available.)

Miscellaneous

With the backing of an ongoing program and the means of taking advantage of opportunities that arise, imaginative projects could aid the total effort. One project which would help all the others would be the collection of signatures for the "Star of Hope" satellite. Those who signed a pledge to work for peace could also indicate which project they would help.

Publicity

The success of the campaign will depend in a large measure on the effective use of the communications media. Making the local newspaper, TV and radio an example of what can be done would serve this end directly and at the same time it would create a greater sense of purpose and responsibility in the communications media.

Conclusion

During World War II, America and the world were amazed at the spiritual and material resources brought into action when people worked together for a great goal. The strength, sacrifice and fervor of war must be given to building a peaceful world. There already exist areas of international agreement and cooperation for world wide goals. (In the United Nations, UNESCO, International Council of Scientific Unions, etc.) These must be vigorously strengthened and extended. There must be support for this from the grass roots. We can fight fear and subversion with faith, when we work together for common goals in which we all sincerely believe. Fortunately, there exists a hard core of human values— freedom, love, wonder, dignity—which is at least dimly understood by all men everywhere. While on the one hand we must guard against the things that threaten these values—most important is the work of extending, around the world, the foundations that support them.

A carefully conducted pilot campaign can achieve a breakthrough in tapping untold spiritual and material resources, not by fear of war and a feverish preparation for war, but by Faith and a joyous preparation for a peaceful world.

Stowaway on a Satellite[1]

By John McConnell

INTRODUCTION

The following article, written back in 1957, almost became the basis for a major motion picture when I presented it to leaders in Hollywood. My wife found a copy of it and I thought it was relevant to what is happening in the world today. It was written at the time I had obtained global attention for my proposal that we launch a visible Star of Hope Satellite.

The central idea in Stowaway on a Satellite is that a U. S. scientist working on a manned space flight project, in a time of desperate international tension and imminent war between U. S. and Russia, conceives and carries out a daring plan to substitute himself for the dummy intended to occupy the capsule in the satellite.

HIS MOTIVE

To be in a position to speak to the whole world from a vantage point which no man on Earth has ever before occupied, on the necessity of marshaling all of mankind's reason and goodwill to stop the plunge toward war and world suicide.

DEVELOPMENT

The first phase of his plan works out o.k. He carries out the substitutions, and the satellite goes into orbit. He starts broadcasting the speech he had very carefully prepared and memorized—mainly an exhortation to think, to use reason, to face all the facts about where the present course

---

1. The ending here is the original. The ending in the abbreviated version in chapter 28 is altered.

of action is leading. Speech is beamed primarily to other scientists and intellectuals. He also stresses need to summon moral energy to match the physical energy recently released by science.

Then he discovers that the receiving part of his radio apparatus is not working. He gets nothing from Earth, and has no way of knowing whether he is being heard.

He is being heard, however.

The first reaction is one of astonishment—and in the U. S. at least—great elation over the fact of having launched a live man into space even earlier than was planned. It is hailed as a great step in the race for "control" of outer space.

People all over the world hear of the man speaking from outer space. Some governments at first try to prevent reception or translation of his broadcasts, but this becomes impossible because the fact is so widely known. All they can do is try to answer his arguments with counter-propaganda—a rather futile attempt.

For nothing else in the airways can compete with the "earth man in outer space." Not only does he swamp all other programs but he makes "business as usual" impossible. More and more people stop to listen when his broadcasts come on (probably at regular times each day).

In the early stages, the effect of this novel event is to increase tension all over the world. Many of the comfortable, complacent ones—and those who were ignorant and unaware of what was happening in the world—are now set "on edge." The whole world gets a terrible case of nerves. For the time being this makes it even more difficult to solve problems and conflicts.

As people listen to what he is saying, the "universal' tenor of his speech causes some on both sides of the Iron Curtain to accuse him of trying to undermine their morale and weaken their fighting spirit. Russia demands that the United States stop him. And the United States, while refusing to bow to Russia's demand, wants to stop him for reasons of its own.

But since his receiving system is not working, nothing can be done, and since he is becoming the idol of the whole world, no government would dare to shoot him down to silence him.

At times his voice literally fills the world, coming from millions of radios at once. (The effect of his broadcasts in different parts of the world and among different people might be shown by repeated sequence of representative scenes around the world, with at least some of the same characters appearing each time in a given scene, so that the audience comes to recognize these figures.)

The hero, not knowing whether he is getting through to Earth's people, keeps trying ever more desperately and earnestly to communicate with them, hoping that perhaps some may pick up his thought, if not his voice. He goes from his carefully prepared speech into ever deeper levels of analyzing man's plight. As a man alone in the universe with his own soul, he senses and expresses the terrible loneliness and alienation which men on Earth have brought upon themselves by not recognizing the fundamental fact of kinship, brotherhood, oneness of humanity.

Earlier in the story, before the hero stows away on the satellite, he is shown to be acquainted with certain efforts on the part of scientists and laymen to reverse the trend toward war by substituting for the policies then in force a more creative course of action , such as:

1. Movement on the part of some scientists to bring all space exploration under the control of a cooperative agency representing every country on earth and eliminate completely the rivalry and the weapons aspect of the program.

2. A laymen's movement to mobilize goodwill on a worldwide scale to find "moral equivalents to war."

It has been urged by both these groups that when their efforts shall have borne enough fruit so that all governments agree to use peaceful means to work out difficulties, and are really laying down their arms, a symbolic "flashing star" satellite be launched to represent the hope and promise of a dynamic peace.

At the beginning of the story, he was not sold on either of these efforts, being somewhat skeptical of "movements" and "crusades." But the same soul-searching which led him to make his daring move has also made him sympathetic with these efforts.

Yet in the early stages of his space flight and broadcasts, he actually slows down the work for peace, along with other work on Earth, by being such a distraction. He pleads for intensified work for peace, but as is shown by various scenes of people reacting to his broadcasts, the actual effect of this world-shaking event, with its tremendous emotional impact, is at first to make people more jittery and confused.

Thus, even though he is being listened to avidly, he seems not to be accomplishing his purpose. Conflicts, arguments and threats continue in the various governing bodies and in the United Nations.

Suddenly the hero tells that his return mechanism has failed and that he cannot get back to Earth. People all over the world are stunned. They have all come to identify themselves with him.

There is a worldwide surge of sympathy and distress for this helpless traveler out in space. Governments are besieged with pleas to help him. But as before, nothing can be done to reach him.

Great sorrow sets in all over the world as people realize they are powerless to help him. Now they hang on his every word and few or none try to argue with his message. Many ministers turn over their regular services and many teachers their classroom to his broadcasts.

His voice is becoming weaker and requires more and more amplification to be heard. But his message becomes more penetrating than ever.

The more he realizes he will not be seeing Earth again, the more tenderly he reminisces on its beauty and his love for the old home planet. (Here could be flashbacks to his life on Earth). He even addresses himself to whatever advanced beings may inhabit other planets, invoking their tolerance and mercy for Earth's blundering but upward striving people—apologizing to the advanced beings for being so provincial as to have patriotic sentiments for his own planet.

Many persons who have organized efforts to save life of hero now turn their energies to actions for peace, petitioning their governments and volunteering possessions and services to help those in need. This happens in communities all over the world, but effect on official governing bodies is still not apparent—and outcome of peace-or-war issues still not clear. Some scenes are shown, however, which indicate a great effort to break through political boundaries and communicate freely about the problems and issues that are causing trouble.

The hero, without knowing it, has by his unique vantage point and the way he made use of it in communicating with Earth's people, succeeded in implanting a worldwide sense of unity that has never before been realized. He has jolted people out of their narrow individual ruts and made them think and feel as they have never thought or felt before. He is becoming very tired and realizes that his strength is just about spent. He has done his best but does not know whether anything will come of his sacrifice.

Suddenly he sees a flash of light. First thought is, 'Have they blown up the World with atomic warfare?" But then he realizes it is not that kind of flash. It appears to be a flashing star. Can this actually be the Star of Hope—symbol of a world that has turned the corner toward peace? He fears it may be a hallucination coming to him in his weakened state. He shuts his eyes for a few seconds and looks again. It is still there, and he realizes it is no hallucination but indeed the Star of Hope.

NOTES

1. The plot should be developed so that the final issue—Armageddon, or an unequivocal turning toward peace—is kept in doubt up to the very end. Yet the developments shown in the course of the story, especially the various reactions to the hero's broadcasts, increasing in intensity as the story progresses, should make the final outcome credible.

2. Since the story cannot be based on the assumption that the hero will be the first man in space, uniqueness will lie in his use of this extra-mundane position to plead for an awakening of mankind and recognition of the fact of brotherhood.

3. The problem of time: how long should the hero be kept broadcasting in the satellite, from scientific and dramatic standpoints?

4. Characterization of the hero: probably he should be fairly young, quiet but determined, not readily going overboard for a new idea, but going all-out to put conviction into practice, once convinced.

5. Personal relationships of the hero. Synopsis does not refer to any, but probably he should have close ties with a few people on Earth. Love interest?

6. Content and wording of his broadcasts are crucial. No long speeches. He talks only a little while each day, and his messages are interspersed with scenes showing reaction thereto. We can send some suggestions about what he says, later, if desired.

7. Before the outcome is revealed by the flashing of the Star of Hope, certain specific events should be shown to be happening on Earth, such as freeing of political prisoners by demand of the people in countries that have such prisoners—as an expression of their awakened sense of brotherhood and universal justice.

Make Our Satellite a Symbol of Hope!

THE TOE VALLEY VIEW
Published every Thursday by the Toe Valley Publishing Co., Inc., and
entered at the Post Office of Bakersville, N.C. as Second Class matter.
John McConnell and Erling Toness, Co-Publishers, Louise Toness,
Editor, Associate Editor—Arthelia H. Brooks. Spruce Pine, Fortner
Bldg.—P.O. Box 605—Phone: Poplar 5-4443
Bakersville, P.O. Box 24—Phone 2711.
October 31, 1957

USUALLY IN THESE EDITORIAL columns we stick pretty closely to local matters. But some issues arising outside our own locality become so universal in importance that they are "local" for everyone in the world. Of course we are referring now to earth satellites and man's venture into the conquest of Space.

What was science fiction only yesterday has become visible—audible—fact today. "After a lifetime of some 250,000 years on earth . . . man has conquered earth gravity and stands poised on the era of universal exploration," writes Norman Cousins in a penetrating editorial in "The Saturday Review" for Oct. 19, called "Sense and Satellites."

But, he points out, the event brings "no universal feeling of release or jubilation," overcast as it is by the chill of a cold war and the threat of extinction by intercontinental missiles utilizing the same principles used in launching the satellite. The answer, Cousins says, is "not to conjure up more effective ways of destroying the world." (How trivial is the whole argument of who or what is to blame for the Russians' getting ahead of us in the armed missiles race—when we consider that the race itself can lead only to destruction!) "The principal need," insists the Saturday Review editor, "is to tap our intelligence and moral imagination to the fullest in creating a working design for a better tomorrow in which all the world's people can share. . . . A great idea looking towards the development of a world community will circle the globe more rapidly than the fastest satellite. It will give us access to the majority of the world's peoples—on whom security really depends. It will also help to make life bearable on this planet before we take off for other ones."

Now is the moment when "Peace on Earth" might have its best opportunity for realization. When men work together for some great goal they share, the forces that make for peace and understanding have the best chance to operate. And a greater goal could scarcely be dreamed of than the exploration of the Universe, in man's eternal search to find and understand his place in the Universe.

What will be the effect upon the world when our own satellite is launched? Will it turn the world toward peace and unity, or away? We need some symbol of peace, to give the world a promise that conquest of space will be for good and not for evil. To create such a symbol would require no new discoveries

The means are already at hand to make the appearance of our satellite as startling an event as the appearance of Sputnik, but startling in a different way. Could not the small satellite to be launched in December according to present plans appear as a brightly shining Star of Hope?

The mechanics of the thing should not be too difficult. The body of the satellite could be covered with some highly reflective material such as aluminum foil. More difficult would be the task of convincing the peoples of the earth that this was not just a propaganda device. Indeed, we would need to make sure ourselves, as a nation, that it was not! The symbol would need to be accompanied by sincere words and convincing deeds in the direction of peace and world cooperation.

It is true that certain segments of humanity do not believe in the Event symbolized by the star of Christmas. But there is no religion or no nation on earth (considering people, not governments) that does not respond with hope and longing to the angel's song of "Peace on Earth, Good Will to Men."

Invitation to the Cities of the World

Proposal to the City of Denver, by John McConnell
—July 15, 2003—
and to All the Cities of the World

SINCE THE FIRST EARTH Day in 1970 there have been repeated efforts that have aided its Earth Trustee agenda: peace, justice and a sustainable future. There have been efforts in different parts of the world in support of its meaning and purpose, but there must be far more support if civilization is to avoid global catastrophe.

A mindless production and communications technology has resulted in explosive waste, pollution and destruction of human liberties. License and anarchy in many cases have replaced freedom and order in human conduct, with liberty the loser. A global crisis now endangers all Earth's people, as well as whales, eagles, trees and plants.

It is incumbent on all informed and concerned individuals to now seek, practice and proclaim those actions which can best break the chains in mind and circumstance binding the spirit of humanity; to reconstitute private and public institutions with functions that will encourage cooperation for the benefit of society and Earth's total web of life.

To this end, we invite the City of Denver, and all cities of the world, to proclaim:

EARTH DAY 2004—will be observed in Denver on the first day of Spring—Nature's symbol of new life and new beginnings. We invite all citizens of Denver to now plan how they will help make Earth Day a time of celebration that will call attention to Earth Trustee actions that can benefit our community—and all Earth's people: a time of jubilee, a time for every individual to join in commitment and actions which we believe will promote life and liberty for all.

PROCLAIM self-regulation as essential for peaceful progress, and determine that we will begin each day with a quiet time of gratitude, worship or reflection, to seek through conscience and faith the inner fire, to set the inner compass for discipline, freedom and love.

PROCLAIM Earth Day, March 20, 2004 (equinox) as a day for people of all religions and ideologies to celebrate life, assessing progress in the care and protection of nature's vital nutrients and joining with friends in a time of prayer, unity and thanksgiving,

PROCLAIM protection of nature. We seek to stop the pollution and waste that is endangering our whole planet, and will take positive, strong actions to change technology from destroying to nurturing Earth's thin skin of life. To this end we urge that all mass-produced products be tested for environmental effects in production and use, with regulations and controls to prevent reckless waste and pollution. We also urge and seek that individuals in labor and management (ourselves included) limit their drive for wages and profit and only produce or buy and sell useful products.

PROCLAIM and urge a new policy and program for all mass media. Since the larger world most of us see and relate to is now that portrayed by TV, radio and press, the media has a special responsibility to convey and portray every possible aid to Earth's rejuvenation. We urge each TV, and radio station, each newspaper and magazine to provide and advance a plan for the coming year that will achieve this purpose. Let them submit this plan to community leaders of their choice, plus all their viewers, readers or listeners for their comments. At least fifty percent of all programs, including news and advertising, should be devoted to ideas, information and actions that will foster Earth Trustee attitudes and actions.

PROCLAIM peaceful liberty. To end the scourge of mass conflict and war and provide a healthy global village where liberty and love can flower and grow, we urge a great campaign of individuals, institutions, cities and nations in a moral equivalent of war. This all-out effort can fully engage the nations of East and West; Muslim, Christian and Jew, in the great task of Earth's renewal. It will overwhelm angry partisans engaged in conflict by providing new alternatives for healthy prosperous lives. The conspiring forces of political and economic aggression will be constantly thrown off balance by the faith and force of a mighty multitude demonstrating that cooperation with nature and one another in the care of our fragile Earth home is the only way to a good life, and right now the only way of survival.

We invite all cities of the world to join us in support for Earth Day and its Earth Trustee Agenda. We appeal to all lovers of liberty to join now in a grand alliance for the care and renewal of Earth, that life may continue and liberty may grow. To this end we will strive to the best of our ability to accomplish the goals set forth in this Earth Trustee Proclamation.

Proclamation:
Earth Care Campaign

John McConnell, Founder
Earth Society Foundation

Presentation December 8, 1982
at Princeton University
Meeting of Y.E.S. (Youth Environmental Society)

O UR WORLD IS IN imminent danger. The objective of the Earth Care
Campaign is to take action that will provide a healthy, peaceful
future for our planet. Impossible as this may seem in the light of thousands of years of failure and the present danger, I believe there are now
elements in our global situations which can be combined in a way that
will synergistically bring about the rejuvenation of Earth.

These elements pertain to the spiritual, the psychological, the financial or economic, the political, and the environmental necessities for
our task. What we are presenting here is a consideration of our planet
and of what we have in common that is sufficiently important to mobilize people everywhere for the care of Earth.

We are initiating a campaign that will ask everyone to select and
work for a project of their own choosing that they believe will assist our
new global task—to take care of our planet. On each Earth Day, March
20–21, we expect to obtain global attention for this task.

The one thing we have in common globally is our planet. The most
important challenge that has ever been faced by the human race is the
necessity now of immediate action for the defense of Earth, the care of
our planet, its life and its people; the restoration of Earth's beauty and
natural bounty.

So the object of the Earth Care Campaign is to saturate media with thinking and feelings about this one goal. And then to illustrate by examples the actions and solutions that can be applied in every block, neighborhood, vocation and institution; showing how every person in the private sector and the public sector can assume a role in this global effort for the rejuvenation of Earth.

In order to accomplish this it is essential that we understand the process of peace. The word peace, "pachem" in Latin, means to agree, to be in accord. All over the world are efforts to understand what is held in common with others and come together for a common purpose. We have organizations like "Common Cause," "Moral Majority," "Solidarity," directly expressing this principle. Of course, any successful organization draws people together because of a common interest or purpose. In every field you find people seeking to strengthen their efforts by joining with others who have something in common with them.

What is needed today is a great unifying purpose, a strong bonding idea that can inter-link all of society. I believe the only thing that can bring this about is the recognition of our planet and a commitment to be Earthkeepers (Earth Trustees), to accept our role as the caretakers of this marvelous planet. And though we may pursue this goal in independent ways, we recognize the essential areas in which we must cooperate in order to succeed, and see the nature of our interdependence. For example, from the knowledge that we now have of biology and the cell, we realize the life-giving elements that are flowing through our bloodstream and that make our physical presence here possible, are linked in subtle ways with every other life cell on our planet. In fact, all life on Earth is, in a sense, one organism, one being. So we must recognize the nature of our independence and our freedom and also the nature of our interdependence and then out of that see the constraints that are necessary in order for us to achieve a dynamic symmetry in our individual and global goals.

In proceeding with an Earth Care Campaign, it is essential that we have a global view with some passion in it. A real awareness of the wonder of our planet will arouse in most anyone a feeling of love for Earth. I am very happy when people have a tear in their eye as they speak about a whale, hummingbird—or a mountain peak. I was little misty-eyed when I heard Ed Gibson just before our 1980 Earth Day celebration telling of his circling the globe 1200 times. What he must have felt as he looked down and saw Earth—like a bright Christmas ornament hanging in the Heavens.

In our Earth Care Campaign, we need a deep sense of common commitment to a purpose and program in which there is honest basic agreement. It is also important to recognize that our accord, agreement and cooperation are limited. The limitation should be recognized, but not stressed.

I think it well for me to talk just a little more about this. One of the books that influenced my life as a young person was *The Recovery of the Spiritual Ideal* by Felix Adler. He stated that whether it is in a relationship between husband and wife, within a group or a country, or in international relationships, if you seek and find an overarching goal that is deeply shared, that is emotionally felt, and you find some way to cooperatively work for that goal, then you find a strange phenomenon, you find that the areas of difference or conflict are diminished or there is accommodation and fair negotiation. Sometimes there are basic changes of outlook, because on each side the people tend to be less defensive and more open when they are working together for a common goal.

So the achievement of a common objective, the discovery of areas of honest accord must be a fundamental aspect of any Earth Care Campaign that is really going to provide a healthy, peaceful future for our planet.

In the United Nations we have a forum where the leaders of nations discuss common global objectives—what is best for the whole world, the good of all of its people. There are many factors, especially nationalism, that limit success in these efforts—but a structure and means of communication are now in place. All recognize the common danger. Provide a solution to which all can agree and vigorous support will ensue.

In our Earth Care Campaign we want to bring to the attention of people globally through effective use of mass media and person to person communication, the fundamental facts that we can all agree to. We want to make these terribly important because if we can work together in what we all have in common we can avoid global catastrophe and have a healthy, peaceful future.

We have stressed that the one thing we have in common is the Earth and that the well-being of our planet, its life, its people is essential. Now viewing this from a different perspective, there are people around the world who have deep religious feelings and it's perfectly in keeping with this for individuals who have a spiritual approach to life to achieve their commitment to Earth through love of God. All great religions teach love of neighbor, the golden rule, and love of Earth. Stewardship and care of Earth is taught in all the major religions.

I am particularly acquainted with what Jesus had to say about it, because I am a Christian. In the Lord's prayer Jesus said, pray "Thy kingdom come on Earth, as it is in Heaven." The beautiful beatitudes in the Sermon on the Mount lead up to people becoming peacemakers. Just before that he said, "Blessed are the meek for they shall inherit the Earth." In the Psalms it says "The Earth hath he given to the children of men." The protection and preservation of Earth's trees, plants, soil and creatures large and small is taught in most religions. I believe that the one thing which will contribute most to global peace is a great spiritual awakening of heart-felt devotion to the nurture and care of our planet. Let the word go forth, "The kingdom of heaven is at hand. A healthy peaceful planet is possible now."

We know the great achievements of theater, art and drama and the wonderful things that are done with music. It is worship, religious experience and the arts that move us, that shape our values and affect our conduct if we let them. In the Earth Care Campaign we will stir the hearts of young and old, from children in kindergarten to senior citizens with symbols, sights and sounds that declare the wonder of Earth—its life, its mystery, and its desperate need for our care. The great responsibility of people in the arts and in media is to dramatize the challenge and the solutions: how we can contribute to this goal in our own block, neighborhood and vocation; in the institutions of which we are a part; to think in terms of Earth Care when we go into the market place and make our purchases; to think of Earth care when we make investments—the way we use our money; to fill our minds with the tremendous challenge, "Help take charge and take care of Earth."

Our generation can bring an end to the bloody history of wars, the degradation and destruction of Earth, and with the grace and help of God see Earth's redemption. We can bring into being the golden age. We have the raw materials, the knowledge, the technology. We have the means today to provide a healthy, peaceful, creative future for every man, woman and child on Earth.

Blocks to achieving this goal are the prejudices and differences that exist all over the world, differences in cultural values and beliefs.

Well now, a difference can often be a creative thing if it's handled right. I remember E. Stanley Jones talking about the many different denominations in the Christian church. He felt that the differences enabled different points of view to be emphasized in ways that contribute to a larger fuller expression of God's grace. For example, in the Episcopal Church there is great formality. The ritual and architecture are a far cry from that of the Quakers or the Friends where you find extreme simplicity. I for one feel that when there is a great devotion to God and understanding of the meaning of worship, each can serve a special purpose. One can complement the other. So also in a common commitment to the care of Earth, there can be great diversity of approach, there can be a great diversity of culture, there can be a great diversity of religions, of ideologies, so long as we are constantly seeking the honest accord that will provide the measure of harmony that is essential for peace and the effective care of our planet.

Once we demonstrate a contagious Earth Care solution, it will spread exponentially and appeal to people of every ideology, climate, and culture. We will see a worldwide effort to change our planet from "Earth Kill" to "Earth Care."

We have a simple, positive, dynamic idea. In the Earth Care Campaign we are asking people to think globally and act locally: in their personal life, to undertake some project they feel will contribute to the care of Earth. In our Earth Care Campaign we invite everyone to have an Earth Care project or activity; that you do this in collaboration with a few other people, with some group, especially some small group. Make this individual commitment and then link up with people of like mind and give at least 10% of your time and money to your Earth Care Project—with follow-through and continuity. You may want to change later on to some other project, but persistence is extremely important in pursuing these goals. Beyond that we suggest that once you have established what you are going to do for the care of Earth, that you tell others, not seeking to proselytize them to your cause or thinking but by a combination of conscience and common sense, to attract them to the Earth Care idea and by your example to inspire them to a like commitment.

I think that person to person communication can be the key to the success of our Earth Care Campaign.

We are seeking to find the maximum use of communication that will contribute to the defense and rejuvenation of Earth—to Earth Care activities and programs.

I want to include here something that has intrigued me for many years, and that is, the nature of exponential phenomena. Dr. Forrester in his book *World Dynamics*[2] has explained the implication of this in a very scholarly way and there has been much since then, but the one little factor that has intrigued me is that two to the thirty-third power is over eight billion. Well, that is more than the number of people that are on our planet. We will take the Earth Care plan I have just described and reinforce it by maximum use of television and radio and the help of leaders, celebrities, and great music. Hotlines and information numbers will enable people to have their local efforts reinforced. A growing commitment will spread in every church, school, block association, and every business organization from the Chamber of Commerce to the corporate board rooms of the world. Throughout this we will seek one common goal: to halt the destruction of Earth before catastrophe strikes, and to change directions with a real dedication to Earth's care. We will do this in ways that we can honestly support and we will see a spreading network of action and hope throughout the world.

In this room today each one of you can decide whether this is a commitment you will make, and that beginning today to do what you can, both by thinking and seeking through contacts and relationships to define and choose your project, your role in the care of Earth, and to spread the word about the Earth Care Campaign. You may help a neighborhood garden, a solar energy project or homestead program for the poor; there are thousands of ways in which you can demonstrate Earth Care. You decide what it is and then make a special commitment to at least one project. Be connected with a group that is working for your objectives and then speak to at least two other people. You might end up sharing your ideas with five or ten people, but at least two people. Tell them what you are doing and expect them to do something with a similar commitment. If we can make exponential growth work in this great task, we can save our planet. Two to the thirty-third power is 8 billion. That means that if the doubling begins this week and continues every week, in thirty-three weeks we will cover the world.

2. Forrester, *World Dynamics*.

Then by constant effort a deeper level of understanding and commitment can be obtained within 30 days. With contagious communications deeper participation will double every month. In thirty-three months we will have a strong global commitment to the care of Earth.

In World War II we managed to turn out second lieutenants in 90 days, so perhaps we should think of a third milestone—in which commitment will be strengthened by further clarification of our duties and opportunities—of new values and relationships that foster Earth Care. If in 90 days we can turn out a second lieutenant we might turn out a real caretaker of Earth and if the doubling of that spreads globally, in 7 years time we could begin to see massive global results.

Now in all of this we have been talking in generalities. You need a general statement, but let me give a few specific examples of what we mean by Earth Care.

Throughout this country and around the world there are individuals and small groups here and there that are demonstrating Earth care solutions. For example greenhouses are being built in increasing numbers to grow food. From wheat sprouts in apartments to neighborhood gardens there is increasing awareness of Earth Care solutions and intensive efforts to increase what is already happening. For example, in Now York City they already have 800 neighborhood gardens, they may eventually have 80,000—this is a possible goal. Think of what the City of New York would be like if it had 80,000 neighborhood gardens. More than that, what if they had a few urban farms where people could come and see fruit trees and farm animals and pick up healthy food to take home with them.

By the same token the efforts for urban homesteads are rapidly spreading. One of the things that will be emphasized in the Earth Care Campaign is not only that the care of our planet is our responsibility but that everyone is entitled to their territorial claim to our planet. The great religions predict the time when every person will have their own vine and fig tree—their own Earth claim. In our own history we had homestead programs where an individual in an earlier time could get 160 acres—good land with trees and fertile soil and flowing streams. By applying his own industry and initiative he could provide a secure homestead and a future for him and his family. Well, I think the Earth is a little too crowded for everybody to have 160 acres but with modern technology and possibilities, certainly everyone could have an apartment, a house or a few acres of land.

We are moved emotionally when we see on television or in a theater, E.T. pointing towards the stars and with loneliness saying "home." I suppose at some point an astronaut may point down to our little planet and say "Home—Earth is our home." But this concept has to be applied to the individual. Every person on our planet in entitled to inherit a portion of the Earth and to have available secure possession of a home with the basic requirements for life on our planet—clean water, fresh air and availability of living growing things. A goal that can obtain common support globally is to provide every family on Earth a homestead, a place where they can live with a feeling of security, a place they can call their home: A home on our planet for every family. We may differ on how to achieve this goal but if we make it a priority and then record how it's being accomplished here and there, territorial claims of individuals will soon take precedence over the territorial claims of nation states. This will meet a global need and diminish some of our basic causes of conflict.

In the Earth Care Campaign we are looking for common goals that can be globally supported and pursued in different ways. Then we want to see an exchange of information that will help achieve these dynamic goals. We are talking here about the care of Earth and the sharing of Earth's natural bounty.

I want to again stress that we are not speaking in terms of ideologies, whether communism, socialism or capitalism. We are just talking plain common sense. We want to see a global community of conscience, of commitment to the care of Earth, and determination to see that every person participates in an increasing way in the benefits of Earth's amazing web of life.

An Earth Care Campaign can lead to a more equitable participation in trade and exchange, here again seeking the special benefits of self-help programs: the advantages of independence and security for basic, local industries—leaving for global trade and exchange high technology mass-produced items that can add to life's benefits. Constantly seeking appropriate use of technology and equitable distribution of Earth's raw materials and technology will stimulate growing cooperation and independence all over the world. It's with this combination that we can build a future.

It is necessary in talking about what the Earth Care Campaign represents and is trying to do to also explain what it is not, and I believe when we say Earth Care Campaign we must not in this mean either efforts for or against the nuclear freeze, or world government, or many solutions which may be good but which do not have and are unlikely to soon obtain the strong support of their opponents. The Earth Care Campaign can appeal to all sides.

As far as the future of freedom and order are concerned, certainly government and industry and all the institutions of our planet need new priorities but the Earth Care Campaign is not seeking to address symptoms. It is seeking change in the basic causes of the crisis we presently have. Addressing symptoms is also urgently needed—but should not be labeled "Earth Care Campaign."

I feel the Earth Care Campaign must call attention to alternatives that are working. Much can be done in spite of present difficulties. The people who are revolutionary in their thinking can find wonderful opportunities through voluntary actions that will diminish inflation and waste. For example, every time you set up a system of barter you are diminishing inflation because much of the work is taking place without the use of money. Another possibility: Ancient religions and present thinking among some economists point to the need for a medium of exchange that can be obtained without paying interest. While no-interest loans require a little benevolence on the part of those who put up the money, they help level the playing field.

It might be a great opportunity for a few bankers to set up a no-interest loan program, appealing to Earth patriots for funds. They could make these loans available to ventures that can provide security that is business-like and responsible, but that are committed to new Earth Care alternatives. Incidentally, the government is providing tax advantages for no-interest loans right now.

We have, for instance, in the energy field, all kinds of alternatives to the present wasteful polluting energy plants. There are right now available Nitinol engines which are more cost efficient than any kind of energy producing equipment that we have; I wish that every possible advantage could be given to those who are developing and are producing Nitinol engines—every home should have one. As we look about for creative alternatives in technology—for industry, communications and education—

we will find basic solutions that will make us better caretakers of Earth. We will discover there are unlimited opportunities in every direction.

The task that we are confronting here is to get attention for our planet and mobilize a global Earth Care Campaign that will capture the imagination of the world and bring the kind of benefits we are talking about. And at the same time create the climate of mutual trust in which disarmament and peace can naturally follow. Believe me, if the world becomes excited about Earth Care concepts and the growing community of conscience that is lifting human thought and vision from the narrow limitation of parochialism and nationalism; if, for example, people in the Pentagon, and in the KGB and around the world suddenly feel a greater loyalty to their planet than to their nation, war will become impossible.

The key to these fundamental changes is a passionate commitment to care of Earth and anything that will assist Earth Care endeavors. This provides a challenge to religious faiths, to different groups and churches that are professing the importance of their religious belief, philosophy or ideology. Demonstrate its value by the things that you do in your Earth Care efforts. This is convincing evidence of love and wisdom.

People still are problem-solving organisms with at least a measure of common sense scattered around the world. Let us make it clear that Earth Care action is already enriching the life and prospects of individuals and communities here and there in many countries. Already we see the benefits of this new world view, this new attitude, this new kind of action. We live in a world of communications where it is very difficult to prevent people from finding out about something terribly exciting and interesting. I think the word can reach every secret corner of the globe that we have an opportunity now to see a healthy peaceful future for our planet. The creative potentials of us and our children can be realized in a way that brings to our mind the dreams of the golden age, the kingdom of heaven on Earth, of a real utopia, where the lion will lie down with the lamb, where the humpback whale can again sing its song, and where in every part of the world people with love and gratitude will plant a tree to symbolize their commitment to Earth. Where wilderness areas will be increased. I think it would be great if Antarctica could be proclaimed a wilderness area and we would agree for at least 100 years not to exploit it, but to leave for future generations, this amazing delicate area of living, breathing life! Again, as custodians and caretakers of Earth, we can bring to our present generation a better life and to future generations unlimited opportunities for love, for creativity, for exploring the universe, learning more about life's great mysteries of spirit and mind. This is our task.

As resources to help you in carrying out your part of the Earth Care Campaign, we have first of all the Earth Charter which is more or less just an outline that might provide connections and inter-linking purposes among participants. It sets forth the idea of being custodians and caretakers of Earth; an Earth Care ethic, Earth Care curriculum and education, and then it has guidelines in production, marketing, advertising, consumption, energy use, land use and communications. The object here is to give a brief general description of the total effort needed for Earth's rejuvenation. This skeleton needs to be filled in with some flesh and blood. We do have an Earth Care Handbook which goes into a little more detail about how this can be done. It would be excellent if locally, nationally and globally there were directories of Earth Care products and activities. Certainly this would be useful in every community if the definitions of Earth Care that are given in the Earth Care Handbook could be used as criteria for the more important programs and projects within each community that will contribute to these goals.

In many organizations there are Earth Care activities. For instance, the Boy Scouts and the Girl Scouts have environmental programs. In churches, block associations and groups of every kind, there are projects that could be appropriately called Earth Care. There will be differences of opinion about what contributes to Earth Care, but I believe the guidelines found in the Earth Charter and in the Earth Care Handbook can develop a broad consensus and help people see the difference between "Earth Kill" and "Earth Care." We feel that there can be communication about the people that are trying to care for Earth and their results. Media can follow through on these activities by giving feature treatment to individuals and programs that are contributing to Earth Care. Then more and more people will come to understand what is meant by the term Earth Care Campaign.

We especially invite communicators, TV, radio, press and magazines, to do what they can to further the Earth Care Campaign by stories and examples. It would be great if media would commit themselves to give half of their time to solutions. We are so overwhelmed by the horror and terror of our problems and all the time there are great things happening that offer solutions.

I recall one woman who was living a very creative and happy life in a bad neighborhood in New York City, and I asked her how she always seemed to be smiling and on top of things, and she said, "Oh, it was very simple. I just got rid of my TV and radio and stopped my magazines and newspaper. Now I am able to function very well and do my part in helping to provide a better life for my neighbors." I don't think this is the solution but it pinpoints the problem. Responsible media will give special emphasis to alternatives and solutions and to those items that are improving the neighborhood and community—and the world.

1983 will be United Nations World Communications Year. Innovative, imaginative use of the telephone can help Earth Care, and long distance rates and use of low-rate hours can be used to spread Earth Care ideas. It is just amazing how much can be accomplished through a few telephone calls. If you have a custom phone where you can have a conference call, all the better. I think that as a part of the Earth Care Campaign, every group should have a telephone tree, some system of communication, sharing information that will be useful to others. Then there is the possibility of data banks and all kinds of other technology that will provide resources and information for the Earth Care Campaign.

We would like to attract the enthusiastic support of the amazing innovative workers in the field of computer technology and video tapes; there is so much that can be done, both in the multi-sense use of mass media, of TV and radio, and also through the data banks and person to person contacts now possible through the computer technology and through the improvements in our telephone systems. Effective use of modern communications for an Earth Care Campaign can work miracles.

Now we haven't even talked about another vital area; there is increasing interest in the mysteries of mind and spirit. There are many differences about the nature of God, of mind and spirit. But who can deny the evidence of ESP, spiritual healing, miraculous answers to prayers, global mental communication between identical twins—and other psychic phenomena that cannot be explained by science. But most will agree that our faith, or thought or feelings, can affect other people—even at a distance. I sometimes feel that every strong loving thought is affecting attitudes and feelings of others. When we become consumed with a love and passion for the redemption of our planet, and our thoughts and our prayers, from the moment we wake to the moment we go to bed at night, are filled with joyous thoughts, with ideas and decisions for a better world and through the grace of God new faith for the redemption of the human family; why something happens that creates a sense of community wherever you go. Suddenly groups are really working together and we see the power of peaceful accord manifesting itself. I think that this is the great thing about prayer—it will get through any defenses when it is motivated by love and faith and by the power of caring hearts.

Through these many different levels of action, we can pursue an Earth Care Campaign that will offer promise of a real breakthrough in the near future—perhaps in 1984. I am not suggesting that all the problems of humanity will be easily solved, no not at all, but we now see a crack in the darkness and the promise of a dawn that will bring light and love and wisdom to the people of this planet. I am reminded of the words of Leonardo da Vinci: "Oh wretched mortals open your eyes!" Now we need to open our eyes and swiftly act to foster Earth's rejuvenation.

Joint Agenda for the Care of Earth

By John McConnell—1983

RECOGNIZING: THAT IGNORANCE AND neglect of our planet, combined with the folly of international rivalries, has now endangered all life on Earth;

That our planet's life is threatened, by nuclear war and by massive pollution of air, water and soil;

That mutual trust is necessary in order to counter these threats;

That only by open communication and joint action, for a greater common good, can mutual trust develop;

That the one thing we have in common is our planet;

That a Campaign for the Care of Earth will create relationships leading to mutual trust and ultimately to reciprocal disarmament and a stable peace. A joint Campaign for the Care of Earth will not cause fear of who is ahead or has the advantage in the Campaign, nor cause excessive concern respecting superior armaments. In the Battle for Earth, success by any participant means success for all. In this new relationship the present meager steps can become larger, more effective steps toward reciprocal disarmament and a stable peace. The larger enterprise of unity in caring for Earth will help us transcend political differences.

That in pursuing peace it is important to identify and emphasize vital matters and the extent and nature of our accord, and to build on this accord;

That peaceful actions beget peace. In every belligerent there is some potential for peace, some chord of thinking or hope that will respond to fair initiatives for peaceful conciliation. We need to recognize points of disagreement, but never use them to diminish cooperation that we agree is for our common good.

That in a world of instant global communications a strong, informed public opinion in all states, dedicated to peace and the care of earth, could become the greatest deterrent to war;

That the greatest challenge in history is the present challenge of destiny involving all humanity, a challenge to reclaim the Earth for all peoples and to free them from the fear of war. (The Earth Care Campaign can provide a "moral equivalent of war.")

That accepting the challenge will bring the measure of trust needed to achieve these goals;

That the peaceful care of our planet cannot be accomplished through halfhearted or insincere efforts, but will require the dedication of all humanity;

That in seeking this basic change in the conduct of governments and their peoples, we acknowledge the failures of all previous efforts. In spite of repeated attempts for lasting peace, during the past thousand years more than a hundred million have died, through failures of peace efforts and repetitions of bloody battles, leaving fatherless children and grieving widows; the best men of each generation have demonstrated valor and heroism—illegitimately in war, and now warfare is conducted through increased resort to terrorism and indiscriminate destruction of young and old, the innocent.

That Nuclear war, ever more frightening and possible, now threatens the extinction of the human race;

That exploitation of trees, vegetation, and wildlife, from ancient times to the present, has decimated or destroyed numerous species and degraded Earth's potential for nurturing life, and that the current acceleration of this process will bring global catastrophe if it is not soon brought to a halt;

That world peace requires a basic long-term commitment to change attitudes and conduct, and to develop structures and programs that will foster peaceful progress in the care of Earth and in our relationships with each other;

That new factors are Space Age global awareness and a deep concern everywhere that something must be done. Our misplaced ambitions and our fears of each other have backed us in a corner with no way out—except through peace, real peace, which may elude us if we fail to grasp this moment of opportunity. We are the generation that will decide Earth's fate.

That we owe to untold generations in our past and future a firm decision for peace and the care of Earth;

That it is time for humanity to take charge and take care of their planet;

THEREFORE, WE JOINTLY ANNOUNCE THE FOLLOWING AGENDA OF ACTION IN SUPPORT OF A GLOBAL EARTH CARE CAMPAIGN:

1. In order to greatly diminish the needless and dangerous degradation of Earth's soil, vegetation, wildlife, air and water, our two governments, U.S. and USSR, will organize, and encourage, Earth Care Campaigns and programs in every one of our communities—seeking to increase tenfold existing programs, and to initiate new programs that will serve these purposes.

2. We will assist other countries, through the United Nations and other international, governmental and non-governmental agencies, to achieve these same goals.

3. The objective of this Campaign is to help make every person a custodian and caretaker of Planet Earth, to sense our common adventure in understanding and managing our beautiful planet; to take pride in it and make it a showcase of Earth Care.

4. To accomplish this we will ask individuals to think about Planet Earth, and then work in their neighborhood or sphere of influence, seeking to learn and follow Earth Care rules and lifestyles that will diminish pollution, waste and destruction, and instead nurture life on our planet. We will assist efforts for grater wilderness areas, local diversified farms and gardens, and sustainable population growth.

5. We will help the transitions occurring in industry that will make technology an extension of, instead of a destroyer of Nature. It is evident that new structure and systems in manufacturing, transportation, community planning and recycling will be necessary if these purposes are to be effectually fulfilled.

6. While Earth Care is a broad concept that affects every area of human activity, in the initial program there are four special areas of concern where Earth Care methods and benefits will be sought. These are: Food, Housing, Energy and Peace.

A. FOOD: All countries should upgrade their food productivity. One way to begin to meet this need is for every family or community to grow its own essential foods. We will pursue this worldwide goal by applying our best minds and resources to this task. Many are already pursuing self-help programs the Earth Care way, in neighborhood gardens, new efficient greenhouses, hydroponics, organic farming, and fish farms. It is most important that every person have an opportunity— regardless of circumstances or resources—to receive basic nutritious food. We will pursue this worldwide goal. FOOD WILL BE SOUGHT THE EARTH CARE WAY.

B. HOUSING: Astronauts and Cosmonauts, looking down on our planet, refer to it as "Home." And indeed it is home. Not only their home but home for every human being. Whether expressed in terms "Gift of God" or "Gift of Nature," the planet is for everyone. We acknowledge that every person has a territorial claim to a portion of the planet; to a secure habitable place which can be called home. Whether through homesteads, in country or city, or in communal living, many governments have recognized the right of individuals to such a share in their planet. A massive effort will be made to provide by the year 2000 a secure habitable shelter for every person who lacks or desires one. We fully support the goals of the United Nations Year of Shelter for the Homeless—1987. HOUSING WILL BE SOUGHT THE EARTH CARE WAY.

C. ENERGY: In the amazing development and benefits of technology a key factor is energy. Wrong kinds of fuel and the misuse of fuel are a major cause of our environmental crisis: resulting, for example, in acid rain, the greenhouse effect, and related threats to our future. It is essential that we wage war against pollution and where possible convert to alternatives now available for clean, efficient, economic energy (solar cells, fuel cells, windmills, tide machines, Nitinol engines, Jojobe plants, Babasu palm oil, and biomass are a few of the solutions now available for cleaner, renewable energy). We pledge to carry out the recommendations contained in

The Plan of Action adopted unanimously by the United Nations Global Conference on New and Renewable Energy at Nairobi, Kenya in August 1981, and further pledge to stimulate research and Worldwide application of new technology in these areas. ENERGY WILL BE SOUGHT THE EARTH CARE WAY.

D.   PEACE: With confidence this Earth Care Campaign will succeed, we each agree to a ten percent decrease in military spending during the coming year and each succeeding year for the next 20 years. Our efforts in the United Nations will seek and expect similar action by all other governments. As global tensions reduce and societies become more stable we will replace our weapons of mutual destruction with mutual understanding of and commitment to peaceful progress. We will seek allegiances to our planet through clear formulation in the United Nations of our rights and responsibilities in its care. With the help of global communications—satellites, telephone, print, TV, radio—a Worldwide community of conscience will make war unthinkable and impossible. Then minimal police force safeguards will be sufficient to guarantee freedom and order for our planet. PEACE WILL BE SOUGHT THE EARTH CARE WAY.

7.   In order to dramatize and assist these efforts to carry out a global Earth Care Agenda, with the help of our sensing devices in Space, we will undertake to provide weekly reports on Earth Care action to the public. (Vigorous efforts will be needed from Media to ferret out and report the solutions that are working to change our conduct from "Earth Kill" to "Earth Care.")

8.   We will participate in the celebration of Earth Day each year on the March 20–21 Equinox and will report each year to the United Nations on progress made. To dramatize our new recognition and care of our planet, on Earth Day satellites will broadcast to the world the annual report on the state of Earth with possible participation of Astronauts and Cosmonauts.

9.   We will do our part and join with all people and all governments in humanity's finest hour—dedication to peace and the rejuvenation and care of our planet.

This paper was written on December 12, 1983. It includes suggestions of Ambassador John McDonald and Rev. Charles Lowry. who reviewed the rough draft. It was given to USSR Ambassador Dobrynin, who said he liked it and would pass it on to his government. It was not acted on. Had it been, the global state of mind in 2001 would have prevented the World Trade Center tragedy.

Earth Changes—Metamorphous for a Golden Age

EARTH CHANGES
By John McConnell
Sept. 21, 1971

INTRODUCTION: EARTH'S PEOPLE

SPIRITUAL

1. Meditation, Global Consciousness
2. Minute for Peace—daily heartbeat of the Global Psyche
3. Earth Hour/Earth Day: Man, Nature and God

COMMUNICATIONS: The New World View—Models for the Future
4. Role and Responsibility of TV and Radio
5. The Press: Headlines for Peace, Features on the Future
6. Public Opinion Press—Communicard

PROPERTY: Each Person Has an Equal Right to Use Spaceship Earth as His Home.
7. Planetary Rights
8. Land Use: Taxes should equal rent on unimproved land

FINANCIAL:
9. Economic Justice: Through a new medium of exchange—based on the products and services to be exchanged.

THE MARKET PLACE: Providing New Motivation for Human Betterment.
10. New Rules for Stock Market: 50% of all stock to be distributed to the poor, with education and training for investing in the Stock Market.

11. Industry: Government subsidy and tax credit for new products and services that demonstrate outstanding improvements with assurance of long term results. Special emphasis on recycling, lowering pollution and helping sustain eco-systems.

12. Merchandizing: Emphasis on consumer service, to foster Earth care.

13. Advertising: Newspaper and TV, radio, magazine advertising furnished by certified non-profit consumer organizations should receive (by law) a specific discount on advertising space.

Heavenly Aeroplane

By Evangelist J. S. McConnell, ~1920

One of these nights about twelve o'clock
This old world's gonna reel and rock
Sinners will tremble and cry for pain
And the Lord will come in his aeroplane.

Chorus:
Oh, ye weary of every tribe
Get your ticket for this aeroplane ride
Jesus our Savior is coming to reign
And take us up to glory in a heavenly aeroplane.

You can talk about your joy rides in automobiles
Talk about your fast time on motor wheels
We'll break all records as we upwards fly
In an aeroplane joy ride through the sky.

There will be no punctures on muddy roads
No broken axles from over-loads
No sparks to trouble or cause delay
As we soar in rapture up the Milky Way.

If you want to get ready to take this ride
Quit all your sins and humble your pride
You must furnish a lamp both bright and clean
And a vessel of oil to run the machine.

When our journey's over and we all sit down
At the marriage supper with a robe and crown
We'll blend our voices with a heavenly throng
And praise our Savior as the years roll on.

****

The above song was written by my father in Walla Walla, Washington, when I was about five years old. It has circled the globe, as you can verify by a Google search. A copyright 1928 version with small differences in wording is in Gospel Quintet Songs published by Thoro Harris, c. 1930. Thoro Harris and my father knew each other. My father was a Pentecostal evangelist and had a major influence on my thinking and actions.

The Great Encounter
by John McConnell
1964

And then I met the Christ
He looked into my eyes
And all the barriers by his gaze were pierced
He reached the depths of me
And from my center I
Was suddenly awakened to life's depths
And heights and majesty
A sense of reverence
And joyous wonder flooded over me
I felt the dignity
And beauty of life
And then I felt reborn
A new and kindly love
Brought with it faith that carried ultimate
Conviction—with a sense
Of great authority
That came, not from possessing wealth or power
But from discovering
(With deep humility)
The wonder, balance, purpose at work in life.

Nova
by John McConnell
1965

No power is greater than love.
But to obtain its unshackled strength
One must become as sensitive to the
Pulsing quivers of the heart as a
Candle flame is to the faint unseen
Breezes of a dark-filled room.

This control at the center of things can only be
Reached by humility, reverence, quietness, and a
Search for beauty.
When it is found, the faintest
Touch can release untold energies . . .

Then a man can stand ten miles tall and send
Thunderbolts crashing through barriers of
Stone and steel.
He can unleash ten thousand
Amazons to quench the world's great desert thirst.

With the serenity of Mount Everest in his mind, and the
Fires of Vesuvius in his heart, he can
Unleash the energies of his faith with the
Sudden brightness of an H-Bomb.

To find and master the delicate secret
Control can be the great quest of a man's life.
The difference between an empty
Meaningless existence and a

Burst of joy that sends one like a
Rocket in search of the stars . . .
Is nothing more than a gentle
Breath that sways a candle flame.

Dear John:

Thank you for entering our recent contest. The judges wish to recognize your outstanding poetic contribution to this anthology. We are therefore pleased to award you our Editor's Choice Award for your contest entry as published in Through the Looking Glass.
Congratulations on your creative achievement.

Sincerely,

The National Library of Poetry
1 Poetry Plaza, Owings Mills, Maryland 21117
1997

Raindrop Shining
by John McConnell
1975

With dirt and grime my window pane
Was getting mighty dreary
Like all the trouble in the world
Which is making things so bleary.

But now I have a spark of hope
A raindrop brought it to me
For when a shower came my way
It left a raindrop shining!

Shining with a mystic light
A spot of Sunlit wonder

The message that it brought to me
Was something most profound
"I am but water from the Sea
The Sun and Sea are life for me.
This means of life and energy
Can give me strength so I can be
A source of love and ecstasy."

So let's protect the Oceans
And use our Sunshine right
Clean Seas and Solar Energy
Can rid us of our blight.

Earth Day

John McConnell
~ 1980

Earth Day . . . Earth Day

On the first day of Spring let the bells of Earth ring
As together we silently pray.
Sun and stars will rejoice as we make our sacred choice
To care for our planet every day.

Earth Day . . . Earth Day

As a Trustee of Earth I will daily seek to choose
The actions of thoughtful love and care.
I will learn, I will work, to improve the life on Earth
By my thought, by my words, by my deeds.

Earth Day . . . Earth Day

Thank you God for the life you have placed upon the Earth
For the flowers, for the trees, for the birds.
Help me live in a way that will benefit and bring
A future of health and peace on Earth.

Earth Day . . . Earth Day

The Earth Day song has been sung many times at the UN Earth Day
Peace Bell ceremony.

The Vision
by John McConnell

The vision that Jesus gave to me
Has given my life a harmony.
The music in my enraptured soul,
Brings love of Jesus every day.

****

Many years ago, in 1975, I wrote the above poem and composed a tune to go with it. It was a great help to me when I spent time in prayer.

Evening Prayer
John McConnell's version

Now I lay me down to sleep
I pray the Lord my soul to keep
Tell me in my dreams I pray
What I should do at break of day.

Life Rhapsody
by John McConnell
November 11, 1978

The vision that Jesus gave to me
Is making my life a rhapsody
There's music in all I hear and see
Since Jesus took my sins away

Faith That Works by Love
Song by Hattie McConnell,
mother of John McConnell

Faith is the hand, that touches God
Until His heart of love,
Is moved to meet the world's dark need,
His strength and power to prove.
God hearkens to our faintest cry,
When looking from above,
He sees behind the prayer we pray,
The faith that works by love.

Chorus 1
Oh the faith that works by love,
Will move the mountains when we pray.
Oh the faith that works by love,
Will turn the darkness into day.

Then faith if borne on wings of love,
Will lift us up to God,
Above the mountain peaks that bar,
When there's no perfect love.
His promises that cannot fail,
With light from Heaven will glow,
Until the need for which we plead,
God's mercy will bestow.

Ah! All have faith, we do not doubt,
But some, as Jesus has told,
Have long been dead, because their love,
To God has now grown cold.
Then would you have the living faith,
That cometh from above,
Just let God's fire consume the dross
Until faith works by love.

Chorus 2
Oh the faith that works by love
Will move the mountains all away.
Oh the faith that works by love,
Will bring the answer when we pray.

Hoist the Sails!
by John McConnell
August 10, 1972

Four billion years ago, our lonely Earth
Set sail on Cosmic seas,
Guided by an unseen hand
Of nature, God or chance.

As life evolved
Through endless eco cycles
Man was born, destined
To destroy or enrich
The precious ship.

And now his hand
Has seized the tiller
But his ear has not
Yet caught the captain's
Quiet command.

The sails are down, the ship becalmed,
Its fragile life at stake. No longer
Do we ride the gentle swells of
Silent seas and breathe the
Fragrant air.

Broken are the rhythms
Of our cyclic plants
And other living things.

But now the captain speaks
Again. Our quiet thoughts
At last reveal his voice.

"Hoist the sails, Earth Man
Set them for celestial winds.
Hold the tiller firm, the course is clear
Better winds are just ahead."

Be he nature, God or chance,
His voice is heard
And we shall head the captain's
Quiet command.

Minute for Peace Poem
by John McConnell
December 7, 1963

Dedicated to the memory of Yehudi Menuhin, d. March 12, 1999

It was three days before Christmas
And on valley and hill
A Minute for Peace
Joined hearts in good will.

We are one human family
Was the message brought
By the pictures on TV
Where before people fought.

This day then began
A Campaign for Earth
To eliminate poverty,
Pollution and dearth.

For when people and groups
Seek a goal all can share
We'll treat neighbor and nature
With heartfelt care.

Our planet is suffering
From shortsighted greed
But as Trustees of Earth
We'll meet our Earth's need.

****

The poem's original title was "Peace-Time Epic," renamed in 1998. It was written just before the first Minute for Peace on December 22, 1963.

Six years before the proposal in 1969 for an Earth Day, this poem expresses the link between "neighbor and nature." Also, it mentions "Trustees of Earth" some 8 years before the term Earth Trustees was first written in 1971.

Bibliography

"Earth on Edge." PBS. Premiered June 19th, 2001. Online: http://www.pbs.org/earthonedge/.

Abbott, John S. C. *Napoleon Bonaparte*. IndyPublish.com, 2002.

Acton, John Emerich Edward Dalberg. 1st Baron Acton. Letter dated April 3, 1887, to Bishop Mandell Creighton. Online: http://www.mcadamreport.org/Acton.html.

Adams, John. "Letter to Abigail Adams" (1775). In Gaustad, Edwin S. *A Religious History of America*. Harper Collins, 1966, 127.

Andersen, Hans Christian. *The Emperor's New Clothes*. 1837.

B., Dick. *New Light on Alcoholism: God, Sam Shoemaker, and A.A.* Paradise Research Publications, 1999.

Bardfield, Morton. "Short Wave Station WRUL." Online: http://www.northernstar.no/wnyw3.htm.

Benking, Heiner. Personal communication.

Booth-Tucker, Frederick St. George. *The Life of Catherine Booth: The Mother of the Salvation Army*. Nabu Press, 2010.

Bready, John Wesley. *This Freedom—Whence?* New York: American Tract Society, 1942.

Chase, Stuart. *The Tyranny of Words*. Chicago: Harcourt Brace, 1938.

Cohen, Eduardo. "What Americans Need to Know—But Probably Won't Be Told—To Understand Palestinian Rage." Online: http://www.globalexchange.org/countries/mideast/palestine/eduardoCohen.html, 2000.

Corwin, Norman. "Could Be." Radio play, September 8, 1949.

Cunniff, John. "Founders Mission: Change World." *The Phoenix Gazette*, March 19, 1974.

Daily, Starr. *Love Can Open Prison Doors*. Los Angeles: DeVorss, 1934.

de Chardin, Pierre Teilhard. *The Phenomenon of Man (Le Phénomène Humain)*. 1955.

Douglas, Lloyd C. *Magnificent Obsession*. Willett, Clark & Colby, 1929.

Earth image. Online: http://eol.jsc.nasa.gov/scripts/sseop/photo.pl?mission=AS17&roll=148&frame=22727.

Finney, C. G. "Power from on High—What Is It?" Tract. Words of Life—Extra Edition, Nov., 1921.

Forrester, Jay. *World Dynamics*. 2nd ed. Cambridge: Wright-Allen, 1971.

Gatty, Harold. *The Raft Book: Lore of the Sea and Sky*. New York: George Gatty Press, 1943.

Gaustad, Edwin S. *A Religious History of America*. Harper Collins, 1966.

Goodman, Paul. *Growing Up Absurd*. New York: Random House, 1960.

Hawthorne, O. Lawrence. "Make Me A Man!" In *The Little Acorn Series*, Omaha, NE: The Acorn Press, n.d. See "The Charlotte M. Smith Collection of Miniature Books," Special Collections Department, University of Iowa Libraries, Iowa City, IA. Reprinted in *Boys' Life*. New York: Boy Scouts of America, XXIX (2, Feb. 1939) 6.

Hayakawa, S. I. *Language in Thought and Action*. Chicago: Harcourt Brace, 1941.

Hock, Sidney. *New York Times Book Review*, May 22, 1966.

Horgan, J. *The End of Science: Facing the Limits of Knowledge in the Twilight of the Scientific Age*. New York: Broadway Books, 1997. Orig. 1996.

Kaye, M. M. *The Far Pavilions*. St. Martin's Press, 1978.

King, Martin Luther, Jr. "Loving Your Enemies." Sermon, Dexter Avenue Baptist Church, Montgomery, Alabama, Christmas, 1957. Online: http://www.salsa.net/peace/conv/8weekconv4-2.html.

King, Martin Luther, Jr. *Strength To Love*. New York: Harper & Row, 1963.

Laubach, Frank C. *Prayer, the Mightiest Force in the World*. Fleming H. Revell, 1946.

Lewis, Bernard. "The Crisis of Islam." *Christian News*, April 28, 2003.

Lowry, Charles. *Communism and Christ*. 2nd ed. Morehouse-Gorham, 1952.

McConnell, John. "Earth Day: Past, Present, Future." Online: http://www.earthsite.org/mc-lee.htm.

McConnell, John. *The Christian News*, February 22, 1993.

McConnell, T. W. "Evangelist T. W. McConnell's Testimony." *Apostolic Faith*. Los Angeles, CA 1(1, Sept. 1906) 3–4. Online: http://www.azusabooks.com/af/LA01.shtml#McConnell.

McDaniel, Carl N., and John M. Gowdy. *Paradise for Sale—A Parable of Nature*. Berkeley: University of California Press, 2000.

Muller, Max. *Lectures on the Science of Religion*. With translation of the Dhammapada ("Path of Virtue"). Kessinger, 2003.

Orwell, George. *1984*. Secker and Warburg, 1949.

Pope John Paul II. "Apostolic Letter Inter Sanctos." AAS 71 (1979) 1509.

Pope John Paul II. *Crossing The Threshold of Hope*. Alfred A. Knopf, 1994.

Pope John XXIII. "Pacem in Terris," Encyclical Letter: On Establishing Universal Peace in Truth, Justice, Charity, and Liberty, 1963. Online: http://www.papalencyclicals.net/John23/j23pacem.htm.

Reed, Edward (ed). *Peace on Earth: Pacem in Terris*. Proceedings: "An International Convocation on the Requirements of Peace." New York: Pocket Books, 1965.

Reeves, Simon. Personal communication.

Sayers, Dorothy. *Mind of the Maker*. London: Methuen, 1941.

Schweitzer, Albert. *Out of My Life and Thought*. Translated by Antje Bultmann Lemke. New York: Henry Holt, 1990.

Shucman, Helen, and Bill Thetford. *A Course in Miracles*. Foundation for Inner Peace. 2nd ed. New York: Viking Penguin, 1992.

Smith, Adam. *Paper Money*. Dell Publishing, 1981.

Steinfels, Peter. "Pacem in Terris: A Retrospective." Online: http://www.vincenter.org/convocation/steinfels.html.

The Holy Bible, New King James Version. Nashville, Tennessee: Thomas Nelson, 1982.

von Foerster, Heinz. "Logical Structure of Environment and Its Internal Representation." In R. E. Eckerstrom (ed.). *International Design Conference*, Aspen, 1962. Zeeland, MI: Herman Miller, Inc., 1963.

Weir, Robert M. *Peace, Justice, Care of Earth: The Vision of John McConnell: Founder of Earth Day*. Kalamazoo, MI: Press On Publishing, 2007. First edition published as *Star of Hope: The Life and Times of John McConnell, Founder of Earth Day*. New York: Swan Books, 2006.

Index

www.ingramcontent.com/pod-product-compliance
Lightning Source LLC
Chambersburg PA
CBHW072037020426
42334CB00017B/1307